FAMILIES, ILLNESS, AND DISABILITY

ALSO IN THE FAMILIES AND HEALTH SERIES

The Body Speaks: Therapeutic Dialogues for Mind-Body Problems
James L. Griffith and Melissa Elliott Griffith

FAMILIES, ILLNESS, AND DISABILITY

AN INTEGRATIVE TREATMENT MODEL

John S. Rolland, M.D.

BasicBooks
A Division of HarperCollins*Publishers*

This book is dedicated to the many exceptional families I have been privileged to work with and learn from in their quest to live well despite illness and disability; to loved ones, my mother and Essie, who lived well in the face of death, and my father, who lives well at ninety; and to Froma and Claire and the rest of my family, whose continued love and support are so important to my life.

Copyright © 1994 by BasicBooks,
A Division of HarperCollins Publishers, Inc.

Designed by Ellen Levine

Library of Congress Cataloging-in-Publication Data

Rolland, John S., 1948–
    Families, illness, and disability : an integrative treatment model / John S. Rolland.
        p.   cm.
    Includes bibliographical references and index.
    ISBN 0-465-02915-9
    1. Family—Medical care—Psychological aspects. 2. Sick—Family relationships. I. Title.
RA418.5.F3R65   1994
155.9'16—dc20
                                                                94-206
                                                                CIP

96 97 ❖/HC 9 8 7 6 5 4

Contents

Foreword

THE IMPORTANCE of *family* in medicine is both self-evident and obscure: we are intrigued by the intuitive evidence that health care and family are intertwined, yet how to think about that link and what to do about it are often tantalizingly vague. Despite the many difficulties associated with this perspective, we can justifiably experience a measure of confidence and excitement in approaching it. The careful work of numerous clinicians, researchers, and theoreticians is yielding solid gains. In the present work, John Rolland summarizes much of the evidence for our optimism and provides an integrated theory that will guide future work and thinking.

The family perspective on health care is part of an intellectual and technological movement toward holistic and ecosystemic approaches to medicine that conceptually unite mind and body and consider people within their particular social contexts. This process is substantially changing medicine and its institutions. Workers from many disciplines are involved: psychologists and psychiatrists; primary-care and family practitioners; public health workers; general and specialty nurses, including nurse practitioners and psychiatric nurse specialists; social workers; family therapists and counselors; researchers studying the family; and a host of other social scientists.

As in families themselves, both individualizing and integrative forces are at work in the professions. Rolland's book draws from and summarizes much of this new body of knowledge, and will be of interest to workers with varying backgrounds. Rather than emphasize the distinctions and differences among the professions, an orientation toward the family naturally tends to rebalance the direction of professional development.

What do we need to know about the family in terms of health? Like answers to other important questions, this one depends on the use we propose to make of the information. At least part of the problem is that there could easily be too much data at our disposal. Organizing these data and setting practical limits to our inquiry are at least as great a concern as extending that inquiry adequately. A measure of caution is called for when we use the term *family*. The natural recognition we all have of the concept, its deep relation to our being human, is profoundly important; yet we cannot assume that common definitions are all we need to understand how family and disease interact.

When we say "family," do we mean present family or the historic, multi-generational family in which the patient grew up? Does *family* mean household, legal, or biological family, blended family, or extended kin network? What part does culture play? How are we to factor in the personal characteristics of the individual actors, their health circumstances, and their place in the life cycle?

I find the concept of normative and non-normative illnesses particularly useful. We hope the aged will not have too bad a time of it in their final illnesses; painful as loss of them may be, in most instances a timely death is not disruptive to families (if it is, therapeutic work may be indicated). On the other hand, when the young die, we say they died "before their time" and mourn grievously. A serious illness in a child seems, as Peggy Penn has observed, to freeze time.

As a parent of a chronically ill child, I can remember bargaining, at every step in his illness, with I-knew-not-whom for my child to be no worse off than he was at any particular point in time. Looking back, I think I wanted to stop time in its tracks; my wife and I had learned that we could endure whatever the moment brought us if only it did not worsen. Rolland is keenly aware of time as a neglected dimension in analysis of the meaning of illness. Importantly, he links the timeliness of an illness to the developmental phase of family life.

Other personal examples: in my childhood I was often beset with asthma attacks (which fortunately stopped at puberty) along with quite painful middle-ear infections—this before the age of antibiotics. Unpleasant? Yes; but much mitigated by the pleasure I gave my mother. I was then an only child; my young mother doted on me and had, in my repeated illnesses, an exceptional opportunity to demonstrate her considerable skills as a nurse-mother. Perhaps we were overly close—but who cared? It was an intensification of the normal role relationship and was culturally quite acceptable.

And many years later, when my father was completely disabled with Alzheimer's disease, my mother was able to set up her home as a small hospital and nurse him through his terminal illness.

The central notion here is *fit*, the degree to which the psychological and role demands of being sick and of caring for the sick are consistent with the personal and social structures of the family. This does not always work out adversely: a family may be enhanced by illness and its demands. Indeed, family therapists have come to recognize that illness may stabilize structures in some families, which frequently become dysfunctional only at the point when the illness improves and the role demands change.

In the personal examples given above, our good fortune—if one can call it that—consisted of a good fit between the illnesses with which our family was coping and the developmental phase we were in as individuals and as a family. Cultural dimensions should also be noted: Is there a clash of cultural expectations with the role requirements of being sick or of being a caregiver? My mother as a young woman did not think of herself as having a professional life other than as a mother and homemaker. Thus, she found child care and nursing her son completely fulfilling—or, more accurately, any discontent with this role (and I think she had a good deal) was masked by the success she had in the role itself. The same was true in her old age as she cared for my father: this was what a "woman of valor," the Jewish virtuous woman, did.

As we all know, things all too commonly do not go this way. I consult to a pediatric AIDS unit of a large urban hospital. Typically, a household being served consists of two orphaned children and their grandmother, perhaps with some other adults, for example, an uncle or a great grandmother; and one or both of the children is seropositive for HIV or has full-blown AIDS. The family is likely to be African American. The children's father was perhaps infected with the virus by using contaminated needles for drugs, the mother, by the same route or through sexual intercourse. This household unit is the "health-care family," valiantly struggling, together with an equally valiant health-care team, to stem the tide of biomedical and psychosocial problems.

The family, for these folks, is a living network of emotional ties seen through the lenses of their culture and place in the individual and family life cycles. Their losses are severe: the children have lost their parents; the grandmother has lost her child. Stresses are unremitting, supplies short, and developmental issues pressing. Senescence and physical exhaustion threaten the grandmother; the street and its blandishments threaten the children. And the seropositive child is also caught in a constantly changing biological drama with a cataract of psychosocial consequences.

Rolland is especially attuned to awareness that, with regard to illness, one is rarely dealing with a static situation, and that the meaning of an illness changes constantly as it is played out against the background of these other factors.

How do we order the almost limitless data that can be assembled about families? In biomedical terms, a family history has most often meant a review of genetically linked conditions, an allergic diathesis, a history of cancer, or whatever. Psychosocial medicine can go much farther. But how do we sail these almost endless seas of data? Recently attention has shifted, in family therapy, to an orientation that is summarized in the expression *the problem-defined system*, meaning an assemblage of persons affected by the problem or having an effect on it, either in terms of maintaining (causing) it or changing (treating) it. This concept allows for fluidity in bringing together the most efficient treatment group and particularly directs our attention to the importance of the provider system in this process since, as a variation on the old adage has it: "If you are part of the solution, you are part of the problem."

Fortunately, the clinical encounter establishes its own necessities and priorities. The clinician must first be clear in his or her mind about what the problem is and then identify the problem-defined system that is relevant to it. Insofar as the family is concerned, we need to be able to delineate the "health-care family," that is, the current natural system that influences health-care outcomes and is affected by them. In some situations this is simple enough: my physician and I regularly include my wife in the information loop about my health so that she can add information and ask her own questions. Physicians who establish some version of this practice with their patients find that it prevents confusion and difficulties, and they come to like it.

Aside from this modest prophylaxis, when should a deeper inquiry about the family system be conducted? Those practicing in high-risk specialties— oncology, pediatric and adult intensive care, transplants, head trauma and stroke, and geriatrics, among others—have learned to include family meetings in their standard protocols. Their patients suffer from diseases or are subjected to treatments that are at the extreme of human stress. In these situations family breakdown can reasonably be expected to occur. A prima facie case is made here that "family" is relevant.

As noted, in many instances informational meetings are all that is required. But there are occasions when the family is implicated in a dysfunctional health-care process and a different kind of psychosocial involvement is called for. (William Doherty and Macaran Baird, in their book *Family Therapy and Family Medicine: Towards the Primary Care of Families* [New York: Guilford, 1983], have described these levels of involvement in primary-care medicine.) Something does not work the way it is supposed to: there is a clinical puzzle, nonadherence to a treatment regimen, a dysfunctional interaction with professional caregivers. One might say that there is a *stuck system* that recycles the same information without showing any change.

Patients and their families in these situations constitute an important, costly, and frustrating subset of people who are often cycled and recycled through the health-care system. They can be understood as presenting psychosocial problems, either in their personal lives or in their interaction with the health-care system, under the guise of biomedical problems. Descriptively, common examples include:

- overutilizers or frequent attenders, a portion of a clinic list that consumes a disproportionate share of the available resources;

- noncompliant and other troublesome ("heartsink")* patients. These are patients who produce feelings of despair and helplessness in their doctors. They usually consult frequently and tend to stick to a chosen doctor. Their symptoms seem to fit no known pattern of illness, yet the intensity and complexity of those symptoms can overwhelm even experienced practitioners.

In many instances, the presenting complaint is couched entirely in somatic terms—low back pain or persistent tiredness, for example—for which no physical or laboratory correlates can be found. Sometimes complaints are orchestrated into a maddening and frustrating din, baffling to patient and physician alike. If one adds the numbers of these patients to those in the high-risk group and then combines that total with the patients presenting with traditional mental health disorders for which family work is increasingly relevant, it becomes evident that the patient population requiring psychosocial help is quite large indeed.

With regard to the place of this work in designing the health-care-delivery models of the future, it seems to me that the complexity involved speaks to the need for clinical teams made up of both biomedical and psychosocial practitioners. The knowledge base and skill requirements for the family-oriented psychosocial therapist are extensive, though not all will be needed in all instances. The traditional one-provider model aims to train biomedical personnel to include family systems thinking and techniques in their work, certainly a most valuable objective. Yet, except for a small number of unusually gifted clinicians, this arrangement is difficult to launch in practice. Biomedical and psychosocial providers neccessarily differ in the position from which they look at clinical events and the logic that they use to interpret them. To preserve both perspectives a collaborative team model is called for.

In summary, the ecosystemic perspective provides a significant new stance from which to view living systems and has a profound impact on service-delivery systems, both in identifying the system to be dealt with and the tools for doing so. Environmental awareness has made the word *ecology* a part of our everyday language, although many who use that term find it difficult to be comfortable with the notion of *social* ecology. The integrative approach set forth in this book is a significant instance of the ecosystemic paradigm applied to clinical work. Indeed, the paradigm defines the area: we ask what the ecological context is of the pattern called illness and note quickly enough that family and the health-care system are most proximate in defining it. In using the term *define* we indicate the importance of language and realize that illness occurs in context and is a social construction.

---

*Term from Dr. J. S. Riddell, according to Dr. Hilary Graham, Highgate Group Practice, London.

This social construction—or perhaps we might better speak of co-construction—is a complex process involving multiple interacting meaning systems. A complex tapestry of meaning is constantly being woven and, in the weaving, redefines itself. Family, as Rolland shows so well, is critical in establishing these meaning structures, as is the health-care system itself. We are learning as well that many baffling clinical situations may very well be the surface manifestation of the clash of conflicting and discrepant currents of meaning within the family, within the health-care provider subsystem, or between these components.

The patient is at the vortex of these currents of meaning and may very well be held immobile or tumbled mercilessly by them. Our task as clinicians is to assist him or her to use the available resources to swim out of those binding psychosocial whirlpools. As scholars and researchers we study the family so as to be able to do that job better. This book will provide valuable help in achieving that goal.

Donald A. Bloch, M.D.
September 1993

Preface

THIS BOOK was inspired by strong feelings about the unmet needs of families living with illness and disability. Family members' personal struggles and suffering often remain hidden from those outside the family, sometimes even from each other.

A fuller awareness of this reality came only when illness struck in my personal life. Although I had completed medical school and part of my residency in psychiatry at Yale University and had been exposed to hundreds of patients and their families, I did not really learn to appreciate the many dilemmas and strains for families with serious health problems until my personal life was directly affected. Within a year, my mother had a stroke and my first wife, Essie, was diagnosed with an incurable form of cancer. Although I was a young physician and came from a highly educated, financially secure, and closely knit family, I was wholly unprepared for the strains of coping with my family members' life-threatening illnesses. As I was growing up, no one in my immediate family had ever been seriously ill. There were stories of tragedy and loss related to being part of a first-generation Jewish refugee family from Germany. But there were no family stories about how to cope with long-term illness.

Over the next four years, I learned through trial and error many of the common excruciatingly painful issues that confront families with an ill, aging parent or couples in which one partner is seriously ill. It was an eye-opening, painful, and humbling experience. I became aware of how little my own professional discipline seemed to have to offer people in my family's predicament. The tendency to focus almost exclusively on individual dynamics did not fit the many issues in family members' relationships with each other or the entire extended family unit. Individual colleagues were supportive, but traditional psychotherapeutic models seemed both too narrowly focused on the individual patient and based too much on theories of psychopathology rather than the normative strains of families coping with adversity.

In situations of illness, there is a tendency for family members to high-light their shortcomings—an "I should have been able to do more" self-criti-cal process. I was no exception. However, I started to ask myself a different question. I thought about what would have been useful information or sup-port for me and my family members at different stages of the illness that would have made a difference in our ability to cope and adapt. This question provided a new and empowering lens through which to view not only my personal experience but to begin to think about a model to help all couples and families challenged by illness or disability. The most immediate and simple answer was, "I wish at the time of diagnosis that a professional had suggested that the whole family meet to discuss the illness and its implica-tions for family life." At the time, I was working at a mental health center connected to a community-based hospital in a predominantly working-class region. In my role providing psychiatric consultations for the hospital med-ical units, I noticed that family members were often present or available in the evenings during visiting hours, and I began to routinely respond to con-sultation requests by meeting with patients and their families. To my initial surprise, the referring physicians were highly supportive and, since this was a community hospital, tended to have some knowledge of the families. I found that I could address the problems of the patient more effectively and efficiently, and simultaneously could deal with the concerns of other family members. And, family members were appreciative.

From this simple beginning, I decided to develop the Center for Illness in Families in New Haven, Connecticut, whose mission was to provide a col-laborative, family-centered approach to the psychosocial needs of families dealing with a range of chronic and life-threatening health problems in chil-dren and adults. A guiding belief was and remains that any family facing ill-ness and disability should routinely be provided the opportunity for a fam-ily consultation around the time of the onset of the condition, as well as continued access to such services over the course of the disorder. Over a six-year period, as a multidisciplinary team of colleagues, we used a family sys-tems approach in providing services to over 500 families. The "health-re-lated family unit" was considered the psychosocial hub for effective coping and adaptation. Our approach was normative and preventive. A variety of consultation, brief-treatment, and ongoing treatments were offered for indi-viduals, couples, and families, or multifamily groups. Clinicians remained available to families as they moved through a variety of contexts, including hospital, extended care facilities, home, and hospice. One particularly strik-ing statistic was that approximately 70% of the families served had never previously seen a mental health professional. Also, a number of physicians learned to use the center's services preventively, involving us routinely as valued team members in the overall treatment plan for their patients with chronic disorders.

Since 1990 I have had the opportunity, with my wife, Froma Walsh, to develop a more comprehensive center at the University of Chicago. The Center for Family Health and its affiliated postgraduate training institute in couples and family therapy, The Chicago Center for Family Health, represent a joint venture through the Department of Psychiatry and the School of Social Service Administration. One of the center's main programs is family-centered health care. This program is designed to provide state-of-the-art clinical training, services to families, and research to promote healthy family functioning, life cycle development, and adaptation to serious, chronic, or life-threatening illness or disability. Clinicians of different professional disciplines and from diverse work settings can take courses or elect a fellowship or part-time training in a two-year certificate program in family systems in health care. These training programs are designed to serve the varied needs of health and mental health professionals from psychiatry, social work, psychology, nursing, marriage and family therapy, and other medical and allied health fields.

The model described in this book represents a synthesis of my professional and personal experiences over the past twenty years. Although research regarding the relationship between family dynamics and health status or treatment compliance has influenced my thinking, the model derives predominantly from the efforts of myself and colleagues to remain clinically relevant and useful to the many real-life family situations with illness we have encountered.

I would like to thank a number of people for their help, support, and friendship in bringing this book to fruition. I am indebted to two outstanding mentors, Dan Levinson and Betty Carter, who taught me about the central importance of individual and family development over the life cycle. I owe a great debt of gratitude to my wife, Froma Walsh, for her tireless love and support, for the many important conversations that helped shape and refine the ideas presented in this book, and for her invaluable help in reviewing all stages of the manuscript. I want to acknowledge Donald Bloch for his leadership in promoting the development of family systems in health care, and for his personal support.

I would especially like to thank some of my colleagues at the Chicago Center for Family Health, who reviewed different chapters in progress: Linda Brown, Gene Combs, Mona Fishbane, Jill Freedman, Joyce Goodlatte, Tony Heath, Laurie Honor, Ronna Lerner, Calvin McGinn, Michele Scheinkman, David Schwartz, Richard Schwartz, John Schwartzman, Virginia Simons, and Karen Skerret. I also want to express my appreciation to William Borden and Celia Falicov for their review of several chapters, and Edie Heinemann for her administrative assistance in preparation of the manuscript. Finally, I would like to thank my editor, Jo Ann Miller, and her assistant editor, Stephen Francoeur, for their patience and first-rate guidance.

CHAPTER 1

Introduction: In Search of a Family Psychosocial Map

S ALLY, A YOUNG MARRIED WOMAN with two small children, received the most up-to-date medical treatment and expert surgical interventions during her four-year bout with cancer. Eight months after her physician pronounced her cured, Sally and her husband, Dave, separated. A prolonged emotional and financially draining divorce and custody battle followed. Dave drank heavily and became verbally abusive. Both children developed behavioral problems at home and at school that required crisis intervention, bringing this disintegrating family to treatment for the first time.

In a twist on the popular aphorism "The treatment was successful, but the patient died," conventional treatments of serious illness may save the patient, but cause irreparable harm to the family unit. The psychosocial strains on a family with a member suffering a chronic or life-threatening condition can rival the physical strains on the patient.

Illness, disability, and death are universal experiences that confront families with one of life's greatest challenges. The impact of a diagnosis of cancer or daily living with a serious disability reverberates throughout the family system, leaving no one untouched. For some families, the quality of life deteriorates, whereas others are resilient and thrive. This book addresses the unmet needs of families in distress by presenting a psychotherapeutic model that fosters healthy psychosocial adaptation over the course of a serious and chronic condition.

Illness and disability can strike any family. What is most significant is at what point in life, in what form, and with what intensity they occur and how long they persist. Perhaps most important is how the experience will affect cherished family relationships. With major advances in medical technology and improved standards of living for many segments of society, people are living much longer and better with conditions that used to be fatal. Cancer, heart disease, and diabetes are just a few examples. Many children with chronic illnesses that in the past were fatal or necessitated institutional care are surviving to adulthood and entering mainstream adult life. The extension of later life has heightened the strain on sons and daughters who must contend with the competing interests of caring for aging parents, child-rearing, and financial pressures, and do so in a society in which families are often geographically dispersed and health care is exorbitantly expensive and often inadequate. This means that ever-growing numbers of families are coping with chronic disorders over an increasingly greater part of the life cycle.

In acute health crises that are resolved within days, weeks, or months, a focus on good biomedical care takes priority. Psychosocial demands on families may be intense, but they are time-limited. Like sleep-deprived parents with an infant, a predictable time frame helps families endure the inevitable hardships and maintain a positive outlook. In chronic conditions, however, uncertainties and ambiguities often extend into the distant future, frequently with the expectation that the patient's illness will worsen and eventually result in death. Over time, a serious psychosocial strain on the family unit is unavoidable. What is needed is a model that can give both clinicians and families a way of thinking that promotes a sense of control and empowerment over a complex and uncertain long-term process.

As a starting point, we need to consider the *family or caregiving system ("health-related family unit"), rather than the ill person, as the central unit of care* (Litman, 1974; Ransom, 1983a). In situations of chronic and life-threatening conditions, there is a need for a biopsychosocial model, defined in systems terms, that addresses the psychosocial needs of all family members and intimate friends. Using a broad definition of family as the foundation of the caregiving system enables us to describe a model of successful coping and adaptation based on family system strengths and vulnerabilities. This is in sharp contrast to most current models of intervention in behavioral medicine, consultation-liaison psychiatry, and psychotherapy that focus narrowly on the patient. At worst, families are relegated to the background: it is recognized that they affect the patient's psychosocial adjustment, but they are not considered to need every bit as much help with their suffering as the patient. Early intervention that acknowledges the importance and pain of all family members prevents their being marginalized and mobilizes their potential as a powerful psychosocial unit in the treatment process.

Families enter the world of illness and disability without a psychosocial map. Often they desperately need a psychosocial guide that can provide support and reassurance that they are handling an illness normally. This raises a fundamental question: What is normative coping and adaptation for families living with a chronic disorder? A basic problem arises in seeking a single, universal definition of the healthy family, as distinct from a dysfunctional or pathological one, in terms of coping with serious health problems. Research is documenting that a broad range of diverse, multicultural family forms and styles of functioning are compatible with normal, healthy family development. This suggests that there is a variety of ways families can adapt successfully to illness and disability and that there is a need to rethink rigid, monolithic models of the ideal family (Walsh, 1993a and b).

Until now, no book has presented a framework to address the full range of experience and treatment issues faced by couples and families one (or more) of whose members suffers a serious illness or disability. What is most needed is a comprehensive way to organize our thinking about all the complex interactions among a family, individual family members, a chronic condition, and professionals involved in providing care—a model that can accommodate the changing interactions among these parts of the system over the course of the illness and the changing stages of the life cycle.

A Review of the Literature

In recent years a burgeoning literature has described the impact of a variety of disorders on family life, and a lesser amount has dealt with the effects of dysfunctional family dynamics on the course and outcome of disease or on compliance with treatment. Thomas Campbell (1986) has provided an excellent, comprehensive review of research in this area through the mid-1980s. In this context, systems theory has been used increasingly as the theoretical lens for clinical intervention and research design.

Since the 1926 Peckham experiment (Ransom, 1983b), carried out in a London community health center, first documented the reciprocal relationship between the psychosocial functioning of the family unit and physical health, interest in the impact of stress on health has gradually increased. Hans Selye's (1956) *The Stress of Life* is a classic work. Meyer and Haggerty's (1962) important research demonstrated a relationship between family stress and susceptibility to streptococcal infection. Holmes and Rahe's (1967) social readjustment scale, which includes many family events, provided early documentation of the relationship between recent stressful life events and increased physical or emotional symptoms.

There have been important advances in behavioral medicine (Antonovsky, 1979; Weiss, Herd, & Fox, 1981) and psychosocial epidemiology (Dohrenwend & Dohrenwend, 1981). In particular, the fascinating subject of psychoneuroimmunology is developing more sophisticated physiological markers for studying the impact of stressful life events on immune functioning and susceptibility to serious illnesses such as cancer (Ader, 1981; Borysenko, 1987; Locke & Gorman, 1989). Rudolf Moos's (1977, 1984) edited volumes and Avery Weisman's (1984) *The Coping Capacity* have addressed some of the important clinical issues in chronic and life-threatening conditions. Investigators such as Henry Richardson (1945) and F. J. A. Huygen (1982), who maintained detailed records in his general practice over a number of years, have demonstrated clusters of illness in families at times of social or developmental stress.

A family systems approach has been applied to physical illness only recently. In a 1972 review on family perspectives of psychosomatic factors in illness, published in *Family Process*, Lawrence Grolnick noted, "There is no body of knowledge regarding applications of family therapy to psychosomatic disorders" (p. 476). In 1977 John Weakland's influential article, "'Family Somatics': A Neglected Edge," served as a challenge and rallying cry to bring family systems theorists into the world of health and illness. Family therapy had been lagging behind other relevant disciplines, notably social work and nursing, whose journals had for decades been publishing articles, by prominent clinicians, on the impact on families of a variety of chronic and life-threatening disorders.

More recent growth in this area can be attributed to the pioneering journal *Family Systems Medicine*, founded in 1983 under the editorial leadership of Donald Bloch. This journal has provided a forum for communication about research and clinical practice, promoting discussion among health and mental health professionals about systems theory, family therapy, health problems, and issues of collaboration. Writing and program initiatives have developed rapidly at the interface of family therapy and family medicine. A number of excellent texts have emerged over the past decade that highlight how family systems approaches can be integrated into family practice and primary care. William Doherty and Macaran Baird's (1983) classic *Family Therapy and Family Medicine* is probably the best known among a number of important works (Christie-Seely, 1984; Crouch & Roberts, 1987; Henao & Grose, 1985; McDaniel, Campbell, & Seaburn, 1990; Ramsey, 1989; Sawa, 1985).

Some important recent contributions have focused particularly on clinical intervention techniques. *Medical Family Therapy* (1992), by Susan McDaniel, Jeri Hepworth, and William Doherty, broke new ground as the first book to describe the various uses and roles of the family therapist in a variety of health care contexts and medical situations. This book, along with Lyman Wynne, Susan McDaniel, and Timothy Weber's (1986) earlier work, *Systems Consultation: A New Perspective for Family Therapy*, and Michael Glenn's (1987) *Collaborative Health Care: A Family-oriented Model*, describe well how systems approaches can be effectively incorporated into a variety of health settings and used to improve the integration of family systems-oriented clinicians into health care and other larger systems. Doherty and Baird's (1987) *Family-centered Medical Care: A Clinical Casebook* is useful in illustrating, through brief case examples, five levels of family systems intervention in common clinical situations.

To date there is less literature on family systems consultation and therapy approaches to chronic and life-threatening illnesses. *Chronic Illness and Disability*, edited by Catherine Chilman, Elam Nunnally, and Fred Cox (1988), *Family Health Psychology*, edited by John Akamatsu, Mary Ann Stephens, Stevan Hobfoll, and Janis Crowther (1992), and *How Do Families Cope with Chronic Illness?*, edited by Robert Cole and David Reiss (1993), provide overviews of some of the current research, clinical, and policy issues affecting families facing health problems. Lorraine Wright and Maureen Leahey's (1987) edited work *Families and Chronic Illness*, though targeted to nurses, is valuable for other professionals as well. In *Chronic Disorders and the Family*, Froma Walsh and Carol Anderson (1988) have edited a useful summary of treatment of severe and chronic mental and physical illness. A number of authors have written helpful books about family experiences with specific disorders, such as AIDS (Landau-Stanton, 1993; Macklin, 1989), alcoholism (Steinglass, Bennett, Wolin, & Reiss, 1987) childhood cancer (Chesler & Barbarin, 1987), Alzheimer's disease (Boss, Caron, & Horbal, 1988), and somatoform disorders (Griffith & Griffith, 1994).

Other clinicians and researchers have developed specific models of intervention, based on particular clinical models. Most noteworthy is the pioneering work of Salvador Minuchin, Bernice Rosman, and their colleagues at the Philadelphia Child Guidance Clinic, in which, based on the psychosomatic family model they developed, structural family therapy was used with children facing childhood illnesses (Minuchin et al., 1975; Minuchin, Rosman, & Baker, 1978). This particular approach emphasizes family patterns of organization, especially regarding hierarchy, roles, and boundaries. More recently, Beatrice Wood's (1993) development of the biobehavioral family model of pediatric illness represents a significant advance beyond the earlier psychosomatic family model and use of the structural approach. She integrates individual and family-level theory, particularly by joining individual biobehavioral reactivity with family interpersonal responsivity. Also, behavioral (Coyne & Fiske, 1992; Fiske, Coyne, & Smith, 1992) and cognitive (Turnbull et al., 1993) approaches have been utilized in other settings.

Peter Steinglass and Mary Elizabeth Horan (1988), in an overview of the research and theoretical literature on family factors in chronic illness, note four major perspectives that have emerged:

1. *The family as resource.* From this viewpoint, the family is envisioned as a primary source of social support that functions protectively to enhance resistance to illness and helps determine successful compliance with treatment when an illness occurs.

2. *The psychosomatic family—a deficit model.* Here the family is not seen as a potential resource, but rather as a potential liability, contributing to onset of illness, an unfavorable course, and poor compliance with treatment.

3. *Impact of illness on the family.* This orientation emphasizes the impact of an illness on the family rather than the way family factors affect the onset or course of a health problem.

4. *Family influences on the course of chronic illness.* This perspective is more systemic, taking into account the interaction between family behavior and characteristics of the illness and how this mutual interaction can have a positive or a negative influence on the course of a chronic disorder.

The Family Systems–Illness Model described in this book combines these ways of thinking, stressing an interactive perspective that views the family as a resource and avoiding the tendencies of the deficit model to overemphasize family pathology.

The Family Adjustment and Adaptation Response (FAAR) model represents an important development of this interactive perspective (McCubbin & Patterson, 1982; Patterson, 1989b). This model combines family stress theory and family systems theory. It is based on the idea that families facing major stressors, such as chronic illness, use their resources and coping capabilities to meet the demands of the disorder. The meaning families ascribe to these demands and capabilities is seen as a critical mediating factor in determining family adjustment and adaptation. Families undergo repeated cycles of adjustment/crisis/adaptation in response to normative life cycle transitions and changes in an illness. Joan Patterson (1988) has applied this model particularly well to issues relative to children with chronic disorders.

The important research of David Reiss, Peter Steinglass, and colleagues at George Washington University has added to our understanding of how families organize themselves when faced with chronic disorders. Their model was built around the concept of a family paradigm in which family identity is based on three family dimensions that predict differences in family problem-solving behavior in a laboratory situation (Oliveri & Reiss, 1982; Reiss, 1981). They conceptualize family paradigm and identity in terms of family members' shared views about order, equity, coherence, and novelty in the social world, and ideas the family holds about itself in relation to this social world (such as competence or durability). Using this model, Reiss and coworkers' research with end-stage renal disease (Reiss, Gonzales, & Kramer, 1986) showed that "in sharp contrast to expectations based on previous data, high [family] scores on problem-solving variables, as well as measures of accomplishment and intactness, predicted early death, rather than survival" (p. 795). This counterintuitive finding suggests that we have much to learn about the complex interaction of family factors, quality of life, and the course of diseases.

Finally, valuable contributions to our understanding have come from first-person accounts of family members' experiences. In particular, Maggie Strong's (1988) *Mainstay: For the Well Spouse of the Chronically Ill* is a moving account of her experience as a well spouse rearing a family after her husband developed multiple sclerosis early in their marriage. Anatole Broyard's (1992) *Intoxicated by My Illness*, Cheri Register's (1987) *Living with Chronic Illness: Days of Patience and Passion*, and Norman Cousins' (1979) *Anatomy of an Illness as Perceived by the Patient* provide insight and inspiration about how to live well with a serious condition.

LIMITATIONS AND NEGLECTED AREAS

The existing literature is limited in several critical ways. Edited volumes lack a coherent framework. No single volume articulates an overarching, comprehensive, systems model for intervention, with couples and families, for the full range of health conditions. Many of the clinical writings address a particular illness or disability. The problem is that insights about a particular disorder can be applied either too narrowly or too inclusively to conditions with markedly different psychosocial demands. Application of a particular type of treatment can become overgeneralized, insufficient stock being taken of the complexities of different disorders over time. The Family Systems–Illness Model described in this book addresses this problem, so that one conceptual model can be applied to a full range of adult- and childhood-onset illnesses and disabilities, including long-term mental disorders.

The *landscape of chronic disorders* is diverse and complex, presenting a vast range of symptoms and trajectories, accompanied by a variety of psychosocial demands over the natural history of the disorders. Although there are elegant and detailed descriptions of the physical demands of particular conditions, these accounts are not expressed in a systems language in which the pattern of demands of the illness over time is put into psychosocial terms that are useful to both clinicians and families and serve as a bridge between the biomedical and the psychosocial worlds (Strauss, 1975). This is a tremendous unmet need.

The dimension of time has been neglected. No model has combined illness and disability in a schema that covers the past, the present, and the future. The literature has generally focused on a specific phase of what I refer to as the "illness life course" (for example, disease onset, terminal phase, or bereavement). There is no schema that considers the unfolding of illness-related developmental tasks over the entire course of a disorder. If developmental issues are addressed, they tend to be restricted to a particular person, usually the patient. With some notable exceptions (Eisenberg, Sutkin, & Jansen, 1984; Turk & Kerns, 1985; Walsh, 1989a), developmental issues with regard to other family members and the whole family unit have been given far less attention. The impact of chronic conditions on the patient, well family members, and key caregivers differs, and depends on when an illness strikes in the family and in each member's individual development. Because the great variation in how different conditions manifest themselves over the course of a condition has been largely ignored, developmental tasks for all family members and the family unit that are associated with the time phases of an illness have not been well articulated. Developmental skews become inevitable during the course of an illness or disability. For all these reasons, work with chronic conditions requires a model that can integrate individual and family life cycle issues into a coherent whole.

Systems thinkers have stressed that a family's present behavior cannot be adequately understood apart from its history (Boszormenyi-Nagy & Spark, 1973; Bowen, 1978b; Carter & McGoldrick, 1989; Framo, 1992; Paul & Grosser, 1965; Walsh & McGoldrick, 1991a). Multigenerational legacies and patterns of adaptation shape myths, beliefs, and expectations that strongly influence how families perceive a current health crisis and guide the kinds of systems they develop in the face of adversity. Roles and expectations based on gender are particularly important (McGoldrick, Anderson & Walsh, 1989).

In sum, with families facing illness and disability there is a need for a *multigenerational life cycle model* that coherently integrates legacies and themes related to illness with the three interwoven developmental threads of the illness, individual, and family life cycles in a manner useful for assessment and intervention.

Belief systems play a central role in shaping family coping and adaptation when confronted with chronic disorders. Arthur Kleinman's (1988) *The Illness Narratives: Suffering, Healing, and the Human Condition* vividly describes, from an anthropological perspective, the kinds of explanations and meanings people attach to health problems. Other excellent work in the area of cognitive psychology, particularly attribution theory, has examined the ways in which people construct beliefs about how things happen, especially significant personal events (Abramson, Garber, & Seligman, 1980; Lazarus, 1991; Lazarus & Folkman, 1984). However, these important contributions to our understanding of meaning systems do not describe the evolution and significance of belief systems at a family level or the ongoing systemic processes in families relative to meaning systems when a member becomes ill.

In recent years there has been increasing interest in families' constructions of reality, narratives, and scripts (Anderson & Goolishian, 1988; Byng-Hall, 1988; Combs & Freedman, 1990; Dell, 1985; Gergen, 1985; Hoffman, 1990; Keeney, 1983; Maturana & Varela, 1987; Reiss, 1981; Sluzki, 1992; Watzlawick, 1984; White & Epston, 1990). This important body of work has only begun to receive attention and application to family beliefs in situations of illness and disability (Griffith & Griffith, 1994; Griffith, Griffith, & Slovik, 1990; Madsen, 1992; Patterson, 1989a; Rolland, 1987b; Seaburn, Lorenz, & Kaplan, 1992; Wright, Watson & Bell, in press).

A basic task for families is to create a meaning for a health condition that preserves its sense of competency and mastery. At the extremes, competing ideologies can leave families with a choice between a biological explanation or one of personal responsibility (Bad things happen to bad people). Families desperately need reassurance that they are handling an illness normally (Bad things do happen to good people). Integration of belief systems needs to be included in a family systems model of illness and disability.

Through a Normative Lens

Over the past ten years, I have had an opportunity, myself or in team consultation with colleagues at the Chicago Center for Family Health and, previously, at the Center for Illness in Families in New Haven, Connecticut, to provide family systems–based consultation and treatment to over 600 families with chronic and life-threatening disorders. Approximately two-thirds of our referrals have involved individuals and families who have never before seen a mental health professional. This is a striking statistic, with profound clinical implications: it underscores the need for any comprehensive model to be useful for average families coping with the usual strains of illness, not just for the severely dysfunctional families commonly seen in mental health settings.

What is called for is a model that describes in normative terms the complex, mutual interactions among the physical disorder, the patient, and the family. There is a considerable literature describing the impact of chronic disorders on individuals and families (Campbell, 1986). Research on families facing illness and disability, like studies of the individual patient, has tended to emphasize pathological family dynamics that are associated with an unfavorable course of the disease or poor compliance with treatment. This leads to paradigms that emphasize dysfunctional illness-based family systems and families with psychosomatic disorders.

The early ground-breaking research of Salvador Minuchin, Bernice Rosman, Lester Baker, and colleagues (1975, 1978) is an example of how conclusions drawn from work with severely dysfunctional families is misapplied to normal families coping with illness. They studied children with brittle diabetes, anorexia nervosa, and asthma who were in and out of hospitals and emergency rooms. They found that these severely dysfunctional, "psychosomatic" families were characterized by significantly disturbed processes, including patterns of enmeshment, rigidity, lack of conflict resolution, overprotection, and making children the third leg of a triangle in unresolved parental issues. Any family with these characteristics is likely to have problems with any chronic disorder. Unfortunately, the findings have been applied indiscriminately by many clinicians and in professional training programs, in which trainees learn that if they observe any of these traits to any degree, a family is to be considered at high risk of disturbance or already disturbed.

This judgment disregards the fact that components of family functioning, such as cohesion, exist on a continuum, and that different types or stages of a condition may require varying levels of family cohesion for optimal coping and adaptation. I have seen very enmeshed families function very well when faced with a rapidly progressive, fatal illness, such as metastatic cancer, because high cohesion is needed, and enmeshment does not necessarily present a problem in this kind of situation; in fact, in the short run, it is adaptive. This example illustrates that defining pathological systems at one end of a continuum does not clarify what constitutes healthy family coping and adaptation to illness.

The impact of individual and family dynamics on illness and disability has historically been defined largely as psychosomatic processes, and almost invariably in pathological terms. As a result many normative biopsychosocial interactions are defined as psychosomatic, an inappropriate label that is associated with a number of pejorative cultural meanings that imply characterological or family deficiency.

A more inclusive model is needed that views psychosomatic interactions from a more holistic, interactive, and normative perspective. All illnesses are then seen as having a psychosomatic component, in which the relative influence of biological and psychosocial factors varies over a range of disorders and stages of illness. Even with regard to highly virulent diseases such as AIDS, there is compelling evidence that family and/or community support affects the patient's quality of life and the course of the illness. From this vantage point, psychosomatic interplay is good news: it provides an opportunity for psychosocial factors, not just medical interventions, to be important influences in the healing process.

A serious health crisis can awaken family members to opportunities for more satisfying, fulfilling relationships with each other. Hence, any useful clinical model should emphasize the possibilities for growth, not just the liabilities and risks.

The Family Systems–Illness Model

This book aims to fill the knowledge gap for health and mental health professionals who deal with families facing illness and disability. It provides a normative, preventive, systems model for psychoeducation, assessment, and intervention with families (Rolland, 1984, 1987a, 1987b, 1988a, 1988b, 1990a, 1990b, 1993a). This model is based on systems theory. Above all, family systems theory emphasizes interaction and context; individual behavior is viewed within the context in which it occurs. From this perspective, function and dysfunction are defined relative to the fit among the individual and family, their social context, and the psychosocial demands of the situation— here, a health problem. Family enmeshment, which may be dysfunctional under other circumstances, can be adaptive during a health crisis where family members may need to pull together and suspend normal boundaries in order to facilitate short-term coping and adaptation. The transactional patterns within the family and between a family and other systems (for example, health institutions) are considered central in shaping individual behavior. Further, in family systems theory, individuals are seen to be interrelated so that change in any one member affects other family members, which, in turn, affects the first family member in a circular chain of influence. Since every action in a sequence is also a reaction, causality is seen as circular rather than linear. Therapeutic interventions are aimed at modifying dysfunctional family patterns in which symptomatic behavior is embedded. Changing the context of a behavior is often considered the best way to produce individual change. In this sense, family or relationship processes are emphasized as much as, if not more than, the content of a problem.

Therefore, for clinicians and researchers alike, *interaction* is at the heart of all systems-oriented biopsychosocial inquiry. In physical illness, particularly chronic and life-threatening disorders, the primary focus is the system created by the interaction of a condition with an individual, family, and other biopsychosocial systems. Engel (1977, 1980) has described a continuum of natural systems that begins at the level of the smallest subatomic particle and extends sequentially through the levels of the person, family, community, culture, nation, and total ecosystem. The Family Systems–Illness Model takes the family as its central point because, from the perspective of clinical assessment and intervention, the family may provide the best lens through which to view these other systems. This choice is made with the recognition that the family is a system interacting with the larger environment, particularly the health-care system, and that the impact of chronic disorders on a family is affected by its own economic resources and extended kin and social network, and the availability and quality of services.

The Family Systems–Illness Model highlights the interactive processes between the psychosocial demands of different disorders over time and key components of family functioning. Beginning with the expected psychosocial demands of a disorder through its various phases, family systems dynamics that emphasize multigenerational patterns, family and individual life cycles, and family belief systems (including those associated with culture, ethnicity, and gender) provide the core of this clinical framework. Figure 1.1 depicts one useful way to present the interface between the illness and family aspects of this model.

The model offers a useful systemic view of family adaptation to serious illness in a child or an adult as a developmental process over time. Considering the family the unit of care, in which a broad range of family forms and biopsychosocial interactions are normative, enables us to develop a model that takes as its central reference point the idea of goodness of fit between a family's style, with its particular strengths and vulnerabilities, and the psychosocial demands of different disorders over time. From this perspective, no single family pattern is regarded as inherently healthy or unhealthy. Rather, the organizing principle becomes relative: What degree of family cohesion is optimal in different kinds of conditions, and how might that change in different phases of various disorders?

The model is designed to help families master the basic issues presented by chronic disorders. To create a functional family-illness system to meet the challenges of such a disorder, families need, first, psychosocial understanding of the condition in systems terms. This means learning the expected pattern of practical and emotional demands of a disorder over its course, including a time line for disease-related developmental tasks associated with different phases of the disorder as it unfolds. Second, families need to gain an understanding of themselves as a functional unit in systems terms. Third, they need an appreciation of individual and family life cycles to help them stay attuned to the changing fit between the demands of a chronic disorder and new developmental issues for the family unit and individual members. Finally, clinicians and families need to understand the values, beliefs, and multigenerational legacies that underlie health problems and the type of caregiving systems they establish. Figure 1.2 represents one way to conceptualize the relationship between these different levels of influence.

The Family Systems–Illness Model provides a conceptual base for approaching clinical practice and research regarding illness and disability from a family systems perspective, with emphasis on the initial consultation and assessment process and the common issues and challenges faced by families as they experience a condition over time. Intervention guidelines are offered, but the model is intended for clinicians who may use different models and techniques of therapeutic intervention. The model is interdisciplinary, and can be applied by both health and mental health clinicians; it has been designed with an awareness that the level of psychosocial intervention will

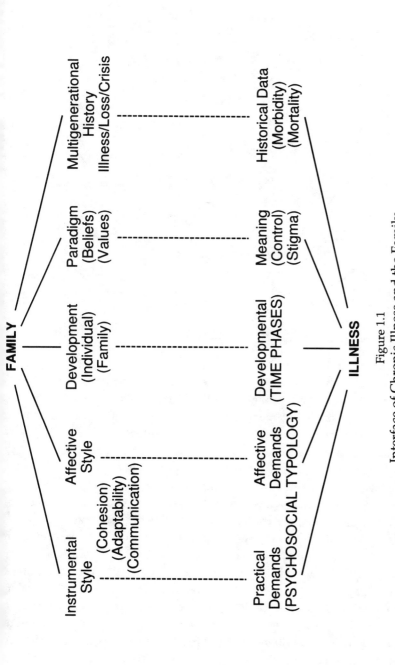

Figure 1.1

Interface of Chronic Illness and the Family

Source: Reprinted by permission from Rolland, J. S. (1984). Family systems and chronic illness: A typological model. *Journal of Psychotherapy and the Family, 3,* 144.

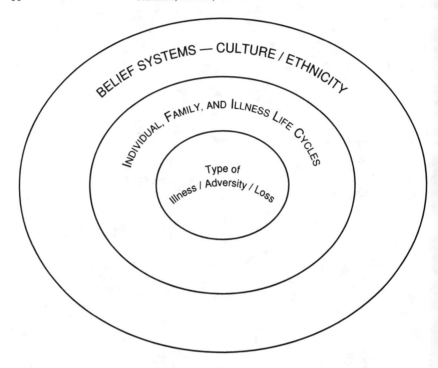

Figure 1.2
Family Systems–Illness Model: Spheres of Influence

vary considerably depending on the context and the professional background and role of the clinician. Doherty and Baird (1986) delineate five levels of psychosocial involvement with families, beginning with minimal provision of medical information and advice, through providing support, undertaking a systemic assessment and planned intervention, and, finally, conducting family therapy. The Family Systems–Illness Model should be helpful at any of these levels of intervention.

I have written each chapter with enough detail to be useful to clinicians needing to conduct more comprehensive assessments or intensive interventions. I will discuss a range of important issues and dilemmas and offer sample questions so that clinicians can get a feel for how I elicit information about various areas of family life. I never cover all questions or all issues in detail with any one family. Those clinicians who function under enormous time pressures and have limited time with families can adapt this approach to make best use of their limited time. For instance, instead of doing a detailed multigenerational history, asking a few well-chosen questions can serve as a "screening scan." If a critical issue is identified, clinicians can decide whether they or someone else need to evaluate the situation further.

The Plan of This Book

This book is divided into three parts. Beginning with the idea that there is an ongoing systemic interaction between chronic disorders and families, Parts I (chapters 2 and 3) and II (chapters 4–8) describe the illness and family aspects of the model, respectively, and provide clinical case vignettes. Part III (chapters 9–11) applies the model in more depth to specific treatment issues for families and couples, and to personal and larger system interface issues for clinicians.

Chapter 2 describes a psychosocial typology of illness in which the pattern of onset, course, outcome, incapacitation, and degree of uncertainty provides a way to understand the practical and affective psychosocial demands of any disorder. Chapter 3 deals with the core time phases in the illness life cycle: the crisis, chronic, and terminal phases and the key transitions that link them. Major psychosocial developmental tasks and clinical issues associated with each phase are described. Together, the psychosocial typology and time phases provide a way to think about the psychosocial demands of different "types" of disorders at different phases of their course. Practical applications of this clinical framework are offered.

On the basis of the psychosocial typology and time phases framework, Part II of the book describes critical family processes in chronic disorders, highlighting the dimension of time (chapters 5 and 6), belief systems (chapter 7), and uncertainty in the face of loss (chapter 8). Chapter 4 provides a brief overview of family dynamics in chronic disorders, including family organizational patterns, adaptability, cohesion, boundary issues, triangulation, and family communication processes. Chapter 5 describes use of genograms and then considers the assessment and clinical importance of multigenerational issues related to illness and loss, covering, with the aid of case examples, legacies, including toxic ones, catastrophic expectations, and areas of strength and learned differences between adults. Chapter 6 draws on and links key concepts from several major individual and family life cycle models to facilitate placing the unfolding of chronic disorders in a developmental context and discusses the ongoing interactions between the illness and the development of the family and its individual members. Issues of timing of onset and future nodal points are highlighted.

Chapter 7 describes the role of belief systems in chronic disorders. The discussion includes key elements of families' health belief systems and the forces that shape them over the course of a condition. Special consideration is given to beliefs about normality, the mind–body relationship, control and mastery, positive illusions, meanings attached to symptoms and illnesses, the cause of and influences on the course or outcome of a disorder, ethnicity, gender, and culture, and the fit of beliefs among family members and with health providers. The chapter examines beliefs that induce blame, shame, and guilt and interventions that foster more adaptive beliefs and promote competency and mastery.

Families facing life-threatening and progressive, disabling conditions often live for years with the painful ambiguities and uncertainties of threatened loss. In contrast to the concept of anticipatory grief, which has been limited to the terminal phase of an illness, chapter 8 addresses issues for families dealing with anticipated loss over the entire course of a chronic or life-threatening condition. Considered are such issues as distinguishing among anticipation of disability, cognitive impairment, suffering, and death and the different strains for families dealing with possible versus probable or inevitable loss. Clinical concerns and intervention guidelines in terminal illness are included in this chapter. Helping families think about anticipated loss in relation to future life cycle nodal points in their personal and family lives is stressed.

Part III addresses salient treatment issues and intervention guidelines. Chapter 9 describes some principles for effective systemic intervention based on the Family Systems–Illness Model. Then, family treatment issues in chronic disorders in childhood, in parental illness and disability, and in coping with aging parents are covered in separate sections. Flexible use of individual, family, and multifamily group interventions is described.

Chronic disorders often wreak havoc on a couple's relationship. Couples must meet the challenges of maintaining a viable, balanced relationship with each other while serving as patient and caregiver and coping with the uncertainties of planning and achieving normative developmental goals in the face of threatened loss. In chapter 10, the model provides a basis for discussion of common couples' problems regarding intimacy, sexuality, communication problems, relationship skews, gender roles, and co-parenting and the use of individual and conjoint treatment.

It is vitally important for clinicians to understand how their own belief systems and multigenerational and life cycle issues related to loss affect their effectiveness. Chapter 11 considers critical interface concerns of clinicians and other providers of health-care, such as dilemmas related to professionals' facing loss and personal limits in the context of work demands while simultaneously trying to maintain a satisfying personal and family life. This chapter also deals with common boundary issues between families and clinicians and health-care institutions, addressing effective intervention with typical dilemmas related to fit and mutual accommodation between these interacting family and provider systems.

PART I

THE EXPERIENCE OF ILLNESS AND DISABILITY

CHAPTER 2

The Psychosocial Typology of Illness

FROM A SYSTEMS PERSPECTIVE, any effective clinical model describing the interaction of chronic disorders and the family must redefine illness and disability in systems terms. In Part I of this book, I shall begin by addressing the illness aspect and its contribution to that interaction.

In order to think in a truly interactive or systemic manner about the interface of the illness and the individual or the illness and the family, one needs a way of describing illness itself in systems terms and a schema that recasts the myriad of biological diseases in psychosocial terms. Illnesses such as cancer or heart disease should be given a psychosocial meaning that patients and their families can use to guide and empower them in their task of living with a chronic disorder. Chapters 2 and 3 provide a framework that facilitates a fluid dialogue between the illness and the family parts of the illness/family system. Such a schema must simultaneously remain relevant to the interactions of the psychosocial and biological worlds and provide a common metalanguage that transforms or reclassifies the usual biological language. Also, for such a systems framework to be useful, it needs to facilitate thinking about the interface of chronic disorders with other important systems (for example, health care, community, religion, education).

There have been two major impediments to progress in this area. First, insufficient attention has been given to the areas of diversity and commonality inherent in different chronic disorders. Second, there has been a glossing-over of the qualitative and quantitative differences in how various diseases manifest themselves over the course of the illness. Chronic conditions need to be conceptualized in a manner that organizes similarities and differences over the course of the disease so that the type and degree of demands relevant to psychosocial research and clinical practice are highlighted in a more useful way.

The great variability of chronic illnesses and their changing nature over time have presented a vexing problem to psychosocial investigators who have attempted to identify the most salient psychosocial variables relevant to the course of the disease or to compliance with treatment. Reviews of psychosocial factors that can affect the impact of stress emphasize a variety of methodological and conceptual weaknesses (Elliott & Eisdorfer, 1982; Kasl, 1982; Stein & Jessop, 1982; Weiss, Herd, & Fox, 1981). The difficulty begins when social scientists or psychotherapists accept a disease classification based on purely biological criteria clustered so as to meet the needs of medicine. This nosology is most useful for establishing a medical diagnosis and formulating a medical treatment plan. In traditional medicine, the process of diagnosis and treatment planning is the primary concern. When a patient is admitted with severe abdominal pain, the main objective is to discover the biological cause of the pain.

One can argue that clinical practice and psychosocial research in physical illness are hampered as much by blind acceptance of this model of medicine as by their own shortcomings. A different classification scheme can provide a better link between the biological and the psychosocial and thereby clarify the relationship between long-term illnesses and the family.

Historically, this specific illness orientation has pushed clinicians' and researchers' views of the relationship between psychosocial factors and physical illness toward one or another end of a continuum. Truths are sought either in each specific disease or in "illness" as a general, quasi-metaphorical concept. In the former, clinical wisdom or research findings are not generalized. Researchers continue to study each illness within a narrow focus. Countless insightful articles have been written by clinicians describing individual and family coping with particular disorders without highlighting the general aspects of adaptation they share with other illnesses. At the other end of the continuum, findings regarding a particular disease are indiscriminately generalized to all illnesses. Both of these extremes hamper the clinician. Lacking guidelines to balance unifying principles and useful distinctions, clinicians may become bewildered by the wide variety of chronic illnesses and apply a monolithic treatment approach to all chronic illnesses, or inappropriately transpose aspects of their clinical experience with mental disorders. Extensive experience with a single kind of illness that requires an intensive focus on separation and loss, such as terminal cancer, may be transferred to a chronic illness, such as stroke, in which other issues such as problem solving and redefining family roles predominate.

Clinicians from different disciplines bring their own assets and liabilities to the interaction of family and illness and disability. Physicians and nurses have a surplus of technical medical information. They can have trouble seeing the psychosocial forest through the technological lens they need to use to help the patient medically. And if they can switch lenses, often they have

trouble deciding which trees in this medical forest are psychosocially important. They may have difficulty taking the 1001 facts about diabetes and dis-
tilling from them the essence of the psychosocial meaning of the disorder.

Mental health professionals without a medical background are often intimidated by cases involving physical illness, particularly if they encounter
patients during a medical crisis or in a setting such as a hospital. They may
express feelings of uncertainty: "I don't have medical training, so how can I
help families with these problems? I feel awkward and don't know how to
apply my professional expertise in this area." From another vantage point,
their not being burdened by the responsibility for medical treatment frees
them to attend more fully to the psychosocial problems. They need a way to
comprehend the essence of an illness in psychosocial terms without first
having to become a medical expert on diabetes.

Several sources of information are helpful. Most physicians, nurses, and
medical social workers assigned to specific medical services (such as oncology) are willing to help mental health clinicians understand the basics of an
illness. Patients and families themselves will recount stories involving the
most important physical symptoms, treatments, and issues of prognosis.
Also, medical encyclopedias and review and continuing-education articles
for primary-care health professionals are useful, and often are written in an
understandable style. Finally, as consumer advocacy has grown, a number
of readable books on specific illnesses have been written for the public.

The psychosocial importance of different time phases of an illness is not
well understood. Clinicians often become involved in the care of an individual or family coping with a chronic illness at different points in the "illness
life cycle." Clinicians rarely follow the interaction of a family-illness process
through the complete life history of a disease. In research, a major problem
has been the relative predominance of cross-sectional, in contrast to longitudinal, investigations. Often, studies include cases that vary widely in terms
of the amount of time families have lived with a chronic illness. Moreover,
separate investigations of the same disease may produce conflicting results.
Debates ensue without either side's taking into account different time phases
as a plausible explanation for conflicting findings.

A few studies have explored short-range psychosocial effects on the
course of a disease. John Gottman and Lynn Katz (1989) found that children's stress-hormone levels fluctuated with the degree of marital distress of
their parents. One study noted a synchronicity of emotional and behavioral
factors with ratings of joint tenderness in people suffering from rheumatoid
arthritis (Moldofsky & Chester, 1970). Others have studied exacerbations of
diabetes and asthma (Baker et al., 1975; Bradley, 1979; Hamburg et al., 1980;
Matus & Bush, 1979; Minuchin, Baker, Rosman, Leibman, Milman & Todd,
1975). Salvador Minuchin and colleagues (1975), in their classic study of children with brittle diabetes, used the accepted medical correlation between a

rise in the level of free fatty acids in the blood and the development of diabetic exacerbations. They demonstrated a sustained rise in these levels when
the children were brought into an interview where the parents were discussing a conflictual issue. Although such studies are important, their contributions concern microfluctuations rather than broad-scale phases of an illness, including crisis, chronic, and terminal phases.

The importance of broad time stages of illness has surfaced periodically in
the literature on chronic illness. One example has been studies that examine
the adaptive and harmful effects of denial, loosely defined as attempts to
negate a problem at different points in the course of the disease. For parents
of a child with leukemia, denial may enable them adaptively to perform necessary tasks during earlier phases of the illness, but may lead to devastating
consequences for the family if maintained during the terminal phase (Chodoff, Friedman, & Hamburg, 1964; Wolff et al., 1964). Similarly, denial may be
functional for recovery on a coronary care unit after a heart attack, but harmful if this translates into ignoring medical advice about diet, exercise, and
work stress over the long term (Croog, Shapiro, & Levine, 1971). These two
examples illustrate how denial can, at certain points in a long-term illness,
reduce the potential for overwhelming affect and help families accomplish
the necessary illness-related tasks. These studies highlight the importance of
a longitudinal perspective (in this instance, in relation to a particular defense
mechanism—denial), but do not offer an overarching framework.

There is a clear need for a model that describes illnesses and disabilities in
psychosocial terms and provides a useful guide for both clinical practice and
research. This chapter and the next describe a psychosocial typology and
time phases schema of chronic and life-threatening disorders that highlight
for all conditions the pattern of psychosocial demands over time. Illness
variability and time phases are addressed in terms of two separate dimensions:

1. Chronic illnesses and disabilities are grouped according to key biological similarities and differences that dictate significant and distinct psychosocial demands for those who are ill and for their families.
2. The prime developmental time phases in the natural evolution of
   chronic disease are identified.

A Psychosocial Typology of Illness

Any typology is a subjectively constructed map for orienting one to a territory (Bateson, 1972, 1979). The goal of the typology presented here is to create clinically meaningful and useful categories for a wide array of chronic
disorders affecting individuals across the entire life span; it is designed not

ONSET: Acute vs. Gradual

COURSE: Progressive vs. Constant vs. Relapsing

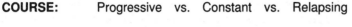

OUTCOME: Nonfatal vs.   Shortened   vs. Fatal
                                  Life Span
                                       or
                              Sudden Death

INCAPACITATION: None vs. Mild vs. Moderate vs. Severe

Figure 2.1
Psychosocial Illness Types

for traditional medical treatment or prognostic purposes, but for examining the relationship between family or individual dynamics and chronic disease.

This typology conceptualizes broad distinctions of the pattern of (1) onset, (2) course, (3) outcome, (4) type and degree of incapacitation, and (5) degree of uncertainty (see figure 2.1). These categories are hypothesized to be the most psychosocially significant for a wide range of illnesses and disabilities. They were also chosen because the type of onset, course, and outcome strongly influences the nature of the developmental tasks associated with each of the time phases of the illness—crisis, chronic, and terminal—described in the next chapter. For example, the type of onset significantly affects the nature of the developmental tasks normally associated with the initial crisis phase. Although each variable is actually a continuum, it will be described here in a categorical manner by selection of key anchor points along the continuum. Consider these anchor points guideposts that can clarify the many shades of gray.

ONSET

Illnesses can be divided into those that have either an *acute* or a *gradual* onset. This division is not meant to differentiate types of biological development, but to highlight the kinds of symptomatic presentation that can be noted subjectively by the patient or objectively by other people. Strokes, heart attacks, traumatic brain injury, and meningitis are examples of conditions with sudden clinical presentation, though they may have long periods of biological change that led to a marker event. Examples of illnesses with a gradual onset include arthritis, chronic lung disease, and Parkinson's disease. For an illness with a gradual onset such as rheumatoid arthritis, the diagnosis serves as a somewhat arbitrary confirmation point after clinical symptoms have appeared.

A condition with a gradual onset presents a different form of stressor to a person or family than a sudden crisis. The total amount of readjustment of family structure, roles, problem solving, and affective coping may be the same for both types of illness. However, for those with acute onset, such as stroke, the emotional and practical changes are compressed into a short time and require of the family more rapid mobilization of crisis management skills.

Some families are better equipped than others to cope with rapid change. Families able to tolerate highly charged affective states, exchange clearly defined roles flexibly, solve problems efficiently, and utilize outside resources effectively have an advantage in managing acute-onset illnesses. Other families' style of coping may be more suited to gradual change: like the tortoise versus the hare, they take a slow and steady approach. Given enough time, they will achieve their goal. Such families adjust well to gradual-onset disorders such as Alzheimer's disease, but may be initially overwhelmed by problems such as stroke. The problem of fit between this family style and the initial demands of an illness calls for a brief early intervention to support family members through this vulnerable phase and help avert long-term dysfunction. Once "in gear," the family very well may have the resources to manage the complexities of a long-term disorder, particularly one without repeated, acute changes or new and unfamiliar symptoms.

The slower rate of family change required to cope with gradual-onset diseases, such as rheumatoid arthritis or Parkinson's disease, allows for a more protracted period of adjustment, but perhaps generates more anxiety before the diagnosis is made. For acute-onset diseases, there is relatively greater immediate strain on the family in simultaneously trying to prevent further loss and death and cope with a new problem (Adams & Lindemann, 1974).

COURSE

The course of chronic disorders can take essentially three general forms: *progressive, constant,* or *relapsing/episodic*. Each will pose differing psychosocial challenges for families.

A *progressive* disease is one that is continually or generally symptomatic and increases in severity. Examples include: incurable cancers, Alzheimer's disease, AIDS, juvenile-onset diabetes, rheumatoid arthritis, and emphysema. The individual and the family are faced with the effects of a perpetually symptomatic family member in whom disability increases in a stepwise or progressive fashion. Periods of relief from the demands of the illness tend to be minimal. Families need to be prepared for continual adaptation and role changes.

At each stage of a progressive illness, such as Alzheimer's disease, the family needs to organize itself to deal with a particular level of disability and degree of uncertainty. Yet, it cannot really "settle in" at any particular stage because progression looms ahead, and must be prepared to keep reforming its system to keep pace with the changing picture of the illness. Increasing strain on family caregivers is caused by both the risks of exhaustion and the continual addition of new caregiving tasks over time. Family flexibility in terms of both role reorganization and willingness to use outside resources is crucial.

In progressive disorders clinicians need to be aware that, like a marathon runner, any family can "hit the wall"—literally come to the end of its physical, emotional, or financial stamina and/or its ability to reform its system. At this point, a family may need to radically restructure its way of handling the necessary changes. In systems terms, this family needs to make more fundamental second-order versus first-order change. Second-order change has to do with altering aspects of one's world view and the basic rules that go with them. It involves a transformation that is more discontinuous with the past than is first-order change. For example, one elderly couple governed by traditional gender roles made it through the initial phases of the wife's progressive respiratory condition by added effort in performing their traditional, gender-defined roles; but as the condition worsened, the couple finally reached a stage at which they could carry on only by redefining their basic roles so that daily tasks could be shared. When families lack the resources or flexibility to make fundamental changes, they may have to allow professional help into their home or consider institutionalizing the ill member.

Thorough, early assessment of a family can help a clinician judge when a family may reach its limits. Evaluative discussions are particularly important when dealing with progressive disabling disorders, in which caretaking demands alone can result, over time, in a family increasingly defining its life mission and source of competency in terms of successful caregiving. Such families may be on a collision course because of the incompatibility of their caretaking ideal and the exhaustion inherent in many progressive illnesses. And, as we shall discuss later (chapter 7), a collapse or perceived "failure" of the caretaking mission can have serious negative consequences that reverberate throughout the family and across generations. Clinicians can help a family avert a crisis by laying the groundwork for basic change that will improve their staying power. It is also important to explore family attitudes about such possibilities as extended, home-based, professional care.

It is useful to distinguish further between illnesses that progress rapidly or slowly. The demands on a family of a rapidly progressive illness such as metastatic lung cancer or acute leukemia are different from those of slowly progressive illnesses such as rheumatoid arthritis, chronic lung disease (for example, emphysema or chronic bronchitis), or adult-onset diabetes. The pace of adaptation required for coping with the continual changes and ever-new demands of a rapidly progressive disease mounts as the time shortens. A slowly progressive illness may place a higher premium on stamina over a long period rather than on continual adaptation and change. With a rapidly progressive illness such as a fast-growing brain tumor, the pileup of psychosocial demands can easily outstrip a family's ability to adapt (much like the body's inability to keep up with the tumor). In such situations families with limited resources may have to decide which tasks confronting them warrant highest priority. This can involve a daunting and agonizing decision, especially if the consequences are great. One lower-income family trying to manage a grandmother's advancing dementia felt torn between overwhelming financial pressures and a commitment to keep the grandmother alive and in the family home. Clinicians can help a family decide what, within its limits, is most important. This is particularly useful when dealing with families that have an ethos of mastering a situation themselves, no matter how great the problem.

An illness with a *constant* course is typically one in which an initial event occurs, but then the biological condition stabilizes. Examples include stroke, single-episode heart attack, traumatic brain injury, amputation, or spinal cord injury with paralysis. Generally, after an initial period of recovery, the chronic phase is characterized by some clear-cut deficit such as paraplegia, amputation, speech loss, or cognitive impairment; or there may be residual functional limitations such as diminished tolerance of physical stress or restriction of previous activities. There may be recurrences, but the individual or family is faced with a semipermanent change that is stable and predictable over a considerable time. The potential for family and patient exhaustion exists, but without the strain of new role demands over time that characterizes progressive disorders.

For families in this situation, it is easier, in a relative sense, to resume normal living than is the case for those dealing with a progressive condition. Once the patient and family learn how to manage the disability, they can plan for the future without the continual uncertainties inherent in progressive illness. In family consultation with a rehabilitation team and me, a man with a spinal cord injury paralyzing him from the waist down was able to devise a slow, methodical plan to return to work within two years. This plan, which depended largely on a predictable trajectory of the illness, required the family to establish and follow a realistic program. The predictability of the man's condition was also essential in assuring his employer's willingness and ability to accommodate to the employee's physical limitations.

Conditions with a *relapsing* or *episodic* course include, among others, spinal disc disorders, inflammatory bowel disease, asthma, peptic ulcer, migraine headaches, multiple sclerosis, and forms of cancer in remission, such as those that are resectable or responsive to chemotherapy. The distinguishing feature of this type of course is the alternation of stable periods of varying length, characterized by a low level or absence of symptoms, with periods of flare-up or exacerbation. Often family members can carry on a normal routine, though the specter of a recurrence hangs over their heads.

Relapsing illnesses demand a somewhat different sort of family and patient adaptability. Compared with progressive or constant course illnesses, they may require the least continuous caretaking or role change. But the episodic nature of the illness may require a flexibility that permits movement back and forth between two forms of family organization—one during flare-ups and the other for periods of remission. In a sense, the family is always on call to cope with crises and handle exacerbations of the illness. Both the frequency of transitions between crisis and noncrisis and the ongoing uncertainty of when a crisis will next occur produce strain for the family. Also, the considerable psychological discrepancy between periods of normalcy and periods of illness is a particularly taxing feature unique to relapsing chronic diseases. These disorders may not be as biologically severe as those with a progressive or constant course, yet, over time, they can be the most psychosocially challenging.

For instance, in one family the father had had a chronic disc problem that had been asymptomatic for several years. Family members, including Dad, had almost forgotten about his problem. One Saturday morning Dad went outside to do some light yard work, unthinkingly lifted something slightly too heavy, and threw his back out, becoming instantly disabled and in severe pain. He then had to be confined to his bed for two weeks. In a matter of hours, the family, rudely reawakened to the fact that the father had a chronic disorder, had to rapidly shift roles and expectations to accommodate to his disability. Flare-ups of relapsing disorders often coincide with periods of great family or other stress, which affects physical health. In this case, the father had been subjected to recent stressors at work that had tightened up his back muscles and perhaps made him more vulnerable to reactivating his disc problem.

It is important to understand a family's expectations about the course of a disorder. In this regard, it is useful to ask each member questions such as the following:

- What information has the medical team or particular professionals given you about the expected course of your or your family member's condition?
- What were you told about how uncertain the course could be?
- Does this information differ in any way from the family's or individual member's expectations about the course and its degree of uncertainty?

These questions help determine what, specifically, has been said to the family and to which members directly. They help clarify whether, despite what the doctors have said, family members have their own ideas, based on previous experience or other sources of information. Clinicians may learn about discrepant viewpoints within the family that can help explain conflicts between members about how the condition should be handled. They can assess who is knowledgeable and who is uninformed, and why. Did the physician choose to communicate with only certain family members? Did key family member(s) decide who should get information directly from the primary source? Were different family members, for instance, the patient or children, given different information, and for what reasons (for instance, age-appropriate distinctions versus overprotection)? Such questions reveal whether the medical team has given consistent information. Divergent viewpoints about the expected course from "the experts" can create tremendous turmoil within a family. Often health professionals are unaware that colleagues have communicated significantly different information to a family or particular family members. Solving these sorts of problems at an early stage can be very useful in helping avert long-term dysfunctional patterns among all concerned.

OUTCOME

The extent to which a chronic illness is a likely cause of death and the degree to which it can shorten one's life are critical distinguishing features with a profound psychosocial impact. The most crucial factor is the initial expectation of whether a disease is likely to cause death. At one end of the continuum are illnesses that do not typically affect the life span, such as lumbosacral disc problems, blindness, arthritis, spinal cord injury, or seizure disorders. At the other extreme are illnesses that are clearly progressive and usually fatal, such as metastatic cancer, AIDS, and Huntington's disease. There is an intermediate, more unpredictable category, which includes both illnesses that shorten the life span, such as cystic fibrosis, juvenile-onset diabetes, and cardiovascular disease, and those with the possibility of sudden death, such as hemophilia or recurrences of heart attack or stroke.

The major difference among these kinds of outcome is the degree to which the family experiences anticipatory loss and its pervasive effects on family life. This subject will be discussed fully in chapter 8. All chronic ill-nesses potentially involve loss of bodily control, key aspects of one's iden-tity, and intimate relationships (Sourkes, 1982). In a life-threatening illness, loss of control entails greater consequences—death and permanent loss of relationships. In life cycle terms, the ill member fears an end to life before his or her life plan can be completed, and being alone in death. The family fears becoming survivors alone in the future. For both there is an undercurrent of anticipatory grief and separation that permeates all phases of adaptation. Families are often caught between a desire for intimacy with and a pull to let go, emotionally, of the ill member. The expectation of loss can make it ex-tremely difficult for a family to maintain a balanced perspective.

A torrent of affect can make a family unable to master the myriad of prac-tical tasks and problems necessary to maintain family integrity (Weiss, per-sonal communication, 1983). Also, a tendency to see the ill family member as practically in the coffin can set in motion maladaptive responses that divest the ill member of important responsibilities. The end result can be structural and emotional isolation of the ill person from family life. This kind of psy-chological alienation has been associated with poor medical outcome in life-threatening illness (Davies et al., 1973; Derogatis, Abeloff, & Melisartos, 1979; Schmale & Iker, 1971; Simonton, Matthews-Simonton, & Sparks, 1980).

Loss is more ambiguous and uncertain an outcome in illnesses that may shorten life or cause sudden death than in those that are clearly fatal, and this ambiguity makes issues of mortality less prominent but more insidious in day-to-day living. It is for this reason that this type of illness provides such a fertile ground for idiosyncratic family interpretations. The "It could happen" nature of these illnesses creates a nidus for both overprotection by the family and powerful secondary gains for the ill member. This is particu-larly relevant with regard to childhood illnesses such as hemophilia, juve-nile-onset diabetes, and asthma (Minuchin et al., 1975; Minuchin, Rosman, & Baker, 1978).

Traditional cultural rights and privileges are associated with the role of being a patient (Parsons & Fox, 1952; Resnick, 1984; Thomas, 1970). Families displaying normal empathy are expected to suspend the usual responsibili-ties and expectations of the ill family member, and the affected family mem-ber can use this status to wield power and control, a condition often referred to as secondary gain. This phenomenon is more likely in the case of a chronic condition, particularly a life-threatening one. In fact, as we shall discuss later, secondary gain is available to all family members in relation to the out-side world. A common example might be a couple in which a husband's dis-ability is used as a legitimate excuse to avoid performing household chores over which they have long struggled.

It is vitally important for clinicians to be informed about prognosis, par-ticularly about the probability and timing of loss; for this, direct contact with the primary physician is often essential. Family members frequently organize themselves and set priorities concerning major life issues in direct relation to their ideas about prognosis. Therefore, the clinician must inquire about each family member's perceptions in this regard. Significant differences about the life-threatening potential among family members or between the family and health providers are critical and often are a source of major conflict.

To assess family perceptions about outcome, I ask questions such as the following:

- What has your physician told you about your family member's (or your) prognosis?
- Do you think your family member's illness can or will shorten his or her life? If so, when do you think this could happen?
- Do your views differ from what you have been told by your doctor(s)? If so, how is this difference managed?
- Is there agreement about the prognosis within the family? If there is disagreement within the family, who disagrees with whom, and how are differences of opinion handled?
- If the illness can be fatal, how does this knowledge affect day-to-day family life (for instance, emotional climate, roles, communication, priorities)? Who talks with whom about it? Who does not, and why not?

This line of questioning allows the clinician to identify coping strategies, areas of misinformation that can be corrected, denial, patterns of communication about threatened loss, and differences in perception that a clinician should assess further.

Typically, disregard of these issues leads to dysfunctional family patterns that pose major, ongoing risks to a family's overall adaptation. These risks far outweigh immediate concern about approaching sensitive and painful subjects with the family. It is important that all family members be given an opportunity to answer these questions. I prefer to do this, when possible, with everyone present, including the patient. In different situations, I may begin by meeting separately with each family member, or with the adults and children separately. The overall goal is to facilitate the family's ability to have timely open discussion about sensitive issues when appropriate over the course of the condition.

To assess a family's preparedness to face a downhill course, particularly in high-risk illnesses, I suggest that clinicians ask the following kind of questions:

- Although we are all very hopeful for a good response to treatments, if things do not go well, at what point will you begin to focus on possible loss (for example, on the basis of what symptoms or information from a physician)?

- What would you, as a family, envision doing differently at that point from what you do now?
- Can you imagine any information that would be useful to your family now, to relieve certain worries (for instance, concerning pain control)?

Posing these questions gives families an opportunity to express their fears and, at the same time, to distinguish the current situation from a later possibility. This is like an insurance policy, which, once drawn up, can be put on the shelf and, one hopes, never be needed. Generally, families find that this process increases their sense of control.

INCAPACITATION

Disability can result from impairment of mental functioning or cognition (as in Alzheimer's disease), sensation (as in blindness), movement (as in stroke with paralysis or multiple sclerosis), decreased energy production, or disfigurement or other physical causes of social stigma. Illnesses such as cardiovascular and respiratory diseases impair the body's ability to produce raw energy, which can reduce peak performance or stamina.

Social stigma is an important cause of disability in many disorders. Conditions such as mastectomy for breast cancer, neurofibromatosis (the "elephant man"), severe burns, or psoriasis are cosmetically disabling and distorting of body image to the extent that the attendant social stigma interferes with normal social interaction. Often treatment procedures produce psychosocial difficulties because of their disfiguring nature or side effects; mastectomy for breast cancer and hair loss from cancer chemotherapy are examples. AIDS is socially disabling because of the combined effects of its perceived high risk of contagion, its long, asymptomatic incubation/carrier period, its current status as incurable, and its links with highly stigmatized groups in our society—homosexuals and users of intravenous drugs. Even during asymptomatic periods, people with AIDS often experience enormous handicaps related to stigma: they may lose their jobs, health insurance, family and friends, and general sense of self-worth. Finally, labeling a difficult-to-diagnose patient with confusing symptoms of persistent tiredness with the chronic fatigue syndrome can be socially incapacitating because of ambiguities surrounding its cause and its current association with underlying mental disorders such as depression.

The different kinds of incapacitation imply sharp differences in the specific adjustments required of a family. For instance, the combined cognitive and motor deficits of a person with a stroke necessitate greater changes in family roles than are required by a person with a spinal cord injury who retains his or her cognitive faculties. Some chronic diseases such as hypertension, peptic ulcer, many endocrine disorders, or migraine headache cause none, mild, or only intermittent incapacitation. This is highly significant in moderating the degree of stress facing a family.

For some illnesses, such as stroke or spinal cord injury, incapacitation is often most severe at onset and exerts its greatest influence at that time. Disability at the beginning of an illness magnifies family coping related to onset, expected course, and outcome. In progressive diseases, such as multiple sclerosis, rheumatoid arthritis, or dementia, disability looms as an increasing problem in later phases of the illness. This allows a family more time to prepare for anticipated changes. In particular, it provides an opportunity for the ill member to participate in disease-related family planning.

As a caveat, several studies cite the importance of the family's expectations of a disabled member. An expectation that the ill member can continue to have responsible roles and autonomy has been associated with both a better rehabilitation response and successful long-term integration into the family (Bishop & Epstein, 1980; Cleveland, 1980; Hyman, 1975; Litman, 1974; Slater, Sussman, & Stroud, 1970; Sussman & Slater, 1971; Swanson & Maruta, 1980). Duane Bishop and Nathan Epstein (1980) found that families had the greatest difficulty deciding realistic role expectations both in mildly disabling illnesses, where demands were very ambiguous, and in the most severely incapacitating ones, because of the sheer amount of role change required.

In sum, the net effect of incapacitation on a particular individual or family depends on the interaction of the type of disability with the premorbid role of the affected family member and the family's overall structure, flexibility, and emotional and financial resources. However, the presence or absence of any significant incapacitation may be the principal dividing line in initially trying to construct a psychosocial typology of illness (Viney & Westbrook, 1981).

A PSYCHOSOCIAL TYPOLOGY MATRIX

By combining the kinds of onset (acute or gradual), course (progressive, constant, or relapsing/episodic), outcome (fatal, shortened life span, or nonfatal), and incapacitation (present or absent), we generate a typology with 32 potential psychosocial types of illness. Each type of illness has a different pattern of psychosocial demand based on its inherent biological features. For instance, a stroke has an acute onset and a constant course after the initial recovery, can shorten life, and is disabling. The psychosocial demands of stroke are determined largely by the combined effects of those four qualities. A traumatic brain injury, which also is characterized by sudden onset, a constant course, and disability, is different in that it does not involve the psychosocial strain of being life-threatening. Using this information, a clinician can think about the psychosocial demands of each condition both independently and in relation to each other. (See table 2.1.)

Certain types of disease, such as fatal illnesses with a constant course, are so rare or nonexistent that, for practical purposes, they can be disregarded. According to the needs of a clinician or researcher, the number of potential types can be reduced further by combining or eliminating certain factors; this would depend on the relative need for specificity in a particular situation.

DEGREE OF UNCERTAINTY/PREDICTABILITY

The degree of uncertainty or predictability of a disorder is vitally important, but has not been formulated as a separate category in the typology. Rather, because of its overarching quality, predictability should be seen as a metacharacteristic that overlays and colors the other attributes: onset, course, outcome, and incapacitation of any disorder. Families coping with highly unpredictable diseases, such as multiple sclerosis, often state that these ambiguities are the hardest aspects to accept and master. The more uncertain the course and outcome, the more a family must make decisions with flexible contingencies built into their planning. Normally complicated life decisions are always layered with a myriad of illness-related ambiguities. This process requires a kind of ongoing, strategic problem solving that can exhaust even the most resilient and adaptive families (see chapter 6 for a detailed case example).

There are two distinct ways in which illnesses can be unpredictable: they can be more or less uncertain in terms of the actual *nature* of their onset, course, outcome, or incapacitation; and they can vary in the *rate* at which changes will occur. Some diseases, such as spinal cord injury, can be accurately typed at the point of diagnosis and have a highly predictable course. Alzheimer's disease has a clear endpoint, but the timetable for getting there is very unpredictable. The course and outcome of other illnesses such as multiple sclerosis, stroke, heart attack, hypertension, or lung cancer are rather unpredictable. In these kinds of disease, the initial prediction of type may change. For instance, if a second episode occurs, a stroke or heart attack can be considered relapsing or progressive. Lung cancer can become incapacitating if brain metastases occur. Some cases of lung cancer progress rapidly; others advance slowly, with a long remission, or not at all (spontaneous cure). Certain illnesses, rheumatoid arthritis or migraine headaches for example, tend to have a predictable, long-range course, but can be highly variable from day to day, and this can interfere more with daily than with long-term planning. This illness typology cannot predict these changes. In a

Table 2.1
Categorization of Chronic Illnesses by Psychosocial Type

		INCAPACITATING		NONINCAPACITATING	
		ACUTE	GRADUAL	ACUTE	GRADUAL
FATAL	PROGRESSIVE		Lung cancer with CNS metastases AIDS Bone marrow failure Amyotrophic lateral sclerosis	Acute leukemia Pancreatic cancer Metastatic breast cancer Malignant melanoma Lung cancer Liver cancer	Cystic fibrosis*
	RELAPSING			Incurable cancers in remission	
SHORTENED LIFE SPAN	PROGRESSIVE		Emphysema Alzheimer's disease Multi-infarct dementia Multiple sclerosis (late) Chronic alcoholism Huntington's chorea Scleroderma		Juvenile diabetes* Malignant hypertension Insulin-dependent adult-onset diabetes
	RELAPSING	Angina	Early multiple sclerosis Episodic alcoholism	Sickle cell disease* Hemophilia*	Systemic lupus erythematosis*
	CONSTANT	Stroke Moderate/severe myocardial infarction	P.K.U. and other congenital errors of metabolism	Mild myocardial infarction Cardiac arrhythmia	Hemodialysis treated renal failure Hodgkin's disease

NONFATAL

COURSE			
PROGRESSIVE	Lumbosacral disc disorder	Parkinson's disease, Rheumatoid arthritis, Osteoarthritis	Noninsulin-dependent adult-onset diabetes
RELAPSING		Kidney stones, Gout, Migraine, Seasonal allergy, Asthma, Epilepsy	Peptic ulcer, Ulcerative colitis, Chronic bronchitis, Irritable bowel syndrome, Psoriasis
CONSTANT	Congenital malformations, Spinal cord injury, Acute blindness, Acute deafness, Survived severe trauma & burns, Posthypoxic syndrome	Nonprogressive mental retardation, Cerebral palsy; Benign arrhythmia, Congenital heart disease	Malabsorption syndromes, Hyper/hypothyroidism, Pernicious anemia, Controlled hypertension, Controlled glaucoma

* = Early

Source: Reprinted from Rolland, J. S. (1984). Toward a psychosocial typology of chronic and life-threatening illness. *Family Systems Medicine, 2,* 245–62. Reprinted with permission of Family Process Inc.

particular case, if important changes occur during the course of a disease, a clinician should make note that the patient has switched from one illness type to another. The family may need help in reorienting to a new set of psychosocial demands and expectations.

Merle Mishel (1988) has described how the experience of uncertainty is affected by a number of factors, including the degree to which the pattern of symptoms is consistent and predictable. Families dealing with diabetes come, over time, to recognize the early warning signs and subtleties of an insulin reaction. In one case in which a grandmother had mild cognitive deficits from a stroke, the patient and her family learned over time to detect subtle cues of "wooly thinking" in the morning that alerted family members that she would have difficulty coping with her usual daily routines. Disorders in which the cues are more complex or in which progression means encountering novel and unfamiliar symptoms or treatments heighten anxieties for families. In these instances, clinicians need to achieve a balance between overloading a family with information about future crises and allaying anxieties by providing useful information concerning uncertainties. Also, it is important to distinguish between helping families reduce uncertainty through knowledge and helping them learn to tolerate living with it. For optimal long-term adaptation to highly uncertain disorders, such as multiple sclerosis, families may need to construct illusions of control (see chapter 8).

OTHER ILLNESS CHARACTERISTICS

Several other important attributes that differentiate conditions, though not basic components of the illness typology, should also be considered, where appropriate, in a thorough, systemically oriented evaluation. The visibility, frequency, and intensity of symptoms; the likelihood and severity of medical crises; and the role of genetics are other disease characteristics with important psychosocial significance. Also, the complexity, frequency, and efficacy of a treatment regimen and the amount of home- versus hospital-based care required by a condition vary widely across disorders. These factors have important implications for individual and family adaptation, including demands on family financial resources.

Symptom visibility

A number of investigators have described the vicissitudes of having a visible versus an invisible disorder. The psychosocial impact of this variable on families has been less well explored. Some symptoms are readily visible: paralysis, disfigurement, and rash, for example. Some signs of a disease such as high blood pressure are invisible, but can be easily measured. Others, pain being the primary example, are invisible and much more subjective in terms of measuring their severity. A physician sympathized with the plight of a woman with chronic migraine headaches: because her appearance did not reveal her condition, people were insensitive to her distress. Physician and patient joked that her family and colleagues would be more responsive if only she had a bandage wrapped around her head!

Although visible signs of an illness or disability have the potential disadvantage of stigma and shame, they do permit others to gauge their interactions with the patient in a relatively more objective way than is the case with invisible disorders. Invisible signs of disease foster ambiguities in several ways. For some patients and family members, denial or minimization is more possible on a day-to-day basis—in other words, "out of sight, out of mind." For others, this ambiguity becomes a constant source of rumination and rehearsal of worst-case scenarios. This is particularly true for invisible disorders, such as cancers in remission, that are potentially life-threatening. Invisible symptoms are more prone to invite different family perceptions and positions: families can be split in their ambivalent feelings, one family member expressing minimization of risk while another worries for the entire family.

Invisible symptoms that can fluctuate, for example, pain, become an important currency in family interactions. They can fuel preexisting dysfunctional relationship problems. They can be used by the patient as a mechanism to control family interactions or the power balance in a conflictual relationship. These possible sources of secondary gain can engender a distrust of the patient by other family members. The fact that various treatments for pain are only partially successful adds to the ambiguities that reverberate through the family's interactions.

These inherent ambiguities with regard to invisible disorders or symptoms are a powerful source of explanatory models and metaphors that become ascribed to pain. The distinction between the literal or physical and the metaphorical is blurred. For families this blurring enhances the possibility that all kinds of family legacies, myths, and beliefs transform physiological pain into a mirror reflecting core family issues. The patient with pain who says to her spouse on one occasion, "I am in pain" and on another, "You are a pain" is extending the meanings of her pain to include the idea that her spouse is a source of her pain, and therefore influences her overall physical condition. We shall explore the power of belief systems in chapter 7.

Likelihood and severity of crises

It is important for families to consider the likelihood and severity of disease-related crises (Strauss, 1975). Fears about illness-related crises are often a major source of a family's undercurrent of anxiety.

A clinician should assess the family's understanding of the possibility, frequency, and lethality of a medical crisis. How congruent is the family's understanding with that of the medical team? Do family members expect a catastrophe? Do they minimize real dangers? Insulin reactions in people with diabetes is one example. Many families worry that a family member who has such a reaction while sleeping could die, which causes parents or spouse to lie anxiously awake at night. In fact, this is not true. Are there clear warning signs that the patient or family can recognize? People with diabetes may perspire, become tremulous, lose their concentration, or act confused or irritable. On the other hand, the increasing blood pressure that may precede a fatal stroke can be completely silent. Can a medical crisis be prevented or mitigated by the detection of early warning signs and the institution of prompt treatment? When a patient or family heeds the early warning signs of a diabetes insulin reaction or an asthma attack, a full-blown crisis can usually be averted. How complex are the rescue operations? Do they require simple measures carried out at home (for example, medication, bed rest), or do they necessitate outside assistance or hospitalization? How long can crises last before a family can resume day-to-day functioning?

It is essential to ask a family about its planning for such crises. In particular, the extent and accuracy of the family's medical knowledge are of paramount importance. How clearly have leadership, role reallocation, emotional support, and the use of resources outside the family been thought through? Who in the family has been trained to give Mom an injection of a glucose formula in an emergency? Frequently, children capable of this have not been instructed and live in terror that they will be alone with Mom and helpless to render aid. If an illness has begun with an acute crisis (for instance, a stroke), then assessment of that event gives the clinician useful information on how the family handles unexpected crises. Evaluating the overall viability of the family's crisis planning is the key to this part of an assessment. Offering clear information and guidelines is crucial in helping families construct viable and flexible planning for possible crises.

Genetic contribution

A family's understanding or ignorance about the possible role of genetic transmission of a disease is another illness variable of major psychosocial importance. It is important for future family planning and for the emotional adaptation of the family to convey whether a disease is (1) not genetically linked and therefore unlikely to recur, (2) definitely genetically transmitted, or (3) more likely to occur in a particular family, though the predisposition can be offset by environmental/social factors. In many diseases that commonly occur in particular families (for example, heart disease, cancer), the role of genetics is acknowledged but, at present, not well understood. Other diseases, such as hemophilia or sickle-cell anemia, have clear modes of genetic transmission. The genetics of illness is a complex subject. There are many biological processes involved that influence whether (1) a disease requires the genetic contribution of one or both parents, (2) a person can be a carrier of a genetic trait without showing it themselves, or (3) a disease is linked to gender.

Clinicians should evaluate the accuracy of the family's knowledge, the family's cross-generational experience with a particular illness, and family mythologies that have developed in connection with a genetic, or possibly genetic, illness. In particular, these kinds of disease provide a powerful nidus for blame, self-incrimination, and victimization. For this type of disease, genetic counseling is an extremely useful adjunct to a comprehensive psychosocial treatment plan (Hsia et al., 1979).

In recent advances with regard to such conditions such as colon cancer and Huntington's disease, a progressive, fatal illness involving dementia, biological markers have been identified that can measure, with increasing accuracy, whether a family member is susceptible to or definitely will develop the disorder. Huntington's disease typically strikes at midlife. Identifying the genetic marker has led to a simple medical test that allows people at risk to determine whether they will develop the condition. Research (Wiggins et al., 1992) suggests that, in general, psychosocial adjustment is better when people know whether they will develop Huntington's disease: eliminating the debilitating anxiety of not knowing often seems to outweigh bad news. By all indications, advances in medical genetics will enable the development of increasing numbers of diseases to be predicted in this way. Clinicians need to use extreme caution in making broad generalizations. Any at-risk person or family should have a thorough opportunity to discuss the psychosocial implications of testing a particular member and be informed about the possibility of preventive medical intervention that may reduce the overall risk.

Treatment regimens

Some treatment procedures involve significant expenditures of time and/or energy (for example, home kidney dialysis) or require another person to carry them out (for instance, postural lung drainage in children with cystic fibrosis). Treatments for other diseases, even severe ones such as advanced hypertension, may involve oral medication and regular checkups that the patient can handle alone. This illustrates the salience of the fit between the demands of the illness and the family pattern of functioning. A relatively disengaged family has far more trouble with disorders requiring regular teamwork (for instance, home dialysis, paralysis) than with those, such as hypertension, that demand a minimum of collaboration. Although they reduce time-consuming dependence on medical centers, treatments that are given at home place a greater onus of responsibility on the patient or family. Therefore, the degree of family emotional support, role flexibility, effective problem solving, and communication in relation to these treatment factors will be crucial predictors of long-term treatment compliance and the appropriateness of home-based care. In this situation, a disengaged family may not be a good fit with the requirements for effective medical care.

Clinicians need to familiarize themselves with a client's treatments. For instance, how complex and frequent are the interventions? Are treatments on a fixed schedule or a more unpredictable one dictated by symptoms? What are the possible side effects, such as discomfort or fatigue? How much energy is required to administer treatments, and are other people required? These considerations have important implications in terms of the level of disruption to family life and the degree of family involvement and teamwork required for successful compliance. Sometimes a fixed treatment schedule can be more disruptive than a flexible one. A daughter's brittle diabetes may require a controlled diet with dinner at 5:00 P.M. This may necessitate separate dinner sittings and multiple meal preparations, add considerable strain to family life, and potentially turn a previously pleasant family ritual into an ordeal.

Treatments that have a considerable impact on a person's life-style, are difficult to accomplish, and have minimal effects on the level of symptoms or prognosis are those least likely to be adhered to (Strauss, 1975). Also, interventions that are visible and possibly stigmatizing can interfere with compliance. This is particularly true for children and adolescents. Cancer chemotherapy that results in hair loss is a good example.

James Coyne and Veronica Fiske (1992), in their research with couples coping with heart disease, have suggested that the degree to which couples or families can have an impact on the course of the disease is a critical variable that distinguishes different kinds of disorders. First, they suggest, clinicians determine to what extent the patient's health and functional capacities depend on the effectiveness and persistence of couples'/families' coping efforts. They mention heart disease as an example of a disease highly responsive to these efforts, in contrast to many forms of cancer in which the relationship between coping efforts and outcome is less clear. Second, they advocate assessing the degree to which couples and families can affect the ultimate outcome (not just morale) rather than immediate stabilization of an illness. End-stage renal disease, diabetes, and congestive heart failure are examples of the latter. On the one hand, we need to be mindful of these significant distinctions, particularly in situations in which family efforts clearly can affect the course of the disease. On the other, it is important to recognize the limits of our knowledge and interventions in this area. We shall return to this topic later (chapter 7) in relation to family efforts to sustain hope or positive illusions.

Age at onset

Finally, the age at onset of an illness, in relation to child, adult, and family stages of development, is a critical factor. The psychosocial demands of any disorder can be understood only in relation to other developmental imperatives for each family member and the family as a whole. This will be discussed in chapter 6, on life cycle issues.

Psychosocial Perspective

Gaining a psychosocial understanding of illness is one of the basic tasks of families entering the world of living with chronic disorders. In terms of each of the variables in the typology that has been described, I am particularly interested in how family members' expectations are in sync with, or differ from, one another and from those of the involved professionals. I ask them the source of their information so that I may begin to understand whether differences are due to contradictory sources of information or to processing the same information through different historical, ethnic, or cultural lenses (see chapters 5 and 7). Routinely, I ask families to discuss these issues either in an initial consultation or as a homework assignment. This exercise is an excellent way to achieve rapport with families that are unaccustomed to dealing with health/mental health professionals or to sitting together as a family to discuss sensitive issues. We begin by talking about what is foremost in their minds—a significant health problem. They are guided to consider their overall understanding of the disorder and to begin building a bridge from the technological to the psychosocial world of illness and disability.

Family members are frequently astonished to learn that they have very different ideas about the expected course and outcome of the illness. This process of revealing differences allows potential areas of conflict to be discussed preventively at an early stage of a long-term endeavor before maladaptive patterns are set in motion. When misinformation is an issue, I advocate to both the family and the physician that a meeting be arranged to discuss the illness and its treatment. To the busy physician, I reframe this extra meeting as "a stitch in time" that will "save nine." I emphasize that this will help avert frequent phone calls and compliance problems and promote family cooperation during times when much technical medical care is required. If appropriate, I offer to be present at the meeting, to facilitate a dialogue that will include putting information in psychosocial terms.

In one case, a young physical therapist, who had developed severe asthma, and her husband were referred because of increased marital conflict following her diagnosis. They fought mostly about what was really the illness and what was not. Because symptoms seemed to crop up precipitously, he felt that she was using her illness as an excuse for anything she did not want to do. In this case, each partner had very different levels of comprehension of asthma. The husband clearly did not understand much about the condition and, since the diagnosis, had left all asthma-related discussions to his health-professional wife and her physician. In this instance, I sent the couple to the pulmonary specialist to explain the wife's disease to them.

CHAPTER 3

The Time Phases of Illness

TO COMPLETE a meaningful psychosocial schema of chronic disorders, the developmental time phases of an illness need to be included as a second dimension. Too often discussions of "coping with cancer," "managing disability," or "dealing with life-threatening illness" approach illness and disability as a static state and fail to appreciate the dynamic unfolding of the illness process over time. Each phase of a chronic disorder has its own unique psychosocial demands and developmental tasks, which require significantly different strengths, attitudes, or changes from a family.

To capture the core psychosocial themes in the natural history of chronic disease, three major phases can be described: (1) crisis, (2) chronic, and (3) terminal. The relationship between a more detailed chronic disease time line and one grouped according to broad time phases can be diagrammed as shown in figure 3.1.

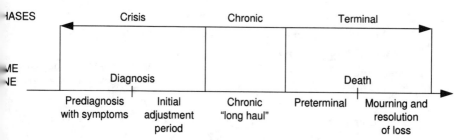

Figure 3.1
Time Line and Phases of Illness
Source: Reprinted from Rolland, J. S. (1984). Toward a psychosocial typology of chronic and life-threatening illness. *Family Systems Medicine, 2,* 254. Reprinted with permission of Family Process Inc.

The Crisis Phase

Frequently, the crisis phase begins with a symptomatic period before actual diagnosis when the individual or family has a sense something is wrong, but the exact nature and scope of the problem are not clear. For some, the physician's suspicions on a routine examination mark the beginning of the crisis phase, which includes the initial period of readjustment and coping after the problem has been identified through a diagnosis and initial treatment plan. For an acute injury or a sudden-onset illness such as stroke or heart attack, the crisis phase may extend through a protracted rehabilitation period.

However the journey begins, families have a strong need for reassurance that they are handling things normally, because they have only a vague road map, or none at all. This initial period is often a time of excruciating vulnerability and uncertainty, in which all experiences seem heightened in intensity and family members grope for ways to reassert control. A time line for accomplishing illness-related developmental tasks can be of enormous help in stabilizing a family: it helps avert the feelings of being overwhelmed that are inevitable when all the tasks over the years of an illness are viewed as compressed into a two-dimensional picture. If we experienced all of life's hurdles that way, most of us would feel crushed by the weight of reality.

The immediate problem for many families is deciding which tasks belong where in the sequence. Some families immediately tackle problems that can be shelved for six months, at which time the long-term picture will be clearer. One woman put her house up for sale, started giving her valuable possessions away, and discussing funeral arrangements with her adult children during her initial treatment for breast cancer when, in reality, she had a small tumor and an excellent prognosis. She had not discussed the prognosis with her physician; and her children, who lived in another part of the country, accepted her portrayal of the situation as fact.

During the crisis phase, there are a number of key tasks for the ill member and his or her family. From the perspective of the Family Systems–Illness Model, the following are most important.

First, family members need to learn about systems ideas, so that they can understand themselves as a functional unit. Viewing themselves and the problem confronting them through a systems-oriented lens provides an organizing framework that fosters empowerment and effectiveness. In my own work, I need to remind myself that this perspective is usually a novel experience for families. I can remember how unfamiliar these ideas were to me when my mother had a stroke during the first year of my psychiatric training. We, as a family, grappled with all the variables, such as role reallocation, communication, and threatened loss; but we did so in a piecemeal and somewhat random fashion, without a framework for effectively approaching the situation.

Second, family members need to gain a psychosocial understanding of the disorder in systems terms. They need to be introduced to the notion of the course of an illness, with developmental tasks associated with each phase. Their grasp of themselves as a system within the context of the pattern of practical and emotional demands of the illness over time provides the groundwork for a viable family–illness system.

Third, the family needs to create a meaning for the disorder that maximizes a preservation of its sense of mastery and competence. I shall return to detailed discussion of family health beliefs in chapter 7.

Rudolf Moos (1984) describes certain universal, practical, illness-related tasks. These include: (1) learning to deal with pain, disability, or other symptoms; (2) adapting to hospital or clinic environments and any disease-related treatment procedures; and (3) establishing and maintaining positive relationships with the health-care team.

FRAMING EVENTS

Initial experiences with the health-care team are immensely important and have far-reaching effects on families. I term these nodal experiences "framing events." Discussions with health providers about the nature of the disorder, its prognosis, and prescriptions for management are all part of the framing event. The initial crisis period fosters a hypervigilant, anxious, trancelike state that makes families highly receptive to intended and unintended messages about how to cope with the uncertainties that confront them. What clinicians actually say or leave unclear or unstated about the nature of the illness and its prognosis is critical. Who is included and excluded from relevant conversations influences how the family frames the experience. As part of every assessment, a clinician should track, in some detail, families' initial experiences with health providers, particularly at the time of diagnosis. What did these experiences mean to them, and how did they shape the patient's and the family's views and behaviors about how to live with symptoms and treatments? How did these experiences affect the formative stage of their relationship with the health providers?

Framing events can go awry for many reasons, which I shall be addressing throughout this book. A major source of mistrust between family and health provider arises when there has been no attempt by the latter to include all relevant family members in discussions about the patient. Neglect of this critical step can be considered noncompliance on the part of the physician. The family generally experiences such an omission as a disregard of its importance in the overall treatment plan. This only heightens a skew inherent in the relationship because of the very technological nature of the initial crisis phase, when the medical team generally is in charge. Families often express their dissatisfaction as "Our doctor doesn't understand us."

Physicians, burdened by relentless demands on their time, confuse the family's need for information and being included in decisions with a desire for lengthy discussions. Many details about illness management can be addressed by other members of the health team, but an initial meeting of the health-team leader with the family promotes the mutual understanding necessary for optimal development of the relationship.

In addition, there are critical tasks of a more general, sometimes existential, nature. First, the family needs to grieve for the loss of the identity it possessed before the disorder began. Second, family members need to move toward a position of acceptance of permanent change while maintaining a sense of continuity between their past and their future. Although life will be different, families need help in affirming positive values and caring and those parts of family life that can remain intact. During the initial crisis phase, a family gathering at the bedside or a ritual to promote healing can be extremely beneficial. Recalling other crises the family has weathered in the past can help establish a sense of continuity. For example, one family recounted its escape from Nazi terrorism and coming to the United States as refugees during the Depression and eventually succeeding as a family. Third, families must pull together to undergo short-term crisis reorganization. And fourth, in the face of uncertainty, family members need to develop a special system flexibility with regard to future goals (see chapter 8).

The question of *permanency* is pivotal, determining whether a family needs to make the transition to a chronic phase and everything that goes with that reality, or whether it can resume life with no mandate for basic change. In many acute illnesses, chronicity is ambiguous at the beginning. The physician may propose a moratorium on this question while trying various interventions. For problems such as trauma, infections, or some surgical procedures, a certain amount of time is needed for natural healing to occur. The physician may inform the patient and family members that there may be residual problems or that in a certain percentage of cases, the condition becomes chronic. During this period the need to accept a long-term disorder is uncertain, but preparation for that possibility is a different story, and should be addressed directly.

First, it is important for clinicians to inquire if family members have decided whether the patient's condition is chronic. How did they arrive at that conclusion? Was the physician or someone else their source of information? If the source was not someone on the health-care team, it is important to know if the decision has emerged from a part of the family's history or culture, or from a particular family member or other powerful person in the system. One family, whose inclination was always to assume the worst, decided, early in the recovery phase, that the father's mild heart attack was totally and permanently disabling, and family members started to reorganize accordingly. The oldest son had already developed plans to drop out of school and take a job to help support the family. In this case, the physician expected a nearly complete recovery that would require only minor life-style modifications.

Clinicians should ask if there is any disagreement about chronicity within the family or between the family and health-care team and how these different viewpoints are being handled. Such disagreements are significant since they may signal that the family is not accepting the physician's perspective or that dysfunctional conflicts exist within the family. Silent but potentially life-threatening conditions, such as hypertension, often create the biggest problems for families. After hypertension is diagnosed, a husband may ignore medical advice and stubbornly continue to eat salty foods, while other family members nag him and fret about his health. One man said, "My father ate whatever he wanted until he died at 85. I feel fine. I plan to live the same way he did." It is extremely difficult for a family to move on to the next phase of adaptation if its members have different views about chronicity since they will then be moving at cross-purposes. This may be a juncture at which family consensus will be necessary for healthy, long-term coping and adaptation.

If the prognosis is still unclear, clinicians should inquire when and how it will be clarified. Frequently the physician has a clear or rough estimate that has not been communicated to the family. Raising this question early allows a family, on the basis of the best information available at that time, to plan and pace itself through a period of anxious uncertainty. In this regard, family members often put plans on hold to help their ill member through this crisis period. It is useful to inquire when the time will come for the patient and other family members to make decisions about the patient's illness and short- and long-range individual and family plans. What significant issues will the family and individual members face at that time? Such questions acknowledge the family's transitional crisis structure and that much is in limbo; they also imply that this structure is useful in only a time-limited way, and would not be appropriate in terms of either a cure or long-term living with chronic illness.

Other kinds of questions raise more specific issues about permanency. Asking the family how it would see the patient and other members functioning differently with a permanent condition in terms of roles, hierarchy, and communication helps assess different aspects of family functioning (see chapter 4). It is useful to find out who would be most likely to assist the patient into the extended future if the condition turns out to be chronic. How would such a coalition affect the rest of the family? How was the caregiver identified? Is the caring role a flexible one that can be shared (an important consideration in progressive illness and long-term disability)? Or is it rigidly assigned to one member on the basis of expectations linked to generation, gender, or sibling position? Frequently an oldest daughter is expected to assume the caregiver role with respect to an ailing parent. Sometimes a son or daughter who never has felt validated and still seeks affirmation from a parent may volunteer to be sole caregiver for that parent.

The meaning of accepting chronicity can be assessed by questions such as the following: If you were to think of your disability as permanent, what about it would be hardest to accept? Who in the family would have the easiest and the most difficult time accepting that fact? For many families the most intense grieving occurs at the time of accepting permanency, because loss must then be definitively acknowledged. Simon (1988) has pointed out that a critical issue for families is relinquishing hope for a cure, yet remaining optimistic. Asking family members what would be their new version of hope if they gave up hope for a full recovery opens discussion of this issue. Finally, if the illness is chronic, clinicians should explore whether any family members, including the patient, feel that they failed, or are blamed by others (see chapter 7).

The Chronic Phase

The chronic phase, whether long or short, is the time span between the initial diagnosis and readjustment period and the terminal phase, when issues related to death and dying predominate. It is a period that can be marked by constancy, progression, or episodic change. In this sense its meaningfulness cannot be grasped by simply knowing the biological behavior of an illness. Rather, it is more a psychosocial construct, sometimes referred to as "the long haul" or the phase of living day to day with chronic illness. Often the patient and the family have come to grips, psychologically and organizationally, with the permanent changes presented by a chronic illness and have devised a workable way to live. At one extreme, the chronic phase can last for decades as a stable, nonfatal, chronic illness. At the other extreme, it may be nonexistent, as in an acute-onset, rapidly progressive, fatal disorder in which the crisis phase is contiguous with the terminal phase.

The ability of the family to maintain the semblance of a normal life under the "abnormal" conditions presented by a chronic illness and heightened uncertainty is a key task of this period. For a fatal illness, it is a time of living in limbo. Certain debilitating but not clearly fatal illnesses, such as a massive stroke or dementia, can make the family feel saddled with an exhausting and endless problem. Paradoxically, some families' hope to resume a normal life may be realized only through the death of their ill member. This highlights another crucial task of this phase: maintaining maximal autonomy of all family members despite a pull toward mutual dependency and caregiving. This autonomy needs to flourish within a context of connectedness that allows for expression of the individual needs and separate pursuits of each family member. Many of the clinical dilemmas for families, couples, and clinicians associated with the chronic phase are addressed in chapters 9, 10, and 11.

The Terminal Phase

The last phase is the terminal period, including the preterminal stage of an illness in which the inevitability of death becomes apparent and dominates family life. It encompasses the periods of mourning, bereavement, and resolution of loss. This phase is distinguished by the predominance of issues with regard to separation, death, grief, resolution of mourning, and resumption of normal family life beyond the loss.

As families enter this phase, one of the key tasks is a shift in their anticipation of the possibility of a terminal phase to its probability and, finally, its inevitability. Hopes for a cure and long-term survival must be relinquished. Clinicians should expect intense grieving related to giving up the often protracted struggle to overcome the disease. This is distinct from the experience of anticipatory grief, in which family members prepare for the loss of a loved one. Mastery in the chronic phase, which emphasized maintaining autonomy within the constraints of the disorder, must now be redefined in terms of a process of preparing emotionally and practically for death.

As in the initial crisis phase, families at this point generally need to accept more intense involvement by health professionals. However, the role of the professional and of medical technology is geared more toward caregiving, the provision of physical and emotional comfort, than toward medical stabilization and improvement. In this sense, families need not only to have increasing contact with health providers but also to see the latter's role differently. Clearly, this change in roles is often more challenging for the health-care team than for the family, because of strong beliefs about equating professional success with life, not death.

Families face a number of practical tasks in the terminal phase. They have to decide when and whom to tell about the transition. If they have not settled such matters previously, the patient and key family members must consider redefinition of family roles in this final stage of an illness; a living will; the extent of medical efforts desired; who has power of attorney if the patient's competency to make sound decisions is compromised; the patient's preferences about dying at home, in a hospital, or at hospice; and his or her wishes with regard to funeral and memorial services. The common clinical issues for families in this phase will be addressed in more detail in chapter 8.

Transition Periods

Critical transition periods link the three time phases. Elizabeth Carter and Monica McGoldrick (1989) and Daniel Levinson (1978, 1986) have emphasized the importance of transition periods in the literature on family and adult life cycles. Similarly, the transitions between developmental phases in the course of a disease are crucial for individual and family adaptation. They offer an opportunity for reevaluation of the appropriateness of the priorities and structure of family life in light of new illness- and disability-related developmental demands. Unfinished business from the previous phase can complicate or block movement through the transitions. Families or individuals can become permanently frozen in an adaptive structure that has outlived its utility (Penn, 1983). For example, the usefulness of pulling together in the crisis period can become maladaptive and stifling for all family members if maintained throughout the chronic phase.

Enmeshed families, because of their fused and often rigid nature, can have particular difficulty negotiating delicate transitions. A certain amount of normative enmeshment is very helpful during the initial crisis of an illness. Relinquishing a certain amount of personal and generational boundaries for the sake of the family group effort is adaptive and strengthens family bonds. "We-ness" is at a premium during this time. However, when issues of forging autonomy within the constraints of chronicity need to be addressed, enmeshed families encounter their Achilles' heel. Autonomy and separateness are historically a source of conflict in such families. Chronic disorders, especially disabling ones, present an ongoing tension between autonomy and dependence that challenges an enmeshed family's vulnerabilities.

These transitions are major turning points at which a family's basic structure for coping and adaptation needs reevaluation. The transition between the crisis and the chronic phases is perhaps the most significant: it is the dividing line between crisis and the long haul; it is the time to draw up a viable family blueprint for living with a chronic disorder. Families can be encouraged to consider midcourse corrections, based on their experiences in the early phase of the illness, before they inadvertently settle into rigid patterns that have outgrown their initial usefulness.

In one case, a 42-year-old single woman had, for the past 20 years, been the primary caretaker of her mother, who was disabled by crippling arthritis. At the beginning, being the oldest of six siblings, she had taken a leave of absence from school to help her father with her mother and siblings. Twenty years later, her siblings had all moved on in life; but she remained the primary caregiver, having sacrificed her career plans and an independent life of her own. Because she had been so effective during the initial crisis, certain rehabilitation possibilities for the mother had been overlooked. The successful crisis structure assumed a life of its own and became permanent. As the loyal oldest daughter in an Italian family, the caregiving daughter had never openly discussed her sacrifice. When the initial crisis phase ended, the family never reevaluated its understanding of the situation and become more flexible in the chronic phase so that the developmental possibilities of all the family members might be maximally realized.

At the other end of the illness life cycle, the *transition from the chronic to the terminal phase* presents families with a different set of developmental demands. A family that is adept at handling the day-to-day practical tasks of a long-term, stable illness but limited in its skills in affective coping may encounter difficulty if their family member's disease becomes terminal. The relatively greater demand for affective coping skills in the terminal compared with the chronic phase of an illness may create a crisis for a family navigating this transition.

A family with three children, aged 18, 12, and 9, had seemingly coped with the mother's breast cancer for five years; they had steadfastly believed in their ability to conquer cancer. Mom had become disease-free, and the family never mentioned her illness. In general, the family seldom talked about feelings. When metastatic spread was discovered, the family became emotionally paralyzed. While new treatments were tried and failed, no one could discuss the next phase. The children, particularly the two younger ones, were emotionally shielded and not prepared for Mom's impending death. The 9-year-old was excluded from the funeral; she became severely withdrawn and depressed within a year. The 18-year-old moved away and limited her contact with the family. The 12-year-old became overfunctional and watched over Dad and her younger sister. Dad, the family wage earner, was ill prepared to provide the nurturing side of family life, especially under such emotionally difficult circumstances.

This family's somewhat rigid style and lack of communication about emotional issues made them vulnerable to a terminal illness. They could live with a chronic condition in which the threat of loss was in the background. When a recurrence of the cancer heralded the next phase, they were unable to adapt.

The Psychosocial Developmental Model

The combination of the time phases and the typology of illness provides a framework for a psychosocial developmental model of chronic disease and disability. The illness time phases (crisis, chronic, and terminal) can be considered broad developmental periods in the natural history of a chronic disease. Each period presents certain basic challenges and tasks independent of the type of illness. In addition to the phase-specific developmental tasks common to all psychosocial types of disease, each has specific supplementary tasks. This is analogous to the relationship between certain universal life tasks and a particular individual's development. Every one of us is both similar to others and unique.

The basic tasks of the three illness time phases and transitions recapitulate, in many respects, the unfolding of human development. For example, the crisis phase is similar in certain fundamental ways to the period of childhood and adolescence. Piaget's (1952) research demonstrated that child development involves a prolonged period of learning to assimilate from, and accommodate to, the fundamentals of life. Parents often temper other developmental plans (for example, with regard to a career) to accommodate rearing children. Similarly, the crisis phase is a period of socialization to the basics of living with chronic disease during which the family frequently puts other life plans on hold to accommodate socialization to the illness process.

Themes of separation and individuation are central in the transition from adolescence to adulthood, particularly for males. Eric Erikson (1950) pointed out that adolescents are granted a kind of moratorium or postponement period during which the identity of childhood gradually merges into that of adulthood; eventually the adolescent must relinquish this moratorium to assume normal adult responsibilities. In similar fashion, the transition to the chronic phase of illness emphasizes autonomy and the creation of a viable, ongoing life structure in light of the realities of the illness. In this transition, a holdup or moratorium on other developmental tasks that served to protect the initial period of socialization/adaptation to life with an illness or disability needs reevaluation. The separate developmental tasks of living with a chronic condition and living the other parts of one's life must be brought together and forged into one coherent life structure. I shall return to this concept of illness development later.

At this point, we can combine the typology and phases of illness to construct a two-dimensional matrix (figure 3.2) that permits the grouping and differentiation of illnesses according to important similarities and differences. It subdivides types of illness and disability according to three time phases, which allows examination of a long-term illness in a more refined way. Each disorder can be typed according to a general pattern of psychosocial demands that will change as a family moves through the time phases of the condition. For instance, the psychosocial demands of a gradual-onset, progressive, fatal, incapacitating illness (GPF+) such as Amyotrophic Lateral

▸NSET	COURSE	OUTCOME	INCAPACITATION
= acute	P = progressive	F = fatal or shortened	Yes = (+)
= gradual	C = constant	life span	No = (–)
	R = relapsing	NF = nonfatal	

	PHASE		
	I	II	III
	CRISIS	CHRONIC	TERMINAL
P F +			
P F –			
P NF +			
P NF –			
C F +			
C F –			
C NF +			
C NF –			
R F +			
R F –			
R NF +			
R NF –			
NESS TYPE			
P F +			
P F –			
P NF +			
P NF –			
C F +			
C F –			
C NF +			
C NF –			
R F +			
R F –			
R NF +			
R NF –			

Figure 3.2
Matrix of Illness Types and Time Phases
Source: Reprinted from Rolland, J. S. (1984). Toward a psychosocial typology of chronic and life-threatening illness. *Family Systems Medicine, 2,* 256. Reprinted with permission of Family Process Inc.

Sclerosis (ALS, or Lou Gehrig's disease) can be thought about in relation to each of the three phases of illness—crisis, chronic, and terminal.

By addition of a family systems model to this matrix, we can create a three-dimensional representation of the broader illness/family system (figure 3.3). Psychosocial illness types, time stages of illness, and components of family functioning constitute the three dimensions. This way of depicting the Family Systems–Illness Model offers a vehicle for flexible dialogue concerning the illness aspect and the family aspect of the family–illness system. In essence, this model allows speculation about the importance of strengths and weaknesses in various components of family functioning (for example, cohesion or affective communication) in relation to different types of disease at different phases in the illness life cycle.

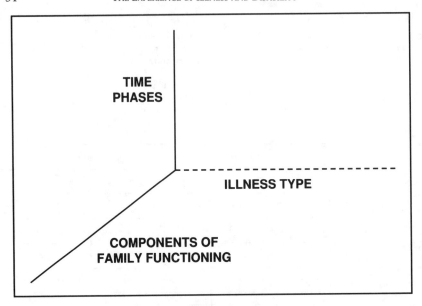

Figure 3.3
Three Dimensions of the Model: Illness Type, Time Phase, Family
Functioning
Source: Reprinted from Rolland, J. S. (1987). Chronic illness and the life cycle. A
conceptual framework. *Family Process, 26,* 209. Reprinted with permission of
Family Process Inc.

A Framework for Clinical Assessment and Intervention

There are several important implications of this part of the Family
Systems–Illness Model for clinical practice. At their core, the components of
the typology offer a means of grasping the nature of a chronic illness in psychosocial terms and build a bridge for the clinician between the biological
and the psychosocial. Perhaps the major contribution is the provision of a
framework for assessment and clinical intervention with a family facing illness or disability. Such a framework enables the clinician to think and plan
with greater clarity and focus. Attention to onset, course, outcome, and incapacitation and the degree of uncertainty facilitates integration of an assessment and focuses a clinician's questioning of a family. For instance, acute-
onset illnesses demand high levels of adaptability, problem solving, role
reallocation, and balanced cohesion. Considerable family enmeshment may
make a family less likely to be able to cope with these demands. Forethought
on this issue should help the clinician evaluate a family appropriately and
target interventions to achieve a more functional balance of cohesion.

The concept of time phases provides a way for the clinician to think longitudinally and better appreciate chronic illness as an ongoing process with
landmarks, transition points, and changing demands. An illness time line

delineates psychosocial developmental stages of an illness, and each phase has its own unique developmental tasks. David Kaplan (1968) has emphasized the importance of solving phase-related tasks within the time limits set by the duration of each successive developmental phase of an illness. He suggests that failure to resolve issues in this sequential manner can jeopardize the total coping process of the family. Therefore, attention to time allows the clinician to assess a family's strengths and vulnerabilities in relation to the present and future phases of the illness.

Taken together, the typology and time phases provide a context for integrating other aspects of a comprehensive assessment, which should include evaluation of a range of universal and illness-specific family dynamics in relation to the psychosocial type and time phases of an illness. The assessment should consider: the family's illness belief system; the meaning of the illness for the family; the interface of the illness with individual and family development; the family's multigenerational history of coping with illness, loss, and crisis; the family's planning for medical crises; the family's capacity to handle home-based medical care; and the family's illness-oriented communication, problem solving, role reallocation, affective involvement, social support, and use of community resources. Parts II and III of this book consider these issues in detail.

The Family Systems–Illness Model clarifies treatment planning in several ways. First, awareness of the components of family functioning most relevant to particular types or phases of an illness guides goal-setting. Sharing this information with the family and deciding upon specific objectives will give the family a sense of control and realistic hope. A laissez-faire family that is not accustomed to rigorous and timely problem solving may need additional guidance in mastering the precise, day-to-day decision making needed for effective management of diabetes, for example. Such knowledge prepares the family to recognize psychosocial warning signs that should alert it to request a family consultation. This knowledge also guides families, which often lack previous exposure to mental health services, in calling upon a family therapist at appropriate times for brief, goal-oriented treatment. In sum, the typology and time stages of illness promotes understanding and prediction of the relative need for family and health-care team involvement and provides a way to optimize the quality of relationships.

Clinical Applications: The Therapeutic Quadrangle

Using the psychosocial typology and time stages of illness as a reference point has important implications for health-services delivery both for the patient's and the family's relationship to health professionals and for the organization of services.

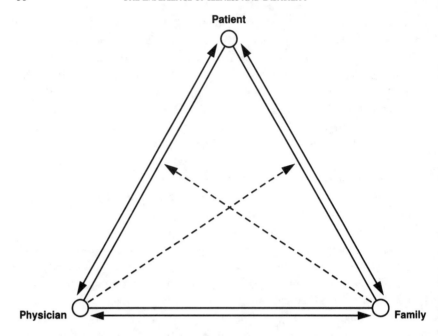

Figure 3.4
The Therapeutic Triangle in Medicine
Source: Adapted from Doherty, W. J., and Baird, M. A. (1983). *Family therapy and family medicine: Toward the primary care of families.* New York: Guilford.

Jay Haley (1976) has observed that helping professionals need to be included in the conceptualization of any treatment system with a family. The application of this idea in the medical world has led to various descriptions of the therapeutic triangle in medicine (Doherty & Baird, 1983). This triangle includes the patient, his or her family, and the primary care provider and health-care team. Doherty and Baird point out the illusory nature of thinking in dyadic terms about patient–family and physician–patient relationships. They stress active participation of the physician in the former and of the family in the latter. A schematic representation of this set of relationships is shown in figure 3.4.

The inclusion of the concept of psychosocial illness types in the scheme creates a system composed of four interlocking triangles (figure 3.5). It is easier to conceptualize the illness as a fourth member if one pictures each illness type as having a personality (which includes the kind of onset and the course, outcome, degree of incapacitation, and predictability) and a developmental life course (which includes the time phases of illness).

A diagnosis of an illness and disability adds a new family member—the condition itself. It also elevates the position of the physician for the family. For years the family doctor may have resembled a distant relative seen occasionally; a chronic illness may transform this distant relative into a central

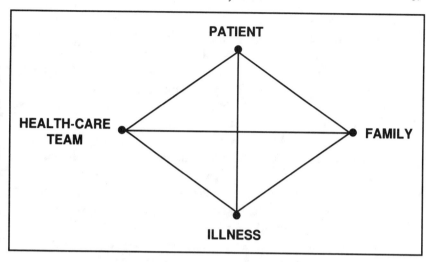

Figure 3.5
The Therapeutic Quadrangle
Source: Reprinted by permission from Rolland, J. S. (1987). Family systems and chronic illness: A typological model. *Journal of Psychotherapy and the Family, 3,* 164.

figure in family life. The physician's centrality in the life of both patient and family will vary according to the level of technological care required by the illness. In life-threatening conditions, such as acute leukemia, the physician and the illness can easily become omnipresent in all significant family interactions and decisions. David Reiss and Atara Kaplan De-Nour (1989) have described the ebbs and flows of this relationship according to the stage of the illness. They highlight the centrality of the health-care team when technological priorities prevail and the need for the family to relinquish significant control to health professionals at such times.

The psychosocial typology and time phases help clarify the personality of this new family member—the illness—and the timing and degree of importance the physician or other members of the health-care team will have within the family. In many disorders, such as incurable forms of cancer, the initial crisis and the terminal phase or periods of flare-up would be natural points in the illness at which technology or decisions involving the physician become more important. This is particularly true if the patient requires hospitalization or regular treatment at a health facility. In progressive or disabling diseases, health-care team involvement may increase gradually over time, without intermissions; and the metaphorical extra family member with special needs becomes a bigger and bigger "elephant in the living room."

The actual impact of these various forces on a family and its relationship with the health-care team depends on: (1) the type and phase of the illness and its relative demand for medical care by professionals (It is important to remember that some illnesses, such as spinal cord injury, are severely disabling, but may require little medical input after the initial rehabilitation phase.); (2) the location of medical care (If in the home, the family may retain a greater sense of control.); and (3) the meaning the family ascribes to this relationship. This last factor will be addressed in chapters 7 and 11.

Clinicians need to be mindful that inclusion of the illness and the physician as powerful members within the family system can be a very sensitive issue, particularly for tightly knit or rigid families. The typology and time phase framework allows a clinician to think about the actual impact on a particular family, based upon an understanding of family dynamics and of the psychosocial type of illness. As major extra family members, the illness and the physician can function as significant third legs in dysfunctional family triangles (see chapter 4). For instance, in a dysfunctional couple, the husband's heart attack can serve him as a powerful ally against his wife: he can blame his heart attack on her incessant nagging. And because heart attacks can recur and be fatal, he can use this life-threatening aspect, along with blaming her for the first attack, as a constant weapon in assuming control of all conflictual aspects of their relationship. We shall return to this triangulation process later when considering treatment issues in Part III.

Another way to use the psychosocial typology and time phases framework is to take the original therapeutic triangle diagrammed in figure 3.4 (the patient, the family, and the health-care team) and see how it is affected by different types of illness. For instance, consider the issue of locus of control in relation to an illness (Wallston et al., 1976; Wallston & Wallston, 1978). This concept refers to how much an individual or family sees outcomes as being influenced by their own efforts. A family's beliefs about the potential to control biological processes can vary along a continuum from an internal to an external orientation. A certain minimal level of agreement concerning this kind of health belief is critical to establishing a viable therapeutic relationship among the patient, his or her family, and the health-care team. The degree of consensus concerning beliefs about control can vary dramatically for this triad depending on the type of condition.

One particular family physician had a good working relationship with a family that had consulted him over the years for minor health problems. When the father suffered a serious heart attack, differences in beliefs about control surfaced in relation to this life-threatening and possibly disabling illness. The stability of the long-standing, healthy, therapeutic triangle became seriously threatened. In this case the physician, aware of increased tensions with the patient and family, thought about his own beliefs regarding serious heart disease and questioned the family about theirs and thus averted a potentially serious rift in their previously excellent working relationship.

Service-delivery Applications

In terms of organization of services, the psychosocial developmental model of chronic disorders has implications for periodic reevaluation of the family in relation to the course of the illness. The time phases and transition points suggest the timing of the evaluations. Strengths and weaknesses in various components of family functioning can be addressed, taking into account all the factors relevant to the psychosocial type of the illness. Scheduling timely, preventive, "psychosocial checkups" is inherently appealing to most families. For example, I consulted several times with a family whose members were anxious about the possibility of life-threatening bleeding episodes in their son, who had just been diagnosed as having hemophilia. A year later, anticipating possible heightened separation fears within the context of these illness-related risks, I offered a family consultation as a preventive measure several months before the child was scheduled to start preschool.

The typology presented here facilitates the development of various preventively oriented psychoeducational or support groups for patients and their families. For instance, groups can be designed to meet the needs of patients dealing with progressive, life-threatening diseases; relapsing disorders; acute-onset, incapacitating illnesses; or the chronic phase of diseases with a stable, constant course. This grouping is especially useful when there are not enough families involved with any particular disorder to form a specific group, and is particularly applicable in rural settings or for less-common illnesses. Thinking about group-oriented services in terms of psychosocial types of illness helps overcome such obstacles while preserving the groups' thematic coherence. More-detailed discussion of the uses of time-limited and ongoing multifamily groups will be found in chapter 9.

Also, designing brief psychoeducational modules, timed for critical phases of particular types of diseases, encourages families to accept and absorb manageable portions of a long-term coping process. Each module can be tailored to a particular phase of the illness life cycle and deal with the family skills needed to confront specific disease-related demands. Such an educational approach provides a cost-effective means of prevention in that it helps detect families at high risk for maladaptation to chronic illness. (See chapter 9 for a more detailed discussion of the uses of multifamily groups.)

PART II

THE FAMILY SYSTEM RESPONSE

CHAPTER 4

Overview of Family Dynamics with Chronic Disorders

Introduction

Part I of this book offered a way for clinicians to rethink physical conditions in systemic terms according to the pattern of psychosocial demands over time. Equipped with the psychosocial typology and time phases of illness framework, we turn now to the family side of the Family Systems–Illness Model. This introductory chapter examines some of the basic components of family functioning under conditions of illness and disability. Succeeding chapters will consider the dimension of time (chapters 5 and 6), belief systems (chapter 7), and dealing with uncertainty in the face of loss (chapter 8).

A NORMATIVE PERSPECTIVE

Clinicians need to consider family functioning from the standpoint of the flexibility, stamina, and depth of commitment that coping with a particular disorder will require. The resilience needed by a family dealing with a slowly progressing but fatal illness such as cystic fibrosis cannot be compared with that necessitated by the demands of ordinary life. Clinicians need to be careful not to append the label "pathological" to families beset by serious illness since standards of normality and dysfunction appropriate to other situations do not apply to them.

The myth that normal families are problem free (Walsh, 1993a) is particularly relevant to families coping with physical adversity. In a family assessment, clinicians need to be mindful of distinctions between symptomatic and dysfunctional or pathological behavior. Most families dealing with disabling or life-threatening conditions can eventually become symptomatic, regardless of how well they initially appear to be functioning in all aspects of family life. Families commonly exhaust their emotional and/or material resources under protracted stress. Just as we should not consider biological decline in an 80-year-old person a failure of the body, so assessment of normality in families dealing with serious disorders needs to be undertaken in light of the magnitude and duration of the situation. This is not to imply that symptomatic family functioning does not need attention; rather, we should view the assessment and intervention process through a normative lens that facilitates the creation of the empowering, collaborative therapeutic relationship that promotes healing. The process of family assessment can be a powerful "framing event" that determines whether families create affirming or destructive narratives about living with a serious condition. This topic will be addressed in detail in chapter 7, on family belief systems.

Components of Family Functioning

Leading systemic models of family functioning incorporate concepts of organization (including power, roles, hierarchy, boundary integrity), adaptability (flexibility versus rigidity), cohesion (closeness versus distance), and communication styles (see, for example, Beavers & Hampson, 1990, 1993; Epstein et al., 1978, 1993; Minuchin, 1974; Olson, 1993; Olson, Russell, & Sprenkle, 1989). These models assume that families face three kinds of life tasks—basic (for example, obtaining food and shelter), developmental, and hazardous (for instance, coping with unexpected life events such as illness and disability)—and that these basic tasks have both instrumental/practical and affective aspects.

Drawing from advances in research on normal family processes, we can identify key components of family functioning (Rolland & Walsh, 1994; Walsh, in press). The framework of family assessment that will be used in the Family Systems–Illness Model is based on evaluation of four basic domains of family functioning:

1. Family structural/organizational patterns.
2. Communication processes.
3. Multigenerational patterns and family life cycle.
4. Family belief systems (for example, shared constructions of reality, family paradigm, and world view).

The Family Systems–Illness Model emphasizes multigenerational life cycle issues and belief systems. These two domains and their clinical significance for families facing chronic disorders will be described in detail in the next three chapters. In this introductory chapter, the significance of family organizational patterns and communication processes with regard to chronic conditions will be briefly highlighted.

It is important to assess all the basic domains of family functioning, but the psychosocial-typology and time-phases framework provides a useful clinical guide, suggesting the areas of family life that will be most heavily taxed by a particular condition. Since all families have areas of relative strength and vulnerability, the goodness of fit between a family and the psychosocial demands of different disorders can vary tremendously. Certain illnesses and time phases may play into a family's strengths, and others, into their weakness. For instance, some conditions, such as well-controlled hypertension, may necessitate little day-to-day communication; patients take their daily medication, monitor their diet, and keep regular medical appointments. On the other hand, a family coping with a child with cystic fibrosis must communicate with each other on a daily basis about complex, home-based, medical procedures and a range of practical and emotional issues.

FAMILY ORGANIZATIONAL PATTERNS

The functioning of any family must be considered in terms of how effectively it organizes its structure and available resources to master challenges throughout the life cycle.

The family constellation

The family constellation includes all members of the current household, the extended family system (including noncustodial parents after separation or divorce), and key people who function as family insiders (for example, close friends and professional caregivers).

In chronic disorders, professionals involved in the ill member's care become part of the "health-related family unit," or treatment system. If a disorder is terminal or life-threatening, health professionals become associated with issues of life preservation, anticipated loss, and dependency. In protracted, disabling conditions, it is not uncommon for professionals involved in home health care to become central to family life; they therefore need to be evaluated as part of the day-to-day system. This is most striking in serious disorders that begin in childhood, the health-care team then becoming a true "second family." Tremendous ambivalence often surrounds including in the family constellation professional caregivers whose functions involve life and death issues and intimate physical and emotional contact with the ill member (see chapter 11).

In disorders, such as AIDS, that are stigmatizing or affect groups subject to discrimination, such as the gay community, caregiving networks emerge that function as a family unit. Clinicians need to inquire about whom the patient considers to be family and be sensitive to possible conflicts that may loom between a family-of-origin and a "chosen" family who may never have met, but who are brought face to face for the first time in a life-threatening crisis.

Family adaptability

Family adaptability is one of the chief requisites for well-functioning family systems (Olson, Russell, & Sprenkle, 1989). Stability (homeostasis) and flexibility are counterbalancing needs. The ability of a family to adapt to changing circumstances or life cycle developmental tasks is balanced by a family's need for enduring values, traditions, and predictable, consistent rules for behavior. Family adaptability or flexibility can vary on a continuum from the dysfunctional extremes of very rigid to the chaotic (Olson, Russell, & Sprenkle, 1989). Particularly in disorders that are progressive, relapsing, or have acute medical crises, family adaptability is essential.

Homeostatic mechanisms are the means by which norms are delimited and enforced to maintain a stable state in the interactional system. All family members contribute to the homeostatic balance by forming or shifting alliances, through silence and distancing, or by rescuing a vulnerable family member in distress. For instance, childhood illnesses that react quickly to emotional stress, such as asthma and diabetes, may predictably flare up whenever parents' marital disagreements escalate beyond tolerable limits. The child's distress diverts attention from the marital conflict and eases the tension between parents as they focus on the child's current crisis. The destructive, noncompliant behavior of an acting out adolescent with diabetes may be offset by the angelic behavior of a well sibling, who contributes in a complementary way to the overall family balance. The reciprocal interplay of these behavior patterns may become obvious only when the ill child leaves home and the angelic sibling starts to misbehave in response to interactional cues like those responsible for the diabetic adolescent's behavior. In instances of serious family dysfunction, an individual treatment that succeeds for the adolescent with diabetes (for instance, in terms of improved compliance with treatment) may have no impact on a dysfunctional system, which may place another sibling, as substitute, in the symptomatic position.

Flexibility is required for a family to adapt to the internal and external changes serious illnesses may require. Internally, the family must reorganize in response to new developmental imperatives brought on by a progressive illness. Also, changes in family organization will be needed as a disorder continues to interact with normal family and individual members' life cycle development (see chapter 6). Sometimes, a basic shift in rules, or "second-order change," is required, as in a transition from one developmental stage to the next, when new phase-appropriate needs and tasks demand new norms and options (Carter & McGoldrick, 1989; Hoffman, 1989).

Families at the extremes of adaptability will have more problems with certain types of conditions. Because rigid families have particular difficulty with change, their style of functioning will be ill suited to the rapid shifting of roles required by relapsing disorders. Such families will function better with constant course conditions, such as a permanent injury. Families that are chaotic and disorganized lack predictable, consistent leadership and have patterns of living that would be problematic in conditions in which strict adherence to regimens is required. For instance, successful management of diabetes needs compliance with dietary rules, specific mealtimes, and timely insulin injections and blood sugar monitoring, all of which are a poor fit with chaotic family functioning.

Major illnesses, such as a stroke or Alzheimer's disease, cause the family sufficient stress to require major adaptational shifts in family rules in order to ensure continuity of family life. A disabled husband may have to alter traditional, gender-based rules to allow himself to assume the role of homemaker while his wife takes a job outside the home.

The following questions are useful to understanding how a chronic condition has impacted, or will impact, on family organization:

- How has the family had to reorganize itself, or how will it need to do so? At present? Over the course of the condition?
- In what ways have pre-illness roles changed for each family member since the diagnosis? Is this different for instrumental or affective roles?
- How much illness-related responsibility does the affected member assume? How congruent is this with family expectations?
- Besides the ill member, who has primary caregiving responsibilities for managing the disorder? How was this decided? How does everyone feel about this arrangement? Could other members share responsibilities to alleviate a disproportionate burden on the primary caregiver?
- Overall, given the psychosocial demands of the condition, does the family organization seem realistic? Is there overcompensation, in which the patient has been relegated to a sick, helpless victim role? Is there undercompensation, the patient bearing too much responsibility, given the severity of the illness?
- How do family expectations fit with those recommended by involved health professionals?

Cohesion

Cohesion, the other central dimension of family organization, has been shown to be a major predictor of family coping with illness (Olson, Russell,

& Sprenkle, 1989). Families must balance needs for closeness and connectedness with a respect for separateness and individual differences. This balance shifts as families move through the life cycle. For instance, in families with small children, there is a relatively greater need for teamwork or cohesion. With adolescence, the family organization typically shifts to less cohesion and more emphasis on differentiation and autonomy of adolescent members. A disabling chronic condition may intensify and prolong these normal transitions. In some problems, such as mental retardation or cerebral palsy, the need for high cohesion may be permanent, derailing family members from normative developmental shifts (see chapter 6).

Clinicians need to be aware of varying cultural norms. A highly cohesive family style is normal in many ethnic groups, and may not be dysfunctional. In Italian families, a health crisis commonly brings the entire family to the bedside. In one case, involving a father in a coma, a six-week vigil was an expression of normal family loyalty, not enmeshment.

Boundaries

Boundaries, the rules determining who does what, where, and when, are crucial structural requisites. *Interpersonal boundaries* define and separate individual members and promote their differentiation and autonomous functioning. Although family organizational styles vary with cultural norms, dysfunctional families tend to be characterized by extremes of enmeshment or disengagement. An enmeshed pattern limits or sacrifices individual differences to maintain a cohesive sense of unity. Members are expected to think and feel alike: differences, privacy, and separation are regarded as threats to the survival of the family (Bowen, 1978b). Typically, identity formation is blocked, there is little sense of self, or a distorted, rigid role assumption is made, based on parental needs and projections. A disengaged pattern of too little cohesion reinforces individual differences, separateness, and distance at the expense of family relatedness, at the extreme fragmenting the family unit and isolating individual members.

Patterns of enmeshment and disengagement are clearly risk factors for successful family coping and adaptation. For any disorder, clinicians need to assess the fit between the psychosocial demands for cohesion and family patterns of closeness. At a pragmatic level, conditions that require teamwork, such as home-based dialysis for end-stage renal disease, will be especially difficult for a disengaged family that avoids closeness and cooperative efforts. Hemodialysis carried out in a hospital with close surveillance and support of a dialysis team usually fits better with the limits of a disengaged family. On the other hand, the minimal demands for teamwork involved in a disorder such a stomach ulcer may not create a problem for a disengaged family since taking medication and going for regular checkups are self-contained.

Enmeshment creates several other key problems. Families may be overprotective and inhibit the development of autonomy with regard to self-care and pursuing realistic life goals. This pattern is most problematic for chronically ill children and adolescents as they strive for normal independence. Also, as discussed in chapter 3, the transition from the crisis to the chronic phase is a particularly vulnerable period. The normative need for high cohesion in a health crisis can mask enmeshment, which becomes more apparent as a family moves toward the chronic phase, in which autonomy is a central goal. Because enmeshed families maintain rigid boundaries around the family unit and tend to be wary of outsiders, conditions that necessitate outside professional help, especially in the home, will be very problematic for them. In such cases noncompliance needs to be understood within the context of perception of medical care as a threat to family well-being.

Generational boundaries, the rules differentiating parent and child roles, rights, and obligations, maintain the hierarchical organization of families. They are established by the parental/marital subsystem and, in turn, reinforce the essential leadership of the parental unit and the exclusivity of the marital relationship. An effective parental/marital coalition with shared leadership is vital, particularly with respect to chronic disorders of childhood (see chapter 9). This helps prevent dysfunctional split roles in which one partner becomes overly responsible as a reaction to distancing and underresponsibility of the other, or a vicious cycle in which one parent becomes increasingly authoritarian as the other becomes more and more lenient.

Generational boundaries may be breached when a child regularly assumes the function of a parental child. In chronic disorders, particularly in single-parent, lower-income, or large families or if a parent is ill, elder children commonly assume parentlike caregiving responsibilities. This is often functional and necessary for family survival, but can become dysfunctional if rigid role expectations interfere with age-appropriate developmental needs (see chapter 9).

Family–community boundaries are also important. Well-functioning families are characterized by a clear sense of the family unit, with permeable boundaries connecting the family to the community. Many families facing serious illness easily become isolated and need social networks for support and connectedness to the community (Anderson, 1982). Clinicians need to familiarize themselves with other systems in which families are involved, such as schools, religious institutions, and workplaces. It is important to explore with families the possible impact of a member's illness on relationships with those systems. For instance, gross misunderstandings about HIV transmission have severely affected the ability of children with AIDS to attend and function normally within schools.

In a closed, enmeshed system, family isolation contributes to dysfunction and interferes with peer socialization and the emancipation of offspring. A chronically ill child generally is at risk of isolation from peers and community activities. When families maintain rigid, closed boundaries with the outside world, this risk is greatly magnified.

The concept of the *triangle* and the dysfunctional process of triangulation has been central to clinical application of systems theory (Bowen, 1978b; Haley, 1976; Satir, 1964). Triangulation refers to the tendency of two-person systems, especially in marital relationships, to draw in a third person when tension develops between the two. Three types of triangles most typically occur. In one arrangement, a couple (persons A and B) may avoid or drop their conflict to rally together in a united front of mutual concern about an ill child (C). If the child is exhibiting behavior problems associated with an illness, such as refusing medication, the parents may unite to blame or scapegoat the child. In a second kind of triangle, one parent (A) may form a coalition with an ill child (C) against or to the exclusion of the other parent (B). Dysfunctional triangles are formed by the breaching of generational boundaries in a covert parent–child coalition against the other parent, or a grandparent–child coalition against a single parent. It is important to note that an excluded member supports this pattern through maintaining distance. In a third arrangement, the triangulated member (C) may assume the role of go-between for the parents (A and B), thus balancing loyalties and regulating tension and intimacy.

Chronic conditions greatly increase the risks of triangulation, particularly when certain unresolved, conflictual family issues already exist. One common cross-generational pattern is seen in couples in which one member maintains a very close relationship with his or her family of origin, one parent often interfering with the couple's developing their own relationship. Here, an illness can serve to shift the balance of power. Imagine a woman caught between loyalty to her husband and to a close-knit family of origin both of which expect and compete for her attention. An illness in any member of this triangle will alter family dynamics. If either the husband or one of her aging parents becomes ill, that person can legitimately expect more of her time and energy. If she becomes ill, the family of origin and the husband may vie for primary caregiving rights. Another typical cross-generational pattern occurs when a mother becomes preoccupied with caring for a vulnerable child and her husband feels shut out or has distanced himself due to gendered role expectations (see chapter 5).

A common triangle presented by divorced families is one in which the parents have not emotionally separated, and conflict persists through their children. The intense emotions and caregiving needs that can be generated by a life-threatening illness, such as cancer in one of their children, can force warring ex-spouses and remarried families together in an implosive way. Sometimes such a crisis can provide an opportunity to lay aside or resolve old difficulties.

It should be underscored that in each case, all three members of a triangle are active participants, and each benefits from a reduction in tension. The more dysfunctional a family, the more rigid are these patterns and the more likely is the formation of multiple, interlocking triangles throughout the extended family system. In fact, models of family therapy that emphasize multigenerational patterns of transmission specifically assess the replication of dysfunctional triangular configurations.

As will be discussed in chapter 10, an illness can function as the third leg of a triangle in a dysfunctional couple's dynamics. The ill partner can use an illness or disability as a means of secondary gain and for wielding power in struggles for control of a relationship, secondary gain here referring to the rights and privileges associated with the "sick role" (Resnick, 1984). In disorders that have ambiguous or invisible symptoms, such as pain syndromes, the potential for manipulation is much greater since it is difficult for family members to gauge the severity of the patient's complaint.

In some cases the hospital, health-care team, or one professional can become the third leg of a dysfunctional triangle. When dysfunctional family dynamics are apparent, clinicians should watch for evidence of splitting: competing family factions may unite against a professional or a whole health institution. This pattern needs to be distinguished from normal situations of despair, such as during the terminal phase of an illness, when families commonly express their grief and suffering by angrily blaming the health-care system.

COMMUNICATION PROCESSES

Effective communication is absolutely vital to family mastery of illness and disability. J. Ruesch and Gregory Bateson (1951) noted that every communication has two functions: to convey content (report), in the form of factual information, opinions, or feelings; and to indicate the relationship (command) between those involved in the communication. The statement "Take your medicine" conveys an order with an expectation of compliance and implies a hierarchical differentiation of status or authority in the particular relationship, for example, that between parent and child. All verbal and nonverbal behaviors, including silence (or spitting out a pill), convey interpersonal messages—in this case, "I won't obey you." In every communication each participant seeks to define the nature of their relationship. In families facing major, long-term, health problems, communication cannot regularly be left unclear or unresolved without pathological consequences or possible dissolution of family relationships. Family units, as ongoing relationships, stabilize the process of defining caregiving roles through mutual agreements or family rules.

In a family evaluation, clinicians assess family members' ability to communicate both about pragmatic (instrumental) and emotional issues related to the relevant disorder. Clarity and directness of communication are important in both areas (Epstein et al., 1993). Specific patterns to note include: toxic or sensitive subjects concerning which communication falters (for example, the possibility of death); gender constraints (for instance, often males are good at instrumental tasks related to caregiving in an illness, but constricted in emotional expression); and specific relationships in which communication is extensive and intimate and others in which it is blocked or distant (for example, anger may be expressed, but not love).

Here are some questions I find useful in determining the effect an illness is having on family communication patterns:

- How has the condition affected family members' ability to talk directly and openly with one another?
- Is the illness or disability discussed openly? By whom? With whom?
- Is anyone protected in, or excluded from, these discussions (for instance, the ill member, children, or aged, frail, or seemingly vulnerable family members)?

Communication about emotional issues is generally more difficult, particularly with regard to disorders that involve threatened loss. Because of this, I ask specifically about the effect a disorder is having on the overall affective climate of a family and on communication about emotional issues. Some illustrative questions include:

- How has the family mood been affected by the disorder? Has it become more or less angry, sad, depressed, hopeless, and helpless, or optimistic, warm, affectionate, and playful?
- Which relationships have become closer or more distant? How?
- What type of feelings seem easiest and most difficult for the family to express?
- Living with chronic conditions can be very frustrating at times. To whom do you express this?
- Do family members refrain from expressing these kinds of feelings to the affected member? If so, how does he or she feel about being protected in this way?
- With whom in the family does each member feel most and least comfortable in sharing feelings about the affected member's condition?

As part of an initial consultation, I often find it useful to meet separately with particular family members to assess constraints to open communication that commonly occur with regard to sensitive topics, such as threatened loss and feelings of shame. Some useful questions include:

- Are there issues related to the illness that you think about to yourself, but do not discuss openly? What issues? Why do you keep them to yourself?

- Under what circumstances would you discuss these private thoughts (for example, when a child is older, when the patient becomes terminally ill)?

- With whom would you feel most and least comfortable talking about these issues (for instance, the ill member, a friend, a minister)? Why?

Family rules organize interaction and serve to maintain a stable system by prescribing and limiting members' behaviors. Relationship rules, both explicit and implicit, provide a set of expectations about roles, actions, and consequences that guide family life. A family tends to interact in repetitious sequences, so that a relatively small set of patterned and predictable rules govern it. Relationship rules serve as norms within a family, as baselines or settings according to which family behavior is measured and around which it varies to a greater or lesser degree. The marital *"Quid pro quo"* (Jackson, 1965; Walsh, 1989b) is an example of rules that are worked out by a couple, a largely implicit bargain regarding how they define themselves in the relationship and their expectations of the relationship. Chapter 10 describes how relationship rules and understandings are challenged when couples face illness and disability.

A serious health problem complicates family rules in several ways. In childhood disorders there may need to be rules for the ill child based on limits and risks imposed by the condition rather than chronological age. This fosters a skew in which younger siblings may have more flexible rules than an older brother or sister, which may create a chronic source of tension and conflict. In relapsing conditions, such as recurrent migraine headaches, a family often needs to establish two sets of rules—one for when the affected family member is well, and another for when he or she has a flare-up. Clear understanding of when illness rules apply can be complicated, especially in conditions such as pain syndromes in which the transition from one mode to another is ambiguous.

Effective *problem solving* is essential for successful coping with chronic conditions. This refers to the family's ability to resolve the normative and non-normative problems that confront it and to maintain effective family functioning (Epstein et al., 1993). Well-functioning families are characterized not by an absence of problems, but by their joint problem-solving ability. Families can have difficulties solving instrumental problems (for instance, reorganizing household responsibilities after a mother's heart attack) and the more affective aspects of problems, such as sharing the grief and fear associated with a diagnosis of cancer. Families can falter at various steps in the problem-solving process. Nathan Epstein and his colleagues identify seven sequential steps in the process: identifying the problem, communicating with appropriate people about it, developing a set of possible solutions, deciding on one alternative, carrying it out, monitoring to ensure it is carried out, and evaluating the effectiveness of the problem-solving process.

A systemic assessment will emphasize the process of the whole group in problem solving, viewing individual effectiveness within the context of such issues as the family's division of labor and power structure, the available resources, and the family's success in solving problems. In a clinical assessment, observation of joint problem-solving processes and inquiry about how crucial decisions are arrived at provide important information about shared power and communication processes.

With ongoing health problems, it is useful to ask families what kind of important family decisions are significantly affected by their family member's condition. Are there particular types of problems they have difficulty trying to solve? For instance, one family with an aging parent with advanced dementia knew the grandmother needed to go to a nursing home and had gathered all the background information necessary to make a sound decision. They discussed the pragmatic aspects of the issue very effectively, but the decision to carry out the plan was so emotionally wrenching that they got stuck at that point in their problem-solving efforts.

Table 4.1
Family Structure: Organizational Patterns

ADAPTABILITY: Balanced stability and flexibility vs. chaotic/rigid

COHESION: Balanced connectedness and separateness vs. enmeshed/disengaged

BOUNDARIES AND SUBSYSTEMS:

  Proximity and Hierarchy
    1. Individual Differentiation
    2. Couple Relationship/Parental Coalition/Power Balance
    3. Generational: Sibling Subsystem; Family of Origin
    4. Family & Community: Permeable Boundaries, Connectedness
       a. Social and Economic Resources
       b. Interface with Other Systems, e.g., Workplace, School, Health-care

---

Source: Adapted from Walsh, F. (in press). *Promoting healthy family functioning.* New York: Guilford.

In summary, no single family style is inherently normal or abnormal (Walsh, 1993a). Assessment should emphasize the fit of a family's organization and communication with the functional requirements of a chronic condition within developmental and social contexts. For optimal functioning, a strong generational hierarchy and clear lines of parental authority are essential. Equal sharing of power in the couple/parental unit is crucial for a healthy gender balance (Goldner, 1988). Family strength requires clear, yet flexible, boundaries and subsystems in order to mobilize alternative coping patterns when stressed by the challenges of illness and disability. (See table 4.1).

CHAPTER 5

Multigenerational Experiences with Illness, Loss, and Crisis

A FAMILY'S CURRENT BEHAVIOR cannot be adequately comprehended apart from its history (Boszormenyi-Nagy, 1987; Boszormenyi-Nagy & Spark, 1973; Bowen, 1978b; Carter & McGoldrick, 1989; Framo, 1976; McGoldrick & Walsh, 1983; Paul & Grosser, 1965). This is particularly germane to families facing a chronic condition. Systems-oriented clinicians see inquiring about a family's history as a way of tracking key events and transitions as well as gaining an understanding of the family system's organizational shifts and coping strategies in response to past stressors. This is not a cause-and-effect model, but reflects a belief that such an inquiry may help explain and predict the family's style of adaptation. For families facing illness or disability, a multigenerational assessment helps clarify areas of strength and vulnerability and identify high-risk families that, burdened by unresolved issues and dysfunctional patterns transmitted across time, cannot absorb the challenges presented by a serious condition.

A historical, systemic perspective involves more than simply deciphering how a family organized itself in confronting past stressors: it also means tracking the evolution of family adaptation over time. In this respect, coping styles, patterns of adaptation, replications, discontinuities, shifts in relationships (that is, alliances, triangles, relationship cutoffs), and sense of competence are important considerations. Monica McGoldrick and Froma Walsh (1983) have described how these patterns are transmitted across generations as family myths, taboos, catastrophic expectations, and belief systems. Gathering this information enables a clinician to create a basic family genogram (McGoldrick & Gerson, 1985).

Clinicians frequently raise questions about the amount of multigenerational information that is necessary, particularly given the significant time constraints of most health and mental health facilities. Whether to gather such information and how much of it are two separate issues. In my experience, it is almost always important to conduct such an inquiry when someone has a chronic condition. How much information is needed depends upon the clinical context and time limitations. A brief screening interview by a primary physician, nurse, or medical social worker is different from a psychiatric consultation or psychotherapy evaluation. Here I present a comprehensive approach, with the understanding that posing only a limited number of key questions may be feasible in a crisis situation or if a clinician has typical time constraints. In situations that involve regular or intermittent psychosocial treatment, I generally gather detailed multigenerational information over a number of sessions toward the beginning of therapy.

The following section describes the uses of a family genogram in assessing the relevance of family interaction patterns to the treatment of illness and disability. For a more comprehensive overview of genograms, the reader is referred to Monica McGoldrick and Randy Gerson's (1985) excellent book *Genograms in Family Assessment*. Following a discussion of the basic family genogram, I shall present a family health genogram and case illustrations of common multigenerational patterns and issues.

Uses of the Family Genogram

THE BASIC FAMILY GENOGRAM

A family genogram is a very useful means of graphically presenting a family tree and showing significant multigenerational patterns. A tool whose use can be learned by less experienced clinicians, it provides a context for other parts of a thorough systemic evaluation and enhances a clinician's ability to see the interplay of important family system events and ways of functioning. It furthers continuity and comprehensiveness of care by supplying a versatile, succinct, clinical summary that can be used to familiarize consultants or other clinicians providing intermittent care with a case quickly.

As McGoldrick and Gerson (1985) point out, "The genogram helps the clinician and family to see the 'larger picture,' both currently and historically; that is, the structural, relational, and functional information about a family on a genogram can be viewed both horizontally across the family context and vertically through the generations" (pp. 2–3). Helping a family or couple view its current situation in relation to multigenerational patterns over time is a valuable learning experience and furthers rapport between the clinician and the family. Often, a family finds this process of sharing its history an easier first step than discussing current emotionally charged problems. Gathering multigenerational information leads the clinician to ask factual questions, which often reduces family members' anxiety. The structured format of the genogram helps families regain a feeling of control, an important therapeutic first step, and promotes the constructive problem solving needed in facing the challenges of serious illness or disability.

The genogram gives the clinician a quick sense of a family's strengths and vulnerabilities in relation to the current situation, and places present issues in the context of multigenerational family patterns. This enables the clinician and family to move back and forth between current and past patterns of problem solving, structure, communication, and beliefs. This clarification helps to reduce confusion among the family and is a way for the family to regain control of the present. Preparing the genogram provides the clinician a way to address family anxieties by beginning to reframe, detoxify, and normalize emotionally charged information.

McGoldrick and Gerson (1985) describe three steps in creating a genogram: (1) mapping the family structure, (2) recording information about the family, and (3) describing family relationships.

The structural map

The basic family structural map is a pictorial representation of nuclear and extended family members and significant nonfamily persons or organizations (such as a church), usually encompassing three generations. Figure 5.1 shows the generally accepted format for presenting individuals and their familial relationships. An identified patient is indicated by a doubly outlined circle or square. The current family unit or network of close relationships should be placed roughly in the middle of the diagram, and any previous marriages and primary relationships, off to the right or left.

Family information

The family structural map is fleshed out by adding information about demographics, functioning, and critical family events. Demographic data include ages, dates of birth and death (causes also being listed), occupation, education, religion, ethnic background, and geographic location of different branches of the family.

Functional information covers medical, emotional, and behavioral functioning of each family member. Recurrent patterns, such as repeated illnesses, are noted; these point to increased biological risk of particular diseases. Less obviously, a wife's excessive anxiety about and overprotection of her husband following a mild heart attack becomes more understandable when it is learned that her father died of a massive coronary when he was the same age as her husband. Key words describing a person or his or her

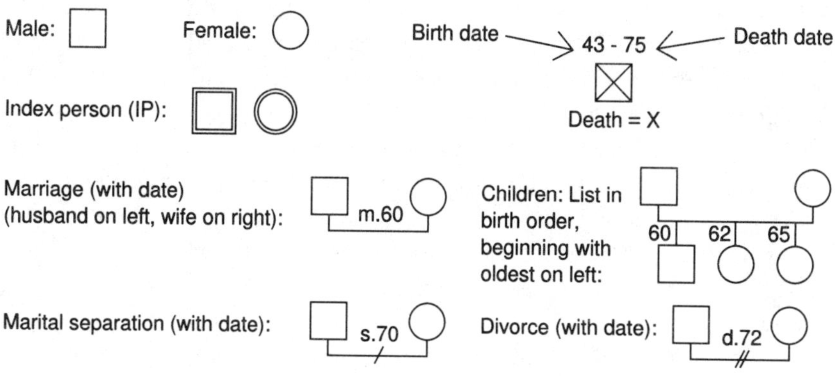

Male: □   Female: ○   Birth date ⟶ 43 - 75 ⟵ Death date

⊠
Index person (IP): □ ○   Death = X

Marriage (with date) (husband on left, wife on right): □—m.60 ○

Children: List in birth order, beginning with oldest on left:
□ ○
60 | 62 | 65
□ ○ ○

Marital separation (with date): □—s.70 ○

Divorce (with date): □—d.72 ○

Figure 5.1
Genogram Format
Source: Adapted from McGoldrick, M., and Gerson, R. (1985). *Genograms in family assessment.* New York: Norton, 154.

role (for example, "long-suffering," "family star," "black sheep") are very useful in identifying central, peripheral, or alienated family members. Research has documented that the impact of an illness is much greater when it involves a central emotional or financial figure (Litman, 1974).

Critical family events should be recorded, such as important shifts in relationships, transitions, migrations, losses, and successes; separations, divorces, remarriages, and job changes should also be included. A visual time line is a useful format in recording the dates and chronological sequence of major family events. This will highlight periods of great stress or change, any pile-up of multiple stressors, and anniversaries that may have special meaning. It is crucial to note the concurrence or timing of such events with the onset or exacerbation of any illness. For example, a child's illness may flare up at the time of his noncustodial father's remarriage, especially if the father's contact and support have been erratic.

Family relationships

Mapping the interaction patterns among family members is extremely important in identifying problematic and healthy relationships. Figure 5.2 shows how to represent some typical family relationship patterns. Conflictual or cut-off relationships and potentially supportive bonds in the nuclear and extended family (for example, between mother and son, father and daughter, or husband and wife) can be noted. Dysfunctional triangles that persist or are re-created repetitively in each generation may be revealed. In cases of divorce and remarriage, relationships with biological parents, stepparents, and step- and half-siblings should be recorded; again, conflictual relationships and cut-offs are especially noteworthy. As a visual map, the genogram is particularly helpful in clarifying complicated relationship patterns that have to be taken into account when a family needs to establish a caregiving system for a chronically ill or disabled member.

Obviously, descriptions of relationships and people's attributes are highly subjective; nevertheless, different constructions of reality and different versions of a key family story are valuable parts of a multigenerational assessment. Though absolute truth or consensus may not be achieved, it is desirable that everyone be present when information for a genogram is being gathered.

Although methods for interpreting genograms are beyond the scope of this presentation (see McGoldrick & Gerson, 1985, chap. 3), an outline of categories of analysis is given in table 5.1.

Several patterns are particularly noteworthy with regard to illness and disability. Repetitions of relationships, symptoms, or patterns of functioning are very significant, as are recurrences of certain triangles, coalitions, cut-offs, and patterns of under- or overfunctioning. Examples include: divorces, alcoholism, conflictual father–son relationships, rigidly defined gender roles, unresolved losses, cut-offs in survivors' relationships when a family member dies, and a recurrent illness in the family. Finally, the impact on relationships and family functioning of change and untimely life cycle events, such as childhood-onset illnesses or a divorce, is important.

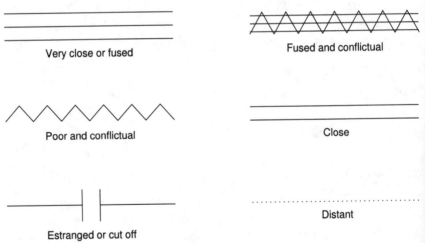

Very close or fused

Fused and conflictual

Poor and conflictual

Close

Estranged or cut off

Distant

Figure 5.2
Relationship Lines
Source: Reprinted by permission from McGoldrick, M., and Gerson, R. (1985). *Genograms in family assessment.* New York: Norton, 21.

Table 5.1

Genogram Interpretive Categories

Category 1: FAMILY STRUCTURE
  A. Household composition
    1. Intact nuclear household
    2. Single-parent household
    3. Remarried family households
    4. Three-generational household
    5. Household including non-nuclear family members
  B. Sibling constellation
    1. Birth order
    2. Siblings' gender
    3. Distance in age between siblings
    4. Other factors influencing sibling constellation
      a. Timing of each child's birth in family's history
      b. Child's characteristics
      c. Family's "program" for the child
      d. Parental attitudes and biases regarding sex differences
      e. Child's sibling position in relation to that of parent
  C. Unusual family configurations

Category 2: LIFE CYCLE FIT

Category 3: PATTERN REPETITION ACROSS GENERATIONS
  A. Patterns of functioning
  B. Patterns of relationship
  C. Repeated structural patterns

Category 4: LIFE EVENTS AND FAMILY FUNCTIONING
  A. Coincidences of life events
  B. The impact of life changes, transitions, and traumas
  C. Anniversary reactions
  D. Social, economic, and political events

Category 5: RELATIONAL PATTERNS AND TRIANGLES
  A. Triangles
  B. Parent–child triangles
  C. Common couple triangles
  D. Divorce and remarried family triangles
  E. Triangles in families with foster/adopted children
  F. Multigenerational triangles
  G. Relationships outside the family

Category 6: FAMILY BALANCE AND IMBALANCE
  A. Family structure
  B. Roles
  C. Level and style of functioning
  D. Resources

Source: Adapted from McGoldrick, M., and Gerson, R. (1985). *Genograms in family assessment.* New York: Norton, 159.

The Family Health Genogram

In the treatment of a chronic illness or disability, a multigenerational assessment involves the same tracking process as that involved in constructing a basic family genogram, though clinicians focus their questions particularly on the family history and past experiences with illness, loss, crisis, and adversity. In each instance it is important to gather information on how each adult's family of origin organized itself as a system in response to these situations, in both current and previous generations, and how systemic patterns evolved over time. A central goal of this inquiry is to bring to light the adults' areas of common experience and learned differences (Penn, 1983) regarding patterns of coping and adaptation.

The psychosocial typology- and time-phases framework helps focus the clinician's multigenerational evaluation. I scan the family history specifically for situations with psychosocial demands similar to those of the present situation, which aids me in making the best use of limited time. Considering family experiences with illness, loss, crisis, and adversity facilitates a comprehensive view of a broader range of family experiences that may be relevant to the present condition.

When appropriate to the type of illness, seeking information on each kind of experience separately allows families to describe other forms of loss (for example, divorce or migration), crisis (for instance, lengthy unemployment, rape, or a natural disaster such as a fire, flood, or earthquake), and adversity (such as that associated with poverty, racism, war, and/or political repression). Tracking family experiences with other kinds of crisis can clarify areas of strength and vulnerability in a family facing an illness with expected crises. For instance, assessment of a family's experience with a flood that destroyed its home provides important insights about how its members pulled together or fell apart in a crisis, juggled strong emotions simultaneously with huge logistical problems, and made use of resources outside the family. For instance, it gives some idea of how the same family might manage a stroke. On the other hand, experience of a protracted struggle, as in poverty, may give vital clues to a family's hardiness when confronted with a persistent condition such as traumatic brain injury or developmental impairment in a child with autism or cerebral palsy—conditions that require endurance, perseverance, and skill in dealing with prejudice.

CRISES

If a condition involves crises, the family's history of coping with crises in general, especially unanticipated ones, should be explored. Illnesses with acute onset (such as a heart attack), moderate-to-severe sudden incapacita-

tion (as in a stroke), or rapid relapse (as in ulcerative colitis, a diabetic insulin reaction, or disc disease) demand, in various ways, rapid mobilization
of skills in facing crises; the family needs to reorganize quickly and efficiently. Other illnesses, such as spinal cord injury, rheumatoid arthritis, or
emphysema, because of their continuous demand for caregiving stamina can
lead to family exhaustion that culminates in a crisis. A family history of effective coping with moderate-to-severe constant stressors is a good predictor
of how a family will adjust to these latter types of illness.

GENERAL ADVERSITY

Families can vary tremendously in terms of their experience and sense of
mastery of illness, despite evidence of adequate mastery of adversity. For example, a mother may have endured the complexities of divorce and abandonment by her father yet never dealt with illness. By tracking key aspects of
the earlier stressor, a clinician can help such a person draw appropriately on
her experience and coping skills so that she can apply them to her current
situation of a husband with a fatal form of cancer. Potentially unresolved issues concerning her abandonment by her father may need to be addressed in
order to ensure a different experience in facing the impending loss of her
spouse and without feeling a repetition of her abandonment as a child.
Strengths she acquired as a child can assist her in dealing with her own children as they confront their father's death. Traumatic experiences that she felt
were beyond her control in her youth are important in the context of an illness whose outcome may be beyond personal control, but the clinician can
aid her in differentiating her present situation from her past. Unlike the
helplessness she felt as a child, there are a number of things she can do to obtain information useful for dealing with her children's distress.

PSYCHOSOCIAL TYPOLOGY AND TIME PHASES

In gathering multigenerational information specifically about experiences
with chronic conditions, the psychosocial typology and time phases of illness framework is extremely useful. Tracking family members' illness experiences gives the clinician a sense both of a family's breadth of experience
and of its history with regard to a particular kind of illness or a specific disease. Clinicians can use their time most effectively by focusing on the most
relevant experiences with illness and adversity—those with psychosocial typology and time phase characteristics similar to the current condition. Yet
there is also something to be learned from a different type of experience. For
instance, some families are able to express emotions in a crisis, but may feel
constrained in a long-term situation. A clinician can track how a family orga-

nized itself to cope with a specific health problem and how the resulting system evolved in relation to the practical and emotional demands of the illness over time.

Organizing a multigenerational assessment within this framework facilitates understanding the historical interplay of family dynamics and the demands of an illness. At the most basic level, the clinician can evaluate each adult's degree of exposure to illness and disability and general skills and beliefs about coping. This will reveal whether the family tried to impose a rigid, monolithic model for adapting, regardless of the demands of different conditions, or was flexible in organizing itself to meet varying problems. Did the family show particular skill or vulnerability in relation to phases of an illness? Although a particular family may have handled crises and loss effectively, it may have been unable to deal successfully with a long-term condition requiring pacing and endurance. Such a family might feel vulnerable in any future encounter with a protracted illness, such as Alzheimer's disease.

What has the family learned from past experiences? One family, despite its psychosocial difficulties with the father's heart condition, learned improved coping skills from that experience and adjusted accordingly when the mother developed a similar illness. Another family may be unable to learn from experience and repeat dysfunctional patterns across generations; confronted with threatened loss and death, such a family may repeatedly reenact patterns of denial, lack of preparation, and flight from mourning and bereavement.

One can direct historical inquiry more effectively on the basis of the anticipated psychosocial demands of the current condition. Consider a family that faces an acute-onset, unpredictable, somewhat disabling, and possibly fatal condition, such as the aftermath of a heart attack. Besides a general inquiry about the family's previous experience, one would ask specifically about illnesses or situations that involved acute or rapid change, uncertainty, disability, living with the threat of loss, and death (since this is a possible outcome). Asking about earlier encounters with heart disease would naturally offer the closest approximation, but similar psychosocial types of illness, such as stroke or certain cancers, would also serve. Experiences with other disorders such as a disabling injury might provide insights about a family's ability to adapt to acute change and disability, but little about its reactions to uncertainty or threatened loss.

Through this kind of assessment, a clinician learns whether a family has certain standard ways of coping with any illness and whether there are critical differences in its style and success in adaptation to different types of conditions. For instance, a family may have consistently organized successfully when faced with illnesses that were not life-threatening, but reeled under the burdens of the mother's metastatic breast cancer. Such a family might be particularly vulnerable if another life-threatening illness were to occur. Another family may have experienced only non-life-threatening illnesses and be uninformed about how to cope with the uncertainties particular to life-threatening conditions. Both families are at risk of coping unsuccessfully with threatened loss and death, but for different reasons: the former because it has been sensitized by a negative legacy, the latter because of lack of experience with this sort of problem. Cognizance of these facts will draw attention to areas of strength and vulnerability in a family facing cancer or any life-threatening illness.

The difference between these two kinds of family experiences can help determine the most appropriate intervention strategy. For a high-risk family burdened by negative experiences and legacies, a brief intervention addressing any multigenerational patterns can help prevent a reenactment of those that are dysfunctional. Simply drawing attention to parallels makes covert linkages overt. This kind of focused intervention allows families to make better use later of psychoeducational or ongoing support groups. Families with no previous exposure to living with chronic conditions respond well to early psychoeducational interventions partly because they are not encumbered by baggage from the past and are relatively unblocked by fears or attachments to dysfunctional coping patterns.

Tracking a family's coping capabilities in the crisis, chronic, and terminal phases of previous chronic illnesses can alert clinicians to possible complications in adaptation at different points in the illness life cycle. A family may have adapted well in the crisis phase of living with a father's spinal cord injury, but failed to navigate the transition to a family organization appropriate for the long haul. An enmeshed family, with its tendency toward rigid overcloseness, may have become frozen in a crisis structure and been unable to deal effectively with issues of maximizing individual and collective autonomy in the chronic phase. Another family, with a member with chronic kidney failure, may have handled very well the practicalities of home dialysis; however, in the terminal phase, their limitations with regard to affective expression may have left a legacy of unresolved grief. A history of difficulty at a specific time phase can alert a clinician to potentially vulnerable periods for a family over the course of the current chronic illness.

LIFE CYCLE COINCIDENCES ACROSS GENERATIONS

A coincidence of dates across generations is often significant. Often we hear statements such as, "All the men in my family died of heart attacks by the age of 55." This comment is a multigenerational statement of biological vulnerability as well as a legacy and expectation of untimely death. In one particular situation, mental and somatic symptoms began as a son approached the age at which his father had died of a sudden, unexpected heart attack in early midlife. This man distanced himself from his wife and family, believing he would spare them the pain he had suffered when his own beloved father died. In a similar case, a man vulnerable to stomach ulcers began to eat indiscriminately and drink alcohol excessively, despite medical warnings, when he reached the age of 43, precipitating a crisis requiring surgery. His failure to comply with treatment created a life-threatening situation. It was only after his recovery and upon his 44th birthday that he remarked that his own father had died tragically at age 43, and that he had felt an overpowering conflict about surviving that age.

Knowledge of such age-related multigenerational patterns can alert a clinician to risks concerning compliance with treatment, blatantly self-destructive behaviors, or realistic fears that may emerge when an illness is diagnosed or when a patient reaches a particular stage of the life cycle. A brief intervention timed to coincide with an approaching intergenerational anniversary date is very useful preventively in this type of situation.

It is not uncommon for the onset of a family member's symptoms, particularly somatic complaints, to coincide with the diagnosis of a serious disorder or death of another member. A similar pattern is sometimes seen in pain syndromes in which a medical workup is inconclusive. Uncovering a temporal relationship between the onset of symptoms and a concurrent or previous traumatic family crisis (such as a serious illness or death) facilitates a clearer treatment strategy. In such cases a timely intervention, based on this historical timing, helps prevent or interrupt the transfer of a multigenerational family pattern in which emotional distress or threatened loss is expressed through somatic pain.

FAMILY DYNAMICS

For any significant chronic condition in either adult's family of origin, it is useful for a clinician to get a picture of how the family organized to handle disease-related emotional and practical tasks.

Structural and practical issues

By asking about organizational patterns developed to cope with chronic conditions in the past, clinicians can get a good idea about the preferred kind of system a family will set up in a health crisis. This includes family hierarchy, roles, and boundaries within the family and between the family and the outside world (particularly the health-care team). Did these structures represent a sharp change for a family? This question provides information about a family's ability to adapt its usual way of structuring itself to the increased and different sort of demands made by chronic disorders. Were these family structures appropriate and functional for the particular situation? Did the family "illness structure" persist dysfunctionally beyond the situation? This question helps determine whether a family became frozen in time at a particular stage of a condition or never completely recovered. How did this happen? Was it through inertia, lack of understanding, or an inability to let go, resolve a loss, or move on? These kinds of questions elicit family strengths and vulnerabilities at a structural/organizational level. What particular role did each adult and his or her own parents play over time in these situations? What did their experience mean to them?

Affective issues

In the same way, clinicians should track how a family managed affective issues. In each adult's family of origin, did communication about illness stick to pragmatics, or was there an ability to share emotions? I am particularly interested in whether certain emotions were taboo—anger, sadness, grief, despair, and fear, for example. Were there gender-related patterns in this regard, men being permitted to display anger, but not grief, and the opposite being the case for women? Were there particular patterns or expectations for adults compared with children? For instance, did no one share feelings? Or was there a generational barrier that allowed parents to communicate feelings, but children were excluded? Were the reasons for these patterns cultural, based on previous catastrophic experiences or fear of losing control, or attributable to other factors? Secrecy, as distinct from communicating information at an age-appropriate level, is usually dysfunctional in chronic disorders.

Past experience with professionals

It is important to assess the history and patterning of relationships with physicians and other professionals. Structurally, did the family tend to delegate one family member (typically the wife/mother) to communicate with the physician? Did the family make its own wishes known, or did it modify a usual style of assertiveness to one of deference to accommodate a physician who wanted to be completely in charge without being questioned? What kind of experience or rules were there about sharing feelings with one's physician? Did family members hide their feelings from the physician? If so, why? Did the physician relate to the family in an unemotional, technical, businesslike way to which the family responded in kind? Did the family have a warm relationship with a family doctor that made it difficult to deal with the segmented, more technological relationships common in large, impersonal hospitals or dictated by a disease requiring a number of specialists?

Personal role

Overall, it is important for a clinician to find out what role individual family members have played in handling affective or practical responsibilities. What did they learn from those experiences that influences how they think about the current illness? What would they want to do similarly or differently? Are there aspects of the current situation that they feel confident, insecure, or terrified about? Whether each member has emerged from relevant experiences with a strong sense of competence, failure, or fear is essential information. It is particularly important to know whether parents, when they were children, were given too much responsibility, parentified or were shielded from involvement in family affairs.

In one particular case involving a family with three generations of hemophilia transmitted through the mother, the father, as a child, had been shielded from the knowledge that his older brother, who died in adolescence, had had a fatal kind of kidney disease. Also, this man had not been allowed to attend his brother's funeral. That trauma had given rise to a strong commitment to openness about disease-related issues with his two hemophiliac sons and with his daughters who were genetic carriers.

Collecting such information about each adult's family of origin enables the clinician to anticipate areas of conflict and consensus. Peggy Penn (1983) and Gillian Walker (1983) have described a common pattern in which unresolved issues related to illness and loss that have been dormant in a marriage may suddenly reemerge, triggered by a chronic illness in the current family unit.

Case Examples

INEXPERIENCE

A recent family consultation highlights the importance of family history in uncovering areas of inexperience.

Joe, his wife, Ann, and their three teen-age children presented for a family evaluation ten months after Joe's diagnosis of moderate-to-severe asthma. Joe, aged 44, had been successfully employed for many years as a spray painter until exposure to a new chemical gave rise to attacks of asthma that necessitated hospitalization and occupational disability. Although somewhat improved, Joe continued to have persistent, moderate, respiratory symptoms. Initially, his physician had told him that once he ceased spray painting, his condition might either disappear, improve somewhat, or progress to include other triggers in his daily environment. The physician was noncommittal concerning the possible chronicity of the asthma and how severe it might become.

Joe had a history of alcoholism that had been in complete remission for twenty years. There was no other family history of emotional difficulties.

During the eight months after his initial diagnosis, Joe's condition did not improve, and he developed symptoms of asthma at home in response to other environmental triggers. His continued breathing difficulties contributed to increased symptoms of depression, uncharacteristic temperamental outbursts, alcohol abuse, and family discord. This finally led to hospitalization for alcohol detoxification and treatment for depression.

As part of the initial assessment, I inquired about the family's previous experience in coping with chronic disease and learned that this was the nuclear family's first such encounter. In their families of origin, they had had limited relevant experience. Ann's father had died seven years earlier of a sudden and unexpected heart attack. Joe's brother had died in a drowning accident.

In this case, neither spouse had had experience with disease as an ongoing process, but both had dealt with sudden death and bereavement. Illness had for both meant either death or recovery. Joe assumed that improvement meant cure. The physician/family system was not attuned to the hidden risks for this family as it underwent the transition from the crisis to the chronic phase of Joe's asthma—the juncture at which the permanency of the disease needed to be addressed. The history of alcoholism presented another risk factor that compounded this couple's difficulty in coping with a chronic illness in which the prognosis was uncertain.

Retrospectively, it is evident that a crisis could have been prevented by taking the uncertain prognosis into account in conjunction with the family histories. This could have been accomplished by the physician's scheduling a physical and psychosocial checkup roughly six months after Joe's diagnosis. At that point, enough time would have elapsed for the physician to offer a revised prognosis, one that involved the likelihood of chronicity; and family members probably would have had sufficient time to deal with their disappointment and make the transition to acceptance of a chronic condition before a downward emotional spiral could lead to a family crisis.

This case highlights the importance of gathering multigenerational information from the entire family. Sometimes one family's lack of, or negative, experience can be counterbalanced by another member's relevant experience and success in coping with a similar type of illness or adversity. One person can teach the other and provide within-family psychoeducation.

In terms of the Family Systems–Illness Model, this family lacked experience with a relapsing, intermittently disabling chronic illness. This, combined with the history of alcoholism, made them vulnerable to the stress inherent in the transition from the crisis to the chronic phase of the illness, particularly in terms of the developmental task of acceptance of the permanency of the condition.

In a contrasting case, a preadolescent girl was diagnosed with severe scoliosis that required wearing a back brace. Her aunt had a daughter six years older with the same condition who had undergone the same treatments and improved, and this young woman was able to serve as a model of successful adjustment and outcome and as a guide for her younger cousin. Moreover, the mother obtained vital support from her sister regarding living with the uncertainties of scoliosis and how best to manage her preteen daughter's natural anxieties about a disfiguring disability.

ILLNESS TYPE, TIME PHASE, AND UNRESOLVED LOSS

A family seen in treatment illustrates the interplay of problems in coping with a current illness that are fueled by unresolved issues related to a particular type and/or phase of disease in one's family of origin.

Mary, her husband, Bill, and their son, Jim, aged 8, presented for treatment four months after Mary had been involved in a life-threatening head-on auto collision in which the teen-aged driver of the other vehicle was at fault. Mary had sustained a serious concussion, and initially the medical team was concerned that she might have suffered a cerebral hemorrhage. Ultimately, it was determined that this had not occurred. Mary's physicians assured her that there was no bleeding and that she could expect a full recovery. Nevertheless, over the following months Mary became increasingly depressed and, despite strong reassurance, continued to believe she had a life-threatening condition and would die from a brain hemorrhage.

During the initial evaluation, Mary revealed that she was experiencing vivid dreams of meeting her deceased father. The clinician learned that her father, to whom she had been extremely close, had died of a cerebral hemorrhage after a four-year history of a progressive, debilitating brain tumor. Late in his illness he had developed frequent and uncontrolled epileptic seizures. Mary was 14 at the time; she was viewed as the "baby" in the family, her two siblings being more than ten years her senior. The family shielded Mary from her father's illness, and at the end, her mother decided not to let her attend either the wake or the funeral. This experience affirmed her position as a child in need of protection, a dynamic that carried over into her marriage.

Despite her hurt, anger, and lack of acceptance of her father's death, Mary had avoided dealing with her feelings about her mother for over twenty years. Other family history revealed that her mother's brother had died of a sudden stroke, and that a cousin had died after being struck on the head by a streetlight. Further, her maternal grandfather had died of a stroke when her mother was seven years old. Her mother had had to endure a wake with an open casket for three days at home. This traumatic experience was a major factor in her mother's attempt to protect Mary from the same kind of memory.

Mary's life-threatening head injury triggered a catastrophic reaction and dramatic resurfacing of previous traumatic losses involving similar types of illness and injury. In particular, her father's, uncle's and grandfather's deaths by head injury and central nervous system disorders had sensitized Mary to this type of problem. The fact that she had witnessed her father's slow, agonizing, and terrifying downhill course only heightened her catastrophic fears.

Her mother's protection of Mary is largely clarified by the genogram in figure 5.3 and sessions in which she was involved. Her mother had been traumatized by the open casket in the living room at the time of her own father's death. As a result, she vowed that she would never let her own children experience the same kind of trauma. As is common in multigenerational patterns, the mother's attempt to spare her own daughter the trauma she endured goes one hundred eighty degrees the other way when her own daughter must deal with death. This unfortunately created a new problem of unresolved loss that surfaced in the context of Mary's head injury.

The pattern of Mary as the child to be protected was solidified at the time of her father's death. One important expression of this pattern was that Mary's mother always communicated important sensitive information through Mary's husband, who, over the years of their marriage, had colluded in treating Mary protectively, which served as a source of power for him in their marital relationship. Mary, for her part, had never discussed her feelings about not being permitted to attend her father's funeral because she felt her mother had had a hard enough life without reviving old hurts.

A clinician might wonder whether Mary was vulnerable to any physical problem or major stressor. In fact, a kidney complication that developed during her first pregnancy had precluded her having more children and, naturally, impacted on the couple's family planning. At that time the couple grieved; but Mary did not develop the sort of disabling, catastrophic reaction that had occurred in the present situation, in which the prognosis was favorable. As happens in many cases, an unresolved loss or catastrophic fear can remain encapsulated and walled off until rekindled by a crisis—in this instance medical—whose characteristics closely resemble the original experience. In Mary's situation, the initially life-threatening involvement of the central nervous system was a sufficient stimulus.

Therapy focused on a series of tasks and rituals that involved Mary's fam-

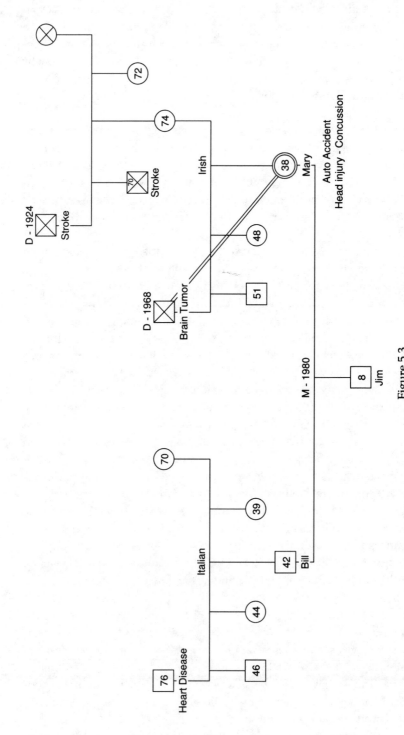

Figure 5.3
Multigenerational Legacies Based on Illness Type, Time Phase, and Unresolved Loss

ily of origin. Her husband participated in most sessions and, on occasion, her eight-year-old son as well. For several reasons it was particularly important to include her husband. First, interventions focusing on changing her pattern of interaction with her mother would likely alter the customary pattern of interaction and hierarchy in the marriage (which closely paralleled that with her mother). Second, Bill had aging parents with heart disease and preferred to minimize the risks of losing them. Mary's addressing issues of threatened loss and death in her own family could have been undermined by Bill because of his fears regarding his own aging parents. Conjoint sessions provided an opportunity for both Mary and Bill to address these issues together.

Because Mary had enormous difficulty expressing anger, she was coached to write a letter to the teen-ager who had been responsible for the accident. Although she did not mail the letter (due to pending litigation), writing and sharing it with her husband were very helpful to her.

Next, Mary initiated a series of conversations with her mother about her feelings of having been excluded from her father's funeral and about the pattern of mutual protection between mother and daughter over the years. A more open relationship between mother and daughter facilitated the next stage of treatment, which involved Mary's saying goodbye to her father. Her first attempts to write a goodbye letter seemed as if she were writing to someone still alive, trying to enable him to catch up on the last twenty-three years. Over a three-month period, Mary did compose a real goodbye letter and experienced the grieving she had bypassed for so many years. It was particularly important to include her husband throughout this phase of treatment because he initially interpreted her grief as regression and it directly stimulated his own anxiety concerning the threatened loss of his own parents.

The final stage of treatment involved a graveside ritual in which Mary, with her family of origin and nuclear family present, read her goodbye letter to her father. This ritual brought closure, for all the family members, to unfinished family issues related to her father's death.

The choice of treatment was critical in this case. At first, Mary was extremely depressed. Many clinicians might have chosen to treat her immediately with antidepressants. Although I considered that option, I found that focusing on the connection between her reaction to her head injury and her unresolved issues related to loss succeeded in reducing her level of depression and panic sufficiently to obviate the need for pharmacological intervention. Making these connections gave her a better sense of control. Validation of her unfinished story by me, the professional, and her husband, her best friend, laid a foundation for reentering, reworking, and finishing the story.

REPLICATION OF SYSTEM PATTERNS

Evaluation of the system that existed and evolved around a previous illness includes assessment of the pattern of relationships within that system.
In many families relationship patterns are adaptive, flexible, and cohesively
balanced; in others, these relationships can be dysfunctionally skewed, rigid,
enmeshed, disengaged, and/or triangulated. Penn (1983) describes how particular coalitions that emerge in the context of a chronic illness are replications or isomorphs of those that existed in each adult's family of origin. The
following case is prototypal.

Mr. and Mrs. L. had been married for nine years when their six-year-old
son, Jeff, developed childhood-onset diabetes. Soon thereafter, Mrs. L. became very protective of her son and made frequent calls to their pediatrician expressing persistent concerns about Jeff's condition. This occurred
despite Jeff's doing well physically and emotionally and despite frequent
reassurance by the physician. At the same time, the couple's previously
close marital relationship became less harmonious: Mrs. L. argued with
her husband, and Mr. L. actively distanced himself from his wife and son.

Mrs. L. had grown up with a tyrannical, alcoholic father. She had witnessed intense conflict between her parents and, during her childhood
and adolescence, had tried to rescue her unhappy mother, attempting to
tend to her mother's needs and cheer her up. She talked frequently to her
family physician about the situation at home. She felt that she had failed
in her rescue efforts since her mother continued, over the years, to be victimized and depressed.

Mr. L. grew up in a family in which his father had disabling heart disease. His mother devoted a great deal of time to caring for his father. Not
wanting to burden his parents, Mr. L. reared himself—distancing himself
from the primary caregiving relationship between his parents. He supported his mother's caregiving efforts largely by taking care of his own
needs, and stoically viewed this strategy as successful. (See figure 5.4.)

With their son's illness, Mrs. L., burdened by feelings of guilt at being a
failed rescuer, had a second chance to "do it right" and assuage her guilt.
The diabetes provided her this opportunity. And, it is a culturally sanctioned, normative role for a parent, particularly a mother, to protect an ill
child. These factors—her unresolved family-of-origin problems and her culturally sanctioned role—promoted enmeshment with her son. Moreover,
since she had derived support from the family physician concerning her situation as she was growing up, she actively sought and expected support
from her son's pediatrician.

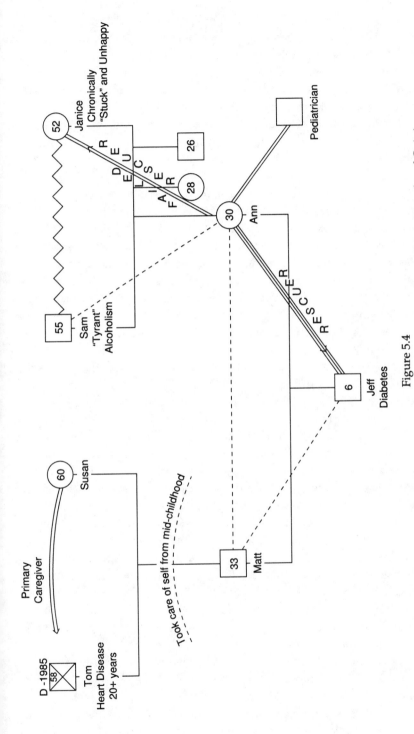

Figure 5.4

Replication of Patterns of Involvement with Illnesses from One's Family of Origin

Mrs. L. unconsciously pushed her husband away, because in her family of origin she had viewed rescuing her mother within the context of battling her father. She fully transposed the pattern of relationships by rescuing her son while keeping her husband at a distance.

Mr. L., though outwardly objecting to the coalition between his wife and his son, honored their relationship, as if it would make up for the one he had forfeited with his own mother. Furthermore, despite his unmet needs as a child, he believed the structure, and his role in it, had worked; hence, he distanced himself to allow the paradigm to flourish: that of the caregiving relationship he saw between his parents and now between his wife and son.

Both Mr. and Mrs. L. have replicated their family-of-origin patterns of triangular relationships and their particular positions in those triangles: Mrs. L. as a rescuer in a family coalition and Mr. L. in a distanced position. Moreover, there is an exquisite complementarity or fit in the positions Mr. and Mrs. L. have assumed in the triangle they have created with their son. The roles of each person in this triangle fit traditional cultural norms: the mother is appropriately concerned about and caring of her ill child; the father is in a more distant, instrumental provider position. Because of these norms, it can be more difficult for a clinician to detect the beginnings of dysfunctional reenactments of unresolved family-of-origin patterns developed around previous experiences with illness, crisis, loss, or adversity.

Early assessment of multigenerational patterns such as these helps distinguish normative from problematic responses. Further, it helps identify the source and degree of commitment to gender-defined caregiving roles. Particularly in crisis situations, such as onset of an illness, couples may fall back on traditional, gender-defined divisions of labor, particularly if they have worked well in previous situations of illness or crisis. A climate of fear and uncertainty is a powerful stimulus to seeking familiar and time-tested methods of coping. Or, as this case highlights, a sense of failure in a gender-based role can lead to resumption of that role in another situation. Here, Mrs. L. is driven to reenact the role of emotional rescuer, a typically female role in which she felt she had failed in trying to rescue her mother from her alcoholic father. Psychoeducational intervention helped her distinguish what forms and degree of responsiveness were appropriate from those that were excessive and unhelpful. Also, conjoint tasks for husband and wife promoted a more balanced, shared involvement in coping with the burdens of a chronically ill child and counteracted the peripheral position of the father.

In this case early referral by the pediatrician was essential to prevent entrenchment of a dysfunctional relationship. At this early stage, the parents were able to reflect upon the situation, because the change represented a recent and dramatic realignment of a previously satisfying family structure that was disrupted by the son's diagnosis. They were able to recognize the connection with family-of-origin issues and to turn away from a destructive path. A brief intervention of three sessions was sufficient. If these kinds of cases are not detected early, they typically progress, over a period of years, to highly enmeshed, intractable systems. Morbidity is high, and may be expressed in lack of compliance with prescribed treatment and a poor medical course, in divorce, or in child and adolescent behavioral problems.

Reenactment of previous system configurations around an illness can occur largely as an unconscious, automatic process. Further, the dysfunctional complementarity one sees in such families can emerge *de novo* specifically within the context of a chronic disease. On detailed inquiry, couples frequently reveal that they have a tacit understanding that if an illness occurs, they will reorganize to cope with unfinished business in their families of origin. Typically, the roles chosen represent a repetition or a reactive opposite of roles they or the same-sex parent in their family of origin played. This process resembles the expression of a genetic template that is activated only under particular biological conditions. It highlights the need for the clinician to distinguish between what constitutes functional family processes with and without illness or disability. For families like Mr. and Mrs. L., placing primary therapeutic emphasis on the resolution of family-of-origin issues may be the best approach to preventing or rectifying an unhealthy triangle.

MULTIPLE CHRONIC DISORDERS

Many families facing chronic disease do not have significant intra- or intergenerational family dysfunctional patterns, but a multigenerational assessment will reveal multiple, stressful, chronic conditions in the immediate family unit or extended family. Couples in later life are a prime example. A typical scenario might involve a couple in the child-rearing phase of the life cycle with two sets of aging parents. It is crucial to inquire about the health of all living parents. A situation in which one of the wife's parents has a progressive disease might be compounded by the fact that the husband's sole surviving parent's health is beginning to fail. In such circumstances it is useful to inquire about any previous caregiving experience with a parent who has already died. Are there any family patterns or expectations of caregiving by grown children, particularly women? What constitutes loyalty for each adult? Has there been any past difference between the spouses concerning how their respective families of origin handled aging parents? Are there areas of potentially significant disagreement that could precipitate a crisis or emerge over time? What are acceptable limits of giving, and how does each family assign priorities with respect to responsibility to aging parents in relation to obligations in child-rearing? In chapter 9, clinical issues for families with aging parents will be addressed in detail.

Any family may falter when faced with multiple superimposed disease and nondisease stressors that appear within a relatively short time. The occurrence of progressive, incapacitating conditions or of illnesses in several family members is a typical scenario. A pragmatic approach that focuses on expanded or creative use of supports and resources outside the family is most productive. In this situation it is useful to know multigenerational patterns and rules of inclusion of extended family, friends, community-based support groups, and professional caregiving services (for instance, home health aides, visiting nurses, and/or mental health professionals). Families with traditionally flexible rules for inclusion of others are at an advantage.

PREEXISTING FAMILY DYSFUNCTION

Families with dormant, encapsulated "time bomb" problems need to be distinguished from those that display more pervasive and long-standing dysfunctional patterns. For the latter, illnesses will tend to become embedded within a web of existing problematic family transactions. In this kind of situation, clinicians can collude with a family's resistance to addressing preexisting problems by focusing excessively on the disease itself. If this occurs, a clinician becomes involved in a detouring triangle with the family and the patient. This is analogous to the kinds of dysfunctional triangles formed by parents with an ill child as a way to avert unresolved marital issues (Minuchin et al., 1975, 1978). When a chronic condition serves as a means of solidifying preexisting family dysfunction, the differences between the family's illness and non-illness patterns are less distinct.

In a subgroup of dysfunctional families, difficulties are expressed in psychosomatic form. It is particularly important to identify multigenerational patterns in which stressors are easily translated into somatic reactions or in which family communication is problematic or blocked and is transacted through bodily symptoms (Griffith & Griffith, 1994). The genogram is useful for identifying both intergenerational tendencies and the type of situations in the past that have triggered this form of coping. This dysfunctional pattern needs to be distinguished from the more normative clustering of illnesses commonly found during periods of major family or personal stress (Huygen, 1982; Richardson, 1945). In the former, the clinician is tracking a persistent pattern that tends toward more immediate somatic reactions as distinct from the physical letdowns that can occur in the exhaustion phase of an illness or in the aftermath of any major stressor.

A family with a multigenerational pattern of psychosomatic complaints is similar to other dysfunctional families, but distinct in its safety-valve mechanisms. For these families, somatic expression signals impending system overload and modulates what are perceived as dangerous situations and transactions. These families can resemble some of those that are coping with chronic mental disorders. When a chronic physical disorder exists the risks of serious recurrences may be higher because the pathway of somatic reactivity now includes a physically vulnerable member. Minuchin and colleagues (1975, 1978) have documented this psychosomatic–illness interplay in certain children with brittle diabetes or severe asthma.

In the traditional sense of "psychosomatic," this kind of severely dysfunctional family displays a higher level of baseline reactivity, so that when an illness enters its system, this reactivity becomes expressed somatically through a poor medical course and/or noncompliance with treatment. Such families lack the foundation of a functional non-illness system that can serve as the metaphorical equivalent of a healthy ego. Such limitations may impede direct interventions by clinicians with family-of-origin patterns with respect to disease. The initial focus of therapeutic intervention may need to be targeted more on current nuclear family processes than on intergenerational patterns. However, a multigenerational assessment of this kind of dysfunction can uncover its origins, severity, and potential resistance to change. The prognosis for this kind of family is somewhat guarded.

In one case, Joe, a 40-year-old man with a history of chronic depression and repeated hospitalizations, was admitted to a psychiatric day treatment program. He had always lived with his parents, and received disability income. He had a long-standing somatic preoccupation with his lips and mouth, considering them deformed. This symptom metaphorically and literally kept his lips sealed about important family matters. His father suffered from a chronic heart condition.

Joe initially responded extremely well to the treatment program and began to open up. Within a week, his father developed a life-threatening exacerbation of his heart condition. In this case the admitting clinician had not made a thorough multigenerational assessment. The history revealed that on at least two other occasions, one in Joe's nuclear family and one in his extended family, open communication had been followed by serious physical crises. Over the years, Joe's mental condition had acted as a thermostat regulating communication perceived as dangerous. Whenever change began, the family's basic mechanism for dealing with unacceptable risk through physical and mental symptoms could be used by one or another vulnerable member, in this case the father.

Had this history been known at the outset, a different therapeutic strategy sensitive to this family's somatic reactivity would have been chosen. It might have included a family assessment in the home at the time of Joe's admission to the day program. This would have included his disabled father, who could not participate at the program site. Also, a more thorough tracking of the possible functions of Joe's symptoms for the family and of the risks to the entire system that change might bring would have facilitated a more strategic intervention. An emphasis on small changes might have allowed family resistances to emerge in a less dramatic fashion.

This kind of more seriously dysfunctional family needs to be distinguished from common presenting situations where communication is blocked because of an exaggerated fear of killing a vulnerable member or causing a medical crisis by upsetting someone. Clinicians need to assess the real medical vulnerabilities and probabilities associated with different disorders. They need to be alert to the possibility of automatically colluding in avoidance of conjoint sessions because of fear of a destructive impact. The issue is how to intervene most effectively. Clinicians need to be active in controlling and interrupting dysfunctional interactions and helping families to communicate within safe limits so that important and needed discussions will be possible.

CHAPTER 6

Chronic Disorders and the Life Cycle

WHEN A CONDITION is long term or chronic, the dimension of time becomes a central reference point. The family and each of its members face the formidable challenge of focusing simultaneously on the present and the future, on mastering the practical and emotional tasks of the immediate situation while charting a course for dealing with the complexities and uncertainties of their problem in an unknown future.

Families and clinicians need an effective way to utilize the dimension of time both for comprehending issues of initial timing of an illness and for looking toward the future in a proactive rather than reactive manner. This task is facilitated by placing the unfolding of chronic illness or disability in a developmental framework. Accomplishing this requires understanding the intertwining of three evolutionary threads—the illness, the individual, and the family life cycles—a highly complex process that remains largely unexplored. In order to think in an interactive or systemic manner about the interface of these three developmental lines, we need a common language and a set of concepts that can be applied to each and yet permits consideration of all three simultaneously.

Two steps are necessary to lay the foundation for such a model. First, we need a language that enables disorders to be characterized in psychosocial and longitudinal terms, each condition having a particular "personality" and having an expected developmental course. The framework combining a psychosocial typology and time phases of illness, described in chapters 2 and 3, provides such a language. Second, it is essential to think simultaneously about the interaction of individual and family development. Because an illness is part of a person's life, it will affect the development of that person and various family members in distinct ways. The particular impact on each person will depend on a number of factors, including age at onset of the illness, the core commitments in the person's life at that time, and the stage of the family life cycle. Within the context of a serious condition, the stage of the family life cycle will significantly shape—and be shaped by—each family member's development. This is perhaps most vividly demonstrated when we consider simultaneously the impact of an illness on a couple's relationship and each partner's individual development. The inherent skews that emerge between the partners highlight the necessity of using both an individual and a family life cycle approach (see chapter 10).

Clinicians and researchers generally agree that there are a normative and a non-normative timing of chronic illness in the life cycle. Coping with chronic illness and death is considered a normal task of late adulthood, that is, of the elderly. The problem with this view is that any significant health problem occurring when we are younger is labeled non-normative because it is untimely (Neugarten, 1976). The richness of individual and family life cycles is reduced in an oversimplified way to old age versus everything else, disregarding the varied pathways through life that have been articulated in models of adult development (Levinson, 1978; Sheehy, 1976).

Advances in medical technology have made this view outdated. People at all stages of the life cycle live longer with serious health problems than used to be the case. Earlier concepts about late adulthood need revision. Many people in their seventies, eighties, and beyond continue to make plans and lead productive and satisfying lives; and younger people who in an earlier era would have died now live for years with a chronic disorder, often achieving a full life span. Cystic fibrosis and AIDS are two examples. In the past, children with cystic fibrosis rarely survived to adulthood; now, significant numbers of those affected are reaching young adulthood and grappling with issues of becoming an adult with a life-threatening illness. Five years ago a person diagnosed with AIDS could expect to die within two years; now, with the advent of new drug treatments, many of the affected are alive five years after diagnosis and are still doing well. In a brief period AIDS has been transformed from a short-term fatal illness to a life-threatening chronic disease. Advances such as these have swelled both the absolute number and the proportion of younger family units living with what would be considered untimely conditions. We need a more refined and useful way of describing the unfolding process for individuals and families coping with chronic disorders, based on the life cycle as an organizing principle.

Nevertheless, illnesses and losses that occur earlier in the life cycle are more out of phase and tend to be developmentally most disruptive (Herz, 1989; Neugarten, 1976). As untimely events chronic diseases can severely disrupt the usual sense of continuity and rhythm of the life cycle. Daniel Levinson's research (1978) has shown that the timing in the life cycle of an unexpected event, such as a chronic illness, shapes both the form of adaptation and the event's influence on subsequent development.

Before addressing how best to utilize the illness, individual, and family life cycles together in clinical situations, we need to link individual and family developmental models through key overarching concepts. The developmental relationship among these different levels has remained largely unaddressed.

Basic Life Cycle Concepts

THE LIFE CYCLE

A central concept for both family and individual development is that of the life cycle (Erikson, 1950, 1959; Gould, 1972; Jung, 1964; Levinson, 1978, 1986; Neugarten, 1976). The notion of cycle suggests an underlying order of the life course where individual, family, or illness uniqueness occurs within a context of a basic sequence or unfolding. At the family systems level, this basic sequence recurs for each succeeding generation over time; and life is planned, to a great extent, in relation to expectation of, and preparation for, this unfolding. Beginnings and endings such as birth, illness, and death are part of the natural sequence. The multigenerational assessment described in chapter 5 tracks key elements in the life cycle as they have appeared in previous generations.

LIFE STRUCTURE

A second key concept is that of the human life structure. Although Levinson's (1978) original description of the life structure was within the context of his study of individual male adult development, life structure as a generic concept can be usefully applied to the family as a unit. By life structure Levinson means the underlying pattern, design, or fabric of a person's/family's life at any given point in the life cycle. Its primary components include: occupation, love relationships, marriage and family, roles in various social contexts, and relation to oneself, including the use of solitude (Levinson, 1978, p. 41). It encompasses a person's or family's reciprocal relationships with various significant others in the broader ecosystem (for instance, person, group, institution, culture, object, or place). The life structure forms a boundary between the individual or family and the environment and both governs and mediates the transactions between them. The life structure evolves over the life cycle, the relative importance of different components (for example, love relationships versus occupation) changing over time.

Illness, individual, and family development have in common the notion of periods or phases marked by different developmental tasks. For instance, a major task of early adulthood is to separate from one's family of origin and establish an independent life structure. In late adulthood, gaining a sense of integrity about the life one has lived in light of one's mortality is a basic goal. Levinson (1978) has described five major periods in individual life-structure development: childhood and adolescence; early, middle, and late adulthood; and late, late adulthood. Each lasts approximately twenty years.

Levinson noted that these life cycle eras are linked by the alternation of *life structure-building/maintaining (stable) and life structure-changing (transitional) periods*, each lasting roughly five to seven years, during which certain developmental tasks are addressed independently of marker events. Figure 6.1

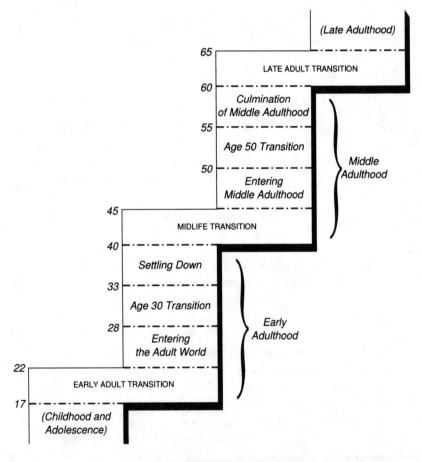

Figure 6.1
Developmental Periods in Early and Middle Adulthood
Source: Reprinted by permission from Levinson, D. J. (1978). *The seasons of a man's life.* New York: Knopf, 57.

illustrates this alternating sequence through early and middle adulthood. The primary goal of a structure-building/maintaining period is to form a life structure and enrich life within it based on the key choices an individual or family has made during the preceding transition period. In a transition period one weighs different possibilities for personal and family life, eventually deciding upon and drawing up blueprints for the next phase. Although the actual possibilities may be very different, depending on issues of race, class, and gender, Levinson's research shows that all of us undergo these phases and certain common processes.

The delineation of separate eras derives from a set of developmental tasks associated with each period. Transition periods are potentially the most vulnerable because previous individual, family, and illness life structures are reappraised in light of new developmental tasks that may require discontinuous change rather than minor alterations (Hoffman, 1989). The concepts of alternating transition and structure-maintaining periods are particularly relevant to chronic disorders.

Family life cycle theory has tended to divide development into stages demarcated by nodal events, such as marriage or the birth of a first child (Duvall, 1977). Elizabeth Carter and Monica McGoldrick (1980, 1989) describe a clinically useful framework based on the following family life cycle stages: (1) the unattached young adult, (2) the newly married couple, (3) the family with young children, (4) the family with adolescents, (5) launching children and moving on, and (6) the family in later life. Predictable developmental tasks and life challenges are associated with each life cycle stage (see table 6.1).

In family life cycle models, marker events (for example, marriage, birth of a first child, departure of last child from home) herald the transition from one stage to the next. Thus, marker events such as an illness or disability can both color the nature of a developmental period and, in turn, be colored by their timing in the individual life cycle.

CENTRIPETAL VERSUS CENTRIFUGAL PERIODS IN THE FAMILY LIFE CYCLE

The concept of centripetal versus centrifugal family styles and phases in the family life cycle is particularly useful in integrating illness, individual, and family development (Beavers & Voeller, 1983; Beavers & Hampson, 1990). Lee Combrinck-Graham (1985) proposes a family life spiral model in which the entire three-generational family system oscillates through time between periods of high family cohesion (centripetal) and periods of relatively less family cohesion (centrifugal) (see figure 6.2). These periods coincide with oscillations between family developmental tasks that require intense bonding and high cohesion, such as early child-rearing, and tasks that emphasize personal identity and autonomy, such as adolescence. Major oscillations over a lifetime may include one's own childhood and adolescence, the birth and

Table 6.1
Stages of the Family Life Cycle

Family Life Cycle Stage	Emotional Process of Transition: Key Principles	Second-order Changes in Family Status Required to Proceed Developmentally
1. Leaving home: Single young adults	Accepting emotional and financial responsibility for self	a. Differentiation of self in relation to family of origin b. Development of intimate peer relationships c. Establishment of self re work and financial independence
2. The joining of families through marriage: The new couple	Commitment to new system	a. Formation of marital system b. Realignment of relationships with extended families and friends to include spouse
3. Families with young children	Accepting new members into the system	a. Adjusting marital system to make space for child(ren) b. Joining in child-rearing, financial, and household tasks c. Realignment of relationships with extended family to include parenting and grandparenting roles
4. Families with adolescents	Increasing flexibility of family boundaries to include children's independence and grandparents' frailties	a. Shifting of parent–child relationships to permit adolescent to move in and out of system b. Refocus on mid-life marital and career issues c. Beginning shift toward joint caring for older generation
5. Launching children and moving on	Accepting the shifting of generational roles	a. Renegotiation of marital system as a dyad b. Development of adult-to-adult relationships c. Realignment of relationships to include in-laws and grandchildren
6. Families in later life		a. Maintaining own and/or couple functioning and interests in face of physiological decline; exploration of new familial and social-role options b. Support for a more central role of middle generation c. Making room in the system for the wisdom and experience of the elderly; supporting the older generation without overfunctioning for them d. Dealing with loss of spouse, siblings, and other peers and preparation for own death. Life review and integration

adolescence of one's children, and the birth and development of one's grandchildren.

In a literal sense, centripetal and centrifugal describe a tendency to move toward and away from a center. In life cycle terms, they connote a fit between developmental tasks and the relative need for internally directed cohesive personal and family group energy to accomplish those tasks. During a centripetal period, both the individual member's and family unit's life structure emphasize internal family life. External boundaries around the family are tightened while personal boundaries among members are somewhat diffused to enhance family teamwork. In the transition to a centrifugal period, the family life structure shifts to accommodate goals that emphasize individual family members' interaction with the extrafamilial environment. The external family boundary is loosened, and the normative distance between some family members increases.

UNIFYING CONCEPTS

These key life cycle concepts provide a foundation for discussion of illness and disability. First, the life cycle contains alternating transition and more stable life structure-building/maintaining periods. Further, particular

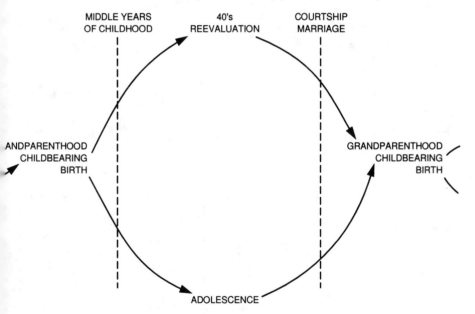

Figure 6.2
System Oscillation between Periods of Higher and Lower Family Cohesion
Source: Reprinted by permission from Combrinck-Graham, L. (1985). A developmental model for family systems. *Family Process, 24,* 143.

periods can be characterized as requiring either considerable (centripetal) or less cohesion (centrifugal) in order to meet psychosocial demands. This set of relationships can be diagrammed as shown in figure 6.3. The Family Systems–Illness Model uses these overarching concepts in concert with specific life cycle events as a way to organize looking at the interaction of individual, family, and illness development.

These unifying concepts of higher and lower cohesion, transition, and stable phases of the life cycle provide a different way of thinking, one substituting a normative versus non-normative mindset with one emphasizing the degree of fit among illness, individual, and family development. Generally, illness and disability tend to push individual and family developmental processes toward transition and increased cohesion. A basic question is: What is the fit between the practical and the emotional demands of a condition and family and individual life structures and developmental tasks at a particular point in the life cycle? Also, how will this fit change as the course of the illness unfolds in relation to the family life cycle and the development of each family member? The nature of the fit among these life cycles will influence the kind of challenges families and individual members will face.

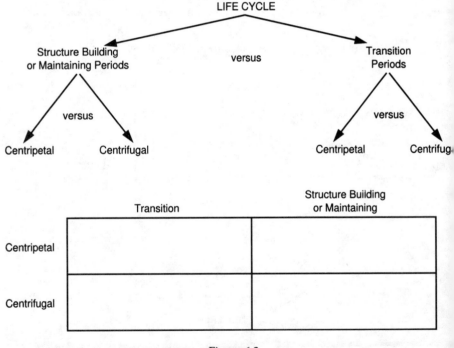

Figure 6.3
Periods in the Family and Individual Life Cycles
Source: Reprinted by permission from Rolland, J. S. (1987). Chronic illness and the life cycle. A conceptual framework. *Family Process, 26,* 215.

Integrating Individual, Family, and Illness Development in Clinical Practice

PERIODS OF HIGHER AND LOWER COHESION

The idea of degrees of cohesion is useful in linking the illness life course to individual and family life cycles. In general, illness and disability exert an inward pull, creating pressures for greater cohesion on both the family unit and its individual members. This tendency varies tremendously according to the specific type or phase of a condition. In family developmental models, periods of increased cohesion begin with the addition of a new family member (infant), which propels the family into a prolonged period of socialization of children. In an analogous way, the occurrence of chronic illness in a family resembles the addition of a new member, setting in motion in the family a process of socialization to illness that requires high cohesion. Symptoms, loss of function, the demands of shifting or new illness-related practical and affective roles, and the fear of loss through death all serve to make a family turn inward.

Periods of less cohesion

If the onset of an illness coincides with a centrifugal period for the family, it can derail the family. The inherently great demands of a new illness for cohesion collide with the naturally lower demands of a centrifugal phase in the family life cycle. A young adult becoming ill may need to return to the family of origin for disease-related care. Each family member's extrafamilial autonomy and individuation are at risk. The young adult's initial life structure away from home is threatened temporarily or permanently. Parents who have recently shifted away from a child-rearing focus may have to relinquish new pursuits of their own outside the family. A recent case involving a brain injury is typical.

Alan, age 25, was a passenger in a serious automobile accident five years earlier, while away at college. He suffered a severe brain injury, and was hospitalized for almost a year, undergoing more than fifteen operations, followed by rehabilitation. Subsequently he returned home to live with his mother, Mrs. S., who had been a widow for ten years. He has an older brother, who is married, has a blossoming career, and lives in a distant city.

At the time of referral, Alan had tried unsuccessfully to return to school, but, finding the work beyond his capacity, had been at home for two years, helping around the house, with no plans for the future. Alan did not drive, and walked only in the immediate neighborhood, which meant that his mother had to drive him to keep appointments or to visit family or friends.

Mrs. S., in her early 50s, has a full-time job and a relationship of six years. After the accident she was forced to table tentative plans to live with her friend. Moreover, she looks after her mother and her father, both close to 80, who still live independently in a nearby apartment. Her father had a minor stroke one year before Alan's accident.

This family is typical of one in a phase of relatively lower cohesion in which both children are young adults with career plans. At 50, Mrs. S. was in a stage of transition, with plans to take the next step in an evolving primary relationship. Alan's head injury halted the family's developmental course, particularly his own and that of his mother, who assumed the role of primary caregiver. They adaptively revived a more cohesive family structure to cope with the demands of the aftermath of Alan's head injury. They were now in the chronic phase, living with long-term disability; but they were at a standstill developmentally.

The goal of treatment was to try to resume, to the extent possible, the initial developmental trajectory within the real constraints of Alan's permanent disability. This meant: (1) Alan's redefining his career goals more modestly by entering vocational rehabilitation; (2) Alan's gradually attempting independent activities (for example, learning the bus system and pursuing the possibility of driving again); and (3) Mrs. S.'s focusing more on her own needs, expecting more of Alan within the home (that is, in terms of cooking meals, doing laundry, and so on), and taking more time to be with her friend.

Two years later Alan got his license, and now drives himself to his job, which involves simple manual labor. He has been exploring the possibility of getting his own apartment. Mrs. S. regularly spends weekends with her friend and is again exploring the possibility of a long-term relationship with him. Her parents have moved into a retirement community that provides meals and other social support services.

When people are diverted from personal developmental goals, they sometimes need to go back to the point at which they were sidetracked and try to get back on the same developmental path, even if it is unrealistic. Clinicians need to help other family members understand that failing to achieve this goal may be a necessary step in the grieving and loss process. Alan's disability precluded going back to college; but he needed to try it, and fail if necessary, before he could more fully accept his limits and move on. This developmental need for closure has to be balanced against any possible physical risks involved in challenging limits or situations of destructive denial. For example, a young man who had a massive heart attack and was at high risk for a life-threatening recurrence had to be restrained from rejoining his training class to become a police officer.

Family dynamics and the severity of the particular condition influence whether the family's reversion to a higher cohesion life structure is a temporary detour within their general movement outward or a permanent involutional shift. A moderately fused or enmeshed family frequently faces the transition to a more autonomous period with trepidation. Their basic family style is more in sync with a period that requires a high level of cohesion. For such a family, a chronic condition provides a sanctioned reason to return to the assumed safety of the previous inwardly focused period of greater cohesion.

The more severe the condition, the more difficulty a family will have resuming its previous developmental course. In the case of Alan, even with a successful intervention, the permanence of his brain damage does impose some real limits on eliminating the need for an ongoing support system; and this need will continue to impose an inward pull on all involved family members' future life cycle stages.

Periods of greater cohesion

Disease onset that coincides with a period in the family life cycle requiring considerable cohesion (for instance, early child-rearing) can have several important consequences. At a minimum, it can foster a prolongation of this period; at worst, the family can become permanently stuck at that stage and enmeshed. When the inward pull of the illness and the phase of the life cycle coincide, there is a risk that they will amplify one another.

In families that function marginally before an illness begins, this kind of mutual reinforcement can trigger a runaway process that leads to overt family dysfunction. Salvador Minuchin and co-workers' (1975, 1978) research on families with psychosomatic tendencies has documented this process in several common childhood illnesses. An illness may reinforce preexisting enmeshed patterns by providing a focal point for other family problems. For instance, Minuchin and his colleagues found that in a family in which there is intense marital conflict, a chronically ill child can function in a triangle with the parents as a mediator of marital distress. Serious exacerbations of the child's illness, such as asthma attacks, become physiologically intertwined with family dysfunction. The threat or occurrence of a serious medical crisis serves to moderate conflict that might escalate beyond control.

In other families this pattern remains stable through childhood, then surfaces dramatically in adolescence, when the developmental push for autonomy conflicts strongly with a long-standing, rigid, overly cohesive system. In such families the added inward pull of the illness and the normative high cohesion stage of the family life cycle have reinforced one another over a number of years, blocking a gradual shift toward a stage of less cohesion that facilitates adolescent development. Finally, the system reaches a breaking point at which the need for change clashes openly with an antiquated system that became developmentally stalled years earlier. Clinicians need to be attentive to such a family's propensity for quietly absorbing an illness when it is organized in an inwardly focused, highly cohesive manner (for example, when rearing small children), yet their rigid, enmeshed patterns will inhibit the natural evolution to a more autonomous, lower cohesion phase later.

When a parent develops a chronic condition during the highly cohesive child-rearing phase of development, the family's ability to stay on course is severely taxed. In essence for more serious conditions, the impact of the illness is like the addition of a new infant member, one with special needs that will compete with those of the real children for potentially scarce family resources. In psychosocially milder health problems, efficient reallocation of roles may suffice. A recent case illustrates how a couple can shift role functions to keep family development on course.

Sally and her husband, Tom, presented for treatment four months after Sally had been diagnosed with chronic fatigue syndrome, which made it difficult for her to manage the demands of caring for their two young children, aged 2 and 4. Tom worked long hours in a small construction business with his father and two brothers. Sally became increasingly upset with his unavailability to share the burdens of housework and childcare that left her exhausted. Tom felt that Sally did not appreciate his job demands and loyalty to the family business, while she resented his rigidness and his placing of family-of-origin commitments ahead of her needs. Marital strain escalated into serious conflict.

For Sally and Tom, sufficient resources were available in the marital system to accommodate her condition and ongoing parenting tasks, yet their concept of marriage lacked the necessary role flexibility to master the problem. The concurrence of Sally's condition with the child-rearing demands in this highly cohesive phase of the family life cycle overloaded the system. The conflict of loyalty between Tom's family of origin and his nuclear family heightened tensions further. Treatment focused on the couple rebalancing their roles, particularly Tom's masculine, monolithic definition of family provider which had, in fact, emerged full force after the children were born.

If the condition affecting a parent is severely debilitating (for example, cerebral trauma or quadriplegia from a cervical spinal cord injury), its impact on a child-rearing family is twofold. A new family member is added, a parent is essentially lost, and the semblance of a single-parent family with an added child is created. In acute-onset illnesses, both events can occur simultaneously, in which case family resources may be inadequate to meet the overwhelming combination of child-rearing and caregiving demands. This situation is ripe for making a child assume the role of a parent or for persuading grandparents to resume active parenting. These forms of family adaptation are not inherently dysfunctional. Nevertheless, a clinician needs to assess these structural realignments in terms of their rigidity. Are certain individuals assigned permanent caregiving roles, or are the required tasks shared and handled flexibly? Are caregiving roles viewed appropriately from a developmental viewpoint? If an adolescent assumes a caregiving role, the family should be mindful of his or her approaching developmental transition to a life independent of the family. In the case of grandparent caregivers, the family should be sensitive to their increasing physical limitations or to the need of one to assist the other.

PSYCHOSOCIAL TYPOLOGY

If we look at illness and disability in a more refined way through the lens of the illness typology and time phases, it is readily apparent that the degree of inward pull varies enormously, with important effects on the family life cycle independent of family dynamics. The tendency for a condition to pull a family inward grows as the level of incapacitation or risk of death increases. Progressive diseases over time inherently require greater cohesion from a family than disorders with a stable, constant course. The continuous addition of new demands as an illness progresses keeps a family's energy focused inward. In contrast, after a *modus operandi* has been forged, a disorder with a constant course (excluding those with severe disability) permits a family to enter or resume a fairly autonomous, less cohesive phase of the life cycle. As the following case illustrates, the added inward pull exerted by a progressive illness increases the risk of reversing normal family disengagement or freezing a family into a permanent state of fusion.

Mr. L., a 54-year-old African-American, had become increasingly depressed as a result of severe and progressive complications of adult-onset diabetes over the past five years, including a leg amputation and renal failure that had recently required beginning home dialysis four times a day. For twenty years Mr. L. had had an uncomplicated, constant course, allowing him to lead a full, active life. He was an excellent athlete and engaged in a number of recreational group sports. Short- and long-term family planning had never focused on his illness. This optimistic attitude was reinforced by the fact that two people in Mrs. L.'s family of origin had had diabetes without complications. Their only child, a son aged 26, had left home after high school and had recently married. Mr. and Mrs. L.

had a stable marriage in which both maintained many outside independent interests. In short, the family had moved smoothly through the launching transition to a more autonomous, outwardly directed period in the life cycle.

The transformation of Mr. L.'s disease to a progressive phase, along with the incapacitating and life-shortening nature of his complications, had reversed the normal transition process to a more autonomous life cycle period for all the family members. Mr. L.'s advancing illness required his wife to take a second job, which necessitated giving up her hobbies and civic involvements. Their son and his wife moved back home to help his mother take care of his father and the house. Mr. L., unable to work and deprived of his athletic social network, was isolated at home and spent his days watching television. He felt he was a burden to everyone, was blocked in his own mid-life development, and foresaw a future filled with only suffering.

The essential goal of family treatment in developmental terms centered on modulating some of the system's overreaction and achieving a more realistic balance. For Mr. L., this meant both coming to terms with his losses and fears of suffering and death and identifying the abilities and possibilities still available to him. This involved reworking of his life structure to accommodate his actual limitations while maximizing his chances of returning to his basically independent way of life. For instance, although he could no longer participate on the playing field, he could remain involved in sports through coaching. For Mrs. L. and her son, this meant developing realistic expectations for Mr. L. that reestablished him as an active family member with a share of family responsibilities. This facilitated their regaining key aspects of their autonomy within an illness–family system.

Relapsing illnesses alternate between periods of drawing a family inward and periods of release from the immediate demands of the condition. However, the on-call state of preparedness required by many such illnesses keeps some part of the family in a centripetal mode despite medically asymptomatic periods. Again, this may impede the natural flow of phases in the family life cycle.

TIME PHASES

One way to think about the time phases of illness is in terms of their involving a progression from a crisis phase requiring high cohesion to a chronic phase demanding less cohesion. The terminal phase, if it occurs, forces most families back into being more inwardly focused and cohesive. In other words, the "life structure of the illness" developed by a family to accommodate each phase in the illness life cycle is influenced by the inherent inward pull of each time phase. The crisis phase, because of its high psychosocial demands and its analogy to childhood (here as a period of socialization to illness), promotes a tendency toward higher cohesion. The chronic phase, which has as a primary task movement toward autonomy within the constraints of the illness, bears a strong resemblance to the less cohesive phase of adolescence and adulthood. The terminal phase, in which increasing psychosocial demands accompany physical decline, is like later life: both foster a pull inward for the family because of increased caregiving.

Thinking in terms of the natural trends toward higher or lower cohesion brings the phases of illness more or less into sync with the stage of family development. For example, consider a family in which onset of an illness has coincided with a relatively autonomous, lower cohesion phase of its development. A typical case might be a family with young adult children in which the father has had a heart attack. Initially, in addition to the sheer level of demand on this family, the inward pull of the crisis phase would conflict with the family's being at an outwardly directed, independent phase at that time. This would increase the level of stress the family experiences. One expression of this added complexity might involve a young adult son or daughter having to put life plans on hold and return home for an indeterminate period to assist in care of the father. This would be in sharp contrast to a family with middle- and high-school-age children still at home that is at an earlier, inwardly focused stage characterized by considerable cohesion.

Often the transition to the chronic phase permits a family to resume, to some extent, its original developmental trajectory. At that point, if the father's recovery from a heart attack is progressing well and he can return to work, the children can revive their early adulthood plans.

Transition periods

Clinicians need to be mindful of the timing of the onset of a chronic illness in terms of individual/family transition and life structure-building/maintaining periods of development. All transitions inherently involve the basic processes of beginnings and endings. Arrivals, departures, and losses are common life events during which there is an undercurrent of preoccupation with death and finiteness (Levinson, 1978).

Illness and disability may precipitate the loss of the pre-illness identity of the family. They force the family into a transition in which one of the family's main tasks is to adjust to possibilities of further loss and untimely death. When onset of a condition coincides with a transition in the individual or family life cycle, one may expect that issues related to previous, current, and anticipated loss will be magnified. Transition periods are often characterized by upheaval, rethinking of previous commitments, and openness to change. This poses a greater risk that the illness may become unnecessarily embedded, or inappropriately ignored, in plans for the next developmental phase. During a transition period, commitments are reevaluated. This process increases the probability that family rules regarding loyalty through sacrifice and caregiving may prevail. Feelings of indecision about one's future can be alleviated by excessive focus on a family member's physical problems, and this can be a major precursor of family dysfunction in illness and disability. By adopting a longitudinal developmental perspective, a clinician can stay attuned to future transitions and their overlap with each other.

The following example highlights the importance of the illness in relation to future developmental transitions.

A father, a carpenter and primary financial support of his family, had a mild heart attack and emphysema. At first, his level of impairment was mild and stable. This allowed him to continue part-time work. Because their children were all teen-agers, his wife was able to undertake part-time work to help maintain financial stability. The oldest son, age 15, seemed relatively unaffected. Two years later, the father experienced a second more life-threatening heart attack and became totally disabled. His son, now 17, had dreams of going away to college and preparing for a career in science. The specter of financial hardship and the perceived need for a man in the family created a serious dilemma of choice for the son and the family.

In this case, there was a fundamental clash between developmental issues of separation/individuation and the ongoing demands of progressive, chronic disability upon the family. This vignette demonstrates the potential clash between simultaneous transition periods: transition of the illness to a more incapacitating and progressive course, the adolescent son's transition to early adulthood, and the family's transition from a living-with-teen-agers to a launching-young-adults stage. This example also illustrates the significance of type of illness. An illness that was relapsing or less life-threatening and incapacitating (as opposed to one with a progressive or constant course) might have interfered less with the son's separation from his family of origin. If his father had had an intermittently incapacitating illness, such as a spinal disc disorder, the son might have moved out, but tailored his choices to remain close to home and thus available during acute flare-ups.

The life structure-maintaining period

The onset of a chronic illness may cause a different kind of disruption if it coincides with a life structure-building/maintaining period in individual or family development. These periods are characterized by the living out of a certain life structure that represents the outgrowth of the rethinking, formulation, and change of the preceding transition period. The cohesive bonds of the individual and family are oriented toward protecting the current life structure. Disorders with only a mild level of psychosocial severity (for instance, those that are not fatal, only mildly incapacitating, and nonprogressive) may require some revision of the individual or family structure, but not a radical restructuring that would necessitate a shift to a transitional phase of development. Some conditions may be so demanding that they force a family to abandon a whole stable life structure and resume a transitional form of life.

Family adaptability is a prime factor in successful coping with this kind of crisis. In this context, family adaptability is interpreted in its broadest sense—a family must transform its basic life structure to a prolonged transitional state. For instance, in the previous example, the father's heart condition rapidly progressed while the oldest son was in a transition period in his own development. The nature of the strain in developmental terms would have been quite different if progression of the father's disease had occurred when the son was more solidly established in a developmental phase that included a beginning career, marital commitment, and a first child. In the latter scenario, the son's life structure would have been in an inwardly focused, highly cohesive, structure-maintaining period within his newly formed nuclear family. To accommodate fully to the needs of his family of origin could have required a major shift in his developmental priorities. Since this illness crisis coincided with a developmental transition period (age 17), however, the youth was unfettered by commitments and therefore available for a caregiving role that could become his permanent life structure.

Later, in his mid-20s, the major complication might have involved the fact that he had made developmental choices and was in the process of living them out. His commitments would have been inwardly focused on his newly formed family. To serve the demands of the transition in the illness, the son might have needed to shift his previously stable life structure back to a transitional state, and that shift would have been out of phase with the flow of his individual and nuclear family's development. This would almost invariably have placed great strain on his marriage. One precarious way to resolve this dilemma of divided loyalties might have been the merging of the two households, thus creating a single, large, very cohesive family system.

For some family members, giving up the building of a new life structure that is already in progress can be more devastating than changes in a more transitional period, when future plans may be at a more preliminary stage and less firmly formulated or clearly determined. An analogy would be the difference between a couple's discovering that they do not have enough money to build a house versus being forced to move out of a house they have already built.

Case Illustration

Thus far this discussion has considered separately the interplay of a chronic disorder with higher and lower cohesion, transition, and structure-building/maintaining (stable) phases of family and individual life cycles. In reality, there is a dynamic interplay of the illness and family and individual family members' life cycles over time. Unless it involves our own family, we rarely have the opportunity to learn about the normative experiences of couples or families with a chronic condition over the course of their lives. I have been fortunate to have close friends who have been willing to share with me their individual and collective stories. One dimension of my dialogue with them has been to evaluate the evolution of various issues related to the development of individuals, couples, and families every few years.

Jim, age 38, and Nancy, age 42, have been married for eight years. They have one daughter, Janet, who is 4 years old. Jim has had multiple sclerosis for twenty-one years. Currently he uses a walker to get around their apartment and at work. His coordination is markedly impaired, particularly his fine motor skills, such as those required for writing. When fatigued or physically ill, Jim's disability worsens. He is legally blind, but can read and work at a computer enhanced for the physically impaired. His keen intellect, warm personality, and strong will are unaffected by his disability. Nancy works full time as a paralegal.

Jim first developed symptoms as a college freshman, at the age of 17. The first three years of his illness were particularly severe, marked by a number of flare-ups and rapid progression. His major disabilities are loss of coordination and muscle strength, difficulty walking, and impaired eyesight. His last major flare-up requiring hospitalization occurred at age 24. Since that time, his condition has progressed very slowly.

During the initial period of Jim's illness, between the ages of 17 and 21, Jim was undergoing his early adult transition. Generally, this is a time for developing a first plan for an independent adult life outside one's family of origin. For men in particular, this usually means starting a career and attempts to form a commitment in an intimate relationship. Before his illness Jim had entered college, with ambitions to become a lawyer, and had had an active social life. His diagnosis and its initially rapidly progressive and life-shortening trajectory became superimposed on this developmental phase. Jim felt he might die an early death, as happens with approximately 10 percent of multiple sclerosis patients. Based on this ominous prognosis, he decided to pursue a career with more immediate gratification for himself and others. He became involved in volunteering his time to help advocate for local and regional environmental preservation. Having revised his early adult transition plans to accommodate more immediately achievable goals, Jim successfully passed through his first structure-building/maintaining period into his late 20s.

Typically, early adulthood is a time of exploring and developing a capacity for intimacy, mutuality, and, often, long-term relationships. The onset of a chronic condition can severely affect this developmental process. Jim described how the uncertainties about his prognosis, his insecurity because of his new disability, and his relative lack of experience with intimacy all interacted to block his pursuit of close relationships. In essence, learning how to manage his illness and intimate relationships simultaneously in the context of threatened loss was too much to handle. After several disappointing experiences, Jim realized that he needed to learn how to cope with his condition before he could resume exploring intimate relationships. This was adaptive. During this vulnerable initial period, he might have found a partner who needed to adopt a caregiving role. In two young adults inexperienced in relationships, a natural skew at this stage of adaptation to a chronic illness might easily have evolved into a dysfunctional long-term relationship. Often, a young adult feeling overwhelmed and insecure, like Jim, might find a partner who is drawn to become a caregiver because of unresolved issues in his or her family of origin, for example, a young adult who, as a child, had assumed the role of a parent or rescuer in a family dealing with a chronic disorder such as alcoholism. Any relationship that begins when one partner is in an initial crisis phase is vulnerable to dysfunction, and this risk is much greater if the couple is also at a stage in their personal development when both are beginning to learn about intimate relationships.

Through his early and mid-20s, the initially rapid progression of Jim's illness ceased and stabilized into a more typical pattern of very slow progression with no major flare-ups. This change in prognosis, coupled with Jim's gradually learning how to live with his disability in a more chronic phase, altered his perspective on time. He could realistically entertain longer-range career and relationship possibilities. Moreover, he had achieved a level of confidence in coping with his condition that enabled him to resume thinking about developmental goals more fully, with less compromise.

As a result of this changed perspective, during his age-30 transition, Jim began a long-term relationship with his future spouse, Nancy. They married when Jim was 31. To Nancy, who was trying to understand his illness, Jim's "willingness to be open, direct, and supportive with regard to my questions and anxieties was absolutely fundamental." Nancy stated, "My ability to set limits on what I would do, to express my own needs and have him accept them as legitimate, was essential to our being able to forge a mutual relationship."

Nancy had grown up as the oldest sibling of an alcoholic mother. During her 20s, she had sought professional help to work out unresolved issues from her family of origin that interfered with relationships. This therapy allowed her to approach a relationship, even with someone with a chronic illness, more assertively. For both Jim and Nancy, their coming together partially reflected the overcoming of obstacles to intimacy they had faced in their 20s.

During the early phase of their relationship and marriage, Nancy undertook additional education to advance her career and then established herself in her first job. During this time Jim continued his volunteer work and supported Nancy during her career transition. Although the disability required time and energy, their relationship was organized to maximize individual goals outside the home.

Three years since their marriage, Jim and Nancy have settled into a comfortable relationship. Jim's illness has progressed very slowly, with no new major complications and at a rate to which they can easily adapt. Nancy is now established in her new career and has turned 37. New life cycle dilemmas surface: they face choices because of competing biological clocks. Nancy is approaching her midlife transition, and her fertility clock, like the one for Jim's progressive illness, is ticking. Initially they had agreed to defer a decision about whether to have a child. Also, to accommodate Jim's need to stay in familiar surroundings, with an elaborate support network to which he was well adapted, Nancy had rejected opportunities for career advancement in a large city and settled for a less interesting and prestigious position. Now, as she enters her midlife transition, she is reevaluating her choices. She decides that she wants either to have a child or move so that she can advance her career more ambitiously. She feels too compromised: giving up both having a child and an active career would be unhealthy for her personally and for the relationship. Her ability to maintain a sense of legitimacy about her own needs, given Jim's limitations, is healthy.

Jim has been medically stable for ten years. He abandoned his original career ambitions in his early 20s because of the threat of an early death, and he did so again at thirty to develop a relationship. He has made active choices with full recognition of his physical limits and the risk of a flare-up if overstressed. His disease is progressing slowly, particularly with regard to his eyesight and his mobility. He feels a pressure to go back to school now, so that he can increase his career options and do so while he still has physical stamina and the ability to read. But he wonders, "Should I even consider these choices, because . . . I don't want to blow it."

As a couple, Jim and Nancy are at a crossroads. Jim's illness dictates a limit on their reserves as a couple. Can Jim handle school? Can they manage an infant? If they choose not to have a child, how will they define the future of their relationship and each person's goals? Decisions that were appropriately deferred must now, under the time pressure of life cycle demands, be addressed. Both Jim and Nancy have had parents die in the past year, which has heightened their sense of life's fragility and the impetus to actively shape their lives and have a child. The illness life cycle weighs on all other developmental choices and forces decision making into more of an either/or framework than would be the case for couples less burdened by adversity.

Consistent with their "can do" philosophy, this couple chose a modified both/and approach. Jim entered graduate school on a part-time basis, in order to feel his way and leave enough slack to overcome any hurdles without overreaching his physical limits. Also, they decided to try and have a child. Nancy quickly became pregnant; and a year after their decision, Jim was attending school and they had an infant.

What Jim and Nancy were least prepared for was the transition from a lower stress family system of two relatively autonomous adults to the considerable demands of an inwardly focused, cohesive family unit with an infant. During prenatal visits, the physician minimized the special needs they might have. As Nancy said, "I too desperately wanted to preserve the glossy picture of raising a child together, so I didn't question things"; but "Jim's limits that normally don't come into play got accentuated." For instance, their baby, Janet, had a period of colic during the first few months. The pediatrician told Nancy that their baby was not getting enough food and suggested that timely and efficient bottle-feeding was needed. Jim could feed Janet; but because of his coordination difficulties, he was slow. The pediatrician's definition of the problem created a dilemma: Jim's disability would prevent "efficient" feeding and exacerbate the colic. Jim argued with Nancy, "I can do it fine, my own way." Nancy was torn between her need to be a good mother and her wish to protect her husband from disappointment. Jim felt inadequate, and their glossy picture of mutual infant care was tarnished. They needed time to socialize themselves to the added complexities of parenthood within the context of a chronic illness that they had mastered in the previous phase of the life cycle. Their story highlights the need for clinicians to be mindful of life cycle transitions that may require helping a family redefine mastery in terms of new developmental tasks.

From this experience Jim learned to anticipate complexities related to his daughter's future development. For instance, he realized that, given his visual impairment, it would be difficult to read bedtime stories to Janet. Instead, he began a ritual of making up bedtime stories that sidestepped his disability while preserving special time with his daughter before sleep.

For Nancy and Jim, having a child made heightened skew in their relationship inevitable. Because of the limits imposed by Jim's illness, Nancy has to bear the bulk of homemaking and child-care responsibilities on top of her job. It is crucial for the well-being of their relationship that they actively try to maintain a balance so that Nancy does not have to assume responsibility for all aspects of family life, which could cause resentment. Although Jim may be limited in his physical capabilities, he can handle any of the family's emotional needs. To keep a balance will require open, direct communication and a willingness to challenge gender-role stereotypes (see chapters 9 and 10 for further discussion).

General Clinical Discussion

From a systems viewpoint, when an illness or disability is diagnosed, it is important, for several reasons, to know the phase of the family life cycle and the stage of individual development of all family members—not just the ill member. First, illness and disability in one family member can profoundly affect the developmental goals of another member. For instance, a disabled infant can be a serious roadblock to a mother's mastery of child-rearing, or a life-threatening illness in a young married adult can interfere with the spouse's need to begin the phase of parenthood. Second, family members frequently do not adapt equally to chronic illness; each family member's ability to adapt and at what rate are directly related to each individual's own developmental stage and role in the family (Ireys & Burr, 1984).

The notion of out-of-phase illnesses can be conceptualized in a more refined way:

1. As described earlier, diseases exert an inward pull and require increased family cohesion. In this sense they are naturally out of phase with families in, or in transition to, a period of more individual autonomy and less cohesion. From this vantage point, illnesses can be particularly disruptive to families in a developmental phase characterized by lower cohesion.

2. The onset of a chronic condition tends to create a period of transition whose duration and intensity depend on the psychosocial type and phase of the illness. This forced transition is particularly out of phase if it coincides with a life structure-building/maintaining (stable) period in an individual's or family's life cycle.

3. If the particular illness is progressive, relapsing, increasingly incapacitating, and/or life-threatening, then the phases in the unfolding of the disease will be punctuated by numerous transitions. Under these conditions a family will need to alter its illness life structure more frequently in order to adjust to the shifting and often increasing demands of the disease. This level of demand and uncertainty keeps the illness in the forefront of a family's consciousness and impinges constantly on its attempts to get back into phase developmentally.

4. The transition from the crisis to the chronic phase of the illness life cycle is often the key juncture at which the intensity of the family's socialization to living with chronic disease can be relaxed. In this sense, it offers a

"window of opportunity" for the family to correct its developmental course.

Some investigators believe that chronic disorders that occur in the child-rearing period can be most devastating because of their potential impact on family financial and other responsibilities (Herz, 1989). Again, the actual impact will depend on the psychosocial type of illness and the pre-illness roles of each family member. Families governed by rigid gender-defined roles concerning who should be the primary financial provider and caregiver of children will potentially have the greatest problems with adjustment. Such families need to be coached to adopt a more flexible view about interchanging clearly defined roles.

Confronted by illness and disability, a family should aim, above all, to deal with the developmental demands of the illness without forcing family members to sacrifice their own or the family's development as a system. Therefore, it is vital to inquire about what life plans the family or individual members have had to alter, postpone, or completely cancel as a result of the condition. The process by which these decisions have been reached is particularly important. Significant factors include gender-based or culturally defined beliefs about who should assume primary responsibility for caregiving functions. Cultures and families are quite diverse in their expectations about the relative priority of sacrifice for the family in time of need versus protecting personal goals and plans. Other family variables, including cohesion, flexibility, and belief systems, dictate group versus individual coping strategies and, ultimately, the kind and degree of life cycle changes made. For instance, if one person (invariably a female) is designated the sole responsible caregiver, then the developmental plans of that person are transformed while other family members may continue their lives with little or no change. A clinical objective might be to help a family become more flexibly cohesive and share responsibilities in such a way that although everyone's life is somewhat affected, no one person's is disproportionately or radically compromised.

The degree of preservation and alteration of individual and family developmental priorities is an excellent barometer of family dynamics. It is useful to know whose plans are most and least affected. What factors (for instance, gendered role expectations) influenced the process that ultimately determined who would be most affected? How does each family member feel about the impact on his or her developmental plans? By posing these sorts of questions, a clinician can learn a great deal about general family functioning.

Clinicians need to determine whether sacrifices are warranted. Often, families overreact in the initial crisis phase of problems, such as a heart attack, that begin in a dramatic or life-threatening manner. On the basis of its initial perception of the severity of the condition, a family may prematurely cancel plans that could be preserved through postponement or creative alterations. When family members change their life plans prematurely, an amplifying cascade effect follows that can tragically alter the whole life course of an individual or an entire family. This is particularly true for conditions, such as a heart attack, in which the uncertainties about prognosis, which may continue indefinitely, can solidify an initial crisis-phase caregiving arrangement that eventually becomes unnecessary.

Early in the experience of an illness, families have particular difficulty separating the need for temporary detours versus permanent changes in life cycle plans. This underscores the importance of timely psychoeducation for families concerning a chronic condition before vital normative life cycle phases are permanently altered. Once developmental plans are derailed, the inherent inertia of chronic conditions makes it more difficult to find one's original path. It is useful to ask family members to evaluate openly which plans they need to change, on what basis, for how long, and when these decisions will be reassessed.

An orientation sensitive to the future means asking family members when and under what conditions they contemplate resuming plans put on hold or addressing future developmental tasks. This enables a clinician to anticipate developmental crises related to independence from, versus subjugation to, a chronic condition. Nodal points of transition to a new developmental phase are typically the most significant. Questions such as the following are useful:

- What individual, family, or illness transitions will be coming up in the next year? In the next five years?
- Are family members aware of major developmental tasks that will become salient at that time? For themselves? For other family members? For the entire family?

Such questions are valuable in a clinical assessment and as a means of encouraging a family to think in life cycle terms. In that sense, posing questions of this nature serves to focus a family on key issues and provides a new frame of reference within which a family may solve problems more effectively. Sometimes these questions are asked with regard to a particular nodal event rather than a general long-term plan. For instance, a clinician might consider asking the following questions of a family with teen-agers in which the father has heart disease:

- In two years, when Joe is 18 and finishing high school, what issues will Joe, other family members, or the whole family need to consider? Whose life might be most affected at that time?
- How will those issues be affected by Dad's heart disease?

- How will those issues be affected if Dad's heart disease worsens (for instance, if he has another heart attack)?
- Given Dad's illness, are there certain expectations about how Joe should plan for the next phase of his life?

These questions help reveal how much life cycle planning is built around the status of Dad's condition. Finding out about expectations is critical because it provides a window into loyalty issues, ethnic or cultural understandings, and beliefs that will become guideposts for decision making during the upcoming transition.

In situations of ambiguity, such as cancer in remission, it is useful to ask, "If Mom were cured tomorrow, what would each person or the whole family do differently in terms of planning for the future?" This question elicits the degree to which life cycle plans have been affected by the condition. It helps a clinician and family see the extent to which a disorder currently organizes and is expected to control family life in the future. Issues suggesting that an illness has assumed too much power over family planning may emerge. This can invite follow-up questions such as: "If you were to view Bill's diabetes and potential complications as less powerful in your relationship, how would that affect your marriage now and your plans together for the future?"

When normative life cycle tasks are truly blocked, anticipation of this possibility before a failure experience ensues can further adaptation. Consider young couples in which one member has a disabling condition, such as multiple sclerosis, that may worsen. Suppose they are beginning to discuss having children. By thinking ahead, a clinician may ask, "Given your interest in having children, and given your disability and the uncertainties of multiple sclerosis, if you were to decide not to have children of your own, are there alternative ways you could satisfy your interest in becoming parents?" "What would need to change in order to accept this alternative as good enough?" When childbearing or child-rearing is precluded, individuals and couples need to be helped to find other ways to express developmental generative needs and dispel feelings that they are inherently deficient if they do not have a child.

A forward-thinking clinical philosophy that uses a life cycle perspective as a way of gaining a positive sense of control and opportunity is extremely helpful for families dealing with chronic disorders. Often beneath a surface optimism concerning the present there is an undercurrent of unacknowledged dread of the future. Much of this is associated with anticipatory loss, which will be discussed in chapter 8. A life cycle framework offers families a way to think about different dimensions of their life structure (for example, work, relationships and family, recreation) now and in the future and the relative priority of each. This facilitates thinking about how each domain might be affected, positively or negatively, by illness or disability.

For instance, consider a man in his late thirties permanently disabled from his profession as an automobile mechanic by a spinal cord injury. The devastating loss of his work identity and self-esteem as a competent male provider for his family can be counterbalanced by helping him see opportunities to achieve a different kind of developmental goal usually relegated to later in life. At midlife many men, after years of driving themselves relentlessly at work, at the expense of developing close caring relationships, reconsider their priorities and try to achieve a better balance. For many men a sense of loss accompanies this realization of missed opportunities. There is both a feeling that they should have been more involved with their children, spouse, and friends and, at the same time, a feeling that their career has not delivered the expected gratifications. One can help this man recognize that his disability has not affected his future developmental possibilities with regard to intimacy and that he has an opportunity to rearrange his priorities before the time when most men finally come to this stage of growth.

CHAPTER 7

Family Health and Illness Belief Systems

ACH OF US INDIVIDUALLY, and as part of our family and other systems, develops a belief system or philosophy that shapes our patterns of behavior in relation to the common challenges of life (Kluckhohn, 1960). Beliefs provide coherence to family life, facilitating continuity among past, present, and future, and offering an approach to new and ambiguous situations such as serious illness. At a practical level, belief systems serve as a cognitive map guiding decisions and action. Depending on which system we are addressing, beliefs can be labeled as values, culture, religion, world view, or family paradigm. In adaptation to physical conditions, I think it vital that clinicians appreciate the contribution and interaction of personal, family, and cultural beliefs.

David Reiss (1981) has shown that families as a unit develop paradigms or shared beliefs about how the world operates. These beliefs shape how families interpret events and behaviors in their environment. One component of the family's shared construction of reality is a set of health/illness beliefs that influence how they interpret illness and guide their health-seeking behavior (Ransom, Fisher, & Terry, 1992; Rolland, 1987b; Wright, Watson, & Bell, in press). Although individual family members may hold different beliefs, the values held by the family unit may be the most significant.

At the time of a medical diagnosis, a primary developmental challenge for a family is to create a meaning for the illness that promotes a sense of competence and mastery in a context of partial loss, possible further physical decline, or death. Since serious illness is often experienced as a betrayal of fundamental trust in our bodies and belief in our invulnerability and immortality (Kleinman, 1988), the creation of an empowering narrative can be a formidable task. Empowering family health beliefs can help us grapple with the existential dilemmas of our fear and denial of death, efforts to sustain this denial, and attempts to reassert control when suffering and death occur.

This chapter will describe how belief systems, particularly those concerned with health and illness, profoundly shape family adaptation to chronic and life-threatening conditions. I will address key elements of families' health belief systems and the forces that shape those beliefs over time, highlighting how to assess and intervene in family beliefs, taking into account issues related to the psychosocial type and phase of a condition. Beliefs that optimize coping and adaptation and, in contrast, those that are potentially dysfunctional and sources of blame, shame, or guilt will be emphasized.

An Overview

Until recently, belief systems have been neglected in systems theory and in models of clinical intervention with families. The power of belief systems needs to be central in our clinical thinking. Constructivism and social construction theory have heightened our awareness that meaning is a social phenomenon that evolves as an unending process through people's interactions and communications (Anderson & Goolishian, 1988; Berger & Luckmann, 1966; Dell, 1985; von Foerster, 1981; Gergen, 1985; von Glasersfeld, 1987; Hoffman, 1990; Keeney, 1983; Maturana & Varela, 1987; Watzlawick, 1984; White & Epston, 1990). From this perspective, meanings and beliefs are represented and continually created in the narratives or stories we construct together to make sense out of our world and our place in it. An innovative application of these theories has been the development of collaborative approaches among health providers, patients, and their families (McDaniel, Hepworth, & Doherty, 1992). These approaches emphasize the co-creation of narratives about health problems that incorporate the belief systems of all concerned.

Arthur Kleinman (1988), in his book *The Illness Narratives*, has eloquently described the need to create meaning systems or explanatory models for effective coping with and adaptation to illness. He delineates three distinct levels of meaning in relation to physical conditions—*disease, illness,* and *sickness*. Disease refers to a purely biomedical description or understanding of a patient's condition. Health professionals function mostly at this level in the biological world of disease diagnosis and treatment. From this perspective, when a physician requests, "Tell me about your pain," he or she wants to know where it is, when it occurs, how intense it is, what medication has already been tried, and what other physical symptoms are associated with it. These questions are intended largely to discover a physical reason for the pain.

Patients and their families live primarily in the realm of illness, which is the human experience of symptoms and suffering, typically in some symbolic form. Illness means "how the sick person and the members of the family or wider social network perceive, live with, and respond to symptoms and disability" (Kleinman, 1988, p. 3). Illness represents a synthesis of biological, personal, family, and cultural meanings that are melded together into a more or less coherent systemic form.

Sickness, at a third level, represents meanings that become associated with a physical problem as a result of larger societal, macrosocial, economic, political, or institutional forces (Sontag, 1978, 1988). For example, some conditions are seen as a reflection of poverty, technological oppression (for instance, pollution), or immoral life-style. Diseases common in inner cities, such as lead poisoning, cancer, asthma, and AIDS, can be viewed through this larger societal lens. The core beliefs about these conditions are derived in part from a larger system perspective, which can profoundly influence the illness experience of an affected family.

From an ecosystemic, family-oriented perspective, Kleinman's description of disease, illness, and sickness can be reworded as the *biological, human experience of individuals and families,* and *societal* levels of meaning. An ecosystemic or biopsychosocial understanding of a condition requires all concerned to appreciate the ongoing mutual influences among these levels of meaning in any particular encounter with, and over the course of, a disorder. In the traditional biomedical model, the health professional decodes and reduces descriptions based on the human experience to biological diseases that can be treated. The family is told a disease diagnosis and, as a result, revises its understanding or beliefs to incorporate this new information. Sometimes the diagnosis will confirm family members' suspicions and thus solidify their initial beliefs or narrative.

As a disease or disability evolves, the circular process continues among new biological information, the personal or family experience of living with illness, and revised meanings. Throughout, we need to remember that the family lives in the world of its personal or family experience of a disease. Belief systems can be conceptualized as the mediator or translator between biological disease and the personal/family experience. This set of relationships can be diagrammed as shown in figure 7.1.

Clinicians need to be able to navigate among the biological, human, and societal levels of meanings of chronic conditions. Some years ago, when I began to interview families about their experience with illness and disability, I asked the medical social service staff at Yale–New Haven Hospital to find typical families from their case loads. Initially I was pleasantly astonished at the overwhelming response. After several interviews, it became clear that for many of these families, it was the first time anyone had taken an interest in the totality of their experience as a family living with a chronic condition. This meant asking about their core family beliefs and their experience of

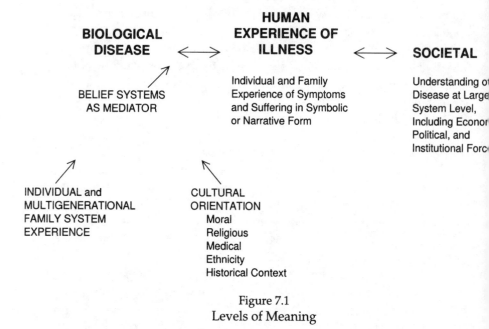

Figure 7.1
Levels of Meaning

their particular disorder from their personal/family or societal viewpoint. Repeatedly families expressed feelings of being misunderstood by the professional staff. What this generally meant was that no one (particularly their physicians) had inquired about their core personal beliefs or the meanings they attached to their family member's condition—their human experience of their family member's disorder.

In chapter 11, I will discuss the implications of the fit of beliefs between professionals and families. The essential point is that the process of inquiry about belief systems and meanings is integral to establishing a mutual, viable relationship, totally independent of any need for consensus between professionals and families. Asking serves as acknowledgment by the clinician of the importance of beliefs for both clinician and family and promotes the establishment of a collaborative biopsychosocial framework for communication. This protects against a cut-off in meaning, the professional operating solely in the world of disease and the family in one of personal experience.

Using a biopsychosocial model that incorporates belief systems, clinicians, patient, and family can move flexibly together and focus on the biological (biomedical treatment), human experience, and societal levels of meaning. In most clinical situations, all three operate simultaneously, and all concerned need to be able to listen and respond on more than one level. Many families can listen to a discussion about their disease, but frequently will partially or completely disengage from the process if they feel unacknowledged or misunderstood in terms of their beliefs and personal/family experience of a health problem. Often we label a dysfunctional outcome of this process as noncompliance by the patient or family. In fact, one can argue that a clinician's disregard of these other levels of meaning interferes with a necessary joining process that, in turn, sets in motion patient and family disengagement. From a systemic viewpoint, one might say that this process represents clinician noncompliance, which, because of the inherent skew of power within the medical system, is considered the patient's or family's problem. Responsibility for the process of disengagement is denied by the health-care team, and the less powerful "victim" is blamed.

Belief systems are a tremendous force in illness. When misused or disregarded, they can wreak havoc on relationships and block healing. When utilized sensitively, they empower all relationships and provide a foundation for biological and psychosocial healing.

Basic Beliefs and the Family Paradigm

When assessing family beliefs, it is useful for a clinician to first get a sense of those basic ones that contribute to a family's overall identity. These are transcendent beliefs that guide family members in daily life and as they encounter life's normative challenges. Such core beliefs provide a foundation on which health beliefs come into play or certain fundamental beliefs (for example, concerning control) may emerge especially forcefully when illness strikes.

Florence Kluckhohn (1960), the anthropologist, has described five universal problems with which all societies must cope and a limited range of possible solutions of, or value orientations toward, each problem within which each society and family sets priorities according to its own preferred world view. Each provides a way (or mythology) to help bring order out of chaos and suggests a coping style to guide family interaction with adversity, such as a physical disorder. These five universal problems and possible orientations include:

1. The *question of innate human nature.* Human nature can be perceived as good, evil, or neutral/mixed and as fixed or changeable. A family's belief about each perception acts as a template for creating meaning about an illness. A view of human nature as basically good serves as a buffer against beliefs about causes of illness that invoke blame, shame, or guilt. Interventions to rescript destructive illness narratives are facilitated when families see human nature as changeable.
2. The *temporal orientation of a family.* Is priority given to past, present, or future? A family that orients toward the past will tend to have more powerful and entrenched multigenerational legacies and beliefs. Families

oriented toward the future may underestimate the effect of past legacies on their current functioning. They may, however, be amenable to trying innovative approaches to healing that involve beliefs that are discontinuous with their past. American middle-class values tend to be future oriented, and may make it difficult for a family to adjust to a progressive, life-threatening illness in which living in the present is more adaptive.

3. The *preferred pattern of human activity*. The three basic styles are being, being-in-becoming, and doing. The first two stress what already is, whereas the third focuses on striving to accomplish something else. Since North American society is a "doing" culture, conditions that hamper action and achievement (such as severe disability) will interfere more with a person's sense of competency if he or she is oriented toward doing rather than being. When someone is terminally ill, just being with that person often becomes more important than doing something. This is one reason North American families often find this kind of situation very difficult to tolerate.

   Being and being-in-becoming emphasize inner feelings and what humans are rather than what they can accomplish; they stress more facets of our being than what can be achieved instrumentally. For someone with a disability, this value allows a wider range of choices for sustaining self-esteem in the face of loss. Continued personal growth is not limited to a "doing" mentality. On the other hand, a doing orientation can focus attention on activities and distract from being-in-the-illness, pain, and so on. In this sense, each orientation entails certain advantages and costs.

4. The *relationship between humans and nature*. The three orientations in this regard are subjugation to nature, harmony with nature, and mastery of nature. These are closely related to beliefs about locus of control, which are extremely important in illness and disability, and will be discussed in more detail below. In beliefs that favor mastery or subjugation, there is an implicit clash between us and the world and us and our bodies; the only difference is in where ultimate power resides. A belief in harmony with nature emphasizes a harmonious fit of meaning between the world and the body. Bodily problems are seen to arise when we have not attended adequately to the forces of nature. For instance, illness can be an inner expression of a world problem (such as cancer as causally related to uncontrolled technological overgrowth that is destroying our environment). Attitudes in the United States promote mastery of illness. As I will discuss later, the fit between this societal value and the ability to control a disorder can vary considerably.

5. The *preferred pattern of relationship between humans*. The basic orientations are lineal (hierarchical/cross-generational), collective, and individualistic. The first two view group life as primary over individual autonomy,

the lineal pattern also emphasizing the continuity of the group through time, with a specified hierarchical succession. The third group gives priority to individual autonomy over commitment to group life. This value is analogous to beliefs about family cohesion, which are very important in chronic illness as they determine the extent to which family members view the family system as the healing unit and value unified thinking and action. In the United States, there is a strong emphasis on individualism, which can make adjustment to disorders that require teamwork or dependency especially difficult, but, at the same time, promote attitudes of self-sufficiency.

Assessment of Health Beliefs

In the initial crisis phase, it is useful for clinicians to inquire about key beliefs that shape families' illness narratives and coping strategies. This means gaining an understanding of a family's overall belief system, of family beliefs brought into play by the strains of a chronic disorder over time, and of meanings associated with the condition itself. A thorough assessment includes tracking beliefs about: (1) normality; (2) the mind–body relationship; (3) control and mastery; (4) optimism/pessimism; (5) rules of communication; (6) meanings attached by a family, ethnic group, religion, or the wider culture to symptoms (for instance, chronic pain), types of illnesses (for example, life-threatening), or specific diseases (such as AIDS); (7) assumptions about what caused an illness and what will influence its course and outcome; (8) multigenerational legacies, stories, and scripts that shape a family's health beliefs and response to illness (see also chapter 5); (9) ethnic, cultural, and gender-related beliefs about expected roles and behavior; (10) family rituals; and (11) anticipated nodal points in the illness, individual, and family life cycles when health beliefs will be strained or need to shift (see chapter 6). Also, a clinician should consider assessing the fit of health beliefs: within the family and its various subsystems (including spouse, parents, extended family) and between the family and the health-care system and wider culture (see chapter 11).

In terms of clinical intervention, we can distinguish the assessment of family beliefs, how to use them in clinical situations as a way of connecting with a family or punctuating important discussions, deciding when beliefs need intervention, and techniques for changing dysfunctional beliefs. I will address primarily issues related to assessment, use of beliefs in clinical situations, and when change may be indicated. I do not make a sharp distinction between assessment and intervention, but rather prefer to think about the process of assessment or inquiry about beliefs as an intervention. There are many specific techniques for changing beliefs; they vary according to the many schools of psychotherapy—a subject beyond the scope of this discussion.

BELIEFS ABOUT NORMALITY

A family's beliefs about what is normal or abnormal and the importance it attaches to conformity and excellence in relation to the average family have far-reaching implications for adaptation to chronic disorders (Rolland, 1993; Walsh, 1993a, 1993b). Family values that allow having a problem without self-denigration have a distinct advantage in utilizing outside help and maintaining a positive identity when chronic conditions occur. Help-seeking that is defined as weak and shameful undercuts this kind of resilience. Essentially, in situations of chronic disorders in which problems are to be expected and the use of professionals and outside resources is necessary, a belief that pathologizes this normative process adds insult to injury.

Two excellent questions to elicit beliefs about how families define normality are, "How do you think other *normal, average* families would deal with a situation similar to yours?" And, "How would a *healthy* family cope with your situation?" The first question gives a good indication of whether family members have a sense of the range of possible experiences and what is typical. Are they making their comparisons in relation to situations that really have similar psychosocial demands, or are they making unrealistic or unfair ones? A family dealing with the initial phase of a member's traumatic brain injury could do itself a disservice by comparing its coping ability and strategies with those of a family facing a seizure disorder or age-peers who are healthy. Does a family compare itself with superstars described in the media and popular literature, or does it have a balanced, realistic view of the average that includes the anticipated challenges and the emotional highs and lows? The second question invites a family to share its views about what is healthy or optimal. Like couples that unrealistically describe optimal relationships as ones free of problems, without conflict or suffering, often families facing illness and disability have a narrow, romanticized view of healthy adaptation that is unrealistic and leaves them feeling inadequate.

In one situation, a courageous young woman with metastatic cancer was filmed for a documentary about coping with life-threatening conditions. The film captured her positive approach extremely well. What was left out was the rigorous and complex process by which she got to that point. During low physical or emotional periods, she would decline, and family or friends would protect her from the film crew. This meant that the film could not record the very poignant, normative, low points at which frustrations and demoralization were expressed and questions about giving up the fight were raised. This does not mean the film was not about a "star" patient: it means that the portrayal of what constituted the real experience of a star was edited and incomplete, that the total process of achieving healthy adaptation was not recorded. The inherent danger is that patients viewing such a first-person account, particularly during the crisis phase, could develop an incomplete and unrealistic idea about what is healthy and optimal.

Families with strong beliefs in high achievement and perfectionism tend to equate normality with the optimal, to define normality or successful family functioning in terms of ideal or problem-free circumstances. Families that define normality in this way are prone to apply to illness standards that are inappropriate because the kind of control they are accustomed to is impossible in this situation. Particularly in untimely conditions that occur early in the life cycle, there are additional pressures to keep up with normative, socially expectable, developmental milestones of age peers or other young couples. The fact that life cycle goals may take longer or need revision may require some modification in beliefs about what is normal and healthy. Sustaining hope, particularly in situations of long-term adversity, demands an ability to embrace a flexible and broad definition of normality.

A young couple's ability to define what is expected or typical is impeded by both a frequent lack of available comparisons with similarly afflicted peers and ambiguities in interactions. For instance, distancing by friends can be interpreted as "You're not normal" when the avoidance may actually represent emotional difficulty for peers in facing an untimely loss that could also befall them and a shattering of their illusion of a guaranteed grace period of health until later life. Overly protective behavior can also reflect emotional discomfort that is misread by affected families as a sign of their weakness and abnormality. The lack of a comparison group is one reason why self-help groups and networks can be so useful to families dealing with untimely conditions: they provide a normalizing context.

Clinicians and families that equate family health with absence of symptoms or problems are at high risk of constant suffering from falling short of a definition of health functioning that is blatantly unachievable. Sensitized by his work with families living in poverty, Minuchin (1974) remarked that all families have problems. From this perspective, having problems is not inconsistent with family health, normality, and successful adaptation to adversity, such as chronic illness. In comparison with families accustomed to adversity, those that have been spared the "slings and arrows of outrageous fortune" may have been better able to sustain a kind of unrealistic standard over many years. Some more privileged families can have enormous difficulty coping with chronic disorders. Their beliefs about normality may have never been tested; and faced with the problems inevitably associated with illness and disability, their standards cannot be maintained.

Successful coping and adaptation are enhanced when a family believes in a biopsychosocial frame for illness that normalizes a psychosomatic interaction. This highlights the importance of the initial "framing event" and whether professionals actively normalize psychosomatic interplay and thus help to counteract any interpretation of family and cultural beliefs as pathological. A physician might say to a family facing asthma, "Many families notice that asthma is affected by stressful times and fear that this will be interpreted as a definite sign of emotional problems. I want you to know that asthma normally gets worse during the inevitable strains that arise in family life. It is important that you keep me informed about major family stresses so that I can decide with you whether adjusting Susan's medication or finding better ways to reduce stress will be the best approach." This promotes a positive attitude toward the potential role of psychosocial factors in influencing the course of the disease and the patient's quality of life. Rather than considering it a shameful liability, a family can approach a psychosomatic interaction as an opportunity to make a difference and increase its sense of control.

MIND-BODY RELATIONSHIPS

The concept of mind-body relationships has been the subject of discourse and debate for millennia. The term *mind-body relationship* has come to represent several related but distinct beliefs that are important to differentiate.

First, some people assume that the mind and the body are separate worlds and that what goes on in each can interactively affect the other. There is tremendous diversity in how this distinction is seen, if at all, and the degree to which the interaction is viewed as equal or more a one-way process. Until recently, traditional Western medicine tended to minimize the potential impact of the mind on the body.

Second, we need to distinguish beliefs about the mind as a logical, thinking process that can determine actions that may help in healing the body (for example, seeking medical care or changing diet or activity patterns) from those of the mind as a source of thought or energy that can directly influence body physiology. The latter include beliefs about the importance of emotional states such as a positive attitude, love, anger, humor, or depression on maintaining physical health and promoting or interfering with healing of the body. They also encompass beliefs about the mind as the locus of responsibility and about the role of willpower in affecting the body. Healing practices such as meditation or guided imagery are based on beliefs about the importance of the mind.

Traditional mental health theories and research have been based on pathology and tended to emphasize character traits or emotional states that affect body chemistry adversely. This perspective acknowledges that emotions can affect the body negatively, but the possible positive influences of healthy attitudes have been neglected. We need to be aware of our own belief biases, often promoted in our professional training; typically, they are based on study of pathology, disease, or dysfunction.

Recently the public has been increasingly drawn to popular literature concerning the importance of positive attitudes in healing (Benson, 1979; Borysenko, 1987; Cousins, 1989; LaShan, 1977; Levine, 1987; Pelletier, 1977; Siegel, 1986; Simonton, Matthews-Simonton, & Creighton, 1978; Weil, 1983). These practitioners stress the unity of mind and body rather than view them as distinct worlds. Also, they describe healing as a state of being involving mind and body, rather than in strictly biomedical terms, where something is done to the body.

We clinicians need to be particularly alert to the fact that families may be more open to these positive possibilities than we are: our own professional thinking may remain antiquated and inclined toward a view of the mind-body relationship that is based on pathology. The danger lies in not inquiring about family beliefs that may promote health. Worse, because of our own rigid mindset, which we may defend on the basis of a lack of hard research data, we may convey to a family our disinterest in these ideas or even dismiss them as unscientific and unworthy. In the process, we may undermine a possible, powerful source of healing, shame a family, and damage the workable alliance necessary for any effective treatment.

Third, we need to understand beliefs about mind that extend beyond the individual to include family, community, or a higher spiritual force (Bateson, 1979). To what extent do family members see the locus of energy that can both harm the body and heal it as residing in these other parts of the larger ecosystem? Anthropologists have found tremendous diversity in the role of family, community, God, or nature as a source of healing. Such beliefs are typically expressed in the form of rituals. For example, in some African tribal cultures, when a member is ill, the tribe engages in healing rituals that involve a continuous line of physical contact ending with the affected person. A combination of rhythmic movement and chanting is believed to promote the flow of healing energy into the ill tribe member (Bateson, 1979). In our society, a family's religious community often organizes a prayer service to promote healing of an ill member.

I find it useful to inquire routinely about family members' basic views concerning the mind-body relationship. How does each member see "mind"? Is it a center directing action? How can the state of mind affect what goes on in the body? In what ways do family members interpret the mind as including the family unit, the community, and religious or spiritual forces? How powerful is the mind in these various areas, particularly in affecting health and illness? The clinician's understanding of family members' beliefs about mind-body relationships provides a basis for joining with the family and in tailoring biopsychosocial treatment strategies more sensitively.

Areas of strength and vulnerability can be identified, and ways of including the family in a complementary fashion in other treatments can be suggested.

FAMILY BELIEFS ABOUT MASTERY AND CONTROL OF ILLNESS

It is critical to determine how a family defines mastery or control in general and how it transposes that definition to situations of illness. Some key thinkers about this issue, such as Aaron Antonovsky (1979), Antonovsky and Sourani (1988), and David Reiss (1981), have distinguished between a belief in the ability to control life events, such as illness, and beliefs that life events are comprehensible or manageable (resources are available to meet life crises). Antonovsky refers to the latter as a "sense of coherence." Others see mastery of physical disorders more in terms of the concept of health locus of control (Dohrenwend & Dohrenwend, 1981; Lefcourt, 1982), which can be defined as a belief about influence over the course or outcome of an illness. I think a combination of both perspectives is most useful. It is vital to determine whether a family's beliefs are based on a premise of internal control, external control by chance, or external control by powerful others (Levenson, 1973, 1974, 1975).

An orientation toward an internal locus of control entails a belief that an individual or family can affect the outcome of a situation, that the energy and ability to create solutions come from within the person or the family. In illness, such families believe they are directly responsible for their health and have the power to recover from illness. They endorse such statements as "I am in control of my health"; "When I feel ill, I know it is because I have not been taking care of myself properly"; or "If I become sick, I have the power to make myself well again" (Wallston et al., 1976; Wallston & Wallston, 1978).

An external orientation entails a belief that outcomes do not depend on the individual's or the family's behavior. Although personal control is minimized, control is viewed as orchestrated from outside oneself. Those who see health control as being in the hands of powerful others view health professionals, God, or sometimes powerful family members as exerting control over their bodies and the course of illnesses. They agree with statements such as "Regarding my health, I can do only what my doctor tells me to do" or "Other people play a big part in whether I stay healthy or become sick." In some families the patient minimizes personal control while investing power in the family. Such a patient may agree with a statement such as "My family has a lot to do with my becoming sick or staying healthy."

Families that view illness in terms of chance believe that when illness occurs, it is a matter of luck, and that fate determines recovery. The potential effectiveness of rational, directed strategies to meet adversity is considered minimal.

It is important to understand that these three orientations often represent tendencies in families rather than fixed and absolute convictions. The balance may shift depending on the type or phase of a health problem. It is not uncommon for a family to adhere to a different set of beliefs about control when dealing with biological problems of the body versus other day-to-day problems. Therefore, it is useful to understand both a family's basic value system and its beliefs about control regarding health in general, chronic and life-threatening conditions, and, finally, the specific disorder facing the family. A family normally guided by an internal sense of mastery may switch abruptly to an external viewpoint when a member develops an illness or, perhaps, only selectively in the case of a life-threatening condition. Such a change may reflect a family's need to conform to society's values, its particular ethnic background, or a powerful multigenerational experience with serious illness.

Clinicians should assess whether a family holds any particular beliefs about a specific illness. For instance, regardless of the actual severity or prognosis in a particular case, cancer may be equated with death or no control because of medical statistics, cultural myth, or family history. At the same time, forms of heart disease with a similar life expectancy as cancer may be seen as more manageable because of prevailing cultural beliefs. For instance, in a family traditionally guided by a strong belief in personal control, if the father, the powerful family patriarch, dies at midlife from a rapidly progressive and painful form of cancer, the family may develop an encapsulated exception to their beliefs about control that is specific for cancer or generalized to other life-threatening conditions.

On the other hand, families may have enabling stories about a member or friend who, despite cancer and a shortened life span, lived a full life centered on effectively assigning priorities to the quality of relationships and goals. Clinicians can highlight these positive narratives as a means of helping families counteract cultural beliefs that focus exclusively on control of biology as defining success.

A family's beliefs about mastery strongly affect the nature of its relationship to a physical problem and to the health-care system. Beliefs about control predict certain health behaviors, particularly compliance with treatment, and suggest the family's preferences about participation in its family member's treatment and healing process. Families that view disease course or outcome as a matter of chance tend to establish marginal relationships with health professionals largely because their belief system minimizes the importance of their own or the professional's impact on a disease process. Just as any psychotherapeutic relationship depends on constructing a shared belief about what is therapeutic, a workable accommodation among the patient, the family, and the health-care team in terms of these fundamental values is essential. Families that feel misunderstood by health professionals are often reacting to a lack of joining at this basic value level. Too often their healthy need to participate has been ignored or preempted by a professional desiring unilateral control.

The goodness of fit between family beliefs about mastery and what the medical situation dictates can vary with the time phase of the condition. In some disorders, the crisis phase involves protracted care outside the family's direct control. For instance, the recovery period after a stroke may begin on an intensive-care unit and entail months of extended care at a rehabilitation facility. This may be stressful for a family that prefers to tackle its own problems without outside control and interference. The patient's return home may increase the work load, but allow family members to reassert their competence and leadership. In contrast, a family guided more by a preference for external control by experts can expect greater difficulty when the ill family member returns home; for this family, the patient's leaving the rehabilitation hospital means loss of their locus of competency—the professional caregiving system. Recognition of such normative differences in beliefs about control can guide an effective psychosocial treatment plan tailored to each family's needs and affirm the family's core values.

For families accustomed to personal control, offering them a way to participate during that initial period requiring intense technological care helps them endure and support treatment. Disregarding such families' normal need to participate (or even ordering them out of the way as a nuisance) alienates them; it can violate their basic beliefs concerning mastery and self-esteem and undercut the very energy the professionals will want to support later in the rehabilitation process. To forge a workable alliance with such families requires clinicians to involve families creatively in some aspect of care right from the beginning, no matter how great the technological needs. In a situation requiring a total takeover by professionals, a clinician can, at minimum, empathize with the family about its need to relinquish physical control temporarily. For instance, he or she can inquire about and encourage family rituals or prayer that complements medical interventions and allows expression of a family's basic beliefs about control and participation.

A family that is comfortable with intense professional involvement and relegates control to the professional will have difficulty at the other end of recovery: the patient's return home can present a crisis. For such families, even if medically unnecessary, it may be psychosocially useful to provide a longer period of home-based assistance so as to help them transform their natural dependence on outside sources of control into greater self-directed competency.

In the terminal phase of an illness, a family may feel least in control of the biological course of the disease and of the decision making with regard to the overall care of its ill member. Families with a strong need to sustain their centrality may need to assert themselves more vigorously in dealing with health providers. Effective decision-making regarding the extent of heroic medical efforts or whether a patient will die at home or in an institution or hospice requires a family–health provider relationship that respects the family's basic beliefs.

CONFRONTING REALITY, HOPE, POSITIVE ILLUSIONS, AND DENIAL

In situations of illness and disability we must be cautious about judging the relative usefulness of positive illusions and minimization of, versus direct confrontation with and acceptance of, painful realities. Often both are needed; and the skilled clinician must thread the needle supporting both the usefulness of exaggerated hope and the need for treatment to control the illness or a new complication. There is greater incentive for a family to confront denial of an illness or its severity when there is hope that preventive action or medical treatment can affect the outcome. Yet, to cope with an arduous, uncertain course, families often need simultaneously to acknowledge the condition itself and minimize treatment risks or the likelihood of a poor outcome.

Most of us cannot tolerate an unrelenting encounter with stark reality: we need mental and physical respite. Shelley Taylor (1989), in her book *Positive Illusions: Creative Self-deception and the Healthy Mind*, describes the normal, healthy need for positive illusions and their importance in successful coping and adaptation. She argues: "The normal human mind is oriented toward mental health and . . . at every turn it construes events in a manner that promotes benign fictions about the self, the world, and the future. The mind is, with some significant exceptions, intrinsically adaptive, oriented toward overcoming rather than succumbing to the adverse events of life" (preface, p. xi).

Taylor cites research supporting the conclusion that exaggerated beliefs about control are correlated with more positive health outcomes and, conversely, that beliefs about a lack of control adversely affect health. This dovetails with Kobasa's (1979) studies of hardiness or resilience, which suggest that people who experience life challenges with a sense of psychological control are protected against the adverse effects of stress on health. Taylor maintains that positive illusions, particularly exaggerated beliefs about control and unrealistic optimism about the future, reduce family terror related to threatened loss and uncertainty.

The healthy use of minimization of the negative or selective focus on the positive and timely uses of humor should be distinguished from the concept of denial, which is considered pathological. Clinical distinctions can be made in several ways. In general, denial and repression are defense mechanisms that increase with the level of threat or the severity of an illness. This may interfere with effective family health behaviors. Optimism as a positive bias rather than an inhibitor of action may facilitate a family's thinking about a formidable challenge in a manageable way and promote its tackling a serious health problem, such as cancer.

In contrast to denial, in which new information is blocked out, exaggerated hope can allow a family to learn and incorporate new and difficult information (for instance, about a treatment complication) and take appropriate action without becoming overwhelmed. A clinician needs to be able to assess when family members have heard essential information about a risky treatment, discussed the risks of loss frankly, decided to try it, and then adopted a highly optimistic belief about the outcome. This is adaptive, just as it would be for a surgeon performing a risky procedure. Once the decision to go ahead has been made, the surgeon will operate most effectively if he or she proceeds with a strong bias to succeed. This is different from a family that completely avoids acknowledgment or discussion of risks and decides for or against a risky procedure blindly.

Families that are optimistic about their ability to master adversity and loss see hopefulness in a manner that extends far beyond biology. They emphasize quality of life and attributes of family identity that transcend the challenge of illness or disability. It is critical for clinicians to distinguish between family beliefs about a positive biological outcome and optimism as an enduring family quality. A clinician confronting a family with a painful medical reality needs to simultaneously support any basic family optimism. In fact, failure to join the family at this underlying level will impede its ability to confront the immediate issue. From this perspective, family members' hopefulness should always be supported, and needs to be distinguished from a narrow view of optimism regarding a particular biological outcome.

When a family lacks a basic sense of its competence, the meaning of biological improvement or worsening often becomes more all-encompassing. For these families hope can flourish or vanish as an illness takes its course. Interventions with such families should attempt to identify other enduring family attributes, so that an illness can be put into a perspective in which hope invested in a biological condition is balanced with optimism about, for instance, the quality of family relationships.

The time phases of an illness provide a useful aid to clinicians in deciding when and to what degree repression, denial, and positive illusions are adaptive. Some degree of minimization can serve a protective function during the initial crisis phase, particularly if there is an extended period of uncertainty, such as in treatment for life-threatening cancer. Another example is a serious head injury with major, long-term implications for a family: thinking about the long-term issues during the immediate, life-threatening period can overload anyone. Minimization allows family members to digest manageable pieces of a short or protracted ordeal. Often a clinician needs to help maintain certain illusions as he or she helps a family focus its attention and resources. Assisting a family in giving priority to immediate goals can significantly reduce its sense of overload and thus alter its need to use self-protective defenses such as denial.

A healthy dose of naive optimism is useful for families while they are trying to become accustomed to the idea of living with an illness or disability; it helps them through an inevitable period of trial and error in learning how best to cope with an ongoing condition without giving up. This situation is analogous to a couple's developing a comfortable style of parenting. If we knew all the trials and tribulations of parenthood beforehand, many of us might never have children, or we might develop very rigid, constricted, protective child-rearing methods devoid of creative spontaneity. Family adaptation to chronic conditions involves a similar socialization process. As families approach the chronic phase, naive optimism is replaced by constructive optimism, based on experience and tinged with positive illusion.

As discussed in chapter 6, any significant transition in the illness, family, or individual members' life cycles are nodal points at which direct communication about such issues as threatened loss are important. Clinicians should not regard this as dashing family hopes. In fact, when such subjects are avoided, dread is heightened that can be counteracted psychologically only by more pervasive dysfunctional individual and family denial. This is accompanied by more restricted and cut-off patterns of family communication. Timely, frank communication preserves a family's ability to sustain functional illusions while maintaining awareness of new developmental issues.

To foster optimal adaptation, clinicians should help families acknowledge the possibility of loss without challenging their hopes. A "what if" inquiry helps families bridge the gap between hope and the possibility of treatment failure or death and begin to envision what might happen and take action as insurance in case their hopes are not realized. This is particularly important in the chronic phase when a disease is progressing and the transition to a terminal phase is likely. As will be discussed more fully in chapter 8, encouraging families to deal with threatened loss by open discussion early in the course of a condition allows maximal participation by all concerned and counteracts denial and distancing among family members.

FAMILY BELIEFS ABOUT THE CAUSES OF ILLNESS AND DISABILITY

When a significant health problem arises, all of us wonder "Why me (or us)?" and "Why now?" We construct an explanation or narrative that helps organize our experience. The larger context within which an illness occurs is a very powerful organizer and mirror of a family's belief system. The limits of current medical knowledge mean that tremendous uncertainties persist about the relative importance of a myriad of factors in the onset of disease, and this allows individuals and families to develop highly idiosyncratic ideas about what caused their family member's illness.

A family's beliefs about the cause of an illness need to be assessed separately from its beliefs about what can affect the outcome. I routinely ask *each* family member for his or her explanation of what caused the illness. Since some families may feel that this question implies that the clinician is blaming them, it is important to frame the query in a curious, neutral manner that invites a collaborative dialogue. For instance, "All of us come up with reasons how or why something happens, but do not get an opportunity to share it. I am interested in what each of you has thought about why Fred had a heart attack." The responses reflect both the family's fund of medical information and its mythology.

Beliefs may include various explanations—biological (for example, virus), supernatural (for example, a vengeful God), societal (for example, poverty or pollution), or individual and family dysfunction. Lyman Wynne and his colleagues (1992) underscore the importance of distinguishing beliefs that are external (such as societal) and viewed as more outside family members' control versus more toxic ones that blame individual members or the entire family system. They also point out that when family systems theory is applied too narrowly or rigidly, clinicians run the risk of inappropriately interpreting dysfunctional family processes as "the cause" for illnesses, thereby unfairly scapegoating families stressed by misfortune.

Negative myths may include punishment for earlier misdeeds (for instance, an affair), blame of a particular family member ("Your drinking made me sick"), a sense of injustice ("Why am I being punished? I have been a good person."), genetics (for example, cancer is common in one side of the family), negligence by the patient (for instance, careless driving) or by parents (as in the sudden infant death syndrome), or simply bad luck. Asking this question can function as an effective family Rorschach and bring to light unresolved family conflicts.

Optimal family narratives respect the limits of scientific knowledge, affirm basic competence, and promote the flexible use of multiple biological and psychosocial healing strategies. In contrast, causal attributions that invoke blame, shame, or guilt are particularly important to uncover because they make it extremely difficult for a family to functionally cope with and adapt to an illness. In the context of a life-threatening illness, a blamed family member is implicitly, if not explicitly, held accountable for negligence or even potential murder if the patient dies. Decisions about treatment become confounded and filled with tension. Every transition to a new stage of loss can escalate the cycle of blame, shame, or guilt. The following case illustrates this point.

Lucy and Tom G., a young couple in their early thirties, have one child, Susan, age 4, who is terminally ill with leukemia. Following diagnosis two years earlier, the initial treatments were moderately successful; but over the past six months, her condition has worsened. The pediatric oncologist has offered the parents the choice between an experimental treatment with a low probability of success or halting treatment; he supports either choice.

Tom's position is "Let's stop; enough is enough." Lucy, on the other hand, feels "We must continue; we can't let her die." The couple cannot reach an agreement, and the physician is immobilized. He requests a consultation for the couple.

The consultant first inquires about each parent's understanding of the options and finds out that both comprehend the choices, but have reached strongly opposing positions.

When the consultant asks, "What is your explanation of how your daughter got leukemia?" the critical story emerges. Tom basically sees it as bad luck. Lucy, however, has a very different belief. During her pregnancy with Susan, Lucy's father had a heart attack and died several months later from a second episode. Lucy experienced this as a time of great stress and grief, which she feels adversely affected the intrauterine life of Susan. After Susan's birth, by normal delivery, Lucy was still mourning the loss of her father, and feels that this affected the quality of her bonding with Susan and led to a hidden depression in her infant. Further, Lucy had read of research linking depression with lowering of the effectiveness of the immune system, which could, in turn, decrease normal surveillance and clearing of cancer cells from the body. She believes this combination of factors caused her child's cancer, and that if she had been a more competent mother, this never would have happened.

Lucy said she had never told this story to anyone, because no one had ever asked, and she was very ashamed. She had hoped for a cure, so that the whole issue could be resolved. She cannot accept stopping treatment because, to her, it means feeling that Susan's death will be her fault. Tom was stunned to learn that his wife harbored such a belief.

This case highlights a number of clinical issues. First, Lucy's beliefs about causing her daughter's illness emerged in full force only in the terminal phase of the disease, although she had had these thoughts from the beginning. Frequently, destructive beliefs about what caused a condition can remain hidden, causing almost unbearable suffering that is kept secret because of intense shame. In this case they surfaced at a clinical crossroads.

Second, the individual pieces of the story are drawn from data and beliefs in the real world: there are accepted theories about inadequate bonding as a cause of childhood depression. Research findings are accumulating in psychoneuroimmunology that show links among depression, immune system compromise, and decreased surveillance of stray cancer cells—and a relationship between bereavement and altered physiology as well. Lucy's story as a whole, however, goes well beyond its individual parts. Most striking is the gender slant of the beliefs. Her story does not include her husband as co-responsible for bonding or supplying a generally nurturant environment for the family that could offset her natural preoccupation with her father's death. In fact, her husband, who disagreed with her beliefs, thought she was exaggerating the extent of her physical or psychological absence. Moreover, he reminded her of his involvement with their child and strongly affirmed her competence as a mother and spouse.

In this case, open discussion of Lucy's beliefs allowed other key people, including Tom and the pediatrician, gently to challenge the story, relate their own versions, and express a sense of co-responsibility. The pediatrician discussed his own second thoughts about whether a different treatment strategy would have been more successful. This process allowed the consultant to offer a revised narrative that both reduced and shared the responsibility among family members and professionals and facilitated expression of grief about the impending loss. After three sessions (the second included the pediatrician), the couple decided to stop further treatment.

A preventive approach that would have identified these toxic beliefs earlier could have helped avert unnecessary suffering. Often, feelings of shame may make it difficult for family members to disclose their true feelings. This is one reason why I usually allow some time during an initial consultation to meet with family members separately, so that shameful feelings can be more easily revealed (see chapters 9 and 10 for further discussion). This need for early intervention is particularly critical when one family member blames himself or herself and the rest of the family concurs. In these instances highly dysfunctional family patterns emerge much earlier. In many cases this type of destructive belief can remain hidden and cause interminable grief and shame, even multigenerational transmission of shame, blame, and guilt driven family systems.

In another case, a husband who believed his drinking caused his wife's coronary and subsequent death increased his self-destructive drinking to alleviate his profound guilt. This led to his being fired from his job and, finally, being involved in a near-fatal auto accident while intoxicated.

In my clinical experience, families with the strongest, sometimes extreme, beliefs about personal responsibility and those with the most severely dysfunctional patterns are most likely to attribute the cause of a condition to a psychosocial factor. In families with a strong inner locus of control, an ethos of personal responsibility governs all facets of life, including the cause of an illness. In these families a relative lack of acknowledgment of "the slings and arrows of outrageous fortune" as a factor in illness can foster blame, shame, and guilt; and in highly dysfunctional families characterized by unresolved conflicts and intense blaming, attributions of what or who is responsible for an illness can give rise to scapegoating and long-term family power struggles.

ADAPTABILITY IN BELIEF SYSTEMS

It is difficult to characterize an ideal family belief about mastery or control in relation to health. A major thesis of systems-oriented medicine is that there is always an interplay of disease with other levels of the system, yet illnesses and the course of disease may vary considerably in responsiveness to psychosocial factors. Distinctions need to be made between a family's beliefs about its general wishes concerning *participation* in a long-term disease process, and its beliefs about its ability to *control* the biological unfolding of an illness. An optimal expression of family competence or mastery depends on its grasp of these distinctions, and the flexibility with which it can apply beliefs about participation and biological control in a balanced manner.

A family's belief in its participation in the total illness process can be thought of as independent of whether a disease is stable, improving, or in a terminal phase. Sometimes mastery and the attempt to control a biological process coincide, as when a family tailors its behavior to help maintain the health of a member with cancer in remission. This may include changes in family roles, communication, diet, exercise, and the balance between work and recreation. Optimally, when an ill family member ceases to be in remission, as the family enters the terminal phase of the illness, participation as an expression of mastery is transformed into a successful process of letting go. In one case, a surviving family member stated, "We were deeply saddened by his death. At the same time, we feel we did what we reasonably could. We were available, in contact, and supportive throughout." Often families have a difficult time deciding what is reasonable in light of the other needs and limits imposed by daily life. Many families feel deficient in comparison with an ideal of all they should have done. In one instance, an oldest daughter needed help in placing her caregiving response in perspective. She felt guilty because she had been unable to spend more time helping her parents when her father was dying of cancer, though she had been constrained by the demands of her job, care of her small children, and geographic distance from her parents.

Families with flexible belief systems are more likely to experience death with a sense of acceptance rather than profound failure. The death of a patient whose long debilitating illness has heavily burdened others can bring relief as well as sadness to family members. Since relief at another's death goes against societal conventions, it can trigger massive guilt reactions that may be expressed through such symptoms as depression and negative family interactions. Clinicians need to help family members minimize guilt and defensiveness and accept the naturalness of ambivalent feelings they may have about a death.

Thus, flexibility within the family and the health-professional system is the key variable in optimal family functioning. Rather than link mastery, in a rigid, circumscribed way, with biological outcome (survival or recovery) as the sole determinant of success, families can define control in a more holistic sense, regarding involvement and participation in the overall process as the main criterion of competence. This is analogous to the distinction between curing the disease and "healing the system." Healing the system may influence the course or outcome of an illness, but recovery from a disease is not necessary to give a family a sense of competence. A flexible view of mastery permits the quality of relations within the family or between the family and health professionals to become more appropriate determinants of success. The health provider's competence is valued from both a technical and a caregiving perspective that is not linked to just the biological course of the disorder (Reiss & Kaplan De-Nour, 1989).

Clinicians need to be mindful that families with the strongest and most rigid beliefs about personal responsibility and control may function very well during earlier stages of an illness, but be extremely vulnerable if the condition progresses. An attitude that conveys "We understand the risks, and we're going to try and beat this thing" needs to be distinguished from "We have to beat this thing." Families that feel the latter are at risk of sustaining two losses: their beloved family member and their belief in their competence as a family. For such a family, disability or death becomes equated with a failure of will or effort. This can have a profound, negative impact on a family's sense of coherence and well-being for generations.

The need for a flexible belief system becomes most evident at major nodal points in illness, individual, or family life cycles. At these times families' mastery of new developmental tasks may require modification of time-honored beliefs or incorporation of new ones. The following case illustrates the problems of rigid beliefs and unresolved multigenerational issues of blame, shame, and guilt that surfaced in the terminal phase of an illness.

Tom and Susan, a young, successful, dual-career couple in their early thirties, had been married for four years when Tom, who had had a lifelong mild case of hemophilia, contracted AIDS from a contaminated blood factor infusion. Tom, who was extremely bright and had an intense belief in personal control and overcoming adversity, decided that he would cure himself of AIDS within a year. The onset of his illness occurred at a time when virtually everyone with AIDS had died within two years. He had always maintained excellent control of his hemophilia, which he inherited through his mother's side of the family. Tom informed himself about

AIDS, kept abreast of relevant research, and sought out new treatments he thought promising.

Tom's mother decided to divorce his father when the boy was 5 years old. Thereafter he had limited contact with his father, whom his mother derided. His father's business failed, and he committed suicide when Tom was a young adult. Tom's mother saw her son as the shining star of the family, who, unlike his father, would be a big success in life. Tom excelled in college, was on the fast track to success, and had a happy marriage.

Susan was an only child; her mother had left her father when Susan was a teen-ager. Her father was described as nice but ineffectual; he had a series of psychiatric hospitalizations for depression. Susan tried to help her father, but felt unsuccessful. Susan saw in Tom a strong-willed, successful man, who, unlike her father, had mastered a chronic illness.

Although Tom, with Susan's full support, tried everything to beat AIDS, his efforts came to nought; and in the second year of his illness, his condition went rapidly downhill. He became demented and impossible to manage at home and finally had to be admitted to a hospice. This was a decision all involved professionals considered necessary and, in fact, was overdue. Tom never accepted death or institutionalization, both of which he saw as shameful defeats. In the end, his mother, who was devastated, blamed Susan for putting him in an institution. Three months before Tom's death, Susan's father died of a heart attack.

This case demonstrates how entrenched, shame-based beliefs and multigenerational legacies can surface and converge, particularly in the terminal phase of a fatal illness involving stigma. In both families of origin, the wives had left their husbands because of their "weakness," and both fathers confirmed their weakness in perceived shameful sequelae—a suicide and chronic depression requiring psychiatric hospitalizations. For both Tom and Susan, their marriage and coping with AIDS provided opportunities to rewrite old scripts: Tom would be strong, conquer his illness, and certainly not die a shameful death or end up in an institution. Susan would not abandon her husband, like both mothers, who felt guilt for the downfall of their husbands after divorcing them. And, through being a successful caregiver, she would make up for not successfully rescuing her father.

Given the fatal trajectory of AIDS in the mid-1980s, this couple was at great risk of failure, particularly when Tom's condition became terminal. In fact, a month before his death, Tom had Susan take over for him, not to help him die, but to assume responsibility for his battle to cure himself. The terminal phase and the decision to go to a hospice became a nodal point of shame and failure. For Tom, it meant not measuring up to a personal value of rugged individualism, which is culturally supported, particularly for men. He could neither conquer his disease nor live outside an institution. Moreover, his disease was rife with stigma. His symptoms of dementia, though beyond his control, replicated, in his mind, the mental disorders of both fathers.

For Susan, a sense of shame and failure was heightened. Because of the strong cultural belief about the role of women as caregivers, her need to institutionalize Tom generated feelings that she was abandoning him (as both mothers had abandoned their husbands) and that if she had been a better caretaker, this could have been averted. Despite the fact that Tom was close to death at the time of admission to the hospice, she believed that putting him there contributed to his death. In this she felt that she was replicating the shame of her own mother. Her father's death during this period only exacerbated her sense of failure: she could rescue neither her father nor Tom. Though she was a devoted wife, she could fulfill neither of Tom's wishes: to be cured and to remain at home. As a result, she bore the burden of his sense of failure in not overcoming AIDS. Moreover, Tom's mother's inconsolable grief and shame about transmitting the hemophilia gene (the reason for both of his illnesses) was expressed in angry scapegoating of her daughter-in-law.

Susan's survivor guilt was heightened because Tom refused to let go and reevaluate his own beliefs about competence. He defined his own death as a failure, and Susan was unable to define her own participation as adequate on her husband's terms. A more flexible belief about mastery would have allowed all concerned to experience Tom's death with sadness and relief at the ending of an ordeal.

Finally, Tom's beliefs about his ability to control anything, including his body, had been cultivated by his lifelong experience with hemophilia. The mildness of his case and the fact that hemophilia is controllable by careful monitoring of one's environment bolstered his beliefs about mastering physical problems. His experience with hemophilia, a very different psychosocial type of illness, did not bring out his rigid shame-based beliefs or prepare him for the inevitable losses associated with AIDS.

This case highlights the need for clinicians to think longitudinally about the viability of strongly held beliefs over the entire course of an illness. What is adaptive at one point may become an albatross later. Interventions that explore the underpinnings of rigidly held beliefs can increase flexibility and thus avert a belief-system crisis later. Questions such as the following can open a dialogue with a family: "You seem very committed to your beliefs about beating this illness. Do any of you foresee any conceivable problems with this?" or "What would it mean for you to redefine your beliefs about success with regard to your (or your family member's) condition in a more flexible way?"

SYMPTOMS/ILLNESS METAPHORS AND NARRATIVES

Beliefs about the cause of a condition are a part of the metaphors and narratives that families construct concerning a physical problem. A full narrative represents the melding of a number of themes, including: the meanings attached to the disease label itself, beliefs promoted by the health-care system, timely cultural metaphors, and personal and family meanings. Clinicians need to understand the meanings about a condition affecting the patient and family as a result of health professionals or larger societal views, as well as those about a condition each family provides from its own unique experience and belief system.

Diagnosis and labeling

The labeling process and the language used to communicate a diagnosis have far-reaching implications. Do family members and professionals refer to diabetes in a family as: "Joe has diabetes," "Joe is a diabetic," or even "Joe's diabetic family"? Each of these expressions conveys a message about the locus and extensiveness of the pathology. The way all concerned communicate about a condition to a large extent determines the meanings and beliefs that become the enduring narratives over time. These narratives, in turn, shape the identity of the affected person and of the family system. When family members refer to Joe's diabetes in terms of his being a diabetic, they are stating that a physical disorder has become the whole, casting its shadow over the entire person or family. Of course, this is particularly common in conditions, such as diabetes, that affect the whole body physiologically. Disabilities that affect only part of the body, for example, one leg, are somewhat less likely to acquire a global label. Conditions with a high level of uncertainty about what causes them or can cure or control them or with stigma attached to them lend themselves to more extensive labels.

Sometimes the label itself has ambiguous or multiple meanings that make it more difficult for families to circumscribe the problem. Couples dealing with fertility problems can come to view their whole relationship as blighted or barren. If they refer to themselves as infertile, this may indicate a problem in their absorbing a significant loss and continuing to define their relationship in hopeful terms despite their inability to have a child biologically their own. In referring to "infertile couples," professionals can linguistically foster a larger meaning that adversely affects couples.

Clinicians need to be mindful of their own way of speaking about an illness or disability and examine any assumptions and meanings hidden therein. Also, they should note how other professionals and family members refer to the particular condition; corrective interventions should be considered from this larger systems perspective. When a family refers to a chronic disorder in somewhat circumscribed terms, this usually indicates a healthy adaptation in which the condition has been given its proper amount of psychosocial space. Families that refer to the ill member or themselves in all-encompassing terms (for example, our alcoholic family) are displaying what Erving Goffman (1986) would describe as a shameful "spoiled identity" that has taken over the system.

Some conditions are associated with embarrassment and shame because of their physical presentation. This is particularly true of those with visible characteristics, such as psoriasis, Tourette's syndrome (which includes uncontrolled tics, guttural sounds, and cursing), musculoskeletal disorders (for example, multiple sclerosis, Parkinson's disease, or muscular dystrophy), seizure disorders, and physical deformities. Other conditions are shameful because of cognitive impairment: mental retardation, traumatic brain injury, and major mental disorders such as schizophrenia, organic brain syndromes (for instance, Alzheimer's disease), and substance abuse. Some conditions, such as inflammatory bowel diseases, can have hidden shameful features (for example, a colostomy) or entail risk of public embarrassment (in this instance, defecating in public). Mastectomy for breast cancer is particularly traumatizing because of the association, in most cultures, of breasts with the beauty and desirability of women. Susan Sontag (1988) maintains that conditions that affect the face induce the most shame and dread—as if there were a split between face and body. Conditions that disfigure the face or produce facial signs of emotional and physical pain become outward, public signs of suffering and the changed identity of the afflicted. The following case is illustrative:

> Bill, a 30-year-old gay man with AIDS, had kept his diagnosis secret for three years, except from his widowed mother. He had carefully concealed his sexual orientation throughout his adulthood, maintaining his social life away from home, in Philadelphia. Loyal to his mother, he continued to live in his home town, a small, conservative community where, he felt, his status and livelihood as a bank teller depended on concealing his lifestyle and diagnosis. He received his medical care in a nearby city, telling neighbors and friends that he suffered from a chronic respiratory condition that fatigued him. A crisis developed when Bill developed Kaposi's sarcomas (large purplish lesions that are characteristic of advanced AIDS), which first appeared on his legs and chest and then spread to his face. Bill could no longer hide his condition, and his mother could not manage his care without outside help.

In the terminal phase, Bill, for the first time, chose to reveal his real life to his extended family and friends. He had always relied heavily on his handsome appearance in social situations. Genuine support in his period of physical decline and facial disfigurement forced Bill to confront his belief that his appearance was his primary source of self-esteem.

When diagnoses involve stigma, clinicians need to differentiate long-standing dysfunctional family processes that contribute to or reinforce a health problem from family behaviors that occur in reaction to a shameful labeling process. For instance, denial of a family member's alcoholism is described as a common characteristic of alcoholic families. However, family avoidance of a shameful labeling process as distinct from its awareness of alcoholism can easily be overlooked. Distinguishing between denial and shame (or denial based on avoiding a shameful label) is critical for effective intervention with such families. In fact, a clinician's failure to make this distinction and then confront presumed family denial will only heighten family members' sense of shame and be likely to increase their avoidance behaviors—which, in turn, could be misinterpreted as further evidence of the initial assessment of family denial.

Metaphors

Metaphors that become attached to biological conditions are critical organizers of families' illness narratives and behavior. Kleinman, in *The Illness Narratives*, maintains that, "To understand how symptoms and illnesses have meaning we must first understand normative conceptions of the body in relation to the self and world. These integral aspects of local social systems inform how we feel, how we perceive mundane bodily processes, and how we interpret those feelings and processes" (p. 13). He believes that this provides the basis upon which we learn how to identify, react, label, and communicate about physical symptoms. In turn, this guides our attributions about illnesses and the narratives families construct about them. For instance, in North American culture, we place enormous value on physical appearance, on such qualities as an unblemished skin and a youthful and sexually desirable body. As the case of Bill illustrated, illnesses or stages of a disorder that are visible tend, in our culture, to create a nodal point of meaning and a crisis in self-esteem.

Some symptoms—pain or fatigue, for example—have an aura of mystery. They are invisible and somewhat poorly understood; they can ebb and flow and be highly responsive to context, such as emotional states or family interactions. Words, like pain, have multiple meanings that can be used to describe both a biological phenomenon and a social quality. Statements such as "I am in pain," "You are a pain," or "You are making my pain worse" can be interpreted literally or metaphorically. Thus, words such as *pain* or *fatigue* have a flexibility of meaning and an ambiguity that promote metaphors. The fact that we often refer to chronic pain and fatigue as "syndromes" is evidence of their current ambiguous medical status.

Families coping with chronic disorders become hyper-aware of bodily functions and symptoms. Over time, their language tends to incorporate medical terms to describe a range of physical states and feelings. Physical fatigue and emotional fatigue or depletion easily become interchangeable in conversation. In a certain sense, a mind–body split eventually becomes linguistically impossible.

The following case illustrates the evolution of an illness metaphor:

Jane is a 20-year-old, single, African-American woman with lifelong sickle-cell disease who lives at home with her mother and older sister. She has been admitted to the hospital with recurrent frequent bouts of pain (a symptom of her disease) and depression. She requires narcotic medication for her pain. In the past two years, she has visited the emergency room with increasing frequency, approximately weekly over the past six months. She does not comply with home medical regimens and routine follow-up visits. She recently entered secretarial school, and is feeling overwhelmed. Her primary physician and emergency-room staff doubt her pain. Jane tells a psychiatric consultant that her main problem is that "No one believes my pain, so why bother?"

Three years earlier, at age 17, Jane was psychiatrically hospitalized following a suicide attempt. At that time she confided that she had been sexually molested by her father since age 13, but had never revealed it to anyone. Hospital notes state that her father denied the allegations and refused family meetings, and that the rest of the family went along with the father's story. Jane was discharged to individual outpatient treatment, which she soon discontinued. Three months later, the father left the family, without explanation; and the topic of sexual abuse was never discussed again. Also, six months after Jane's discharge, after she turned 18 (the customary definition of having reached adulthood in terms of delivery of medical services), Jane was transferred from the pediatric service at one hospital to the adult service of another affiliated institution.

In this case pain and abandonment are central themes in which "disbelief of pain" has become the metaphor describing the totality of Jane's experience. Her feelings about family disbelief and denial of her claims of sexual abuse and the subsequent loss of her father are now being replicated. In the context of a life-threatening illness, Jane, at 18, has lost not only her father but the health professionals and hospital-home to which she was very attached. This loss, like the loss of her father, has not been dealt with. Her family has not heeded her emotional or physical pain. She felt disregarded by the psychiatric service when the abuse issues were dropped after her father's and family's denial of her claims. And now her complaints of physical pain are questioned as manipulative by her new doctors.

In life cycle terms, Jane is in her early adult transition, a time when leaving home and setting up an independent life are normative tasks. For anyone with a life-threatening illness and disability, issues related to threatened loss are heightened. Emotional pain related to the complexities of achieving the typical goals of early adulthood is taking its toll on Jane. She feels this most acutely as she encounters the superimposed strain of college and her physical limitations. This life cycle-generated pain is superimposed on her underlying pain.

Effective intervention with Jane required affirmation of her "pain" and losses by both the therapist, the family, and health professionals. Ambiguities related to her father's leaving and disbelief of her story of abuse needed clarification. And, exploration of issues of threatened loss as a young adult needed attention to transform what had become her dysfunctional communication about pain (see chapter 8).

Larger system illness metaphors

Sontag (1988) has described how certain conditions that are poorly understood, in terms of cause and treatment, and are highly lethal, such as AIDS and cancer, can tap into larger, timely, societal issues and evoke powerful, multilevel metaphors. She believes that "societies need to have one illness that becomes identified with evil, and attaches blame to its 'victims'" (p. 16).

At any point in history, certain dilemmas come to the forefront of society. For instance, before the advent of AIDS, cancer had become the illness associated with fears about death beyond our control and, metaphorically, with certain dilemmas of modern civilization, such as the overgrowth and unlimited technological expansion of society and our polluted, stressful, urban environment. Also, cancer has been associated with beliefs about personal responsibility, that link a predisposition to cancer with familial or personal characteristics, for example, individuals and families with repressed feelings or who feel psychologically defeated or helpless.

AIDS has joined cancer as a metaphor for our fears about our mortality. Because to date AIDS is inevitably fatal, it has become an even more powerful metaphor than cancer. Metaphors about evil, deviance, and unnaturalness are associated with AIDS because of its connections with homosexuals and abusers of intravenous drugs. Fears regarding contagion become irrational in the same way as our fears of becoming homosexual or addicted to drugs, and physical proximity to the afflicted is considered very risky.

At one hospital, patients with AIDS were seen in the dental clinic only on Friday afternoons, when no other, non-AIDS patients would be scheduled. Fridays were chosen so that the offices could be cleansed over the weekend before use by other patients. AIDS patients and family members participating in a support group perceived this arrangement as further humiliation and rejection by the health-care system. The clinic's arrangement only heightened families' fears and sense of isolation as undesirables.

AIDS as a metaphor is linked to important moral, ethical, religious, and political issues. Societal struggles about sexual freedom and identity, monogamy, and hedonism or general permissiveness versus restraint are deeply embedded in the metaphor. There is a substantial unspoken belief about AIDS, similar to beliefs about diseases centuries ago, that restoration of health is possible only after proper atonement and absolution have been made for immorality and sin. The perceived need for moral justice is heightened by the deaths of those victims who are worthy of sympathy because they did nothing to deserve AIDS (for example, infants and people who received tainted blood products). Some speak of the need for a moral cleansing of our dark side and eradication of those morally beyond hope as a necessary prerequisite for societal absolution. In this context, affected families are victimized and suffer interminable grief and shame that has much to do with a larger societal struggle about normality.

Clinicians should routinely ask families about the meanings of illness to which they have been exposed in the broader culture and how these have affected them. Some families withdraw in humiliation; others become energized, reacting to the indignation of false accusations and society's betrayal. These families often become involved in some form of activism to change cultural beliefs. Multifamily self-help groups are particularly useful for conditions associated with stigma and societal prejudice: they alleviate isolation and, by facilitating contact among typical families, promote a normalizing process that restores family self-esteem.

Illness narratives

The story or narrative that family members construct about an illness experience is a synthesis of their attempt to create order out of chaos and fear and their core family themes and beliefs. The narrative typically includes efforts to answer such questions as Why me?, Why us?, Why now?, and What can I/we do?. A simple direct question often suffices: Tell me about your illness and what it has meant for you and your family.

A central clinical task is to elicit family members' narratives and share them amongst each other. In this process, different accounts can become the basis for exploration, clarification, acceptance of different realities, and/or consensus-building. Fundamental life themes can be gleaned from accounts of courage, overcoming adversity, and injustice. Clinicians need to affirm each member's narrative, using them as a basis for the joining process needed in any therapeutic intervention. This ought to be done in an empathic, respectful manner, without blame, emphasizing family strengths where possible. As Kleinman (1988) points out, "The personal narrative does not merely reflect illness experience, but rather it contributes to the experience of symptoms and suffering" (p. 49).

The role of eliciting a narrative for purposes of perspective and closure has been overlooked. From a life cycle vantage point, one of the central tasks of old age is to develop and share one's life narrative as a coherent account that represents a final statement about one's life (Erikson, 1959). In the same way, a *retrospective narrative* can be extremely therapeutic during the course of a chronic condition and after a final loss. It can be used to reaffirm core beliefs, to strengthen positive ones acquired through the ordeal of a serious illness, or to help revise a story laden with destructive or shameful beliefs.

In one case a young woman had valiantly endured her husband's cancer for three years. She and her husband had sought couples therapy with me during this time. His treatments had been arduous, with many complications; and in the terminal phase, he developed difficulties that required professional caregiving at home against his wishes. During his illness the wife had put her budding career on hold to help him. Nevertheless, because she ultimately could not manage him without outside help, she felt guilty.

One year after her husband's death, the young woman was speaking publicly about her experience with cancer. Though she was no longer in treatment, I asked her if she would be willing to talk about her experience for a teaching videotape. The interview offered a chance for her to recount her story. My main contribution to the interview was to suggest that we proceed sequentially through the phases of the illness experience. She emphasized the terminal phase, punctuating his suffering and her shortcomings and sharply condensing the other thirty-three months. I intervened only to the extent of recalling vignettes of her tireless efforts, their quality of life as a couple earlier in the illness, and my recollections of the sadness we all experienced at the end in a medically hopeless situation.

Several weeks later, the young woman called to thank me for the interview, saying it had been very therapeutic. She told me that this had been the first time since her husband's death that she had let herself recount the whole story and that it had been important to do this with someone she trusted who had been involved in the experience. She felt that it had been useful to do this now that sufficient time had elapsed since his death. The interview had rebalanced her final picture of the experience, which had been heavily weighted toward the final period. (This is quite common in situations of chronic illness, an emotionally charged scene—here, part of the terminal phase—taking over the whole narrative.) My suggesting that we go through the story from the beginning and inserting forgotten scenes facilitated this rebalancing and reframing process.

On the basis of this experience, I now routinely propose a session in which families can do a retrospective narrative. This is particularly useful for families that have been burdened for years by a condition or when death has occurred. In situations of loss, this is often best scheduled some time after the immediate mourning period. When family members share their illness stories, they frequently offer each other suggestions for reworking their narratives in a more positive direction. In general, Froma Walsh (1989a) and Carter and McGoldrick (1989), in *The Changing Family Life Cycle*, have noted the value of a life review for older couples in order to share accounts of their life together.

ETHNIC, RELIGIOUS, AND CULTURAL INFLUENCES

Ethnicity, race, and religion strongly influence family beliefs concerning health and illness (McGoldrick, Pearce, & Giordano, 1982; Zborowski, 1969). Significant ethnic differences regarding health beliefs typically emerge at the time of a major health crisis. Cultural norms vary in such areas as definition of the appropriate sick role for the patient; the kind and degree of open communication about the disease allowed; who should be included in the illness caregiving system (for instance, extended family, friends, professionals); who should be the primary caregiver (almost always wife, mother, daughter, or daughter-in-law); and the kind of rituals viewed as normative at different stages of an illness (for example, hospital bedside vigils and healing and funeral rituals).

Health professionals need to become familiar with the belief systems of various ethnic, racial, and religious groups in their community, particularly as these translate into different behavior patterns during illness. For instance, it is customary for Italians and Jews to describe physical symptoms freely and in detail whereas people of Irish or White Anglo-Saxon descent tend to minimize or conceal ailments. One can surmise the potential for misunderstanding and tension that might arise between Italian and Jewish health-care providers and Irish or White Anglo-Saxon patients and their families: a mutually frustrating cycle of health professionals' pursuing a distancing family could develop. At a minimum, dissatisfaction would ensue; at worst, a family might leave treatment, its perceived negative experience reinforcing its alienation and isolation from adequate care.

Clinicians need also to be aware of the cultural differences among themselves, the patient, and the family as a necessary step in forging a workable alliance that can survive a long-term illness. Disregarding such issues can lead families to wall themselves off from health providers and the available community resources—a major source of compliance problems and treatment failure. Sometimes professionals may have to suspend flexibly their need to dominate the situation, especially in relation to family/cultural beliefs that proscribe certain standard forms of medical care (for example, blood transfusions for Jehovah's Witnesses). This requires acceptance that the patient, not the physician, has final responsibility for decisions concerning his or her body.

RITUALS

Rituals are a primary means by which families maintain, store, and convey their identity and core beliefs. Rituals provide stabilization and continuity over time; can facilitate transformation of beliefs; and are particularly important in situations of illness and disability, in which they can be used as a form of therapeutic intervention to facilitate change or healing.

Evan Imber-Black, Janine Roberts, and Richard Whiting (1988), Imber-Black & Roberts (1991, 1992), and Steve Wolin and Linda Bennett (1984) provide excellent overviews about the uses of family ritual in assessment and intervention. They suggest that families have four kinds of rituals: (1) *Daily routines* and regular patterned family interactions, such as mealtime or bedtime rituals and evening or weekend activities. (2) *Family traditions*, such as birthdays, anniversaries, annual vacations, and reunions. These rituals are unique to each family and solidify and convey family identity. (3) *Celebrations* such as Thanksgiving, New Year's, and religious holidays, which serve as cultural symbols connecting families with a larger group identity. (4) *Life cycle* rituals such as births, retirement, weddings, funerals and memorials, as well as unexpected life cycle events such as illness.

Clinicians should routinely assess a family's general commitment to rituals in each of these four areas. Often, rituals are discontinued or interrupted when an illness or loss occurs. For example, Pauline Boss, Wayne Caron, and Joan Horbal (1988) has described how families coping with Alzheimer's disease will discontinue a holiday ritual after the disease has advanced, particularly if the holiday ritual traditionally has been held at the affected member's home. Finding out the process by which a ritual is lost provides a window into a family's beliefs. Why have they discontinued a ritual? Does it reflect their overwhelming grief? In some situations, it can represent the premature extrusion of a member who might still be able to participate in family life in a modified form; in such cases, grief is expressed through discontinued ritual, rather than replacing rituals with new ones or transforming old ones to fit the reality of the illness. Typically, this loss of ritual reflects other, more basic changes in family dynamics, such as the affected member having been excluded from family conversation and decision making.

Rituals also can be lost when families have difficulty adapting old rituals to new circumstances; here, the loss can reflect a deeper despondency in a family. A family may believe they have failed in their efforts to conquer a condition, and their sense of failure may be expressed as having "nothing left to celebrate." Families lacking flexibility and having rigid definitions of success based on controlling natural biological processes are most vulnerable to this kind of loss of their core identity. Assessing rituals in families thus can provide an avenue for exploring other family dynamics and beliefs affected by a disorder.

Research by Steve Wolin and his colleagues (1980) found that for families coping with alcoholism, those that preserve family rituals have decreased intergenerational transmission of alcoholism. This finding likewise applies to families coping with illness and disability. Families that preserve rituals or transform them in positive ways are more likely to sustain empowering family beliefs than those families who lose their rituals. Clinicians can facilitate this process of preservation and positive transformation of rituals for families.

A serious illness can heighten awareness in a family that each gathering and ritual may be the last together. Clinicians can help families deal with threatened loss by promoting the timely creation and use of rituals involving celebration and inclusion. For instance, a reunion can invigorate family members and serve to coalesce the families' healing energies in supporting the ill member and key caretakers. Family celebrations thus offer an opportunity to affirm and improve all family relationships. Emotionally distant and cutoff members can be reconnected to family life as the threat of death and final, permanent separation shatters illusions of infinite time. Often, this awareness shakes family members out of procrastination and indifference, creating the possibility of change for all family members and parts of family life.

Rituals are also useful in situations where a celebration did not take place, such as a child being born with a handicap. In other situations, a loss was not adequately marked. Examples include the occurrence of miscarriage, infertility, or suicide. Sometimes, family members distance themselves from such events; professionals, likewise, may collude such a process by minimizing the significance of the loss or by not inquiring into its impact on a couple or family.

In one case, a young couple had endured two ectopic pregnancies as well as a lengthy fertility workup and interventions over a period of two years. Because the physician detected no apparent physiological problems, he encouraged the couple to continue their efforts to have a child, and emphasized to them the odds in their favor. This fatigued couple, however, had not taken time to mark their losses or allow a sufficient respite period.

After this loss became apparent, the therapist suggested an initial ritual to this couple. They were coached to take a vacation together in order to reaffirm to one another their relationship, which had been strained by their ordeal. The couple selected their favorite place, a location they had first visited during their courtship. The wife felt strongly, however, that she wanted first to mark the losses of her two ectopic pregnancies. Her husband, on the other hand, was reluctant, wanting to forget the past. The therapist supported both the wife's need to mark these losses, and explored with the husband whether he would help his wife get over her grief. Subsequently, the wife asked her husband to quietly join her and participate more actively if he felt like it, to which he readily agreed.

Based on some images in recent dreams about her losses, the wife designed a ritual where she would release two roses (one representing each lost pregnancy) at the waterfront as the tide was going out. Symbols of letting go (the tide), precious life (the rose), and healing (water and gentle waves) were central to her ritual. She also read a brief eulogy for her lost children as the tide took the roses away. Her husband was spontaneously moved to speak for his own sense of loss. The ritual was timed to occur before the couple departed for their vacation; in doing so, the wife felt that first marking the losses of the pregnancies would enable her to experience renewal of their relationship most positively.

In the above case, the clinician actively suggested the idea of a ritual, yet the couple spontaneously designed it according to their own beliefs and symbols. In situations of illness and loss, clinicians need to be flexible with regards to participation of different members in a family ritual and likewise to support the need for personal rituals. For this couple, both types of ritual were necessary. Part of the wife's experience was highly personal as a woman who had endured substantial physical pain and medical operations to end two pregnancies, yet her personal ritual was respectful of other family members who had to adapt at their own pace and in their own way to the same situation.

This case highlights the usefulness of rituals in helping families endure chronic disorders or even transform the disorders into something positive. Rituals such as a timely family celebratory reunion or a couple's private vacation can selectively promote hidden opportunities for relationships, healing, and qualities of life besides those of a healthy body. Also, in such situations families are often feeling overloaded emotionally. Rituals can provide an anxiety-reducing way to handle affect. Because rituals are bounded in space and time, they facilitate family members experiencing strong affect with lower anxiety.

The extent to which a family views an illness as a symptom or disturbance of social relations or the cosmic order suggests the type of rituals that would be effective. Where the family, community, or larger society are seen as participants in either the cause of the illness or the healing process, rituals that incorporate different levels of system would be most effective. In some situations, rituals that involve an extended network of friends, family, or a religious congregation may be important.

The Health Belief Fit among Family Members

It is a common, but unfortunate, error to regard the family as a monolithic unit that feels, thinks, believes, and behaves as an undifferentiated whole. Clinicians should inquire both about the level of agreement and tolerance for differences among family members' beliefs and between the family and health care system. Figure 7.2 offers one way to diagram this set of relationships. Within a family is the rule: "We must agree on all/some values" or are diversity and different viewpoints acceptable? This general rule corresponds to the dimension in Reiss's model called family coordination, which he describes as family members' commitment to developing a group solution to a problem (Reiss, 1981, 1983). How much do family members feel the need to stay in sync with prevailing cultural or societal beliefs, or with family tradition? This general family rule has multiple determinants, including cultural norms, historical context (era of family consensus versus each member acting independently), and multigenerational family beliefs.

In general, family beliefs that balance the need for consensus with both diversity and innovation are optimal and maximize permissible options. Where consensus is the rule, individual differentiation implies disloyalty and deviance. If the guiding principle is that different viewpoints can be held, then diversity is allowed. This is adaptive because it facilitates novel and creative forms of problem solving by the family that may be needed in a situation of protracted adversity, such as serious illness.

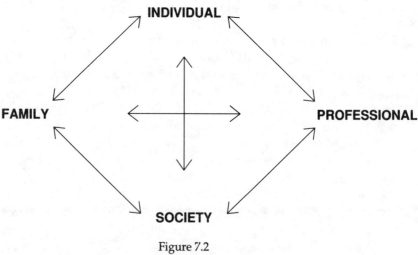

Figure 7.2
Fit of Beliefs

When working with health beliefs in a family where consensus is the rule, attention to the entire family is mandatory. This contrasts with families allowing diversity, where there is inherently greater latitude to work separately on psychosocial issues with the patient or other members without mobilizing family resistance. One useful treatment goal can be to help families negotiate their differences and to support the separate identity, needs, and goals of each member.

Next, it is important to look into the *actual* level of agreement with regard to health beliefs both among family members and between the family and health-care system (see chapter 11 for discussion of interface issues with clinicians and health care systems). How congruent are a family's basic beliefs about control with their beliefs about health? A family that is uniformly external will adapt best, generally, if psychosocial interventions are tailored to that fact. On the other hand, another family that generally believes in an internal locus of control may feel the opposite with a particular condition such as cancer. This family may, through exploration of underlying reasons for this discrepancy, be able to realign their beliefs about being powerless in the face of cancer to beliefs that fit their basic value system. It is critical to keep in mind that beliefs about control refer to a family's attitudes about the importance of their participation in the total illness process rather than just their beliefs about a condition's curability.

THE FIT OF BELIEFS AMONG FAMILY MEMBERS

One should think about the fit of beliefs as an evolving phenomenon, where the degree of fit changes over the course of a disorder, particularly in relation to the illness, individual, and family life cycles. Nodal points or transitions in these life cycles are key junctures where a clash of beliefs may emerge or increase to dysfunctional proportions. In the following case, normative differences among family members' beliefs developed into destructive conflicts during a health crisis.

Assad and Carla, married for eight years, had two children ages 5 and 7. Assad was from an Arab background, while Carla's family was Puerto Rican. A long-standing smoldering triangular conflict had existed for the couple in terms of Carla's divided loyalties between her strong relationship to her family-of-origin and to her spouse. Her family resented his possessiveness, while he disliked her family's expectations of her, which he saw as intrusive and disrespectful of him. In Assad's culture, a wife should have undivided and absolute loyalty to her husband. When Carla's aging father had a serious heart attack, Carla felt it was her duty to help her mother with caregiving. This precipitated a serious marital crisis.

In such situations, clinicians need to sort out normative cultural differences from pathological enmeshment. In this case, all concerned behaved according to their own cultural norms. In Puerto Rican culture, it is normal to maintain close ties to one's family-of-origin after marriage and to expect that a daughter would help her family-of-origin in a health crisis. A daughter would be disloyal not to offer to help. This sharply differs with Arab traditions of the husband. As a result, each side pathologizes the other, creating a conflictual triangle with the wife caught in the middle. In such situations, the clinician who affirms normative multicultural differences promotes a transformation of process from blaming or pathologizing to one of accommodating different cultures.

This case also illustrates how belief system differences in two- and three-person relationships can erupt full force into dysfunctional conflict at the time of a health crisis. The smoldering triangle of Carla, Assad, and her family-of-origin had been manageable over the years, yet the power of a health crisis, coupled with the increased need to use basic beliefs in the face of loss, changed the balance. In this scenario, Carla could be forced to take sides in a coalition either opposing her family-of-origin or her husband. This two-against-one triangle, based on beliefs about how to behave in the face of threatened loss, could easily drive the marital relationship apart or precipitate a cut-off from one's family-of-origin

It is common for differences in beliefs or attitudes to emerge at major treatment or illness transition points. For instance, in situations of severe disability or terminal illness, one member may want the patient to return home while another prefers long-term hospitalization or transfer to an extended care facility. Since the primary task of caregiving is usually assigned to the wife or mother, she is the one most apt to bear the chief burdens in this regard. If such a family also operates under the constraint of traditionally gender-based role assignments where the wife or mother defers to her spouse as the family decision maker, she may not make her true feelings known and may become the family martyr, assuming the nursing tasks without overt disagreement at the time of critical decisions made with health professionals. Clinicians could be misled by a family that presents this kind of united front. A family able to anticipate the collision of gender-based beliefs about caregiving with the potentially overwhelming demands of home-based health care for a dying family member and to flexibly modify its rules would avert the risk of family caregiver overload, resentment, and deteriorating family relationships.

CHAPTER 8

Anticipatory Loss in Physical Illness

A NTICIPATION OF LOSS in physical illness can be as challenging and painful for families as the actual death of a family member. Relatively little attention has been given to families' anticipation of future loss and how their experience with protracted threat of loss evolves with the development of the illness, the individual, and the family. Most of the literature on loss has focused on bereavement in terminal illness, when loss is imminent and certain. Overlooked are the enormous challenges to families over the course of disability and life-threatening illness as they live with uncertainty and face tragedy. A myriad of feelings and transactions associated with anticipatory loss complicates all aspects of family life over time. This chapter will offer a clinical framework to address the interweaving of family efforts simultaneously to sustain hope, cope with varying degrees of uncertainty, and prepare for loss over the course of an illness.

Eric Lindemann (1944) first described the phenomenon of anticipatory grief in his study of spouses' adaptation to wartime separation, noting the essential signs of true grief experienced in preparation for bereavement. Subsequent research has focused on the effects of anticipatory grief on parents with terminally ill children and on key survivors (for example, spouses) of terminally ill adults (Clayton et al., 1973; Friedman et al., 1963; Futterman, Hoffman, & Sabshin, 1972; Gerber et al., 1975; Glick, Weiss, & Parkes, 1974; Natterson & Knudson 1960; Parkes 1976; Parkes & Weiss, 1983; Rando, 1983; Schoenberg et al., 1974). The findings have been inconsistent and often contradictory about both the value of time in anticipating loss and the kinds of coping strategies that are most helpful in long-term adaptation (Fulton & Gottesman, 1980).

In the literature on family systems the attention to loss has focused on the impact of previous unresolved losses on later family life (Bowen, 1978a;

Coleman & Stanton, 1978; Herz, 1989; Paul & Grosser, 1965; Rosen, 1990; Walsh & McGoldrick, 1988, 1991a). Anticipation of loss touches more closely on the existential fact of our own mortality as a future event we may need to deny (Becker, 1973; Kubler-Ross, 1969, 1975).

This chapter offers a systemic, interactional view of anticipatory loss over the entire course of an illness. From this perspective we can examine the mutual influence of family dynamics with: (1) family members' threatened loss of the ill member, (2) the ill member's anticipation of losing his or her family, and (3) the ill member's expectation of disability and/or death. Consideration of the threat of loss needs to encompass the person, family relationships with the ill member, and the intact family unit. The threatened loss of the intact family unit is the level most easily overlooked or not directly articulated, despite its importance. A family member's lament that "we will never be the same" is one expression of this kind of loss. Families that emphasize high cohesion (for instance, Italian families) or small families with only one surviving parent or an only child are examples of types of families more likely to anticipate the loss of the intact family unit if a member becomes ill. This is particularly true if the ill member has a central role in the family.

Unlike the concept of anticipatory grief, which refers narrowly to individual emotions in the terminal phase, the experience of anticipatory loss involves a range of intensified emotional and interactional responses over the course of an illness, including separation anxiety, existential aloneness, denial, sadness, disappointment, anger, resentment, guilt, exhaustion, and desperation. There may be intense ambivalence toward the ill member, vacillating wishes for closeness and distance, and fantasies of escape from an unbearable situation. Especially in chronic illnesses involving long-term threats of loss, families often become hypervigilant and overprotective. They may repeatedly rehearse the process of loss and imagined scenarios of family suffering and hardship. These complex emotions can powerfully influence families' dynamics as they try to adapt to threatened loss. Family members' emotions often fluctuate between these painful feelings and more positive states such as a heightened sense of being alive, of life's preciousness, intimacy, an appreciation of routine daily events, and hope. It is essential to keep in mind and facilitate for families these positive opportunities. Otherwise clinicians may reinforce family narratives that are skewed toward hopelessness and helplessness (see table 8.1).

A systems-oriented model that views the experience of anticipatory loss within a developmental framework clarifies how the meaning of possible loss evolves over time with changing life cycle demands (Rolland, 1987a, 1987b, 1988b, 1990a). Also, the salience of anticipatory loss varies according to members' multigenerational experience with actual and threatened loss: with the kind of illness, its psychosocial demands over time, and the degree of uncertainty about prognosis.

Table 8.1
Characteristics of Anticipatory Loss

1. COMMON EXPERIENCES

Minimization ⟺ Denial

Hypervigilance ⟺ Overprotection

Separation Anxiety

Heightened Sense of Existential Aloneness

Disappointment ⟺ Anger ⟺ Resentment

Sadness

Guilt

Exhaustion ⟺ Desperation

Ambivalence: Closeness vs. Distance
         Family Inclusion and Exclusion (Boundary Ambiguity)
         Escape Fantasies
         Death Wishes

2. POSSIBILITIES

Heightened sense of: Being Alive
         Life's Preciousness
         Intimacy
         Appreciation of Daily Routines
         Perspective on Problems

The quality and degree of anticipatory loss depends on the developmental phase of the illness (Rolland, 1984). Therefore, it is essential to differentiate between a family's awareness of the possibility, at an early point in an illness and its expectation of inevitable loss in the terminal stage. It is also crucial to assess anxieties about *disability* and *suffering* as distinct from *death*, since patients and families often express their greatest fears about helplessness in confronting uncontrollable suffering. In contrast to families in acute grief, such families are faced, early in the illness, with seemingly incompatible psychosocial tasks: they try to sustain vital membership for a person who is expected to become disabled or die as they simultaneously attempt to maintain family integration by reallocating the ill member's role functions. These critical distinctions are easily overlooked, particularly at the time of diagnosis.

Shared belief systems powerfully shape how families view and respond to life-threatening situations. The meanings ascribed to disability and death and a sense of competence to influence the outcome of events will affect how family members act in the face of threatened loss. Unresolved issues of blame, shame, and guilt can strongly affect their view of the cause of an illness and the meanings attached to threatened loss and seriously impede adaptation (Rolland & Walsh, 1988).

Recent studies by Camille Wortman and Roxanne Silver (1989) maintain that traditional assumptions about healthy mourning are largely myth. Their research strongly suggests a much broader range of nonpathological grief reactions and casts doubt on theories of stages of loss (Kubler-Ross, 1975). The present discussion is also based on awareness that there are many effective strategies for coping with threatened loss. Using the Family Systems–Illness Model, this chapter provides a useful framework for clinical assessment that will improve decision making and intervention in a range of situations faced by families dealing with anticipatory loss (see table 8.2).

The Illness Time Line and Threatened Loss

The psychosocial types and stages of illness provide a time line of potential nodal points of loss, including disability and death. Families begin to develop their own time lines when a diagnosis is made. Discussions with health providers about the nature of the disorder, its prognosis, and prescriptions for management constitute a "framing event" for family members. Generally, this is a highly emotional and vulnerable period. Families face a loss of life as it normally was before the diagnosis plus possible further loss through disability and/or death. The resulting hypervigilant, anxious, trancelike state makes families highly receptive to intended and unintended messages about how to handle the uncertainties that confront them. What clinicians say, do not say, or leave unclear about the prognosis is critical; and who is included and excluded from these conversations influence how the family frames the experience.

One family, accustomed to open, frank discussion, described how the physician came to the mother's hospital room and took the family to a separate room to inform them that the mother had cancer and to discuss her

Table 8.2
Anticipatory Loss in Context

---

1. KIND OF ILLNESS
   Possible vs. Probable vs. Inevitable Loss
   Threat of: Death vs. Disability vs. Suffering
   Physical vs. Cognitive Loss

2. STAGE OF ILLNESS

3. STAGE OF FAMILY and INDIVIDUAL LIFE CYCLE

4. MULTIGENERATIONAL EXPERIENCE WITH ILLNESS / LOSS / ADVERSITY

5. FAMILY BELIEF SYSTEMS

---

prognosis. At this vulnerable moment, the family felt it was implicitly being instructed to exclude the mother from any discussion of her condition. The collective fear of the family at that critical moment blocked its normal ability to share important information, even very bad news. The physician, who was extremely busy and perhaps feared an emotional scene with the patient and family that would be time consuming and beyond his emotional comfort zone, chose a self-protective method of dealing with the family.

A physician should lay the groundwork for such a moment by inquiring earlier about each family's preferred way of receiving important information, particularly the results of a medical workup. This can be communicated by saying to the family, "I will be needing to share important information with you over the next few days. Generally I find it best to talk with everyone together. Does this fit your way of getting important news, or do you like to handle things differently?" Asking this question conveys respect for the family and serves to identify family patterns of communication that are potentially problematic, such as avoiding sensitive subjects related to loss with the patient, children, or emotionally vulnerable family members. In the above case, as family members regained their equilibrium, they discussed feeling that the physician had disregarded their normal style of dealing with adversity. The anger this generated adversely affected the family's relationship with the physician. This difficulty was further compounded by the physician's choosing to interpret the family's anger as arising solely from their difficulty in accepting the diagnosis, rather than recognizing his disregard for the family's style of communication.

I believe it is essential for clinicians to ask about family preferences about receiving information from providers and sharing that information with each other even when a family says it does not want to hear certain information or share it. At a minimum, it provides the clinician an opportunity to share with a family the possible risks of remaining in the dark or protecting certain family members from knowledge (for instance, children or aging or frail members). Rather than heightening resistance families often rethink their rules about communication in light of such discussions with a professional. It allows the clinician to anticipate possible crossroads in a progressive disorder at which initial family decisions about the dissemination of information among all concerned might create a crisis (for example, upon entering a terminal phase).

A different kind of problem can also occur: some families may hear the same discussion through very different historical/ethnic/cultural filters, which can lead to conflictual and dysfunctional patterns later. Beliefs about the likelihood and timing of further disability and death strongly influence the relationship rules established in the face of threatened loss.

In one family, the husband had a benign skin cancer removed, and was reassured by the dermatologist that he need have no further worry about the growth. Over the ensuing weeks, marital conflict developed because his wife expressed increased terror about a possible life-threatening recurrence. Wisely, the couple sought help. During the initial consultation, when I inquired about prior experiences with illness and loss, the wife tearfully revealed that her father had died, during her adolescence, from malignant melanoma a year after reassurance by his physician that he had removed a benign tumor. The wife's traumatic experience, unknown to the physician, led her to distrust the prognosis and live in terrified anticipation of her husband's demise. Although the husband knew that his father-in-law had died from cancer, he was unaware of the kind of cancer and the history of misdiagnosis that led to a major loss. This gap in shared knowledge about his spouse's family of origin affected his understanding and sensitivity to his wife's fears.

It is extremely useful to ask each family member about his or her expectations concerning the anticipated course and outcome of the particular condition. Generally, it is best to have the couple or family discuss this together so that differences in outlook are acknowledged openly rather than acted out in escalating cycles of conflict or distancing without anyone's understanding the basis of the conflict or the source of differences in outlook. If strong and tenacious differences exist among family members, at minimum a clinician can facilitate mutual acceptance of divergent viewpoints about prognosis.

PROGRESSIVE DISEASES

Progressive diseases such as Alzheimer's (Boss, Caron, & Horbal, 1988) or multiple sclerosis involve a number of losses that occur in succession. In Alzheimer's disease, although the timing of these losses is variable, their inevitability is not. Family members anticipate and mourn each loss as it is suffered. With disabling conditions, at key points of transition in the illness, family functions may need modification to shift to a new phase of adaptation. Clinicians should be sensitive to nodal points that may require discontinuous or fundamental change for the family. The timing of these crisis points involves a race between increasing disability and each family's unique ability given finite resources, to keep up with the resulting demands without reaching the limits of its adaptation.

Often the most serious crisis occurs when a family has come to the point of exhaustion and confronts decisions such as institutionalization of the ill member or changing rules about who else can provide caregiving. To continue keeping the ill member at home may mean changing time-honored family principles about handling problems without outside assistance, especially in the home. It may require the family to revise basic assumptions about gender-based rules that only women can serve as caregivers. Loss at such crisis points involves grieving for the biological decline of the ill member and loss of family ideals such as never putting a member in an institution.

For instance, one family tried at all costs to preserve the deteriorating father's role functions in order to maintain its strong belief in mastery. As the father's disability increased, it became more and more difficult for the family to deny, through the use of elaborate facades and coverups, that the father was no longer the same person. Successful adaptation required grieving and acceptance of what could not be changed. Achieving acceptance forced the family to revise a monolithic definition of mastery to include a dignified and normal view of bodily decline. Giving up restrictive beliefs about mastery that could not work in this situation involved grieving for the family. However, a major part of the family's collective suffering was alleviated when family members could redefine mastery in terms of action rather than outcome.

Both the "if" and "when" of death have an enormous impact on the family. Most studies of anticipatory loss, by focusing on terminal illness, have not addressed the "if" aspect and have narrowed the timing to the last phase. At diagnosis most illnesses are uncertain on both counts. The real question is the *degree* of uncertainty and *when* anticipatory loss will become salient. For instance, when a family member's lung cancer is in remission, tremendous fear surrounds a possible recurrence. Every appointment with the physician and every ambiguous symptom bring apprehension. The loss of the first remission often shatters a family's hope for a cure and arouses its worst fears. Medically, it means that the best treatment has failed to eliminate the possibility of early death and that second attempts are even less likely to succeed. The ambiguous boundary between remission and cure stokes embers of anticipatory loss indefinitely.

Even twenty years after treatment for cancer, a vague symptom can immediately rekindle fears of recurrence and death. This boundary is also blurred because, in many life-threatening conditions such as cancer, the five-year survival point has been reified as a "medical cure". This nodal point in the illness life cycle, although highly arbitrary, can easily become a psychological parting of the ways between the medical team's view of a cure and the family's continued anxiety about a recurrence. Families can experience the five-year landmark with sharp ambivalence: joy can be mixed with a sense of abandonment by the medical team, the family feeling left alone to deal with real ongoing uncertainty. Physicians may cloak their own anxiety about losing a patient (a medical failure) by using this five-year definition of cure to label a particular case a success no matter what the future brings.

Clinicians can help a family at this point by inquiring about and validating the normalcy of members' experiencing a range of conflicting emotions. Stopping regular checkups with the cancer specialist, appointments so dreaded for so long, suddenly is experienced as an anxiety-filled loss. Clinicians need to be sensitive both to mutual separation issues and the distinctions between professionals' comfort with a statistical medical cure and actual ongoing uncertainties for families.

RELAPSING ILLNESSES

Relapsing illnesses such as asthma or heart disease can flare up or cause sudden death. Stable periods or ones with few symptoms alternate with periods of exacerbation so that issues related to anticipatory loss wax and wane. Families are strained by both the frequency of transitions between crisis and noncrisis and the ongoing uncertainty of when a life-threatening recurrence may strike. In the event of life-threatening crises (for example, in angina or a heart attack or in hemophilia), anticipated loss may preoccupy a family. Families fear most those crises that arise suddenly, without warning, and require immediate help to avert a catastrophe. One woman with long-standing diabetes, abruptly and without warning signs developed severe episodes of hypoglycemia resulting in loss of consciousness. She and her husband feared that an episode could endanger the safety of their small children as well as end her life.

Frequently, rules are shifted to protect a family against life-threatening situations. For instance, when a parent has had a heart attack, the family rule of open communication may shift to one of conflict avoidance as protection against a fatal recurrence. Because dangerous relapses can often be triggered by emotional upheaval, family members, particularly the well spouse, need explicit guidance about when recovery is sufficient to allow them to resume their normal disagreements, sexual life, and so on.

Often when a husband has had a heart attack, the physician has not clearly specified when it will be safe to resume sexual relations. The wife may feel protective and decline her husband's sexual advances not because of a basic change in her desire or attraction, but because she fears losing him through a fatal recurrence. The husband may feel a need to reassert his intactness as a man and to master his own fears about death by performing sexually. An escalating cycle of conflict or avoidance may result in which the husband experiences his wife's protectiveness in declining sex as rejection or as confirmation of his weakened state. In response, he may double his efforts to have sex with his wife, start an affair or turn to other forms of physical exertion, sometimes recklessly, to prove his wholeness. In a circular fashion, this increases the wife's anxiety that her husband needs monitoring and increases her protective behaviors. The driving force behind these kinds of interaction is unacknowledged fears of death coupled with a lack of professional guidelines. In such contexts what is typically labeled a caregiver's controlling behavior needs to be reinterpreted as a part of an interactive cycle representing an attempt to master threatened loss.

Such patterns developed early in a chronic disorder can have a major impact on the entire family system and profound effects on other relationships. The following case illustrates this.

A man sought therapy for help with repeated problems of commitment to relationships with women. He feared marriage would rob him of his freedom and expression of his zest for an adventurous life-style. He viewed his "controlling" mother, who monitored his father's actions and refused to allow him to engage in the sports and traveling he loved, as the source of his concerns.

In family systems-oriented individual therapy, the young man came to realize that what he viewed as his mother's controlling behavior had begun with his father's heart attack (when he, the son, was 5 years old), and was part of a relationship bargain that preserved his father's sense of masculinity and kept him alive. The father denied the seriousness of his condition, failed to comply with doctors' orders to cut back his activities, and threatened to run off on impulsive and risky adventures. He tacitly put his wife in charge of controlling his behavior and thus could maintain a macho bravado and blame her for setting limits on him (actually for him). Had health-care professionals met with the couple soon after the father's heart attack, they might have been able to interrupt this pattern and help the father accept his condition and the need to take responsibility for his own health and, with it, his family's well-being. This template for relationships, driven by unacknowledged and unresolved fears of loss, became an impediment to intimacy for the next generation.

This case points out the importance of inquiring about multigenerational legacies related to illness and loss. For this client, understanding the connection between his father's life-threatening heart condition and the interaction of his parents with regard to the disorder was necessary for addressing his own problem with intimacy. Previous therapy had not succeeded in altering—had, in fact, reinforced—his view of his mother because it left out essential parts of the story.

THE RELATIONSHIP BETWEEN COGNITIVE AND PHYSICAL LOSS

Illnesses vary in terms of the balance between expected physical and cognitive disability. Cognitive loss involves a range of deficits that impair participation in family life. In disorders such as severe stroke, psychological death occurs long before physical death.

Cognitive loss is especially painful for a family because it is associated with progressive loss of intimacy. With physical decline, intimacy can suffer if the family withdraws emotionally. Premature distancing can occur when family members are torn between their wishes to sustain intimacy and to let go emotionally of a member they expect to die. All relationships are predicated on the existential dilemma of choosing intimacy in the face of eventual separation or loss, and life-threatening illness heightens this universal form of anticipatory loss.

Pauline Boss and her colleagues (1984, 1988, 1990) describe endpoint situations in which an ill member becomes psychologically dead to the family, but remains physically alive, as in Alzheimer's disease. She defines these situations as examples of ambiguous loss, the ill member being dead on one level and alive on another. She asserts that uncertainties about the course of the illness impel families either to reorganize without the affected member or to minimize the demands or existence of the illness and unrealistically expect the ill member to maintain his or her usual family responsibilities. Both strategies are attempts by the family to gain a sense of control over the excruciating uncertainties of threatened loss.

The timing of such a family decision depends both on the type, degree, and timing of anticipated loss and on family characteristics such as cohesion and adaptability. For instance, a highly cohesive family may have less tolerance for ambiguity when faced with threatened loss. The need to maintain a cohesive family unit can lead to prematurely extruding the ill member or to tenacious denial.

A useful way to determine whether a cognitively impaired member has been extruded is to inquire about his or her continued participation in family rituals (Imber-Black, Roberts, & Whiting, 1988). Often an important family celebration is eliminated as a way of eluding the pain of loss. For instance, if a mother has advancing Alzheimer's disease, the family may skip a holiday celebration or completely eliminate her traditional participation in the particular ritual. The more adaptive alternative is for the family to acknowledge the loss and struggle to revise the mother's role, allowing her to participate to the extent possible and assigning another member to the rest of her former role.

Clinicians should note communication patterns that bypass the ill member. Typically, a question directed by the clinician to the affected member will be automatically answered by another family member, or family discussions will not include the cognitively impaired member, as if he or she were not in the room or in the family circle.

Threatened Loss in the Crisis and Chronic Phases

Some family developmental tasks in the initial *crisis phase* facilitate family coping with long-term anticipatory loss. Families must mourn the loss of customary life as a family unit that they had before the illness. In progressive and life-threatening disorders families must accept expected hardship and the possibility of further disability or death. A family must learn to live in limbo and grieve for the ambiguities they must endure over the long term. A family's efforts to resist acceptance of chronicity may express its wish to avoid living with threatened loss or "death over their shoulder." Coping with threatened loss for an indeterminate period makes it much harder for a family to define present and future structural and emotional boundaries. Helping families establish functional patterns early in the illness furthers later coping with and adaptation to loss.

Facing loss can shatter a family's myth that life-threatening illnesses happen only to others. A family's loss of its sense of control can be one of the most debilitating experiences, leading to frenetic behavior or immobilization. In a period of intense uncertainty, families desperately need to reestablish a belief in control of the situation, even if the belief is illusory. Assisting families in setting priorities and encouraging direct actions such as gathering information about the illness and community resources are especially useful in helping them reestablish a sense of mastery, which is highly valued in our culture. It is also helpful to promote patient and family involvement in self-help groups concerned with particular disorders. Educating families about significant versus minor physical symptoms may avert unnecessary alarm. Helping families distinguish the expected emotional roller coaster from their fears of going crazy can lower reactivity at this stage.

The *chronic or long haul phase* presents different dilemmas for families. Caregiving demands often give rise to exhaustion and ambivalence as financial and emotional resources become depleted; the emotional tide of anticipation can shift from a fear of to a wish for death that is fraught with enormous guilt and shame, but often not discussed. In my clinical experience, often during a period of increased suffering, the patient expresses the wish to die and end the ordeal. People with unremitting pain or severe, progressive disability may say, "If I have to feel like this every day, then I wish I would die." Although upsetting for loved ones to hear, usually they understand the dilemma for the patient and do not interpret such statements as pathological.

On the other hand, family members who witness the patient's suffering and who are drained by caretaking roles that frequently deprive them of much of an independent life feel intense shame for thinking, "Yes, I wish you would die so I could be free to move on with my life." The patient, who is physically and psychosocially shackled, is given implicit sanction for such thoughts: they go with the rights and privileges of patienthood. Other family members who are only psychosocially stuck as caregivers do not feel entitled to such pessimistic thoughts. The groundwork for this discrepancy is heightened when the patient directly or nonverbally expresses inevitable anger at his or her plight, anger that may be communicated to other family members as "You are fortunate to have your health, and I am jealous." In a moment of frustration, the patient may say, "I wish you could be in my shoes for a minute; then you would understand what this is really like."

The basic problem is that the emotional currency is defined in terms of physical burden. The caretaking burden is underappreciated because physical death or disability as a universal fear cannot be compared with anything else. Only by suggesting the possibility that psychosocial burden is equally valid currency and that the patient and caretakers live in somewhat separate and distinct worlds, each with its own forms of intense psychosocial burden, can the skew that fuels survivor guilt be addressed. I will address issues related to relationship skews in detail in chapter 10.

In my experience, in the chronic phase it is rare for patient and family not to entertain escape fantasies and thoughts of wishing an end to the situation. Because of the shame associated with open acknowledgment of these feelings, I often introduce this subject by making a statement such as, "I haven't heard anyone mention a wish to have this over with; maybe you will be the family to make Ripley's believe it or not." Or if the patient has made a comment along these lines, I may say, "It seems okay for Bill to voice his frustration, but I wonder if the rest of you feel like many families, that they shouldn't have such horrible thoughts about someone they love dearly." Frequently the simple fact of the professional's introducing and normalizing these kinds of thought in this kind of statement lowers the family's shame and anxiety level enormously. Even if family members have not had such experiences, inquiry and comment from a professional can serve a preventive, normalizing function. The task of what the family needs to do about its exhaustion and frustration remains, but the pejorative meanings attached to such toxic thoughts are alleviated, allowing for more open, productive dialogue. If these emotions remain underground, they invariably contribute to survivor guilt. In fact, sometimes such thoughts and feelings can be the seeds of survivor guilt that surface years later. Psychoeducational family interventions that normalize such emotions related to threatened loss help prevent cycles of blame, shame, and guilt.

In long-term disorders, customary patterns of intimacy in couples become skewed by discrepancies between the ill member and the well spouse/caretaker over time. This is particularly true in untimely disorders in which other normative life cycle plans are blocked by the possibility of loss. As one young husband lamented his wife's cancer, "It was hard enough two years ago to absorb that even if Ann was cured, her radiation treatment would make pregnancy impossible. Now I find it unbearable that her continued slow, losing battle with cancer makes it impossible to pursue our dreams like other couples our age." For instance, life-threatening or severely disabling illnesses that coincide with family planning are particularly poignant. For the well spouse, the desire to have children may remain an active fantasy because he or she is physically capable of having a child, but is blocked by the dilemma of the spouse's illness. The ill spouse may become more permanently absorbed in a life or death struggle. This discrepancy can powerfully alter the sense of unified goals and togetherness in the marriage over time.

Clinicians need to distinguish the normal ambivalence that arises in an extended ordeal and a preexisting conflict in a relationship that has become heightened by the prospect of possible loss. This is best assessed by thorough inquiry about the couple's or family's relationships before onset of the disorder.

Medical care for life-threatening illnesses is often provided in specialty clinics, where patients and families coping with similar disorders may develop significant relationships, even in the clinic waiting rooms. Even if patients keep to themselves, they can be acutely aware of other patients who come on the same day to see the same physician. Progression, relapse, or death of another patient can trigger fears of "Will I (we) be next" and reduce family morale. A physician coming out to the waiting area and mentioning to a clerical assistant that another patient should be scheduled for a series of diagnostic tests can rekindle terror among other patients already well aware that new diagnostic tests mean physician concern about serious trouble ahead. It is useful for clinicians to inquire about such clinic contacts and offer family consultations when appropriate.

Terminal Phase Issues

The boundary between the chronic and terminal phases of illness, when death is no longer uncertain but inevitable, is often ambiguous. Medical technology and the imperative to "leave no stone unturned" often reverse or delay these natural transitions. It is now possible to induce a third or fourth remission for cancer. Such persistent medical interventions designed to prolong life can be difficult to distinguish from caregiving attempts to comfort a dying patient. Also, medical training tends to promote ambiguous communication with families, to advocate caution about prognosis, and to discourage admission of uncertainty. The resulting wait-and-see attitude often generates heightened anxiety and ambiguity that confuse a family about the stage of the illness, as in the following case.

Mr. and Mrs. L. were referred for consultation when Mrs. L. was rehospitalized for a lymphoma of ten years' duration and their daughter suddenly refused to visit her mother in the hospital. Three previous recurrences had been easily treated, but this time a number of attempts had not worked. With a highly optimistic physician and a stable course of the condition, the family had never openly discussed the possibility of death. The daughter's behavior signaled a needed change. Mrs. L. continued to feel worse and thought she might be dying, but her physician maintained that she was "doing well" and that he had a number of as-yet-untried treatments (which the consultant recognized as long shots). Discussion with the oncologist revealed his steadfast belief in continued, aggressive treatment that would be undermined by any discussion of death with the family. The family's loyal belief in their physician blocked transition to a final stage of anticipatory grief. It was only 48 hours before her death, when in a coma, that the physician agreed to discuss with the family the fact that Mrs. L. was dying.

LIVING DURING THE TERMINAL PHASE: LEARNING FROM HOSPICE

Hospice, a professional caregiving system designed for the terminal phase of illness, provides perhaps the best guide to the evolving needs of dying patients and their families in the final stage of anticipatory loss. Designed to be autonomous of mainstream health care, the hospice concept, simply stated, is that the patient and his or her family is the unit of care, with services to be available 24 hours a day, 7 days a week, for palliative and supportive care, with emphasis on the biopsychosocial and spiritual needs of the patient and the family.

Drawing on the hospice experience (Lynch, 1989, personal communication), the patient, family, and professional caregivers become a tightly knit group as, together and separately, they move through three distinct subphases common to the terminal phase of anticipatory loss: (1) *the arrival phase*, (2) *the here-for-now phase*, and (3) *the departure phase*.

Once in the terminal phase, the only question is the amount of time left to prepare for death and survivorship. As described in chapter 3, the basic family tasks in this phase are:

- completing the process of anticipatory grief and any unfinished family business;
- supporting the terminally ill member, including helping the survivors and dying member to live together as fully as possible together in whatever time remains;
- beginning the family reorganization process.

For the terminally ill member, the most important needs are controlling pain and suffering, preserving dignity and self-worth, and receiving love and affection from family and friends. Clinicians need to distinguish the need for families to accept the fact that death will occur from the more difficult task of making peace with the fact that the dying member must lose all that he or she has loved (Rando, 1984).

When families are coping with anticipatory loss in the final phase of an illness, the quality as much as the quantity of time becomes a priority. Perhaps more than at any other phase, families function best when they can create an atmosphere in which needs and emotions can be openly expressed without fear of causing resentment or disapproval. Clinicians need to explore a family's fears about the process of dying and about the loss itself. Anticipation of a family member's increasing pain and suffering is often of greater concern than death. This is especially common in long-standing progressive disorders in which the anticipation of death has been rehearsed many times. Early reassurance about effective means of pain control and informed discussion with the family concerning the ill member's wishes about life-saving measures can alleviate a major source of anguish.

The arrival phase

In the arrival phase, families typically are depleted from their protracted efforts to save a member's life. Clinicians need to help the patient and family accept that from now on, medical interventions are intended to maximize caregiving rather than cure. Having hospice help come into the home or admitting the patient to a hospice facility acknowledges the ultimate hopelessness of the situation and the transition from curative to palliative care. This transition is fraught with possibilities for blame, shame, and guilt. The family may blame the medical team for failing to provide a cure, especially if physicians have earlier given an overly optimistic prognosis. The patient and family members may blame themselves or one another for having lost their battle with threatened loss. This is particularly true of families guided by a strong sense of personal responsibility and control.

Sally, 52, had metastatic breast cancer for four years and now was terminally ill. Being independent and a tenacious fighter throughout her life, she had vowed to control her illness in the same way of "exceptional" cancer patients she had read about in popular literature. She also wanted to distinguish herself from her weak alcoholic mother, whom she resented for having died a "broken" person in a nursing home with a dementia caused by alcoholism. When Sally developed brain metastases and became demented and unmanageable at home, her husband and adult children were left with no alternative but to hospitalize her. The family, especially her husband, were burdened by intense guilt in assuming responsibility for her failure "to control" the illness and the fact that she would die in an "institution" with symptoms similar to her mother.

Family therapy focused on both of these issues as a way to unlink the family's sense of failure from the inevitability of death. The failure of Sally's mother to control an addiction needed to be differentiated from Sally, as well as Sally's family's valiant effort to control a fatal illness.

Clinicians can function as a guide for families, helping them gently relinquish their hopes for cure, initiate a humane plan for palliative care, and instill hope in developing a pathway for the experience of death. Their task is to join with the family at a time when members are preoccupied with thoughts of a final separation. In an inpatient facility, such as a hospice or a nursing home, clinicians need to sensitively orient patient and family to a new, unfamiliar setting.

Parents of terminally ill children often find this juncture one of the most difficult. Clinicians need to keep in mind that parents' resistance to turning over care to professionals may represent not only profound grief but also guilt at not being able to save their child. It is very important to help parents participate in terminal care of their child in any possible way. During this phase, siblings frequently become distraught because of the added attention being given to the dying child and because of the increased responsibilities they may have to assume as part of family coping. The inward pull and focus on a dying child is especially difficult if the terminal phase becomes prolonged. Parents may need help maintaining a balance between their devotion to a terminally ill child and other family and professional responsibilities.

A terminal illness can make families feel as if everything is out of control, and clinicians can help them regain a sense of mastery over this painful process. Involvement of all family members, including children, in some aspect of caregiving normalizes the process of dying, provides a sense of control through participation, and counteracts anxiety and feelings of helplessness. At the same time as I try to convey respect for family members' limits, I communicate that the processing of painful feelings and closure are very important.

Painful feelings are more tolerable when families can be helped to experience the joys and pleasures that are available despite inevitable loss. Reading together, recounting good family times, and enjoying a good meal together are just a few examples. Families need to be reminded that premature sorrow can block these positive possibilities. Helping families see how they can stay involved with the dying member even during a gradual process of letting go is very useful.

One of the most painful aspects of a terminal phase for the patient is to witness other family members gradually take over important family roles. One man with terminal cancer felt devastated when he had to turn over to his oldest son management of the family business that he and his now-deceased brother had begun over forty years earlier. When families avoid the need to reallocate functions the affected member can no longer handle, sometimes scapegoating of the patient results or tensions build between other family members. In one family, the relationship between the husband and his mother-in-law became very conflictual as each tried unobtrusively to cover up for the disability of the wife/daughter whose progressive dementia was precluding her management of normal household responsibilities. They fought because of their shared grief and because neither could bear to tell the wife/daughter that her dementia had reached a point where someone else had to take over. The grief associated with this can be lessened when being valued and loved are validated as qualities that transcend physical limitations.

Family members often experience increased feelings of anxiety, guilt, and anger in this phase of an illness. Some of the issues contributing to heightened anxiety include increased and more intense thoughts about a final separation from the dying member, feelings of helplessness to control the outcome, and ruminations about one's own mortality. The patient must deal with anger about unfulfilled personal dreams and expectations. All family members can experience anger about unfulfilled relationship dreams and expectations with regard to the ill member that must now be abandoned. Guilt feelings common to the terminal phase are related to such issues as escape fantasies, being repelled by the wasting away of a dying person, any respite or enjoyment, expression of anger toward the dying person, and tending to pragmatic matters such as finances.

In the context of the intense strains of coping with a dying family member, irrational outbursts of anger and frustration are to be expected. However, in families with rigid and controlled styles, this may be experienced as shameful, especially if directed at the patient. Where possible, clinicians can support family members by normalizing and placing angry feelings in a more realistic perspective, reminding them of their extraordinary efforts and underlying caring for each other. Sometimes a family member feels extremely guilty about not being a good parent, son, or daughter. His or her hope is that caring for a dying member can serve as restitution for earlier sins.

The only way to alleviate these painful feelings is to accept the experience as normal, let go of old issues and disappointments while acknowledging the positive in a relationship, and/or try to deal with unfinished business by openly communicating with appropriate family members. Teresa Rando (1984) has beautifully written "Suffering is pain without meaning" (p. 343). The terminal phase of an illness can provide an opportunity for families to heal old wounds and find caring and love that can lessen suffering. In this phase clinicians need to avoid reflexive thinking that it is too late and, when feasible, offer family consultations directed toward emotional and relational healing.

It is useful to affirm family needs to prepare for practical realities. Because of gender-based socialization, women with a dying spouse often feel terrified about having to manage financial matters. Unfortunately, these fears are often stoked by an avalanche of medical bills incurred during a terminal illness. In such situations pragmatic help must be given even before the funeral is over. In other situations a breadwinner father may need help learning how to care for small children when his spouse is dying.

The here-and-now phase

The here-for-now phase is a period of waiting in which anticipation of the when of loss is narrowed to a day-to-day experience. Families may need assistance redefining hope as focused on the present rather than the future. The patient and the family need mutual understanding of unpredictable mood swings and the courage and strength to live in the moment. The patient hopes for compassion with regard to unpredictable responses to pain and its relief, and not to be abandoned while still alive. It is useful to encourage the dying person to contact absent family members in order to see them once more and to say good-bye. One man wanted to call a cousin whom he had not seen in many years, but who had been a close boyhood friend.

Exhausted family members may need assurance that the dying member's effort to withdraw from the struggles of daily life is not rejection of the family or a rebuke for its not having done enough. At this point, clinicians play a critical role in bridging the ever widening gap between the patient and family. They can help the family to stay involved with the patient while preparing themselves for the final separation. The family's dilemma is in certain respects isomorphic with a clinician's involvement in a time-limited form of therapy, needing to set immediate objectives and plan termination. Clinicians need to learn to not expect or need another visit to accomplish goals.

Once death's imminence has been accepted by patients and families, clinicians can deal more openly with practical matters, such as funeral and will, and with unfinished relationship issues. Clinicians can facilitate families' active participation in planning funeral rituals, burials, or cremations. Helping families to be involved and to develop meaningful rituals counteracts our culture's commercialization of this most important experience; especially in acute losses, a stunned family may turn the process over to professional funeral directors, which may result in an impersonal funeral. It is helpful to ask the dying person about such things as how he or she would like to be remembered, what favorite music should be played at a memorial service, and how he or she would like others to express their sympathy or remembrance, for example, with flowers or donations to a favorite cause.

The departure phase

In the final departure phase, the patient lives in a world of diminishing concerns that center on control of pain and suffering and hope of having people they care about with them in their fading hours. The family's task is to share final moments and then to experience being left behind. Family members may feel shame because of a sense of abandonment or relief at the termination of a burdensome or complicated relationship. This is quite common after illnesses, such as Alzheimer's disease, which have been protracted ordeals in which the affected member may have psychologically died for the family much earlier. In long illnesses family members typically start much earlier and more actively to contemplate a future after the patient's death, which can contribute to survivor guilt and should be normalized.

Family members need to understand that the patient's withdrawal is not rejection or abandonment, but a natural and necessary part of the dying process. This is often perplexing and hurtful to friends and family who were closest to the dying person, who may have romantically fantasized a final death scene in which beautiful and meaningful words were to be exchanged. Clinicians can help family members understand that this final hour is analogous to the moment of childbirth, when the focus is naturally inward. At death, it represents a transition toward a journey that must be made by each of us alone. Yet, family members should be reminded that a universal fear is that one will be left to die alone and that they should not pull away emotionally. Even when the patient is in a coma, the presence of family members and talking to the patient can be helpful, since hearing is the last sense to deteriorate.

Our cultural orientation toward action often makes us uncomfortable when there is nothing more to do. Just being with the dying person, sitting beside him or her, holding hands, and/or listening to favorite music together can be extremely comforting. Relatives too busy to come to the hospital may be reflecting discomfort and avoidance of loss and their own mortality.

Sometimes, a hospital room or intensive care unit full of equipment and tubes inserted in the patient can terrify a child. Clinicians can suggest flexible alternatives, such as making a special card or speaking to the dying person by telephone. I make a clear distinction between this form of participation during a terminal phase and the need for all family members to be present at a funeral or memorial service.

When family members are urged not to procrastinate, but to communicate their affection or to deal with unresolved issues earlier, deathbed disappointments and pathological grief reactions can be avoided. This type of healthy communication facilitates family members taking needed respite from caregiving or a death watch. Family members often fear they will not be present at the moment of death, especially when they live far away and can make only occasional visits. Sometimes this concern represents love or cultural respect and loyalty; but at other times it signifies unfinished business that family members may not know how to deal with. Sometimes with far-advanced illnesses, it may be too late to rectify an unresolved relationship. Clinicians can support such a painful recognition empathically and offer help in overcoming these issues later.

It is important to encourage family members to let the dying member know that he or she will not be forgotten and what positive forms the remembrance will take. One example would be saying something such as, "Every time I go to Truro Beach on Cape Cod, I will remember the wonderful times we spent together."

There is tremendous variation among families and cultures concerning tolerance of and experience in saying good-bye. Clinicians need to be mindful of the wide range of normative responses in helping families through this process. Moreover, seasoned clinicians learn to let go of each departure without losing themselves each time (see chapter 11).

The Family Life Cycle

A family's experience of threatened loss can best be understood through a life cycle perspective, particularly in terms of multigenerational encounters with threatened/actual loss and timing of life-threatening illness within the individual and family life cycles (Rolland, 1987a, 1988b).

THE PAST: MULTIGENERATIONAL ISSUES

Genogram information related to previous family encounters with death, disability, threatened loss, and living with ambiguity is especially important (Herz, 1989; McGoldrick & Gerson, 1985; Rolland, 1987a; Walsh & McGoldrick, 1988, 1991a and b). It is useful to track patterns of coping in previous situations of anticipated loss. Inquiring about family experiences with other forms of uncertainty or loss such as poverty, divorce, violence, abandonment, or dangerous occupations (for instance, military service, law enforcement) in addition to illness events provides valuable information about family hardiness in the face of adversity. Historical inquiry can uncover family members' learned differences, areas of knowledge and inexperience, and the sense of competence or helplessness one might expect in the present encounter with anticipated loss.

A history of unresolved, traumatic, or unexpected loss may generate catastrophic fear when one is confronted with the threat of loss. The risks unfinished business presents in sudden loss have been emphasized. Yet, a history of being a caregiver in a protracted illness can leave fears that one can never again endure the process of such an ordeal. This may be expressed in a heightened preoccupation with one's own or other family members' physical health. Physical symptoms, especially those without a clear, immediate explanation, can unleash a cascade of fear that history will repeat itself.

In this situation it is important for clinicians to distinguish between issues of unresolved loss and sensitization based on a previous ordeal. The latter is akin to the long-term sequelae of post-traumatic stress disorder. Other people, with the same history of traumatic loss will deny the existence or significance of clear bodily symptoms as a way to assert control over profound fears. Some may respond to a loved one's illness, or even the possibility of one, by distancing, emotional cut-off, or separation. One man who had lost his first wife to breast cancer started an affair and filed for divorce from his second wife within weeks of her diagnosis and surgery for breast cancer despite a good prognosis in her case.

Sometimes a preoccupation with threatened loss concerning oneself or a family member can begin at the same point in the life cycle at which a significant family member has died, especially if the loss was untimely, unexpected, or traumatic.

Sam, a married man with small children, at the age of 40 developed somatic symptoms that he was convinced indicated serious heart disease. Several thorough medical workups revealed he was in excellent health; but he remained skeptical, and his symptoms kept increasing. During an initial consultation, when I inquired about past experiences with illness and loss, Sam revealed that when he was 9 years old, his father had died suddenly in his forties of complications of rheumatic heart disease. At that time, Sam and his mother arrived at the hospital only to find out his father had died unexpectedly.

After the funeral and over the years, Sam and his mother almost never discussed his father's death. When he turned 40 and had children almost the same age as he was at the time of the loss of his father, Sam felt he had entered a health danger zone in his life.

Sam had been sensitized to the possibility of sudden, untimely loss, which in his mind would begin at 40. Failure to discuss his father's death had left many unresolved issues about the loss buried. This only heightened the intensity of Sam's anxieties, and when turning 40 triggered his own fears about death and abandoning his family. Reassurances that complications of rheumatic fever had nothing to do with a genetic predisposition to heart disease could be heeded only when these underlying issues were addressed in therapy.

PRESENT AND FUTURE TIMING WITH THE LIFE CYCLE

Anticipatory loss poses different complications depending upon its fit with current or future family developmental imperatives. The impact will vary with a family system's oscillation between centripetal periods of high family cohesion, as in early child-rearing, and centrifugal periods of greater family separateness, as in families with adolescents or young adults (Combrinck-Graham, 1985; Beavers & Hampson, 1990). For instance, a family launching a 20-year-old daughter when she develops a disabling brain tumor that may prove fatal must shift gears developmentally to pull together. The daughter must forgo her budding independence, and the parents must postpone plans for themselves.

Ontime versus untimely

The onset of serious illness is expected in late adulthood, when the quest for meaning, integration and acceptance of one's own personal and family life, and anticipation of death are normative, universal tasks (Herz, 1989; Levinson, 1978, 1986; Neugarten, 1976; Rolland, 1987a; Walsh & McGoldrick, 1988). When a disabling or life-threatening disorder occurs earlier, it is out of phase in both chronological and social time. When such events are untimely, spouse and family lack the psychosocial preparation and rehearsal that occur later, when peers are experiencing similar losses. The ill member and the family are likely to feel robbed of their expectation of a normal life span.

In the case of young couples, the threat of loss is out of phase in that it occurs simultaneously with hopes of child-rearing and career development. They are forced to confront prematurely life's painful fact of intimacy in the face of eventual loss. Although for both a serious illness breaks through denial of death and the promise of a full life span, for the well spouse preparation for disability and death is not on his or her horizon. The hard fact is that the family life cycle with the ill spouse will be severely altered and possibly abbreviated. As one young woman whose husband had metastatic cancer confided, "As long as Jim has cancer, we have no future." Suffering is compounded for couples when peers distance themselves from them because they want to avoid facing the possibility of a similar loss of spouse or child. These issues heighten differences between the well and the ill spouse and isolate the family.

Life cycle transition periods

In all life cycle models (Carter & McGoldrick, 1989; Duvall, 1977; Levinson, 1978), developmental transitions involve beginnings and endings, as in births, launching young adults, retirement, divorce, and death. Commonly, preoccupations about death, life's limits, and anticipation of separation and loss surface at such times. The diagnosis of a serious illness superimposes the illness life cycle onto that of the individual and the family. One of the family's primary developmental tasks then becomes accommodating to the anticipation of further disability and possibly untimely death (Rolland, 1987a).

Families in life cycle transitions may be more vulnerable to the emotional upheaval generated by anticipatory loss associated with illness. For example, suppose a family is in the stage of launching a young adult when the father has a serious heart attack. The threat of the father's death may heavily influence young adult members in transition to alter their life decisions in ways that compromise their own independent strivings.

In long-term threat of loss, as families move through normative life cycle transitions there may be a resurgence of earlier feelings of anticipatory loss families thought were worked through. The following case illustrates how a very positive celebratory family transition can stir up "old" feelings.

A family presented for treatment when the younger daughter was about to graduate from college. Her older brother, Tom, age 25, had developmental disabilities related to damage sustained at birth during a complicated forceps delivery. His disability involved some mild right-side weakness and learning difficulties, particularly with mathematics. Despite his disability, with persistence, substantial commitment by his parents, and the help of professionals, Tom was attending college, but had been struggling to finish for seven years. Most of his age peers had moved on and were settling down in careers and/or marriage.

His sister's impending graduation was a marker that forced more open acknowledgment and acceptance of Tom's being passed by his sister, something all family members had dreaded for years. It heightened Tom's sense of inadequacy, of being left behind, and fears that he would never be able to master adulthood. It rekindled his mother's unjustified feelings of guilt surrounding his delivery and both parents' feelings that if they had done enough, their son would not experience suffering.

This event enabled the parents to work through a deeper level of acceptance of their own heroic efforts and to let go and allow their adult son to handle his own suffering. It provided an opportunity for Tom to address more fully the part of himself that linked self-esteem with performing equally with others in all areas. He needed to learn to accept his limits and work around them without sacrificing his self-esteem.

At times of transition, developmental tasks of the next stage in the life cycle may need to be altered, delayed, or given up when unrealistic. At each transition intense grieving can occur over opportunities and experiences that may have been anticipated but must now be definitively relinquished. Family members often need to mourn the loss of future hopes and dreams. For instance, when a mother learns of her daughter's diagnosis with a terminal form of cancer, she must mourn the loss of anticipated experiences, which might include school graduations, the daughter's marriage, and her own grandparenthood. Clinicians should inquire about losses related to future life stages and explore options for alternative positive experiences.

ISSUES RELATED TO CHILDHOOD VERSUS ADULT ONSET

Threatened loss will impact families in new ways as they encounter developmental tasks at each stage of the life cycle. Such differences can be illustrated by examining timing issues in childhood- versus adult-onset disorders as they affect the marital life cycle.

Childhood-onset, congenital, and inherited disorders

In childhood-onset, congenital, and inherited disorders, a child's socialization and belief system are influenced by a continual interplay of developmental milestones and the limitations and future risks of the illness. In many inherited disorders, family beliefs about mastery and the rules for social interaction are shaped over generations to be in sync with anticipatory loss (Rolland, 1987b). For example, in hemophilia life-threatening bleeding episodes can be triggered by trauma, intense affect, or extended periods of stress. Because sudden death is ever present, parents often teach affected children a finely tuned form of mastery over their bodies that is juxtaposed with fear of social interaction. Emotions are carefully monitored in the interest of self-preservation. Anticipation of loss guides this interweaving of belief system and developmental processes.

In hereditary or childhood-onset disorders, the developmental experience with threatened loss is brought to adult relationships. Couples develop their relationship with the factor of possible loss overtly acknowledged or covertly overshadowing their commitment. It is important for clinicians to promote communication about the impact of possible disability and premature death on such areas as child-rearing, career, and divisions of labor so that the couple can develop the flexibility necessary to adapt to the added strains of a life-threatening illness. Such couples also need to discuss subjects such as disability and life insurance, and wills, issues often postponed by healthy young couples.

In long-term illnesses, such as diabetes and hemophilia, concerns about future loss become embedded in life cycle planning in more subtle and covert ways, as illustrated in the following case.

Greg, a 45-year-old man with lifelong hemophilia, was referred for severe depression. Extensive disability required his using crutches to walk. He had divorced three years earlier; his only daughter had just left home for college.

Evaluation revealed that his mother's family had a 200-year history of hemophilia, involving scores of cases. A brother had died in childhood following an injury, and only one member with hemophilia had lived beyond age 50.

When asked about how he had conceived his life from childhood, Greg stated that at age 8 after his brother's death, he decided that if he could survive the higher risks of trauma in childhood (his brother being a vivid reminder), he had enough time to marry and rear children, but that given statistics and his lengthy family history, life beyond 45 seemed unlikely. After 40, he began to view his life as "pre-dead." He had no vision or plans for life beyond 50 except anticipation of death.

This case demonstrates how a person can structure his entire life cycle to conform to an expectation of disability and death at a particular phase in life. The timing of Greg's divorce coincided with an only vaguely conscious plan to spare his wife's having to deal with his becoming a burden and dying and gave him control over the end of the relationship. His daughter's launching left him alone with his own depression and suicidal thoughts reflecting his hopeless outlook.

Greg's story highlights both the potential danger of anticipatory loss's becoming a runaway process and the need for a preventive clinical framework. Greg had a version of anticipatory loss developed as a child that was inevitable and timed rather than possible and of uncertain timing. He had developed these ideas as an 8-year-old child, but he had never discussed this with anyone, and no one had ever asked. Also, the runaway process accelerated at the most vulnerable point in his life cycle. An earlier intervention that took stock of how his multigenerational experience influenced his personal illness time line could have predicted the time of highest risk and helped him plan for life after 40 in a way that acknowledged the possibility of disability and early death but did not preclude meaningful life goals and relationships within a context of heightened uncertainty. This case highlights the need to ask ill children their beliefs about how their condition will affect their life expectancy.

Adult-onset disorders

The main issue in adult-onset disorders is the necessity for the affected person to shift fundamental beliefs, hopes, dreams, and expectations to accommodate loss and threatened further loss. If the illness began before an intimate relationship and the affected person has had sufficient time to learn to live with his or her condition, then the couple tends to enter the relationship with more congruent expectations. If diagnosis occurs after marriage, couples must alter their original relationship contract to accommodate actual or possible barriers to their hopes and dreams.

Serious illness that occurs early in a couple's relationship is particularly stressful because they are still forming its foundation. For well-functioning couples, if onset of a disease occurs later in the family life cycle, strains are counterbalanced by a firmer relationship base. If there are dysfunctional patterns before the illness, then the threat of loss is more likely to drive the couple farther apart.

When a relationship is started during the crisis phase of an illness, there are significant risks. There is likely to be an inevitable skew that can foster a permanent caregiver–patient relationship bargain in which no more balanced relationship ever existed. Also, an affected person may develop a relationship with someone who is vulnerable, because of unresolved family-of-origin issues, to becoming a rescuing-oriented caregiver. Examples include a person who grew up as a rescuer in a family with alcoholism or as a parentified child with a parent who had a chronic disorder.

NODAL POINTS OF ANTICIPATORY LOSS FOR COUPLES

The type of illness and time frame of anticipated loss influence how a couple responds to threats to their life plan. Consider diabetes as an example. In an illness such as diabetes, the possibility of disability or a shortened life span frequently remains distant. Often the person with diabetes has learned to accommodate to possible negative outcomes through denial and minimization.

In the process of forming an intimate relationship, the well partner will need to be educated about diabetes, in an attempt to gain a sense of mastery in the face of threatened loss of his or her partner and to sustain intimacy with a person with a chronic illness. The well partner's fears may be expressed by hovering over the person with diabetes, questioning his or her dietary habits, and being overprotective about any behavior that could mean hypoglycemia. The person with diabetes may respond angrily, "You are treating me as my parents did. It took me ten years to get them off my back." The need for the well partner to master his or her fears is confused with earlier parental control issues (also related to threatened loss). Also, the ability of the person with diabetes to inform the well partner can be blocked by not wanting to re-experience fears about deterioration, abandonment, and death that are sensitive, loaded subjects for both partners. Clinicians need to be aware that often these issues related to anticipatory loss become obscured in pronouncements such as, "It's my illness and I'll handle it myself."

Another common nodal point occurs when a couple with an ill member faces a decision about having children. Often such couples' ambivalence about having a child is directly related to issues of threatened loss that have not been openly acknowledged. The couple must consider risks of pregnancy complications for both an ill mother and the unborn child. Other concerns include: (1) fear of genetic transmission to offspring who will carry the burdens of loss; (2) anticipation of loss of a "dream child" who may contract the illness at some point; (3) anticipation of illness complications that would interfere with effective parenting; (4) fear that the ill spouse might not survive to rear children to adulthood; and (5) associated financial and psychosocial burdens for the surviving/well spouse. Frequently, fears have been exaggerated by failure to receive or seek accurate information (for example, about the risk of genetic transmission of diabetes).

A third nodal point in diabetes occurs at the time of the first complication. In one young couple, the wife had had diabetes since childhood and never had any complications. The discovery of a small hemorrhage in one eye during a routine checkup caused an emotional crisis. All her fears about the well-known circulatory complications of diabetes that had remained suppressed since childhood came flooding back. Fears about going blind, painful neurological complications, possible amputations, and heart and kidney failure preoccupied the couple at a time when they were considering long-term plans. A brief couples treatment helped both partners discuss their fears, affirm their commitment to the relationship, and build greater flexibility into future plans. Previously the wife had worked as a video technician, a position in which good eyesight is critical. After this crisis, she decided to apply for a job to develop and administer a new visual arts program at the regional high school. This job allowed her to use her professional skills in a new, creative way that was not so dependent on her eyesight.

Belief Systems

In confronting possible loss, creating a meaning for an illness that preserves a sense of competency is a primary task for a family. As discussed in chapter 7, a family's beliefs about what and who can influence the course of events are fundamental. When a family member feels responsible or is blamed for a disorder involving threatened loss, any illness exacerbation or disease progression can cause these issues to erupt into a full-blown family crisis.

In one case, a mother who both blamed herself and felt blamed by her husband for her teen-aged son's diabetes (her own mother had had diabetes) was unable to set limits on her son, who was flagrantly noncompliant with his diet and his insulin injections. In this case, the mother believed that her possible genetic contribution and full-time career were the primary reasons that her son developed diabetes and was doing medically poorly. Her husband, who had always been uncomfortable with their dual-career marriage and felt chronically neglected and competitive with his wife's career, concurred with her self-blame. These beliefs were unknown to any of the professionals involved and only surfaced by direct questioning during a consultation when the son was hospitalized during a life-threatening episode.

Ambiguities about what can cause or affect illnesses, especially psychosocial factors, blur what family behaviors can affect the odds of a tragic outcome. This increases the likelihood of blaming attributions whenever disease progression can be linked to errors of omission or commission. It is crucial for clinicians to help families obtain clearer medical prognoses and management guidelines. In situations of threatened loss, women are more subject than men to attributions involving blame, shame, or guilt because of societal role expectations of primary caretaker responsibilities for their children, husband, aging parents, and the extended family.

In childhood disorders, parents and siblings are at heightened risk of survivor guilt. Siblings close in age to the ill child and in whom rivalry is strong are the most vulnerable to survivor guilt. Surviving family members may feel guilty for being spared physical suffering and threatened death. Parents ruminate about possible negligence as a causal factor. In some family members, especially siblings, this feeling can be expressed as a general somatic preoccupation or catastrophic fear of suffering the same fate. A child whose apparent influenza turns out to be leukemia can trigger family panic if any other member shows the mildest respiratory symptoms. Family members may become overprotective of surviving children. In other cases, guilt can take the form of self-destructive behaviors (for example, alcoholism, recklessness).

As described in chapter 7, severely dysfunctional families and those with particularly strong beliefs about personal responsibility tend to overemphasize psychosocial factors in the cause and outcome of an illness. In this regard conditions involving threatened loss are particularly high-stake situations. A relative lack of acknowledgment of "outrageous fortune" as a factor in an illness can create a powerful nidus for blame, shame, and guilt. For such a family, disability or death implies a failure of will or effort. Anticipatory loss becomes loaded with a second life-versus-death struggle: that of willpower and, possibly, the family's belief system. This sort of family will tend to hold on tenaciously to an ill member. In contrast, families guided by an externally oriented belief system, centered on fate, risk premature extrusion and grieving for the ill member.

Making peace with self, family, and world is a fundamental task in coping with threatened loss, especially in the terminal phase. Several kinds of beliefs complicate this normative process. In particular, unresolved issues of blame, shame, or guilt seriously compromise movement toward closure and acceptance. Second, some families' beliefs about mastery are rigidly defined as an ability to control the biological unfolding and outcome of an illness. A more flexible definition of competence involves active participation in the overall process. To sustain a family value in personal control during a progressive or terminal phase of an illness, participation in a successful process of letting go needs to replace mastery of biology. The difference between a family experiencing a loss with a sense of competency versus defeat is connected to this kind of flexibility in its belief system.

LARGER SYSTEM VALUES

Historically, prevailing American, male, middle-class values emphasize individual achievement and mastery. We live in an era that especially promotes personal responsibility and effort as the road out of adversity. From national policy-making to popular psychology (Siegel, 1986; Simonton, Matthews-Simonton, & Creighton, 1978), there is a tendency to internalize and localize problems in the individual or family. This societal value can interact powerfully with belief systems in a family facing threatened loss. The consequences of a losing battle with disability and death can become infused with a profound sense of public shame and failure. This negatively interpreted experience can alter a family's paradigm for generations. Clinicians need to guard against advocating too strongly a philosophy that the loss could be prevented if only the family took enough responsibility for the illness.

Societal stigma: the example of AIDS

AIDS dramatically illustrates how the process of family coping with anticipatory loss and bereavement are severely compromised by societal stigma. The beliefs/metaphors attached to AIDS (Sontag, 1988) and larger system attitudes that victimize families can rival unresolved family problems as a potential cause of interminable grief linked to family guilt or shame. Threatened loss is too often experienced in a context of secrecy that fosters isolation in the face of an ignominious death. Clinicians can help to remove such blocks, to promote positive rituals and facilitate community support for patients and their families.

AIDS is unique in several other ways. Because it is an epidemic, families and caregivers often experience multiple losses and are dealing simultaneously with a number of friends or family members who are at various stages of AIDS and therefore different stages of anticipatory loss. Clinicians need to be sensitive to the continual immersion in waves of impending death and bereavement surrounding families in high-risk communities. People with AIDS must cope with their own fears of death at the same time as they may be intimately involved with the threatened loss of a partner or another member of their family or community. One or both parents of a child with AIDS often are confronted with their own diagnosis at the same time as they learn about their infant's. In such families with other siblings, clinicians need to build extended family supports for the nurturance of the children and for planning for a future that may not include their parents.

Conclusion

Overemphasis on anticipatory loss can itself become emotionally disabling if not counterbalanced by ways to use that experience to improve the quality of life. In this regard, clinicians can be extremely helpful in assisting families to achieve a healthy balance. In illnesses with long-range risks, families can maintain mastery in the face of uncertainty by: (1) acknowledging the possibility of loss, (2) sustaining hope, and (3) building flexibility into family life cycle planning that conserves and adjusts major goals (for instance, with regard to child-rearing) and circumvents the forces of uncertainty. Clinicians can help families agree about the conditions under which further family discussion would be useful and whom it would be appropriate to include.

From a life cycle perspective, illness, individual, or family transitions are critical times for examining issues of threatened loss and weighing them in light of other developmental considerations. Open discussion and shared decision-making at these junctures will help prevent later blame or guilt if loss occurs.

A young adult whose father has cancer in remission may have difficulty leaving home partly out of fear of never seeing the ill parent again and/or a sense that he or she will be disloyal in avoiding the day-to-day caregiving role. This conflict may be expressed in declining school performance, drug use, or other destructive behaviors. Promoting frank discussion of feelings between parent(s) and their young adult children can be useful in preventing such self-destructive patterns. Furthermore, there is greater incentive and importance for a family to confront denial of an illness when there is hope that preventive action or medical treatment can affect the outcome.

A brush with death provides an opportunity to confront catastrophic fears about loss. This can lead to family members' developing a better appreciation of and perspective on life that result in clearer priorities. Active creation of opportunities can replace procrastination and passive waiting for the right moment. Threatened loss, by emphasizing life's fragility and preciousness, provides families with an opportunity to deal with unresolved issues and develop more immediate, caring relationships. In illnesses in a more advanced stage, clinicians should help families emphasize quality of life by defining goals that are more immediately attainable and that enrich their everyday lives.

Finally, clinicians working with families facing loss need to consider their own experiences and feelings about loss. Such factors as our multigenerational and family history with threatened or actual loss, our health beliefs, and our current life cycle stage will influence our ability to work effectively with such families.

Fears about our own vulnerability are easily triggered when working with families coping with untimely illnesses. This is especially likely if the patient and family are at the same stage of the life cycle as the therapist. Self-awareness is particularly important if one has the same disorder or is at high risk of illnesses involving loss (for instance, a strong family history of cancer or heart disease). Because these situations are so compelling, clinicians who work with a family for an extended period tend to shape their hopes and beliefs with those of the family. This can lead to excessive optimism and forgetting that loss is really possible.

Finally, our own unresolved issues related to actual or threatened losses and fears about our own mortality can lead to maintaining excessive emotional distance, avoiding important, often painful discussions related to threatened loss, or becoming overly involved with a particular family. As we come to accept the limits of our ability to control the uncontrollable and work through unresolved personal losses, we can work most sensitively with the excruciating dilemmas of families facing loss (see chapter 11).

PART III

ASSESSMENT AND TREATMENT GUIDELINES

CHAPTER 9

Treatment Issues with Families

THE Family Systems–Illness Model described in parts I and II helps clinicians to understand the fit between the psychosocial demands of a disorder over time and critical family processes, highlighting life cycle issues and belief systems. In part III, this model is used to inform treatment guidelines with families and couples and interface issues for clinicians. This chapter will describe basic principles for effective systemic intervention using the model, and will address treatment issues for chronic disorders in childhood, parental illness and disability, and aging parents.

Basic Principles for Intervention

The Family Systems–Illness Model is used most effectively in a preventive, normative manner. This means that all families facing illness and disability ideally should, from the beginning, have a psychosocial component in their care that includes the members of the family system. Optimally, all families in these situations would routinely have a family consultation in the crisis phase, near the time of onset. As a preventive measure, this accomplishes three vital therapeutic tasks: (1) it defines a systems-oriented psychosocial consultant as a member of the health-care team, (2) it defines the family as the central psychosocial unit of care, and (3) it normalizes the expectation of common psychosocial strains for the entire family in a nonpejorative, non-blaming manner that enables families to utilize psychosocial assistance effectively and minimizes stigma and shame. It also reduces feelings of helplessness that can lead to family withdrawal and isolation. Inviting a family into this kind of collaborative process at an early stage promotes open and flexible communication among all professionals and family members involved in the caregiving system.

REFERRAL AND JOINING THE FAMILY SYSTEM

When referrals for psychosocial intervention occur later, in the chronic or terminal phase, there is a much greater likelihood that families will experience feelings of shame or being blamed. Professionals may contribute to this process by making a referral when they feel exasperated. This often coincides with a time when biomedical treatment has reached its natural limit, treatments have failed, or a condition has progressed to the next phase (for example, when it is terminal). At these junctures, families can easily confuse a physician's frustration at not succeeding, according to his or her own professional standards, with judging them ineffectual and in need of mental health care. Clinicians need to be sensitive to families' potential sense of shame when a referral is made in the chronic phase, when the course of the condition has worsened, or, especially, when an expected cure or improvement has not materialized. A family's natural disappointment can easily be compounded by the tendency for all involved to seek an explanation for personal inadequacies. Families often assume that the fact that no psychosocial consultant was included earlier was an indication that they were doing well, in the eyes of the health-care team; thus, when a referral is made, it has to mean that they are coping poorly.

This is extremely unfortunate since, in many situations, physicians are not accustomed to thinking in terms of using a family systems consultant in a preventive fashion and do so only when medical care has reached a limit or the natural strains of living with a chronic disorder have piled up beyond a family's limit. Sometimes, physicians also experience feelings of failure and shame at the time of a referral, a common underlying thought being "If I had done a better job, this family wouldn't have to suffer." Such feelings are heightened if family members have directed normal feelings of anger at the physician for not being able to control or cure an illness that may not be controllable even with the best medical care.

In most situations, during my first contact with the referring clinician and the identified patient, I convey my philosophy about the family or caregiving system as the most important unit. Regardless of the reason for referral, I want to communicate the idea that chronic disorders are problematic for the entire family, and that I am interested in the well-being of all family members. My primary goal is to join with the whole caregiving system.

A family-oriented assessment provides the best foundation for making decisions about the most appropriate kinds of interventions, which may include therapy for individuals, couples, or the whole family. A key goal of my initial consultation is to determine the relative usefulness of each. Rather than interpret a request for an individual consultation as resistance to including others, I assume many referring clinicians and families are unfamiliar with a systems model of intervention. Regardlesss of whether I go ahead

with an individual meeting, I want to use the initial contact with both the referral source and the family system to inform them about my approach and
learn how this fits with their own ideas of intervention. This is not intended
to convey a rigid stance that I will meet only with the whole system, though
if I do go ahead and meet with one person, I have established that part of our
agenda will include discussion about the pros and cons of including other
family members.

As much as possible, I want to normalize my joining their family effort to
master their situation so that they see me as a positive resource rather than a
source of punishment or shame. At the time of referral, I find direct inquiry
about any feelings of shame the best approach. To help counteract such feelings, I routinely tell families that 75 percent of the families who come to our
center have never seen a mental health professional before. Emphasizing
family strengths and what they have done well in the face of adversity is
very helpful. Often, families are surprised when I compliment them during a
consultation. They literally have had no way to measure their skill at coping
and usually are overly harsh in their judgments about their competence.
Rarely do I find that this approach encourages avoidance or denial. When I
first meet these families, most of them are overwhelmed, emotionally depleted, and demoralized. Affirming their strengths first gives me greater latitude to begin to address areas of dysfunction.

Several other strategies facilitate the joining process. I want to communicate my flexibility. Where appropriate, I will meet families according to the
demands of the disorder. If the affected member is in a recovery phase, I
may meet them in the hospital at the bedside or in their home; this establishes me as part of the larger health-care team and helps dispel myths families and and other health workers may hold that mental health professionals
form rigid, secretive, therapeutic relationships confined to their offices. Privacy is essential, but clinician distancing and secrecy can heighten these families' feelings of stigma and shame.

I almost always communicate directly with the primary health-care
providers. Frequently a referral comes from a hospital social worker. If I limited my contacts to a referring mental health professional, I would be reinforcing a dysfunctional split between medical and psychosocial care. Many
mental health professionals are intimidated by the notion of directly calling
the primary physician: the inherent power discrepancy and the lack of medical training make them uneasy about such an encounter. In this regard, the
psychosocial typology provides a useful middle ground for therapists in understanding the essence of an illness in psychosocial terms, thereby facilitating their ability to communicate effectively with a health professional without being medical experts. Calling the physician, going to the hospital,
meeting with other health-care professionals, and having the family see the
consultant involved in such interactions all facilitate a functional joining

process and demythologize the therapist's role (Sargent, 1985). Also, it counteracts the common mind–body split in which disconnected biomedical and psychosocial care symbolize a lack of connection between these two worlds at all levels.

These initial joining strategies serve as a model for families to integrate the medical and psychosocial aspects of their experience with illness and disability. A number of families have commented that seeing me with their primary physician discussing their situation greatly facilitated such an integrative process.

TIMING OF INTERVENTIONS

The psychosocial typology and time phases of illness, combined with an understanding of individual and family life cycles, offer a coherent framework for timing interventions. Understanding the natural trajectory of a condition clarifies common transitions and nodal points in the evolution of a disorder (see chapters 2 and 3). Key psychosocial developmental tasks associated with successful coping and adaptation are connected to such a time line. Since most individual and family life cycle transitions will be affected by a chronic disorder, normative life cycle tasks will need to be considered in the context of the condition. The interplay of the illness, individual, and family life cycles provides a useful way to think about the timing of psychosocial interventions (se chapter 6). Rather than automatically suggesting "psychosocial checkups" every six months, I often use important life cycle and illness transitions as a guide for timing consultations and brief interventions. Families can be educated to anticipate nodal points and the kinds of psychosocial demands that will have to be faced and to recognize warning signs of a need for help and request a consultation in a more preventive manner.

Family gatherings afford natural opportunities to intervene in the system. Because serious illnesses make families more aware of the preciousness of time, holidays, such as Thanksgiving, that were taken for granted may suddenly take on new meaning. The awareness that each family gathering may be the last can be emotionally disabling or empowering. Clinicians can propose consultations to coincide with family get-togethers or coach family members in initiating important conversations or designing meaningful rituals. One family approached the mother, who was in failing health, with the idea of a family celebration to honor her life. Her reply was, "That's a terrific idea, but let's get together so we can all honor each other as a family."

TREATMENT MODALITIES

The Family Systems–Illness Model can be flexibly applied to a range of treatment modalities. A systems-based assessment provides an excellent basis for making appropriate clinical decisions about the relative usefulness of individual, couples, family, multifamily, or self-help group interventions. I like to consider such an assessment the hub of a therapeutic wheel from which various individual needs can be addressed in an integrated manner and in relation to the impact on the rest of the system.

As discussed in chapter 4, open, sensitive, and age-appropriate communication among family members is essential for successful adaptation to illness and disability. The relative need for communication about practical or affective issues will vary according to the psychosocial demands of the disorder over time.

Individual and family interventions

Questions about how to balance individual needs, especially those of children, with those of the family unit naturally arise. Within a systems orientation, this becomes a both/and rather than an either/or issue.

Optimally, an initial consultation should be flexible enough to include time with the whole family, an adult couple, and/or individual members. There is no substitute for getting a picture of the entire system. Understanding patterns of communication, particularly concerning illness-related issues, is vital. Deciphering patterns of protection—an affected member, aging parents, or children—is important in an assessment. Because patterns of protection and secrecy are so common, I routinely allow, and may require separate time for each family member. For couples, certain issues related to shame or guilt (see chapter 10) may be best addressed separately first. For example, a woman coping with issues related to self-esteem and body image after a mastectomy may be more comfortable revealing her concerns in an individual session before she is able to share them with her spouse or other family members. Also, some conversations, such as intense anger toward a dying, fragile, or cognitively impaired family member, may be more appropriately dealt with in individual sessions.

Clinicians need to be aware that any decision to advocate an individual intervention has to take into account the potential long-term consequences for communication patterns within the family. In chronic disorders, especially those involving threatened loss, there is a natural tendency toward protective and secretive communication. Particularly with children, encouraging them to open up in individual sessions may be adaptive in the short run; but if there is no attempt to foster open communication within the family, a child may use this experience of private communication as a model for the future in relation to illness; and over time, this can lead to an emotional cut-off from one's family of origin.

In one instance, individual sessions with a sibling in the crisis phase of her brother's diagnosis of cancer, when her parents were at the hospital almost constantly, helped at the time, but served as a framing event that generalized to not discussing any concerns directly with her parents. This pattern of holding back because of her ill sibling led to strong resentment against her parents and her brother (who survived) that became overt in destructive behavior early in adolescence. A family session could have demarcated the end of the crisis phase and affirmed the need for direct communication between the girl and her parents.

Clinicians need to recognize the additional strains in single-parent families. Single parents do not have another adult at home to provide validation and support of their efforts to cope with the physical and emotional needs of an ill or disabled child. In such families it is especially important to invite the participation of extended family or significant friends in sessions since they may represent an essential part of the caregiving network. In some ethnic groups, such as Italian or African-American families, use of the extended families is common; in other cultural traditions, the extended family is an untapped resource.

Skews in adaptation

The natural rhythm of coping and adaptation in families facing chronic disorders is often skewed. This is partly because of family members' being at different stages of personal development and because of variations in the pace of their adaptation according to the psychosocial demands associated with their roles in the caregiving system. When family members are helped to understand these inherent skews, sensitive communication appropriate to the developmental abilities of children is enhanced. Also, patterns of adult members being in and out of sync with one another is normalized. Different family members may need to process parts of their experience according to their own time schedule. Permission to develop and utilize one's own coping mechanisms is crucial, and for this, individual sessions can be extremely useful.

The psychosocial typology and illness time phases can help clinicians understand how these skews are manifested. For instance, when a child suffers a traumatic brain injury, the skew between that child and the rest of the family is very sudden and immediate. In this situation parents may be overwhelmed by caregiving demands at a time when their other children most need support. When a child has a slowly debilitating condition or one with a constant course, such as cystic fibrosis or mild mental retardation, the discrepancy between the affected child and his or her siblings may become apparent only gradually and increase with time; this latter situation permits siblings a longer time in which to adjust to inevitable skews and losses. Preventive education is necessary concerning the expected psychosocial demands of the condition over time.

Typically, family treatment of illness and disability requires clinician flexibility in moving back and forth between different family configurations and individual sessions. Sometimes meeting with members of each generation separately is useful, for example, with a sibling group when a parent or sibling is ill or disabled. When a parent is seriously ill, siblings may form a primary support network so as not to burden further either parent especially the well parent, who may be the primary caregiver. In this case meeting with the siblings separately may uncover a rich network of communication that is hidden when the parents are included. Such sessions can promote bonds of support and caring among siblings and reduce competition and loneliness.

Multifamily groups

Multifamily group approaches are very helpful for families facing chronic disorders. This form of intervention was first used as an adjunctive treatment for young hospitalized adults (Laqueur, 1980). Developments in its technique and format have taken two directions: first, a short-term structure has evolved that can vary from a single, day-long workshop (Anderson, Reiss, & Hogarty, 1986; Falloon, Boyd, & McGill, 1984) to a specified number of meetings, such as six to eight; and second, an educational component has been added to a purely psychotherapeutic format. A modular, time-limited arrangement is particularly useful in a wide range of chronic physical and mental disorders (Gonzalez, Steinglass, & Reiss, 1989).

The group context provides opportunities for families to learn from other families and gain support in trying out new adaptive patterns of relating and coping. Family members can identify with the experience of their counterparts in other families, gain a perspective on their own crisis situation, reduce guilt and blame, and feel less stigma and isolation with regard to their problems. The mutual support of the group makes changes in family relationships less threatening, and allows families that are isolated to establish support networks that may extend well beyond the group sessions. This is particularly important in disorders such as AIDS or conditions involving disfigurement, in which stigma can foster extreme family isolation.

When our center first proposed forming a family support group for AIDS, the medical team and I were very concerned about families' being reticent to discuss their problems openly. We prepared for this possibility by designing some "warm-up" communication exercises to facilitate the group process. We were completely surprised when, within the first ten minutes of the group session, a family involving a gay man and his Irish Catholic police officer father began to discuss issues related to terminal care and the rest of the group was immediately supportive and shared their own similar concerns. For many of these families, this was their first chance to discuss dealing with AIDS, and making good use of their limited time together was essential.

Sometimes multifamily support groups can empower families in their struggles with other systems. In one situation, a time-limited group was offered to families coping with occupationally related respiratory diseases resulting from chemical sensitivity. Many of the cases involved litigation with previous employers concerning who or what was responsible for the condition. These families often felt isolated and rejected. At the last meeting of the psychoeducation series, the group decided to form an information, advocacy, and self-help network for themselves and other similarly affected families throughout the state.

Ongoing multifamily or couples groups are useful alternatives or adjuncts to other types of treatment. This is particularly true in dealing with the constant, inevitable, biopsychosocial strains involved in progressive, relapsing, and life-threatening conditions. As described in chapter 3, multifamily discussion groups can be organized according to the psychosocial type and phases of illness. Bringing together families coping with conditions with similar psychosocial demands promotes a sense of group identity and coherence. Designing brief, psychoeducational modules that are timed with key phases in the illness and address phase-related developmental challenges guides families in mastering issues in a sequential fashion. By giving priority to manageable segments of an overall process of coping and adaptation, this approach helps prevent feelings of being overwhelmed.

I have found very useful sequential use of a time-limited psychoeducational module followed by on-going weekly or monthly multifamily group sessions to address continuing family strains from a disorder in the chronic or terminal phase. For instance, in one oncology service, a multifamily orientation group is formed every few months for families in the crisis phase following a recent diagnosis. This series of four meetings is designed to inform families about salient issues related to cancer, including: understanding themselves as a system; learning about key tasks in the crisis phase and how to think about cancer in relation to family, couples, and child development; effective methods of problem solving; communication of emotional issues; learning to live with uncertainty; available community support services; and guidelines on when to seek professional help. The first meeting includes the oncologist to help families understand the illness, its treatment, and the common psychosocial demands of living with cancer.

After completing this orientation series, families have a number of options. Some families or particular family members identify issues they want to address in individual, couples, or family sessions. Others enter individual or family support groups designed to deal with issues related to the chronic phase.

Multifamily groups can be designed more flexibly, so that families can use the group as needed, have invited speakers to discuss specific topics, and so on. Groups may offer different meetings for specific subsystems, such as couples, siblings, and well partners. A recent national development has been the formation of the Well Spouse Foundation, which offers self-help support groups for well partners (Strong, 1988). Another group, run in conjunction with a hospice program, is intended for families dealing with terminal illness and issues of bereavement following a wide range of fatal conditions.

In general, multifamily groups are cost effective; they provide flexible, long-term continuity of care at regular intervals or at nodal stress points and offer a valuable alternative or adjunct to traditional psychotherapy.

Chronic Disorders in Childhood

One of the most difficult of all human experiences to accept is serious illness or disability in the young. The profound sense of loss and unfairness inherent to this experience makes it one of the most challenging for families to master. Chronic illness and disability are very common in childhood and adolescence, affecting a reported 10 to 15 percent of children (Pless & Perrin, 1985). This translates into a figure approaching 8 million. As Joan Patterson (1988) has written, "With advances in medical technology, children who are born with illnesses such as cystic fibrosis or hemophilia or acquire conditions such as leukemia or end stage renal disease are living into adolescence and adulthood" (p. 71). This good news comes with additional psychosocial burdens that must be borne chiefly by families (Roberts & Wallander, 1992).

When a child develops an illness or disability, the family experiences certain basic challenges, including:

- The need for parents to keep the child safe often conflicts with the affected child's needs for increased autonomy.
- The child needs to be integrated into his or her own peer group and be allowed to play in ways that are age-appropriate and consistent with reasonable safety.
- Affected children need to be encouraged to take an increasingly major role in their own care. Because parents often develop a sense of pride and self-worth through caring for an ill child, as the child becomes more competent, the parents may experience some sense of loss. In this regard, parents often need permission from professionals to tend to their own adult needs and relationships.
- When parents have significant strains or conflict in their relationship before a child's health problem becomes known, attention to those issues may be displaced by focus on the affected child, which increases family dysfunction.
- Ill and disabled children need to be reassured about their intrinsic value

and guided to develop life cycle goals that promote self-esteem, hopeful-ness, and a positive sense about future possibilities.

- Families, out of necessity, must learn how to interact and assert them-selves effectively with many other systems within the broader social ecology that may be discriminatory or inadequately structured to deal with the special needs of ill or disabled children, their siblings, and par-ents (Kazak, 1989). Important examples include: school, work, and the legal systems.

CRISIS-PHASE ISSUES

Psychosocial typology

Diagnosis of a chronic disorder marks the beginning of a protracted jour-ney of grief and anticipatory loss, particularly for parents, who must mourn the loss of a physically healthy child. Education about the psychosocial de-mands of the disorder over time in relation to child and adolescent develop-ment can give parents a better sense of control. Progressive and life-threaten-ing conditions are the most taxing because parents have to live with the uncertainty of whether their child will survive to reach the next developmen-tal phase and, if he or she does, what the extent of his or her disability will be by that time and how it will interfere with specific developmental milestones. In a progressive condition, there is a natural collision course between a disor-der that imposes ever-increasing limits and individual development that nor-mally proceeds toward increasing independence. In a relative sense, a disor-der with a constant course, such as cerebral palsy, presents fewer ambiguities.

Because physical activity is so important in children's play, the disorders that are most disruptive are those that affect physical abilities and motor skills (for instance, cerebral palsy or muscular dystrophy) or involve defor-mities. These conditions inhibit a child's natural exploration and learning processes and limit the options for spontaneous play and creative expres-sion. In the short run, such disorders interfere with the formation of peer re-lationships more than do life-threatening diseases such as cancer. Other chil-dren may avoid the ill child because he or she cannot keep up with them or because they fear his or her differences; sometimes they ridicule a child with disabilities. In relapsing conditions, the affected child and siblings need reas-surance that a flare-up does not mean progressive deterioration or a life-threatening crisis.

Family beliefs

Family beliefs developed in the crisis phase are critical. The meaning given to the loss the illness entails has profound implications for the family's well-being. During this phase it is useful for clinicians to inquire about parents' beliefs and expectations concerning a normal child. It is important to help them think of a child with diabetes as just that rather than as a diabetic child, thus making an important distinction between physical disability in a normal child and the blemished identity of a completely abnormal one. This distinction is directly connected to acceptance of a condition as one aspect of the child's being and keeping that condition in perspective. When illness comes to represent everything about a child or a family, denial is more likely because the meaning of the illness becomes more devastating and total. The resulting attitudes ultimately are based on shame and set the stage for dysfunctional patterns of adaptation, especially in communication. The child's illness becomes a focus for resentment, guilt, blame, and hopelessness. When this occurs, parents may dutifully provide care, but on a deeper level give up psychologically and abandon the child. This fosters feelings of rejection, inadequacy, and being a burden in the affected child; and siblings may feel an abnormal obligation to please the parents to make up for their tragic disappointment.

Families that adapt best to a childhood disorder maintain a balance between the illness and the rest of family life (Beavers et al., 1986). Others may become dysfunctionally centered on the ill child, fail to meet the needs of other siblings, and thus delay or disturb normal life cycle development. Ideas about competency that are perfectionist and based on stereotyped ideals interfere with maintaining balance, and may need to be challenged. Success in meeting this challenge rests largely on families constructing meanings and narratives that are affirming and can become foundation stones in a long-term process.

The notion of keeping an illness or disability in its place (Gonzalez, Steinglass & Reiss, 1989; McDaniel, Hepworth, & Doherty, 1992) helps all family members continue to see the affected child as a competent human being with specific limitations and prevents extreme patterns of either denial of the illness or treating it like an "elephant in the living room." From a balanced position, parents can expect an affected child to meet reasonable developmental goals; to the extent possible, the child needs to be a contributing member to the family's daily life. This enhances the child's self-esteem and normalizes his or her sharing family responsibilities.

Gender issues

Under duress, gender roles can easily become more skewed. In dual-career families, a mother may sacrifice her job and possibly her career to stay at home to take care of an ill child. A mother's taking a few days off in an initial health crisis can easily develop into a long-term arrangement when discussion about future caregiving needs is bypassed. Added financial pressures, coupled with the fact that father can earn more per hour than the mother, may result in a pragmatic decision that has long-term relationship implications. Social policies that limit workplace flexibility regarding medical leave only exacerbate this problem.

Parental self-blame, especially in mothers, who are held primarily responsible for their children's well-being, increases the likelihood that patterns of overprotection will develop. To avoid self-blame, a parent may make unreasonable demands on his or her own time and energy. Parents are especially sensitive to professionals' comments that can be construed as implying neglectful behavior. One woman remembers the pediatrician's asking "Why didn't you bring Billy to me sooner?" as a condemnation of her as an inadequate parent responsible for her child's diabetes. As the result of this kind of framing event, a mother may come to see herself and her child as permanently inferior and abnormal, and this is a serious risk to normal parenting and child development. As discussed in detail in chapter 7 on belief systems, beliefs that involve parental guilt need to be addressed in the initial crisis phase.

When an infant or small child becomes ill or dies, both parents, but especially the mother, are extremely prone to blame and guilt. Because infants are so dependent and vulnerable, parental feelings of responsibility for them are at a peak during this phase of child development. Conditions such as sudden infant death syndrome that have no known cause easily prompt parents to wonder whose fault it was. Each parent may feel unlovable and unable to be loving toward his or her spouse at this time. Early intervention can help prevent the interminable grief and unending cycles of recrimination that contribute to the high divorce rate among such couples.

In one case, a family was referred because the mother was seen as being overprotective of her withdrawn, five-year-old son. The family background revealed that an older son had died of a high fever in infancy. The husband and his mother had blamed the wife, saying that if she had been more attentive, the deceased son would have received medical attention sooner and been saved. The beliefs expressed in this story resulted in the husband's withdrawing from the marriage and reestablishing closer ties to his family of origin, while the wife withdrew into her next pregnancy vowing to protect the replacement child, who was now symptomatic. In the face of a tragic and ambiguous loss, blaming the mother reflected a common, gender-biased reaction that filled a vacuum.

Control issues

One of the most painful aspects of the diagnosis of a chronic disorder is that parents have to cope with the loss of control of their ability to protect their child from physical harm and suffering. Families are challenged to redefine mastery and control in terms of a chronic condition. Clinicians can help families overcome feelings of helplessness by defining aspects of their situation that are controllable, such as information gathering and participating in caregiving. If the initial crisis phase requires intensive medical care in a hospital, clinicians should attempt to include parents in the caregiving process in any way possible so as not to exacerbate feelings of helplessness and inadequacy. Allowing a parent to remain in the room overnight and seeking advice about their child includes parents in the process from the beginning. The health-care team's displaying respect for parental knowledge and preferences empowers the parents and reduces chances of resistance and withdrawal.

COMMUNICATION

When beliefs about competency and normality can be sustained flexibly, then decisions about communication are less apt to produce tension. The situation is somewhat analogous to adoption: if adoptive parents see themselves as not the real parents and adoption as a negative life event, then shame-based patterns of secrecy may follow. Similarly, when a family can accept a child's illness or disability, then communication can be thought about flexibly, not in either/or terms, but in light of what is appropriate for the child's age.

A substantial body of research documents that children are aware of the seriousness of a condition at an early age. Although cognitive development affects children's ability to understand the nature and implications of a serious condition and the meaning of possible death, awareness is present and changes with development. Gerald Koocher and Bonnie McDonald (1992), reviewing the literature, emphasize how data show that children as early as age five have a real comprehension of the seriousness of their disorder; and even younger children display clear reactions to parental strain related to life-threatening illness, such as visits to an oncology clinic. Important research by Vernick and Karon (1965) has shown that children not only have an understanding of the seriousness of a condition but are eager to talk about it. Their reluctance to ask direct questions was found to be correlated with parental anxiety that had led to protective patterns of communication within the family, and the children's reluctance to talk openly was related to their fears about their parents' discomfort in discussing their disorder. In this regard, Kellerman, Rigler, and Siegal (1977) found an inverse relationship between depression and a child's open discussion of his or her illness with parents. Patterns of closed communication were associated with a heightened sense of isolation in children. Secrecy promotes children's fantasies, which typically are terrifying and lead to a profound sense of aloneness.

Fundamentally, I do not think children should be deprived of an understanding of their conditions. How a child understands cystic fibrosis and the level of detail he or she may need will change with cognitive maturation and encountering new developmental milestones. If a child has a disorder that has life-threatening risks that need to be avoided, to survive he or she must begin to deal with real issues of anticipatory loss from an early age. Death is not an abstract issue from which a child can be completely protected. There is no substantial evidence that seeing death or facing personal risks in childhood leads to pathological development. Murray Bowen (1976) commented that he never saw a child hurt by exposure to death, but only by the anxiety of other surviving family members. In fact, many of the most resilient adults I have met are those who had to cope with physical adversity in childhood. They grew up with an increased sensitivity to children who have personal struggles and to the fragility and preciousness of life that enhances their lives and relationships; they know that survival is possible during and in the aftermath of traumatic experiences.

Milton Seligman and Rosalyn Benjamin Darling (1989) have described how closed communication is a major risk factor when a child has a health problem. Often the affected child and siblings are curious; but parents discourage inquisitiveness, turning it into fear by deflecting invitations to answer questions and concerns. As they do regarding sexuality, children ask questions about chronic conditions when they are ready for an age-appropriate answer. One child with cancer asked his parents whether he might die. The parents response "No; you'll be fine" served more to protect parental fears about displaying their feelings than met the child's need to be protected. A response such as "Yes, it is possible; but the doctors have very good treatments for your cancer and are very hopeful" honestly acknowledges the illness by name, the possibility of death, but in a hopeful context. Families need to learn that avoiding the term *leukemia* is not helpful; others will use it, and saying it directly is not the same as saying, "You are going to die."

LIFE CYCLE ISSUES

Families coping with chronic disorders of childhood will find that the psychosocial demands of the condition will interact continually with normative psychosocial and cognitive tasks of development (Patterson, 1988). An illness and disability will take on new meanings as the child and family encounter each new developmental phase, with different psychosocial types of conditions creating their own unique pattern of challenge. A major therapeutic goal is to help families find a workable fit between normative developmental goals and what the disorder will permit at each phase of the life cycle.

A common difficulty for families is being able to distinguish normal developmental problems from those caused by an illness. For instance, age-appropriate rebelliousness and oppositional behavior are common in adolescence. At the same time, any chronic disorder can normatively cause anger and irritability that may be expressed in oppositional behavior. Some conditions, such as diabetes, can physiologically cause intermittent irritability and oppositional behavior as a consequence of hypoglycemia. It can be very confusing for parents to know how to interpret such behaviors and intervene properly. If hypoglycemia is the cause, then getting sugar into the child is essential. If irritability signifies trouble in coping with chronic illness, then addressing the impact of the illness on the child will be most helpful.

If the problem behavior represents normal developmental growing pains, then parents need to set appropriate limits. When oppositional behavior has a medical component, parents need to differentiate, to some degree, interventions with an ill child from those suitable for healthy siblings. The dilemma is that in many disorders, these influences are interwoven. Also, it is very difficult for some parents to relinquish control over the daily testing and necessary restrictions in the care of an illness like diabetes; their sense of their proper role in facilitating a child's development toward independence may have become clouded, and they may benefit from professional advice.

Defining reasonable goals

One of the most frustrating problems for parents is determining what are reasonable developmental expectations for a child with a chronic condition. It is useful to inquire into each parent's understanding of which developmental milestones and goals will be unaffected, delayed, subject to alteration, or unachievable. It is important to encourage parents to talk about their similar or divergent views and note how their perceptions dovetail with the professionals' beliefs. The psychosocial typology and time phases can provide professionals and parents with a common language for these discussions. It allows clinicians to frame future-oriented developmental questions that are relevant to specific disorders. For instance, in addressing parents and their teen-age daughter with cystic fibrosis, a clinician might inquire, "How do each of you think about Sally's plans after high school, given the possible complications of her cystic fibrosis? Is there anything you think she cannot or should not do?"

Often parents are aware of a complication that will affect a future developmental goal, and the question becomes if, when, and how to communicate it to the child or adolescent. In one case I had a consultation with parents of a five-year-old daughter who had been cured in infancy of a cancer near the pelvis (neuroblastoma). The treatment had required radiation of the pelvic region, which precluded normal reproductive development. When asked when and how they would discuss this problem with their daughter, the couple became very emotional and argumentative. One parent felt that the history of cancer should be openly discussed and that the daughter should be forewarned before adolescence. The other felt that she should not be told about her cancer experience and its complication, but left to discover her reproductive limits herself. They had never discussed this issue together. My own bias was toward openness; but at this stage it was essential, first, for each parent to express his or her position and feel understood before professional advice was given.

Developmental/psychosocial versus medical goals

In many conditions there are ambiguities about whether developmental goals can be achieved, to what degree, and what the physical consequences will be. Parents may differ on what are acceptable risks. Some illnesses, such as hemophilia, can worsen under stress and lead to a life-threatening recurrence. One adolescent boy had a nearly fatal bleeding episode while cramming to get good final grades so that he could be accepted to a more competitive university. His drive to succeed academically was motivated largely by his wish to please his father, to whom he felt he had been a disappointment because of the physical limits imposed by his illness. Decisions about whether a child should be involved in such activities as sports can be highly conflictual. One parent may adhere to a somewhat conservative philosophy while the other may believe in "going for it" despite moderate risks. Some disorders, such as hemophilia or severe asthma, require strict limits to achieve medical control. In these situations there is a tendency for parents to be too permissive in setting limits on other behaviors because they want to compensate for the necessary illness-related losses the child must endure.

Parents with chronically ill children must constantly consider the psychosocial quality of life both in terms of acceptable medical management of the condition and normative developmental tasks; often one must be compromised for the sake of the other. Accurate biomedical information about the course of the illness and the risk factors involved is essential in weighing pros and cons. Ambiguities about what activities can make a disorder worse can fuel intense, conflictual family interactions. As part of an initial assessment, it is always important to ask all family members—adults and children—their understanding of risks. When appropriate, clarification from a health professional may be sought. The psychosocial typology and time phases can provide a tool for families and professionals to think together about such dilemmas. Parents often set aside their own developmental needs because of a perceived or actual necessity to be the daily supervisor of the child's health. This leads to poor self-care for the adults, including neglect of the marital relationship and, sometimes, job and educational needs.

This tendency highlights the need for respite from care in the more severe childhood disorders.

Whether, and how, to include children and adolescents in deliberations about balancing medical management and psychosocial development is an important question. Adults are considered mature enough to make decisions about various trade-offs as they affect the quality of life. Children, at any age, deserve explanations about parental decisions. Actual participation in the decision-making process is more complex, particularly with adolescents. When autonomy and independence are central developmental tasks, a chronic disorder can seriously impede the natural movement toward independence. Generally, when children have been overprotected, they respond in adolescence either by remaining fearfully dependent or by vigorously defying parental control. When parents have established a pattern early on of including chronically ill children in discussions about the illness, then in adolescence a more natural, less reactive, gradual transfer of decision-making authority can occur.

Autonomy and control in adolescence

Children can learn to use their condition to manipulate parents and siblings. This is especially true for conditions that can have life-threatening crises and are very responsive to emotional factors. Many children with asthma describe how they can induce an attack. Adolescents with diabetes can threaten not to take their insulin injections, disregard dietary restrictions, or claim to forget them, with immediate and dire consequences. Such behaviors are a powerful way to express anger about having to cope with a chronic condition or to try to take control. Adolescents with diabetes can hold their parents hostage, using their illness as a weapon. Clinicians can help families sort through the multiple issues being communicated through such behaviors.

Heightened feelings of ambivalence about autonomy and control versus dependence are inevitable when a chronically ill child reaches adolescence. Adolescents have a great need to be like others, to belong to a desired peer group, feel powerful, and develop "dreams" about their future. These issues pose a developmental challenge because fears related to anticipatory loss surface. Normal cognitive development enhances the adolescent's ability to look into the future and contemplate loss (Piaget, 1952).

In life-threatening conditions, such as cystic fibrosis, denial and an attitude of invincibility may represent a defense against feelings of despair. An adolescent with diabetes or cerebral palsy experiences normal life dreams through a lens of possible future health complications and the limits imposed by disability. Fears about living independently, infertility, sterility, and genetic transmission that may affect possibilities for intimacy and a family life often emerge. These concerns need to be clarified and adolescents helped to modify either/or thinking and develop positive alternatives when necessary. Denying the need to take one's insulin or follow a diet can indicate a wish to deny the illness and all its possible ramifications for the future. Self-destructive behaviors can reflect fears about being unable to take care of oneself because of the chronic illness. Acting out is one way an adolescent can express ambivalence, since it forces parents to monitor health behaviors more closely and apply stronger limits.

Parents' reactivity to an oppositional adolescent can represent their own anger about the lack of appreciation for their tireless efforts to help the child master his or her illness. The adolescent can interpret these normal feelings as signs of being a burden and a disappointment to his or her parents. In a vicious cycle, this can further fuel self-destructive behavior. The situation is further complicated by adolescent tendencies toward impulsive, immediate gratifications, difficulty with a long-range perspective, and peer pressures for risky behavior. In adolescents with a progressive or life-threatening condition, these normative features of adolescent behavior can be taken to extremes because of underlying feelings of despair about their future. All family members need affirmation and, when possible, normalizing of their struggle at this stage of the life cycle.

In cases that present in this way, clinicians need to be cautious about blaming parents for faulty child-rearing patterns of overprotection or inadequate limit-setting. Often in life-threatening disorders, the family may have had early almost fatal experiences with a child that sensitized them. Health professionals may have reinforced a cautious approach in the crisis phase without considering the psychosocial impact over the long haul. And, in genetically transmitted disorders, such as hemophilia, multigenerational legacies of traumatic loss may underlie beliefs in the need for protection. When there are ambiguities about appropriate caution, a family consultation with the primary physician can be extremely helpful in establishing suitable limits.

The transition to early adulthood

The transition to early adulthood is a major crossroad for all family members. Often there is a powerful resurgence of issues related to anticipatory loss and unresolved problems relating to blame, shame, and guilt. Limits, unrealistic hopes, and issues of permanent dependence come to the fore in the context of the major developmental tasks of this phase, which include: emancipation from parental controls, leaving home, and setting up a first independent life structure in which the "center of gravity" shifts from the family of origin to a new home (Levinson, 1978). A realistic appraisal of independent living must be made. The possibility that a young adult will be permanently dependent and need family support raises developmental challenges for the parents, who typically look forward to the time when child-rearing demands are over and individual or couples' goals can be pursued more freely.

All family members can experience tremendous ambivalence about this phase. The late adolescent may feel a need to prove he or she can keep up with peers. Parents may want to protect the affected adolescent from experiencing limits and disappointment. The real letting go at this phase has more to do with letting adolescents assume responsibility for their own suffering, which they may have to endure while finding their niche in the world. Parental guilt at this phase represents a combination of several themes. One source, most commonly experienced by mothers, is resurgence of the former feeling that "This condition was my fault." Also, parents may define adequate child-rearing as producing a young adult who will experience no suffering in spite of illness or disability.

Siblings can feel guilt about the prospect of succeeding or surpassing their affected brother or sister. Developmental nodal points such as when a sibling leaves home, embarks on an independent life, or begins a serious intimate relationship can arouse such emotional reactions. In some instances siblings and parents may block their own achievement or abandon their own life ambitions out of "wellness" guilt or an attempt to protect the impaired child from emotional pain. Parents' overcoming their feelings of blame, shame, and guilt will help healthy siblings and the affected adolescent move ahead in their own development. Optimally, realignment of the old parent–child relationship will maximize the adult child's ability to assume authority and responsibility for his or her own well-being.

ISSUES FOR SIBLINGS

Particularly in life-threatening and disabling disorders, siblings can easily become forgotten family members. Resentment about not receiving as much attention as an ill sibling, guilt-ridden fantasies about how they might have wished or even caused their brother's or sister's condition, fears about the death of the affected sibling, and/or concerns about their own or their parents' vulnerability are just a few of the common experiences of healthy siblings that require therapeutic attention (McKeever, 1983).

Stoneman and Berman (1993), in a thorough review of research on the impact of childhood illness and disability on sibling relationships, found mixed results. Some studies report a range of individual, peer, family, and school-related problems (Breslau, 1983; Cadman, Boyle, & Offord, 1988; Tritt & Esses, 1988; Wood et al., 1988). Others cite positive influences on such variables as self-esteem, resilience, assertiveness, and family closeness (Daniels et al., 1986; Harder & Bowditch, 1982; Tritt & Esses, 1988). Daniels and co-workers (1986) listed increased family cohesion, an expressive family environment, and the health of the mother as being associated with better sibling adjustment.

Younger siblings, in particular, usually need information and support with regard to their most basic questions:

1. How did my brother or sister get ill?
2. Did I have anything to do with causing it?
3. Will this happen to me, or someone else I care about (parents, teachers, close friends)? Is it contagious?

Like adults, children adapt best when they can develop narratives that promote a sense of competence and mastery. Direct and clear information and supportive reassurance from parents are the best preventive medicine for well siblings. Because of embarrassment, conditions that have visible symptoms are usually the most disturbing to siblings.

Guilt

Especially when working with younger children, it is important to elicit any magical fantasies so that they can be explored and clarified. Siblings sometimes have beliefs that angry feelings toward a brother or sister caused the illness. This is particularly likely in situations of intense sibling rivalry or in families characterized by patterns of blaming during times of stress. One child said, "I gave my brother cancer when I kicked him during a fight." Such beliefs can cause feelings of guilt and a need to be punished that can be expressed as withdrawal, depression, suicidal ideation, self-destructive and aggressive behavior, declining school performance, and seeking punishment. These feelings can be reinforced by parents if they do not allow a child to express guilt feelings by being overly and too quickly reassuring. This reaction is often based on parents' faulty assumption that talking about the illness will upset siblings and encourage lingering unease. Avoidance of this kind can serve the function of protecting parents from stirring up their own self-blaming thoughts. When sibling guilt is not openly addressed, a child can harbor fears, such as of losing control of his or her anger and physically harming or killing someone.

Anger

Caregiving demands and parental preoccupation with the needs of an ill child are the most common causes of well siblings' anger. During the transition to the chronic phase, families need to review the pattern of psychosocial demands that can be expected. For instance, considering whether caregiving demands will be constant, periodic, or increasing can guide parents' discussion, given these realities of the illness, toward effectively balancing the needs of well siblings with those of the ill child. If there will be predictable periods of intensified focus on the ill child, parents can plan ahead to provide additional supports for the well siblings (for example, through grandparents or other members of the extended family). Also, they can plan special times that compensate for medically demanding periods, thus reducing feelings of discrimination. Sometimes well siblings become angry and feel rejected in the aftermath of a health crisis. Children need attention to reaffirm that they are important and that everything is all right again. Unfortunately, parents' exhaustion, depression, and financial pressures may undercut their ability to give quality time to their other children. Extended family members can be valuable resources, giving special attention to siblings and taking them for a day or weekend to give parents needed respite.

Disorders that require constant monitoring and are life-threatening affect siblings more powerfully, fostering more jealousy and conflict. Usually younger children experience the greatest role asymmetry in relation to each other, and this gradually diminishes as they become older. The reverse is often true when one sibling has a disabling chronic disorder: then the discrepancy between them grows and becomes more apparent as they pass each developmental milestone.

The willingness of siblings to accept from and give care to each other can become an increasing source of conflict as they enter adolescence. The desire for independence can make both siblings resentful about these roles. Natural adolescent concerns about body integrity and image can heighten fears about vulnerability for the well sibling and humiliation for the affected sibling when they need to interact in giving and receiving care. Parents often do not realize these complexities and assign increasing caregiving responsibilities to well siblings as they get older because of greater trust in their maturity.

Sometimes guilt and anger merge. Particularly in situations in which a child has a serious disability, such as mental retardation, or dies, as from leukemia, a well sibling may be designated to make up for the loss. A family's inconsolable grief can become displaced in a romantic fantasy of heroic proportions to be lived out by a sibling. This is a tremendously burdensome task that can never be fulfilled.

A highly competent pediatric resident entered therapy with intense feelings of guilt and anger toward his mentally retarded brother and his parents. During the initial visit he exclaimed, "No matter what I do, I never feel I can do enough to make everyone happy." This family situation was compounded by his father's seeing the disabled son as a source of shame. The other son's career choice, to become a pediatrician, was motivated partly by his deep desire to overcome his own guilt and shame by rescuing other children with chronic disorders. Sessions with his family of origin helped enable him to experience feelings of self-worth and accomplishment in his personal and professional life.

Somatic preoccupations

A sibling's illness shatters children's myths that serious health problems and death happen when a person is old; they lose a sense of immunity. Siblings often develop fears or phobias that even the smallest symptom may be serious. Parents can counteract this tendency by giving clear explanations of the affected child's condition and differentiating it from the usual acute childhood illnesses. Also, children can develop negative attitudes and fears about doctors and hospitals. Often this is compounded by having overheard parents' complaints about the physicians caring for the affected child.

Well siblings may develop somatic complaints, such as sleep and appetite problems, headaches, and abdominal pains. Typically, these represent anxiety about becoming ill. Often such complaints coincide with changes in the status of the affected child's disorder. In some families somatic symptoms may become a dysfunctional way of expressing a need for attention. A well sibling may feel that physical complaints are the only valid form of currency that can compete with a chronic disorder. The following case illustrates this point:

Mr. and Mrs. C. presented with behavior problems in their 12-year-old daughter, Sue, who had severe asthma and crippling juvenile rheumatoid arthritis that required the use of crutches. Sue's asthma was volatile and had resulted in increasing visits to the emergency room over the past year, including two life-threatening episodes. Mrs. C. had chronic back problems that flared every few months, necessitating days or weeks of bedrest. Mr. C., who worked at a desk job, had chronic bronchitis and emphysema that limited his energy and ability to do more than basic household chores. The couple had a chronically conflictual relationship, in which physical complaints were regularly used during disagreements as a lever to gain control and sympathy. Their 7-year-old son, Jimmy, was presumably fine.

During the initial assessment, I asked Jimmy, who had been very quiet up to that point, how he got attention with all these serious physical problems in the family. Jimmy got up, grabbed his sister's crutches, and demonstrated how well he could use them. His parents confirmed that during periods of family stress, he would take the crutches and walk around the house and neighborhood using them in front of the rest of the family; this usually coincided with conflict between Mr. and Mrs. C. or with Sue. Jimmy then said, "If things get really tough, I do this." He went to the center of the room on the crutches, feigned extreme pain (like his mother's), dropped the crutches while grabbing his throat with both hands as if gasping for air and coughing (like his sister and father), went into a dramatic "death twirl" such as he had seen in the movies, dropped to the ground, and lay motionless.

This case highlights the power physical symptoms can hold in family life. Jimmy as a small child had learned how to get attention, gain control, and deflect conflicts between other family members by means of physical symptoms. Without adequate family communication, his tactic also provided him a way to try and master his fears of becoming ill or disabled.

The timing of this particular crisis coincided with the ill daughter's entering adolescence. This life cycle transition was superimposed upon unresolved family problems, including struggles for control over physical problems, power issues among family members, dysfunctional communication patterns, and parental conflict and exhaustion. Often a well sibling, like Jimmy, will protect parents by hiding his or her own feelings or distracting them by acting out. Healthy children sometimes feel excluded from the family and different because they do not have physical symptoms. In response, they develop somatic complaints as a way to get attention. Frequently this is not a conscious process, and may be resistant to change.

TRIANGULATION PATTERNS

Salvador Minuchin, Bernice Rosman, and Lester Baker (1978) have reported how, in childhood psychosomatic disorders, a vulnerable child can become triangulated into unresolved conflicts of other family members, most notably parents. They describe *detouring* triangles, in which parents, to avoid addressing marital discord or dissatisfaction, band together to protect a vulnerable child or attempt to control disruptive, problematic behavior. Families also form *cross-generational coalitions*, in which an ill child and a parent form a mutually overprotective alliance against or excluding the other parent. In a dysfunctional family, an ill child provides a focus that stabilizes the system. A circular pattern of interaction develops in which the child both acts and reacts in order to maintain the child focus of the parents and thus protect them against having to deal with their own adult developmental issues.

In a previously functional family, if the mother is designated the sole primary caregiver, such a cross-generational coalition may be formed. When there has been no parental negotiation about the implications of this caregiving decision, it can foster strong resentment, particularly in disabling conditions. Over time, this family's dysfunction whose difficulties stem from faulty structural and communication patterns in response to the illness, can become indistinguishable from a family with long-standing preexisting dysfunction. Preventive intervention is useful in both cases.

Parental Illness and Disability

When a parent in the child-rearing phase of the life cycle becomes ill, many of the issues described above will be similar. Here I will focus on the impact of a parent's illness on children. Chapter 10 will address challenges for couples in which one partner has a chronic condition.

COMMUNICATION

Ill parents struggle over how much, if anything, their children should be told about their condition. Obviously, in visible disorders (for example, spinal cord injury) or when home treatments are noticeable (home dialysis), some form of explanation is unavoidable. One case dramatically illustrates how unqualified reassurance and blocking of further communication about a major illness can cause serious emotional problems in a child, which may assume the form of symptoms that are ascribed to something completely unrelated.

Mrs. L. called the child psychiatry clinic, concerned that her daughter, Janice, aged 5, had been compulsively masturbating for the past three months, and that this was an indication of sexual abuse. When the child assessment revealed no evidence of abuse, the therapist inquired about other recent stressful events in the family. Only at that point did the mother reveal that her husband had had most of his stomach removed nine months earlier because of stomach cancer, and that three months earlier, he had been rehospitalized for further tests that proved inconclusive. When Mrs. L. was asked what the children had been told, she reported that, after her husband's surgery, they had told the children only that, "Daddy had a tummy ache, so the doctors removed Daddy's stomach so he'd feel better."

The therapist then inquired whether Mrs. L. was concerned about her husband's health. She replied, "Of course, I think about it constantly!" The therapist then asked if they ever talked together about these concerns and if they would like to come in together to discuss them, to which Mrs. L. replied, "He won't come in. After the surgery he was adamant that he did not want ever to talk about it. He went back to work almost immediately, and has insisted that everything is fine."

The clinician asked Mrs. L. if she thought this medical crisis had had any impact on the children, especially Janice. Mrs. L.'s response was, "Well, she doesn't tell me about any worries. But now that you ask, at dinner every night, when we say grace, Janice prays out loud for Daddy's stomach." No one in the family ever commented on this.

The therapist then suggested to Mrs. L. that her daughter's compulsive behavior might be her way of expressing her worry and confusion about her father's "stomach problem." She commended Mrs. L. for her desire to respect her husband's wishes about not discussing his cancer, but felt that her daughter's behavior signaled a need for more communication in the family. She coached Mrs. L. to communicate to her husband that the therapist wanted to talk to both parents first so that they could decide together on the best way to keep their children informed about their father's condition. With communication opened up, the daughter's symptoms resolved rapidly.

The therapist later revealed to her supervisor that she had resisted the supervisor's suggestion to push for inclusion of the husband because her own husband had been diagnosed with cancer two years earlier and had made it clear that he did not want to discuss it. This highlights the need for clinicians to be mindful of presenting problems that may represent isomorphs of past or current concerns and communication patterns in their own families.

This case highlights the uncanny ability of children to sense danger and threat of loss despite secretive communication. Ill parents need to confront their own vulnerability and despair about the possibility of not seeing their children to adulthood. A spouse, unable to express his or her own fears of loss, may project that worry onto a child through overprotective behavior. One must not underestimate a child's resilience and need to hear about, understand, and come to terms with adversity. Children need to know they will be secure. Blocked communication only fuels anxieties. When age-appropriate, open communication is established, parents can inform children about realistic and exaggerated fears concerning a parent's condition. Catastrophic fears and fantasies held silently are far more destructive than realistic concerns that are aired and relieved by and with parents.

ROLES

Families coping with chronic conditions need to apply flexible definitions of normal involvement of children in caregiving and child-rearing responsibilities. Understanding the pattern of psychosocial demands of a condition over time can help parents decide on the realistic need to include their children in helping with caregiving and other family responsibilities. Flexibly moving in and out of such roles is greatly facilitated when the whole family understands the course of a disorder. In relapsing conditions, in which disability is intermittent, it is easier and less risky to assign responsibilities to older children, because the time frame of such role changes can be bounded by the duration of a flare-up. Knowing the timing of treatments and length of recovery reduces ambiguity and facilitates family caregiving that may involve children. In progressive, life-threatening, and severely disabling conditions, a parent's limitations are always present and increasing. In these situations, it is more likely that a lasting shift in role functions may occur and create a permanent parentified child. Conditions that involve cognitive impairment are perhaps the most difficult, because a child must witness a parent reduced to a childlike state. Sometimes, as in a fatal illness such as metastatic cancer, older children may adaptively need gradually to assume certain responsibilities to buffer the transition to life without one parent.

The key factor is how role shifts are determined and whether they are sensitive to issues of fairness and the competing tasks of a child's or an adolescent's development. Have parents realistically assessed the need for role reallocation? In two-parent households, have the parents first considered changing the balance of responsibilities between them? In families governed by strict and traditional gender-defined roles, this step may be bypassed. If a mother becomes ill, her responsibilities may be automatically transferred to the oldest daughter without first examining how father and brothers may do their part. If a father becomes disabled, an oldest son may feel pressured to drop out of high school and find work to support the family rather than see his mother take a job outside the home, to which Dad is now confined. In such situations, clinicians can facilitate parents' renegotiating rigid role definitions to meet the demands of a chronic disorder.

When children have to assume new responsibilities, families should be encouraged to discuss issues of balance, flexibility, and shared participation. Balance means that if a child needs to care for a parent, it is important for the ill parent to remain a parent to the child nonetheless. One mother with a spinal cord injury maintained her role as listener and advisor to her children despite needing extensive caregiving support from her husband and children. To the extent possible, added responsibilities should be shared equitably among all family members. It is important not to split role assignments so that one child is designated responsible and the others free of responsibility. Burdens should be shared and altered flexibly as natural shifts in demands on different siblings arise. This reduces the chance of resentment and promotes family problem-solving that will maximally preserve each member's individual developmental goals. Establishing time boundaries for added responsibilities, especially caregiving, can counteract a child's feelings of being trapped and permanently stuck in a parental role. In general, how well parents function as a model for handling issues of skew in their relationship is a strong predictor of children's adaptation to the same role issues (see chapter 10).

If grandparents and other extended family are nearby and healthy, they may be available to help. The inclusion of an ill parent's own parents needs to be carefully considered in terms of the rebalance of power this may imply. Such a solution may be inadvisable if it causes an adult child to feel infantalized, overly dependent, or dominated by a historically controlling parent, who may also be seen by the spouse as an intrusive in-law. On the other hand, it may provide a second chance to form a satisfying relationship if family members can rise to the occasion. One single-parent woman, in a year-long recovery from a serious accident, reluctantly allowed her mother to move into the household and cook and care for her and her children. This nurturing healed old wounds from having felt neglected in favor of her brother. Often adults are surprised that relationships can change dramatically in adulthood. When families consider this option, I encourage full discussion of the implications by the parents separately, between the parents and the grandparents, and by the entire family unit.

Crisis and rescue procedures

Children should be familiar with how to perform crisis or rescue procedures in an emergency. Frequently parents do not include children in these matters out of a desire to protect them and minimize anxiety. Often, this can have the opposite effect. One 7-year-old child whose mother had diabetes was terrified that he would be caught alone with his mother when she had a hypoglycemic reaction and might die while he stood by helplessly. In fact, this child had seen his mother, in an extreme reaction accompanied by an epileptic seizure, saved by an older teen-age son's intervention. The younger child needed to learn what caused hypoglycemia; how to give sugary foods; how, in an emergency, to administer an injection of glucose, which alleviates severe reactions; how to protect his mother if she had a seizure; and how to dial 911 and report a medical crisis. By comparison, most children with diabetes give self-injections by his age.

OTHER RISKS

Seriously ill parents need to be careful about certain risks in relating to their children. Those with life-threatening illnesses, in anticipation that they may suffer an untimely death, may push their children too quickly toward independence. Conversely, they may spoil a child out of guilt that they are not being good enough parents or that they will not be alive very long. This is especially common in disorders that require much self-care, so that the demands of the illness conflict with those of parenting. This may also occur when a parent's illness is hereditary and the affected parent experiences guilt because of the future suffering, like their own, that their children may have to endure. Parents may overprotect their children out of fears that the world is an unsafe place; this pattern is most likely when an illness or disability is seen as having been caused by neglect or a victimizing experience.

In single-parent and lower-income households, all these problems are greatly magnified. A single parent may use a child as a sounding board because there may be no one else available to talk with. Also, if disabled, a single parent will need to rely more on children to assume a wide range of responsibilities. In these situations, children are apt to be reluctant to burden a sole parent with their own needs and therefore suppress them. Children fear being orphaned by losing a sole parent. Thus, it is important to assess potential involvement and support by a noncustodial parent or member of the extended family.

In lower-income households, unbelievable financial strains may force an older child to drop out of school and go to work just to help the family survive. One second-grader, caught stealing food at a grocery store near school during lunch hour, said, " My mommy is sick and needs food, so I bring her lunch every day."

Aging Parents

One of the most common dilemmas for families involves caring for aging parents. It is always painful to witness a parent who once healthy and vigorous become frail and dependent. Conditions that cause mental deterioration or physical pain are perhaps the most difficult to bear.

Several trends in contemporary society have made coping with this problem a particularly difficult challenge. Because of advances in medical technology, many more adults are living into their eighties and nineties. As life expectancy has been extended, many more people in their sixties and seventies are still dealing with aging parents. Although most older adults remain healthy until advanced age, many others are living longer with chronic conditions that can be medically controlled much better than formerly. What this means is that all of us can expect to deal with aging parents for a greater proportion of our adult years.

Although only 5 percent of the elderly live in institutions, 86 percent of people in later life have chronic health problems that require increasing medical expenditures and family caregiving (Cantor, 1983; Zarit, Todd, & Zarit, 1986). These additional financial and caregiving demands often become the responsibility of adult children at a time in their lives when they typically have their own competing demands of child-rearing and financial pressures (for instance, the costs of college education). Moreover, intergenerational caregiving has become more complicated because of increased geographic distance and mobility compared with families in the distant past, who may all have lived throughout their lives in the same community.

Families function best when adult children and their parents have discussed wishes and expectations regarding caregiving. Normative filial obligation includes responsibilities toward parents in later life for both financial and caregiving support. Like wills, funerals, or advance directives, discussion of this anxiety-laden topic is too often avoided and postponed, though almost everyone has given it some thought. Optimally, the possibility of having to care for aging parents should be considered and openly discussed at various junctures in the family life cycle—for example, at the time a couple makes a long-term commitment and, particularly, when they embark on family planning; when children leave home; or upon retirement.

MULTIGENERATIONAL PATTERNS OF CAREGIVING

Multigenerational patterns of caregiving are important in terms of how loyalty is defined and shapes the models adults follow in thinking about their own family. After my mother had a stroke, I became keenly aware, for the first time, that my parents could become ill and die and that I was unsure of their expectations of me regarding caregiving. My own grandmother had lived with my family until her heart disease worsened and she moved to a nursing home; this happened when I was an infant. Growing up, I began to realize that this arrangement had been complicated. I wondered whether having an infant forced my mother to make a choice between her mother and me. I also wondered whether my father had felt that my mother's devotion to her mother and an infant left too little of her time and attention for him. As a young adult, only when my mother had a life-threatening illness, did I ask questions about my past and what would be expected of me. On the basis of their past experience with my grandmother, both my parents strongly preferred residence in a retirement or nursing home rather than moving in with and "burdening" me or my brother and our families. Our discussion clarified family stories about caregiving for aged family members in previous generations and decreased my anxiety about not knowing about preferences and expectations. It brought my parents into a larger group conversation that could include my brother, sister-in-law, and my nuclear family.

My personal experience highlights a common myth that older parents never discuss such morbid issues. Often adult children mistakenly feel that they need to protect their parents from such discussions. When this form of protection occurs, it fosters an often unnecessary role reversal in which aging parents are viewed and treated as childlike by their own adult children. This compounds caregiving burden by blocking open communication and creating anxieties and ambiguities about what the parents would want under different circumstances. When such myths are challenged, an open dialogue between generations is facilitated and a more balanced sharing of roles occurs.

Family traditions concerning the involvement of children and adolescents in caregiving functions are important. In many families in which a parent needs to provide care for a grandparent, an oldest child, usually a daughter, may be expected to keep the family from overload by tending to younger siblings. She may quietly accept such a role without resentment, following a tradition of self-sacrifice by women for the collective well-being of the extended family. Clinicians need to question this skewed arrangement when family well-being comes at the expense of self-sacrifice of any member or group, such as women.

For most children an aging grandparent is the first encounter with chronic illness, disability, and death. Eliciting memories of those experiences can help adult children recall the impact on the family and the roles played by grandparents, parents, their siblings, and themselves during that period. This can serve as a guide to decision-making about important traditions and aspects of the experience they wish to preserve or do differently.

ETHNICITY

It is important for clinicians to inquire about ethnic traditions. For instance, Italian families traditionally have strong intergenerational ties to families of origin. In many Italian neighborhoods, three-story homes are built to accommodate three or four generations. Houses are designed with the cultural understanding that aging parents will be attended to by the younger generation in the same home. In other ethnic groups, such as African-Americans, families may not live in the same household, but a rich and extensive network of shared responsibility among immediate and extended family members effectively supports the needs of aging parents. Family members may take turns phoning, visiting, or running errands for older adults.

Awareness of ethnic and multigenerational traditions can help clinicians distinguish normative patterns of caregiving from pathological disengagement and enmeshment. The United States is a very individualistic, youth-oriented culture that often devalues the older generations; but it is a myth that Americans do not care for their elders and dump them in nursing homes (Walsh, 1989a). Still, United States culture is very different from others, such as that of the Chinese, in which reverence for and devotion to one's elders are paramount. Understanding such cultural beliefs is essential for intervening skillfully with families struggling with problems related to aging parents.

GENDER AND CAREGIVING

Traditionally women have been primarily responsible for caring not only for their own parents but also their husband's. This long-standing role of women has become more complicated because of societal changes. Though an increasing proportion of women are entering the work force, there has not been a commensurate change in expectations that women will bear responsibility for child-rearing and caregiving of infirm parents. Women in the child-rearing stage of the life cycle often are expected to handle up to three full-time jobs: their employment, rearing children, and caring for their own and their husbands' aging parents. Problems of overload are inevitable unless men share these responsibilities more equitably.

Clients need to be helped to examine socialized patterns in which men are to be protected from pragmatic and emotional strains. Often an understanding has developed in the family, particularly between mother and daughter, that men cannot be relied upon or that they are incapable of nurturing. There is a tacit agreement that if the father becomes ill, the daughter will help the mother, and that if the mother becomes ill, the daughter will tend to her and then take care of the father if he is left alone. On the other hand, men may feel disproportionately strained by expectations that they will bear all financial burdens.

It is quite common for a woman to present for treatment of anxiety, depression, or physical symptoms when her spouse's parents become seriously ill. This is most apt to occur when the husband has no female siblings and expectations concerning caregiving fall on the daughter-in-law. In this situation it is important to convene both husband and wife. Asking couples how they decide caregiving roles and about patterns related to gender in each person's family of origin is a useful way to initiate a dialogue. Rigid, gender-defined rules may need to to be revised to avoid overload, resentment, and deterioration of a marital relationship. Sharing any caregiving burden is important. Similarly, if a woman becomes involved in skewed caregiving for her own parents, convening other siblings with the goal of sharing responsibility for the ill or disabled parents is a useful strategy.

DIFFICULT SITUATIONS

Families with small children

The most difficult situation occurs when a couple has small children at the time a parent's health declines. Despite increased life expectancy, this is common among people who have postponed childbearing or have children in a remarriage. Their own family life cycle demands a focus inward on the intense demands of child-rearing; but at the same time, a parent's decline from a disorder such as Alzheimer's disease may require extensive involvement with an increasingly dependent and childlike parent. The course of a progressive, dementing illness with a four-to-five-year prognosis conflicts with child-rearing demands that will probably continue beyond the illness. An unavoidable issue of limits will have to be addressed.

Pragmatic solutions may include home-based professional care, nursing-home placement, or shared caregiver responsibilities among siblings and other members of the extended family. Acknowledging limits to caring for one's own parents or giving higher priority to one's own nuclear family than to them can present an excruciating conflict of loyalties. A desire to repay an existential debt to one's parents in full measure (Boszormenyi-Nagy & Spark, 1973) may be unrealistic. Although parents may have borne the responsibility of rearing their children through to adulthood, it may not be possible for their adult children to care as extensively for them until their death. Almost certainly, it is not realistic if the responsibilities are loaded onto one designated caregiver; it may be more feasible, however, if all the adult siblings discuss and plan together how each can share the burden according to his or her abilities and limits.

The fantasy of being able to repay parents in this way needs to be tempered by the realities of certain types of disorders that may entail psychosocial demands incompatible with home-based care or other life cycle demands, such as child-rearing (Brody, 1974). Beliefs about what constitutes sufficient loyalty need to be addressed as part of a process of defining limits. Otherwise, any choice will risk arousing feelings of shame and guilt that may later find expression in interminable grief or self-destructive behaviors.

Not uncommonly, family strains involving an aging parent may remain hidden behind complaints or symptoms elsewhere in the system. A presenting problem will be defined as child- or adolescent-focused, when in fact an aging parent is the central issue. Regardless of the identified problem, inquiring about grandparents or aging parents is always useful, as the following case illustrates.

Ms. H., a single-parent with a full-time job, contacted the out-patient psychiatric clinic complaining that her 10-year-old son, Jim, was refusing to go to school and was difficult to control at home. The initial family consultation revealed that her son's problems began six months earlier at the time when Mrs. H.'s aging mother with advanced Parkinson's disease had moved in. Jim acknowledged that he frequently cut school and spent all day in his room, which was next to his grandmother's. Ms. H. tearfully described the overload of tending to her mother's advancing disease, which required around-the-clock attention. She felt especially anxious since her mother had developed serious balance problems and had fallen several times. Ms. H. worried and felt helpless that something terrible would happen to her mother while she was at work, and that she would not be there to assist. In this case, it became increasingly clear that Jim's truancy was intended to fill the gap at home and to alleviate scarce caretaking resources available for the grandmother.

A resented parent

A different dilemma occurs when an adult is resentful about caring for a parent who has been experienced as nonnurturing, absent, or abusive. Intense ambivalence may be present, and a parent's expectations of being taken care of may reawaken strong, negative feelings toward that parent. When feasible, a frank dialogue about old hurts may need to precede any effective caregiving. Clinicians should not automatically accept assumptions that it is too late, especially if a parent is seriously ill. Open discussion of forbidden topics and foregiveness may be important for the parent and the adult child, facilitating closure and reconciliation before death.

If this is not possible or is considered too threatening, clinicians need to respect such limits and empathize with the adult child's dilemma. When clinicians can understand not caregiving as an acceptable option, often the adult child feels that his or her pain is validated and can then participate at least in some limited manner. To one patient whose terminally ill father had been a physically abusive alcoholic, I said, "It must be incredibly difficult for you to imagine being around your father at all, let alone touching him."

Family enmeshment

Difficulties may also arise when there has been a history of enmeshment and an adult may have struggled many years earlier, during adolescence and early adulthood, to extricate himself or herself from a fused family. Such an adult child may feel a tenuous hold on his or her own autonomy and independence. The onset of a parent's chronic disorder that is disabling or life-threatening and requires caregiving can rekindle powerful fears of becoming reentangled in the family web.

In dysfunctional families the aging parent may elicit guilt by communicating feelings of abandonment or betrayal by an adult child who struggles with divided loyalties between his or her nuclear family and family of origin. This kind of situation is often accompanied by increased marital tensions for adult children and their spouses. Intense conflict, characterized by mutual blame and guilt, can ensue between an adult child and aging parents. Sometimes this can escalate into physically and verbally abusive behavior around caregiving interactions. Clinicians need to be mindful that intervention with these families may be very difficult because of entrenched protective patterns, rigid and sometimes impenetrable family boundaries, and suspicious views of outsiders.

Clinicians need to distinguish long-standing patterns of enmeshment from common situations in which overdependence has been fostered. Adult children may express fears associated with anticipatory loss by hovering over an aging parent and taking away role functions they are still capable of handling. Often this coincides with the parents' own anxieties, the healthier spouse taking over for the ill partner. This is most common in life-threatening conditions, particularly ones, such as a stroke, that have begun with a serious health crisis marked by disability and intensive care. Because of fear and uncertainty, crisis-phase needs can easily become permanent unless professionals confer with the family about changing risks or caregiving needs. Frequently, patterns of overresponsibility escalate, leading to vicious cycles of helplessness, burden, and resentment.

In some situations adult children assume polarized and extreme positions when an aging parent becomes ill. The following case poignantly demonstrates these tendencies:

Mrs L., a 70-year-old widow, was hospitalized with multiple somatic problems exacerbated by symptoms of early senility. She had two sons, Herb, age 44, and Tom, age 41. The sons reluctantly agreed to come in for a family interview. On the phone, Herb stated that, in his opinion, the hospitalization was merely a ploy for sympathy on his mother's part, an attempt to make him feel guilty for not being at her beck and call as Tom was. He said he had learned years ago that the best relationship with her was no relationship at all. In contrast, Tom, who had always been devoted to his mother since adolescence, had become increasingly responsible for her caregiving needs, particularly since her cognitive impairment had worsened. Yet the more helpful he became, the more dependent and helpless she became in managing her own life. At the point of hospitalization, Tom felt drained by his mother's growing neediness.

This case required two stages of therapeutic work. First, the overly responsible son was coached that he could be more helpful by challenging his mother to do more for herself. Herb, who was underinvolved, was asked to help his brother by taking on several specific, limited, caregiving tasks. Both sons were coached to communicate with each other and directly with their mother. They were warned that their mother might initially resist these changes, and that they would have to be patient and understanding. Mrs. L., seeing her sons cooperating, began to show significantly improved functioning.

The second phase of treatment involved a family life review technique developed by Froma Walsh (1989a). This approach "extends the process of reminiscence which promotes resolution of the tasks of acceptance of one's life and death, to include the perceptions and direct involvement of significant family members who are central to such resolution" (p. 321). In this case, using family albums and scrapbooks as a stimulus to elicit crucial memories, Mrs. L. and her sons were helped to explore and better understand emotionally laden and unresolved developmental periods in family life that were being reenacted as the mother's health had deteriorated. For instance, Herb and Tom's long-standing sibling rivalry was discussed and placed in better perspective.

Herb's cut-off became better understood in recalling that during his adolescence, as the oldest son, he had felt terribly burdened by having to help his mother take care of his father, who suffered from emphysema caused by chronic smoking. He had had an intense conflict with his mother, which he handled by leaving home angrily, severing contact, and vowing to protect himself by remaining self-reliant and avoiding entangling commitments. His relationship with his parents, which had become frozen in his early adult transition, could now finally be discussed. His brother, Tom, had become the good son who inherited Herb's job, faithfully helping his mother with caregiving tasks until his father's death, and then watching over his widowed mother.

Both Herb and Tom had remained single—Herb, because of fears of any relationship commitments, and Tom, because of his ongoing caretaking obligations to his mother. Everyone's anger at the father for smoking himself to death without considering the impact of his life-threatening illness on the rest of the family finally was "aired." Also, each member revealed feelings of guilt that they might have been able to stop him. Herb and his mother were able to see that their conflict had largely represented displacement of feelings that were not expressed directly to the father. Family therapy facilitated mourning together the loss of the father in the context of better understanding, reconciliation, and renewed caring among the surviving family members.

The last parent

When there is only one surviving aging parent, there is additional strain on adult children. Without the possibility of mutual support between spouses, it can feel harder to set limits on providing companionship as well as caregiving. This touches upon a powerful fear with which we can all empathize—of dying alone or in an institution without the presence of family members.

The terminal phase of an illness of the last parent can be particularly emotional for adult children. It signifies the death of the last member of the older generation, moving adult children for the first time into the senior position and making them the next to face issues of aging and their own mortality. This heightened awareness may cause symptoms of anxiety, depression, or sudden preoccupation about one's own health and mortality. Such concerns may find expression in the adult child's marital relationship in distancing or increased dependency needs.

With increasing life expectancy, many adults do not deal with aging parents until they themselves are past the child-rearing stage. Although they are less encumbered by the conflicting demands of rearing children, they may have their own health problems and reduced financial resources because of retirement. One man's own disability related to heart disease limited his capacity to help his aging mother, who had developed severe rheumatoid arthritis. Also, people beyond child-rearing age may have planned for a golden period of greater leisure and independence from the heavy demands of early adulthood, and an ill older parent can present an obstacle to such long-standing plans and become a source of resentment.

Institutionalization

When painful issues related to institutionalizing an aging parent surface, families often become emotionally stuck in either/or thinking. To reduce feelings of burden, clinicians can help orient families to a range of options and community services that may obviate the need for nursing-home placement. Often families are unaware of home and community-based services such as supervised apartment programs with medical backup, adult day care, senior citizens programs, Visiting Nurses Associations, and respite care, all of which can help maintain aging parents in their homes and communities. Informing families about and promoting linkages to these various community supports can instill a greater sense of hope and mastery and counteract feelings of fear and helplessness (Pinkston & Linsk, 1984).

This is particularly helpful to adult daughters, whose disproportionate responsibility for caregiving can leave them most vulnerable to blame, shame, and guilt when the specter of institutionalization arises. One woman with a demanding professional career and small children had to shuttle back and forth across the country to arrange simultaneously for her mother's nursing-home placement and changes and for her father's hospitalization and funeral. Here, having a supportive spouse who could flexibly step in and assume greater child-care responsibilities and support his wife was essential to coping with the various family demands. When feasible, using a child-care program can greatly reduce strain.

Timely family consultations that include aging parents early in an illness allow the whole family to weigh preferences and options together. This permits taking into account the strengths and limitations of both aging parents and adult children, sharing feelings and concerns, and arriving at solutions and decisions together.

CHAPTER 10

In Sickness and in Health: Helping Couples Master the Challenges

O NE OF OUR MOST important marriage vows requires us to care for a mate "in sickness and in health," yet most of us celebrating a wedding have little idea about what life together with an illness would mean. Chronic disorders can have devastating consequences for couples. To master the difficulties and complexities, they must maintain a viable, balanced relationship while caring for an ill partner and cope with the uncertainties of planning and achieving normative life cycle goals despite the threat of loss. A partner's serious illness or disability powerfully challenges couples' relationship rules and sacred boundaries. In this chapter the Family Systems–Illness Model will provide a base for interventions in common couples' problems regarding intimacy, sexuality, relationship skew, gender roles, and co-parenting.

Intimacy in Illness and Disability

All couples' intimacy functions within a comfort zone that evolves over their life cycle. Couples' dynamics determine whether this comfort zone allows intimacy to grow with the seasons of life or become constricted and erode. Like other life challenges, illness and disability offer both an opportunity for growth of the relationship and the risk of deterioration and distance.

The onset of a chronic disorder forcefully challenges the emotional and physical boundaries of a couple's relationship. The disorder is an uninvited guest that must be incorporated into the couple's lives. The psychosocial type of the condition will determine the nature and demands of this "intruder" and how it will develop and make its presence felt over time. A severe disability such as a spinal cord injury always has an effect on a relationship. A relapsing condition, such as disc disease, does so intermittently. Cancers in remission may not necessitate day-to-day pragmatic issues, but the undercurrent of threatened loss can nonetheless invade all aspects of couples' lives.

WHAT IS INTIMACY?

One of the difficulties in discussing intimacy is that it is an elusive concept that is difficult to define. Intimacy may have a variety of meanings for different couples and each partner depending on such factors as gender, culture, social class, and stage of the individual and couple's life cycle. For instance, in U.S. middle-class culture, intimacy is framed in terms of sharing feelings, interests, and friendship; for a working-class couple, however, it may have more to do with helping each other survive, sharing responsibilities, and mutual protection. Also, it is important to bear in mind that intimacy may be qualitatively distinct in different aspects of a relationship, such as the sexual, the spiritual, the intellectual, the recreational, and the professional.

Three central attributes of intimacy will help discussion of couples facing health problems. Lyman and Adele Wynne (1986) consider intimacy in terms of a set of processes, emphasizing the possibility for both partners to expose themselves in verbal and nonverbal ways, trusting that the other person will be understanding and not betray that trust. Second, Murray Bowen (1976) and Harriet Goldhor Lerner (1989) suggest that intimacy requires that each partner be able to maintain autonomy, with clear individual boundaries, and, at the same time, have the capacity to bring "the self" into the relationship. Third, as Katherine Weingarten (1991) has noted, each partner needs to be able to enter temporarily into areas of concern or interest of the other partner and thus participate in creating meanings together.

INTIMACY WHEN FACING LOSS

"There is no love without loss" (Lifton, 1975, p. vii). All of us must grapple with the fact of our own mortality and the realization that intimacy occurs in the face of eventual loss. Serious conditions confront both partners with a powerful reminder of these existential dilemmas. When we are young and in good health, we tend to minimize this reality and defer consideration of these issues until later. Our cultural avoidance of these basic facts promotes patterns of intimacy based on denial of illness and loss, romantically relegating them to later life and hoping for a peaceful death (Becker, 1973; Walsh & McGoldrick, 1991a).

Healthy coping with and adaptation to chronic disorders depend largely on a couple's willingness to address these basic issues. Often the diagnosis of a serious condition can heighten feelings associated with loss in such a terrifying way that couples either draw away from each other or cling to each other in a fused way. Couples adapt best when they learn to deal with these facts of life and use consciousness of them in an empowering manner so as to live more fully rather than constrain their relationship. They can learn to use the awareness that all relationships are time limited to live more fully in the present and enjoy what they have now despite imperfections, rather than postpone fulfillment based on an illusion of infinite time. Whenever I hear someone say, "I know I need to talk to him before he dies," I think, "If not now, when?"

We need to challenge beliefs that chronic disorders and threatened loss are associated only with negative emotions of terror, loneliness, and meaninglessness, and that well-being can be experienced only when chronic disorders can be avoided or denied. When we can forthrightly address these issues with couples, we instill in them confidence to face loss and enhance relationships. Couples that believe in their capacity to face loss together are best able to tackle all the practical and emotional issues of a chronic condition, including its ambiguities and uncertainties. In general, couples adapt best when they revise their closeness to include rather than avoid issues of incapacitation and threatened loss.

When a disorder is chronic, one of the main reasons both partners may try to distance themselves from each other is that the relationship becomes a constant reminder of the universality of loss. Being a caregiver, receiving care, or observing the visible signs of illness or emotional strain can become implosive reminders of loss.

When couples can broaden their experience of intimacy, they can improve the quality of life and help offset the dark side of illness and disability. Learning to live with limitations or a shortened life expectancy is humbling. Couples have an opportunity to reconsider what is really important and what is trivial. For instance, when a condition may compromise sexuality, couples adapt better if they can experience greater companionship. Couples in later life often make this change naturally. When younger couples can see that possibility not as a sign of old age but as the natural maturing of a good relationship, then they can explore new and deeper ways of sharing not as a consolation prize, but as something most younger people do not learn to appreciate until later.

Couples have an opportunity to reconsider what is really important and what is trivial. For instance, competitive strivings between partners can diminish as a couple sees rivalries as wasted energy that detracts from enjoying each other. One 35-year-old man disabled by a construction accident felt a tremendous sense of relief when he really accepted his limitations. On one occasion he exclaimed, "For the first time in my life, I'm letting myself enjoy my wife and family without turning everything into pressured competition.

I fought it like hell for a while, but I just couldn't make my body do what I wanted it to. When I finally could let go, I became a different person. I noticed possibilities I was blind to before. It may sound odd, but I feel healthier now than I did before my accident."

Clinicians need to help couples facing illness or disability consider specific dimensions of intimacy such as open communication about beliefs, desires, and off-limit topics. This process usually includes identifying and normalizing difficult feelings, establishing clear boundaries, and rebalancing common relationship skews.

COMMUNICATION

A long-term health problem and threatened loss present one of life's most powerful challenges to a couple's communication skills. Throughout this book, I have emphasized sensitive, age-appropriate, open, direct communication among family members about a range of issues that are intrinsic to living with chronic disorders. For families headed by a couple, the focal point and responsibility for effective communication reside in this relationship. The couple's comfort zone and patterns regarding openness will drive the rest of the system. Levels of personal disclosure that may have been functional before a disorder appeared often become inadequate. Discussions about living with threatened loss may represent new territory.

Important discussions for couples include: understanding the illness and its psychosocial demands over time; beliefs about who or what caused the disorder and what can affect its course; how to live with threatened loss; personal and relationship priorities; the roles of patient and caregiver; how to maintain a balanced, mutual relationship; and wills and directives concerning a possible terminal phase. One couple facing the husband's terminal cancer found the quality of their relationship enormously enhanced by early discussions about limiting life-saving efforts in the terminal phase. It gave the husband a sense of control over his death that reduced unbearable uncertainties and enabled him to focus his energies on living. It reduced fears for his wife about having to make life-and-death decisions without knowing his true feelings. To foster a balanced position, I always suggest that both partners discuss their desires, draw up a will, and so on. While acknowledging the immediacy of the ill partner's situation, one should minimize differences between the two and illusions that loss is a concern of the patient alone.

I propose that each partner discuss with the other any topics he or she thinks should be off limits, and why. Common reasons include: tentativeness about exploring new territory, concerns about hurting the partner or worsening the condition, or fears that the relationship will not survive openness in certain areas. If certain topics are going to be restricted, couples should consider the consequences and reach a mutual decision. Paradoxically, often this process of defining taboo topics helps dispel myths about acceptable limits. Couples need to appreciate that each partner may need to discuss important illness-related concerns at different times. Often this is problematic because the partner who needs to talk may be intruding on the other's period of mental respite, when painful conversations are purposely avoided. When both partners can share responsibility for initiating such discussions, stereotypes of "worrier," "spoiler," and cycles of pursuer-distancer are minimized. Sometimes helping couples establish a structured time and process for talking about these serious matters alleviates struggles for control about communication.

As is true for relationships in general, I do not advocate that everything should always be shared between partners: a functional balance is necessary. However, many couples enter treatment at later stages with problems connected to areas of communication that have been completely blocked or avoided since the beginning of the disorder. Most common are discussions about death and dying.

Not all thoughts need be communicated. Sometimes it may be functional for a well partner not to share a pessimistic belief concerning the anticipated outcome. In one situation, the husband, Paul, was fighting metastatic cancer. Although the physician had given the couple a one-to-two-year prognosis, Paul maintained a belief that he could beat cancer. His wife, Ann, believed he would die from it; but she confessed, "I never wanted to interfere with Paul's goal, so I kept my feelings that he was going to die to myself or discussed them only with close friends. When Paul became terminally ill and needed to accept the inevitable, we talked more openly." In situations like this, I think couples can have initial "what if" discussions about the future that can prepare both partners for what may come, particularly the well spouse, while permitting different outlooks on the probabilities.

Shameful thoughts and feelings are a major impediment to openness. Normalizing in advance that feelings such as irrational anger, ambivalence, death wishes, or escape fantasies are typical can help counteract secrecy, shame, and well partner/survivor guilt. Couples need to be forewarned that having intense and seemingly irrational emotions toward one's partner is natural in situations of illness and disability. The ill person may, in a moment of desperation or intense pain, wish someone else could be in his or her shoes. One woman with intractable pain shouted at her husband, "I wish you could feel what this pain is like for five minutes." At a moment of exhaustion and exasperation, a caregiver may exclaim, "I wish you would die already, so I can get on with my life!" Often, such thoughts are expressed in ways that under other circumstances would be labeled pathologically cruel. Most of us can allow such thoughts open expression only within our closest relationships. The biggest problem in these situations is that heightened emotions and reactivity are sometimes inevitable. Couples need to understand and forgive themselves and their partner for hurtful comments made in the heat of the moment.

Anger is universal for both partners living with chronic disorders. It should be expected that sometimes anger will be expressed in the relationship, overtly or covertly. Most people living with serious conditions will experience feelings of outrage at being victimized by the illness and fear losing control over their body or their life course. Unfortunately, these feelings can easily be directed at one's partner. Couples function best when they are able to tolerate such strong emotions from either partner without applying shameful or pathological labels. Both partners ought to feel entitled to have and express their own intense emotions. At the same time, they may need help in not becoming reactive to a partner's outburst. Clinicians can help couples redirect their anger from the partner to the illness. Externalization is helpful in this regard.

Some people are extremely fearful about feeling or expressing anger. This is common in someone who grew up with a history of physical or verbal abuse or whose culture values keeping feelings under control. A serious illness or disability can normally generate levels of upset well beyond anything such people have ever experienced in the relationship, and this can be terrifying. Clinicians can help such people differentiate normal outrage within the context of a chronic disorder from pathological anger or abuse.

Rebalancing Relationship Skews

When a serious illness or disability becomes part of a relationship, a variety of skews is inevitable. This section addresses some of the most common skews and ways that clinicians may intervene to help couples compensate for structural and emotional changes.

MY VERSUS OUR PROBLEM

When illness strikes, defining the problem as the exclusive domain of the patient will inevitably skew a couple's relationship. Most framing events foster a fundamental split between the patient and the well partner. The highly technological, medical focus on the patient's condition around the initial diagnosis and crisis phase promotes a definition of the problem as the ill partner's. Optimal couples' functioning depends largely on the willingness of both partners to challenge this fundamental assumption.

Facing and accepting loss should not be limited to the ill partner. It has never been limited to one partner and never will be. Because of his or her disability, the immediacy of loss may be heightened for the ill partner, but the well spouse faces many of the same dilemmas. There is no guarantee that the well spouse may not die first; no one can know or pick the moment of death (Wright & Nagy, 1993). A health crisis provides an opportunity for couples to face this truth. Paradoxically, a serious illness in which one partner is more physically vulnerable challenges this basic assumption. If living with illness or disability is defined without question as one person's problem, then all significant couples' interactions will become skewed by this premise, and their relationship will be an unequal one. As a result, negotiating issues of power and control can become increasingly dysfunctional and lead to resentment, guilt, distancing, and general erosion of intimacy.

One woman described how her relationship with her husband, who had had a serious, degenerative, neurological disorder had become more distant over the years. Finally, a marital crisis brought them back to basic beliefs that had been tacitly agreed upon in the initial crisis phase. She said, "We never really acknowledged the fact that Bill had a terminal illness. We never talked about the fact that I would die someday too, maybe before him. Because we never discussed these key issues, our relationship became hopelessly unbalanced. He felt entitled, and I felt it was my role to satisfy his needs. Only when our relationship came to the brink of collapse did we deal with these assumptions, which had guided our behavior for so many years. We needed to contemplate death together to reestablish our intimacy. Our last year together was our closest. So many problems could have been avoided if only someone had guided us early on." After their marital crisis, they asked her husband's neurologist why he had never urged them to talk about the life-threatening aspect of his condition. His forthright response was, "It was just too painful for me."

If the illness-framing event in a couple's relationship is defined strictly as "my disorder and my problem," it places the illness within the individual. This increases the risks of skew, enabling the affected partner to exert power and control through the role of sick person. If the condition is framed as a conjoint issue, then the psychosocial impact is defined in terms that acknowledge physical and psychosocial burdens and include the illness-related roles of both partners—patient and caregiver. Couples are more empowered when they can view their predicament in a balanced way as a relationship issue shared by both. This also helps counteract the dangers of triangulation discussed later, in which the disorder may be used by the ill member or caregiver as an ally against the partner concerning issues of control, entitlement, or sacrifice.

By introducing this concept of "our problem" early on, clinicians provide an opportunity for couples to examine cultural and multigenerational beliefs about the rights and privileges of ill and well partners. In one situation, a well spouse came from a family in which she saw her mother care for her father, who suffered from a chronic respiratory disease, and never ask anything from him in return. She and her sisters were instructed not to bother their father with their needs. For this woman, powerful multigenerational beliefs and scripts dictated extremely skewed gender-based role relations in which the burden on a daughter and/or wife of caring for an ill father or husband was never acknowledged: chronic illness belonged to the husband or father, and female family members adjusted to that fact. The psychosocial experience of all family members was clearly subordinated to the biological condition of the father.

ESTABLISHING HEALTHY BOUNDARIES

A major risk for couples is that their relationship will become completely identified with a chronic disorder. A key developmental task in the crisis phase is grieving the loss of life as normally led before the condition appeared. Part of this experience involves couples' acknowledging that their relationship will never be the same. Living with illness carries only negative meanings if this painful process becomes associated with an invasion of the entire fabric of the relationship by disability and loss, without possibilities for growth. When this occurs, couples' narratives become burdened with metaphors of decline and loss. Living a normal life is external to the relationship and illness is within it. Although this process becomes more apparent in the chronic phase, the difficulty originates with the framing assumptions about how a couple incorporates a disorder and defines boundaries.

Chronic disorders have an insidious tendency to become embedded in even the healthiest relationships. A major risk is that all interactions will become fused with the condition. Obviously, this becomes most difficult in disorders such as Alzheimer's disease or traumatic brain injury, in which cognitive impairment is always present and directly affects all interactions. This also characterizes life-threatening conditions, where fear about further loss persists (for example, following a heart attack). The risk is even greater in conditions that are permanently disabling, progressive, or require continuous care, such as chronic pain syndromes, multiple sclerosis, or a spinal cord injury. In these situations the disorder is ever present, demanding continual practical and emotional energy from a couple.

Creating limits is particularly difficult as couples emerge from a crisis phase that has been medically intensive and necessitated a period of immersion in learning about the condition. This is particularly true when the crisis phase was marked by a life-threatening onset or a protracted period of disability requiring partner caregiving. Couples tend to lose perspective about how and where appropriate boundaries can be established beyond these illness realities. Patterns initiated in this early period can persist unless reconsidered and updated.

To help counteract this split between couple–illness–decline–death inside the relationship and the world of health and normality outside, clinicians must help couples learn how to circumscribe the time and space occupied by the disorder in their relationship transactions. Often this requires help in learning to distinguish interactions that must explicitly include the disorder from those in which it can become a dysfunctional form of currency. This adaptive minimization needs to be distinguished from denial, which absorbs considerable psychic energy that compromises couples' relationships.

There are some simple strategies for keeping the condition in its place. Where possible, couples should arrange for times that are devoted to self-care and caregiving or discussing the illness and times that are preserved for other activities and discussions that do not become dominated by the disorder. Specific areas of a home can be off limits to illness-related functions. For instance, not discussing the illness in the bedroom can help preserve romance. Couples often stop inviting friends to their home because it has become associated with illness. They should be encouraged to socialize with friends in their home, to try and preserve parts of their home life that have been pleasurable and connected them to their wider social network. This helps counteract the tendency for what is normal to become associated with what is outside the home and relationship. In this regard, establishing clear caregiving boundaries within the home helps.

Couples need explicit guidance about when an initial life-threatening crisis has passed. Misinformation about perceived risks heightens the power that the disorder and associated anxiety will wield over a couple. For instance, in sudden-onset conditions such as heart attacks, a narrow escape from death requires an initial period of reduced stress (both emotional and physical) for the patient that infuses the framing event with ambiguity and fear. In a situation in which a life-threatening crisis can recur suddenly, couples tend to cling, in a ritualistic way, to medical advice originally intended only for a limited period of time. Freedom to talk about emotional issues or to express anger or sexuality is often blocked to avoid another life-threatening recurrence; if a couple needed distance before, this will reinforce it. Or, couples can unnecessarily sacrifice healthy patterns of relating for fear that interacting normally might kill the affected partner. One Italian couple dropped normal lively discussions about the wife's large extended family to avoid getting the wife, who had had a heart attack, too excited. Both the power of an initial life-threatening crisis and the insidious effects of slowly progressive or permanently disabling disorders can block couples' normal abilities to assess long-term risks to their relationships.

In light of the psychosocial demands of a disorder, early exploration with a couple about their usual patterns of communication and intimacy creates a foundation for education about the realistic need for caution over time. For example, after a heart attack, couples need to know when and to what extent they can resume their sexual life. They may avoid normal disagreements out of protective intentions. Because conflict avoidance takes a heavy toll on a relationship over time (Gottman & Levenson, 1992), it is important to help couples develop ways to express and resolve their normal differences. Are there any restrictions they need to incorporate now, six months from now, or even permanently? Such questions will help clarify a couple's patterns of communication in different areas of their relationship.

Externalization

Functional boundaries are promoted when a chronic disorder is put in its proper perspective. Michael White and David Epston's (1990) notion of externalizing the disorder or symptom is useful in this regard. A clinician might refer to a couple's struggle in coping with cancer in the following terms: "The cancer seems to be getting the upper hand lately, interfering with your experiencing the close times together you were accustomed to." Framing a serious disorder in this ways helps establish a boundary between the condition and the couple. This externalization unites the couple in relation to the disorder, which becomes a shared dilemma; and it functions as a reminder that the person is not the illness, and that he or she and the relationship are more than the disorder. The process of externalization promotes a belief in the possibility of greater control over the psychosocial processes generated by cancer in their lives.

Disorders such as cancer or AIDS give rise to destructive metaphors that suggest a lack of control or a complete takeover of one's being. Such metaphors become isomorphically extended, invading all aspects of a relationship. The lack of a boundary between the person and the cancer parallels the cancer's impact on a primary relationship. The notion of spoiled identity (Goffman, 1986) can permeate the ill member and the entire couples system. Healthy use of externalization needs to be distinguished from denial or a "not me" defense, which are regarded as pathological. Externalization can help reduce feelings of being overwhelmed by establishing a functional boundary between the disorder and the couple, enhance their sense of control, and reduce the need for denial as a defense.

Triangulation

As discussed in chapter 9, a chronic disorder can become a powerful third member in any dyadic family relationship. In some relationships governed by unresolved struggles for control, a chronic condition can help the affected member gain the upper hand. For instance, for one couple with long-standing gender-related conflicts, the wife's chronic back pain legitimized her demands for her spouse to do more of the housework. The danger with an illness or disability's serving as the rationale for change is that the change often remains dependent on continued symptoms or the threat of loss. For the woman in this relationship, this blocked her getting well or reporting feeling better because the relationship shift had become possible only with illness. In such situations clinicians need to address the underlying issues related to power and control as a way of removing the disorder from the triangle.

A preventively oriented psychosocial consultation in the crisis phase provides timely psychoeducation to couples about the common challenges to their relationship. Also, it can anticipate any risks that the disorder will become a third party in preexisting unresolved problems.

KEEPING THE ROLES OF PATIENT AND CAREGIVER WITHIN BOUNDS

The skews inherent in the long-term caregiving and dependency needs of an ill partner are almost always problematic, leading to inevitable ambiguity and inherent dilemmas concerning hierarchy, power, and reciprocity (Scheinkman, 1988). A couple's expectations for shared, balanced role functions often become blatantly impossible to maintain when one partner becomes disabled. A new version of balance needs to be negotiated; otherwise, old relationship rules become a "hollow shell" creating role strain and confusion for the couple.

Both partners need to realize that sustaining intimacy depends largely on establishing viable caregiving boundaries. Even the strongest relationships are strained by the ambiguities and discrepancies in shifts between two forms of relating: patient–caregiver and equal partners. Couples function best when they can discuss such problems openly.

A preventively oriented psychosocial consultation in the crisis phase provides timely psychoeducation to couples about the common challenges to their relationships. Early education about the physical and psychosocial demands of a condition over time gives couples a guide to the degree and timing of caregiving demands and helps couples take greater control of their lives. Some progressive disorders, such as Alzheimer's disease, require an increasing amount of caregiving that will eventually become total and permanent. In such conditions, couples have the most difficulty creating a workable boundary between the future time when they will relate as patient and caregiver and the present, when they can relate as equal partners. Other conditions, such as arthritis, may necessitate intermittent care when flareups occur, but have clearer boundaries. Disorders with an uncertain course and outcome make planning more difficult. The psychosocial typology and time phases framework can guide couples concerning periods, during flareups or later stages of progressive disorders, when skew will be inevitable. The type of disability predicts which aspects of a relationship are likely to become skewed and which will be preserved. Although a physically disabled man may no longer be able to share physical tasks or provide income equitably, his potential for helpful communication about practical issues and for emotional support may be unaffected.

Couples need clear professional guidance concerning which aspects of caregiving can be realistically carried out by the patient, which require another person, and which need professional assistance. Also, couples need to know under what circumstances (for instance, when symptoms become severe) care needs to shift to another person or warrants professional intervention. This basic information helps them establish healthy boundaries, so that the inertia of the ill partner's dependency needs and fears and the well partner's sympathy do not take over. Given this basic information, couples can then discuss a range of questions that address possible needed caregiving shifts. Under what circumstances would the couple want to turn over caregiving to a professional or a hospital? What will it mean to their relationship to have professional help with caregiving? What will this mean to the affected partner?

In one couple coping with the wife's severe, advanced Parkinson's disease and increasing dementia, both partners came from families with powerful multigenerational legacies concerning shameful loss. Her mother had died disgracefully in a state hospital, with a dementia resulting from years of chronic alcoholism. Her mother's condition had been a source of intense family conflict and embarrassment within their extended family and local community. His mother had had a progressive illness, and he had left caregiving to his sisters, which resulted in unresolved guilt feelings after his mother's death. These themes severely restricted this couple's options regarding limits as the wife's illness worsened. For him, any version of not remaining the primary caregiver until the end would represent a shameful repetition of abandoning his ill mother. For her, institutionalization with symptoms that could not be adequately controlled would represent a humiliating repetition of her mother's inability to control her alcoholism. In the terminal phase, when the wife's motor and cognitive disability became overwhelming, the couple's restricted options caused an impossible situation in the home, finally resulting in admission to a nursing home after an excruciating ordeal and intense pressure from the primary physicians.

This case highlights the importance of assessing the availability and willingness to utilize extended family members or adult children as supplemental resources to give respite to the well partner.

Other questions are important. How does the well partner feel about caregiving? Are there certain aspects that are too frightening or repelling? Frequently the well partner, particularly women, feel they should handle everything; historically, for women values related to self-respect and loyalty are closely tied to adequacy in nurturing and caregiving roles. Yet, because of this value, other parts of a relationship may suffer. One woman found that tending to her husband's advanced psoriasis interfered with her feeling attracted to him. She had assumed this function without questioning whether he could manage it himself or any discussion about the possible adverse impact on their relationship.

Couples need to negotiate understandings about the caregiver–patient roles that fit the realities of the disorder. Does the couple have a sense of limits? Or, are they driven, like the couple facing Parkinson's disease, by multigenerational legacies and belief systems that promote unrealistic and ultimately dysfunctional relationship bargains concerning these roles? Couples with preexisting issues concerning control or attention are most vulnerable to unhealthy relationship caregiving bargains based on who is indebted to whom.

When caregiving is extensive, both partners require sensitivity to the need for a transition to other ways of relating. Sometimes time alone is important, or sharing in a conversation about lighter or humorous topics can help the transition. When this kind of pacing is bypassed, one or both partners can feel emotionally blocked or violated. An avoidable cycle of anger, hurt, and rejection can ensue at a time when a couple may desperately need to reconnect in old comfortable ways. A disabled husband who wants sex may easily offend a tired partner who may need close, quiet time together with or without sex.

In the crisis phase, and initial recovery period, patient-caregiver relationship skews are heightened. This may be both functional and necessary in order to return home and facilitate recovery. The basic problem is that couples do not have a good sense of their stamina or when it may be advisable to renegotiate a crisis-phase arrangement for the long haul. This process influences successful mastery of one of the key tasks of the chronic phase: maximizing autonomy for all family members given the constraints of the disorder. During the transition to the chronic phase, when issues of permanency and the long haul need to be addressed, clinicians can be very helpful in encouraging frank, open discussion of how the couple can best handle the emotional and practical demands of the disorder and protect their relationship. As has been mentioned, silence by professionals can be interpreted by couples as encouragement that they should retain the structure of their relationship in the crisis phase indefinitely.

Depending on the type of disorder, couples commonly tilt into a number of skewed patterns including: ill versus healthy, disabled versus able, in pain versus pain free, dependent versus independent, and confined versus out in the world. These asymmetries can easily foster feelings of resentment and guilt. Often well partners develop a pattern of concealing personal needs and goals so as to not offend their disabled partners. When this becomes a long-term pattern, mutual resentment and guilt are almost inevitable. Patients resent their illnesses and their partners' ableness; at the same time, they feel guilty about being a burden and preventing partners from living normal lives. Sometimes, to alleviate feelings of being burdensome, the patient behaves in provocative ways to drive the well partner away. Especially in young couples, the well partner often feels both resentful about constricted life cycle options and shame about such feelings. Because of gender-based socialization, women as well spouses are much more likely to accept limits on their own needs and development stoically and without question.

Normalizing this process is a good starting point. Then couples need help devising ways to make flexible autonomy possible. The inequalities in the relationship should be acknowledged. It cannot be stressed enough that the long-term viability of the relationship may depend on openly discussing and legitimizing both partners' needs. I have seen countless relationships deteriorate or end when these issues have not been addressed.

Open communication about caregiving limits may be very painful, but for clinicians to collude in avoiding this subject is a prescription for disaster. The well partner, especially, may need permission to voice concerns and reasonable limits. This is most difficult for the well person when a partner is acutely symptomatic. A profound health skew between two partners typically makes the well partner's claim of entitlement to any semblance of equality seem shameful, yet defining limits is a critical nodal point at which long-term relationship bargains around an illness or disability are solidified. Facilitating this process early on promotes resilience and helps to reduce the ambivalence, escape fantasies, and survivor guilt that so often surface in a dysfunctional way later.

One spouse, facing her husband's slowly progressive, very disabling, fatal illness said that her open decision not to be her husband's primary caregiver allowed her to commit to the long haul. When feasible, such a decision can be very adaptive in confronting an illness that is very incapacitating and protracted. On one level, her decision was rationally accepted by her husband; it lessened his anxiety that he would burden her. On another level, it generated intense anger and sense of abandonment, which, unfortunately, did not surface until much later, during a marital crisis. Sadly, his natural reaction was not openly discussed at the time of the caregiving decision.

TOGETHERNESS AND SEPARATENESS

Any healthy relationship depends upon a balance between togetherness and separatenes (Olson, Russell, & Sprenkle, 1989). For couples facing chronic conditions, finding a workable balance is extremely challenging.

Often intense feelings of anger or abandonment are experienced at key junctures at which boundaries are being negotiated. The need for intimacy to be defined within the context of separateness is especially important in these situations. In life-threatening disorders, couples adapt best when they can acknowledge different needs for separateness. The ill partner's increased need for dependency typically fosters a desire for greater closeness. At the same time, the well partner may need time and space apart from the implosiveness of the illness and prepare for a future that may not include the ill partner. This process can be very painful and threatening to the ill person, who may feel abandoned. As in the case vignette above, this fear is often expressed as intense anger. If this woman had not taken a position about limiting caregiving, she might have felt powerless and totally controlled by her husband's condition. Over time, this could only lead to strong resentment, wishes for his demise, or a decision to leave him when life became intolerable. Instead, her husband had to face a limit and boundary between her needs and his. In this instance, the immediate physical skew and the tragedy of his life-shortening illness had to be acknowledged. At the same time, the basic entitlement of two committed, equal individuals to make personal decisions needed to be affirmed. Couples adapt best to chronic disorders when they can transform their understanding of "we-ness" to include a new version of separateness that acknowledges different needs and realities.

Often the initial crisis phase of a life-threatening illness has a very different impact on each partner's need for togetherness. The ill partner may experience strong needs related to fears of disability and death and may seek more closeness and dependency whereas the well partner may instinctively pull away in an initial detachment that represents preparation for the final separation of death. Couples, especially the well partner, need reassurance that this initial reaction is natural and not a profound statement about loyalty to the relationship. Such reassurances help counteract feelings of shame that contribute later to survivor guilt or unresolved grief.

Clinicians need to be mindful of the distinction between each partner's need for separateness within healthy intimacy and situations in which distancing occurs because of fear. Exploring couples' worst fears in a normalizing manner can diffuse myths, such as concerns about inadequate pain control. Often fears are shared by both partners, but silence prevents their giving each other support. Open sharing of concerns and clarifying limits and expectations often facilitate mutual comforting. One man distanced himself from his wife out of fear that he would need to take complete charge of the dying process for her, including actively helping her die. In an open discussion, his wife specified what she would want and, learning about his fears, agreed to take a more active role by talking with her doctor about assisted death rather than make her husband primarily responsible for helping her.

One of the illusions of a committed intimate relationship is that it offers a way to deny one's separateness and existential aloneness. A serious illness challenges both partners' defenses against that recognition. When couples can use a serious illness as an opportunity to confront this issue, they help counteract tendencies to see each other in unequal terms. For someone with a terminal form of cancer, it means facing the fact that one must die alone. Often fears of separation from loved ones and facing death alone may equal those concerning uncontrolled suffering. A desire to be with a spouse in one's final hour cannot change the fact of separateness and separation.

RECOVERY SKEW

Often the pace of adaptation to diagnosis of an illness or to a crisis is different for each partner. Discrepancies of this kind can be a major source of misunderstanding and conflict, and dealing with this possibility is essential. Clinicians need to distinguish arrested or blocked adaptation, characterized by denial, from normative differences based on personality style or different roles during the crisis phase. The following case illustrates skewed psychosocial recovery for each partner.

Jerry had suffered a serious head injury in a near-fatal car accident. After months in a coma, he regained consciousness and began a two-year recovery that, by all accounts, was miraculous. During this time, he had cognitive and speech deficits that slowly resolved. Late in his recovery, he and his wife, Marge, sought treatment for a pile-up of strains in their relationship. He complained that Marge seemed depressed and unable to celebrate his return to almost normal health. She complained that Jerry was unavailable to talk and attend to her need to discuss what had happened. As he had regained his former state of health, Marge had become more irritable and vocal about how hard life was. Both felt unvalidated.

Jerry, who had an iron will and was fiercely independent, had come to terms with his injury and its meaning for him alone over the weeks and months of recovery. During that time Marge had been totally absorbed in tending to him and their three children as the bulwark for the family unit while he was incapacitated. Her all-encompassing caregiving and parenting roles had, until recently, not allowed her time to process the events. As is often true for the primary caregiver, processing what had happened became possible only near the end of Jerry's recovery, when he was no longer so vulnerable and could handle her being upset. This couple was completely out of sync with each other for two reasons. Jerry's personal style was geared toward working out emotional issues alone, while Marge needed a collaborative process. Also, he was more focused on personal recovery and less aware than she of some of the needs for the relationship to recover. The pace of adaptation for each needed to be validated and normalized.

In a similar situation, a woman had recurrent depressions over a two-year period that required repeated electroconvulsive treatments that caused amnesia for the time of her illness. She was perplexed by her husband's anger once she recovered. As though awakening from a dream, she was unprepared for the aftermath and could not comprehend the anger directed at her.

Both cases demonstrate that when there is an extended period of cognitive impairment, the affected partner, because of problems with recollection and different perceptions of time, may have difficulty understanding a partner's needs. Also, after intense suffering, often the ill partner may have difficulty reliving the experience. This can be considered a form of post-traumatic stress disorder in which processing events with one's partner is like a flashback experience. Clinicians can help the healing process by facilitating a gradual sharing of two equally valid realities.

COGNITIVE IMPAIRMENT AND SKEW

Conditions involving cognitive impairment are among the most difficult for couples (Borden, 1991). Unlike other forms of disability in which the potential for intimacy is preserved, cognitive disability often necessitates a real loss of aspects of intimacy and certain co-parenting roles that cannot be salvaged. For many people, a major attraction in the choice of a partner involves a fit at an intellectual and emotional level. A balance of cognitive abilities is a critical element in the growth of most healthy relationships. Loss of this vital part of intimacy is often devastating. As one woman described the impact of her husband's stroke, "The most painful part is that he's not the same person anymore." To the degree that this occurs, the old relationship has died. This is often a profound crisis for a couple: a new relationship has to be devised, and the possibilities for intimacy are often very different, limited, and skewed.

In fatal conditions, surviving partners typically describe the actual death in anticlimactic terms. The significant loss of the person and the normal relationship may have occurred much earlier. In these cases much of the grieving process has already taken place when the caregiver has felt that his or her partner has psychologically died for them. Unfortunately, continued optimism by health providers and the patient's denial may have made it much harder for a caregiver's natural grieving process to take its course. Clinicians can help avert unnecessary suffering both by affirming the caregiver's experience as normal and by informing professionals involved in a case that a well spouse might need to let go and mourn the loss of an intimate relationship long before they let go of a case medically.

Situations of mild to moderate cognitive loss are often the most complicated, because of inherent ambiguities. The impaired person is often painfully aware and self-conscious about such deficits as forgetfulness, difficulties comprehending previously manageable tasks, and an inability to keep up with a partner. Often a person with milder deficits can appear relatively normal to others, but be experienced as a different person by the well partner. The well partner may report that certain conversations are no longer possible. Errors of judgment may occur in an erratic, unpredictable fashion that reduces a sense of trust.

Often cognitive deficits fluctuate in severity, being very susceptible to fatigue. The ambiguity in these fluctuations can be an additional powerful source of frustration, confusion, and secondary gain. As with regard to other invisible symptoms, such as pain, the well partner can become exasperated.

Problems are compounded when the disabled person denies or minimizes his or her deficits. With milder deficits, the cognitively impaired partner may vacillate between two extremes: "I'm O.K," which reflects denial or minimization of difficulties, and "I can't do anything right," which represents the sense of devastation and helplessness beneath the denial. Both extremes leave the well partner feeling helpless and isolated and impede the couple's moving to the next step in adaptation. Yet, the need for the well partner to protect and act as a buffer between his or her impaired partner and the world makes confrontation very difficult. Often this pattern of protection escalates until a needed confrontation does take place. One man had been left with cognitive deficits from a postoperative encephalitis. He could handle one task or person at a time, but not conversations involving more than one person or multiple trains of thought. For a long time, his wife protected his self-esteem. Finally, in one therapy session, she turned to him and exclaimed, "You can still play each instrument well, but the mixer is broken!" This overdue confrontation represented a first step to openly revising relationship patterns in a way more suited for the long term.

A well partner often struggles with ambivalent feelings about whether to continue to invest in a revised version of intimacy or redefine the relationship in basically caregiving terms. Often couples get mired in thinking either the relationship must be restored to its original state or all is lost. It is useful for clinicians to highlight unaffected areas of a relationship and emphasize the development of new shared interests, such as less cognitively oriented activities (for example, hiking or bicycling). When important aspects of a relationship are no longer possible, the well partner needs help deciding which needs can be met in different ways or with others in a manner that does not threaten the relationship. Both partners may underestimate a relationship's resilience and flexibility because it has never been tested by adversity. Affirming the possibility of positive changes is vital.

When a couple's relationship becomes limited to caregiving, it is akin to that between parent and child. Pauline Boss and co-workers' research (1984,

1988, 1990) on family boundary ambiguity is useful here. Boundary ambiguity within the couple's relationship needs to be considered somewhat separately from that of the whole family system. When a couple's relationship is transformed to a parent–child one, adult intimacy, which was the basis of the couple's relationship, no longer exists. Often well partners experience relief at this point because this ambiguity has been clarified. In progressive dementias, a spouse may understandably reach this transition point earlier than would be the case in a disorder with a constant course, such as a traumatic brain injury, because of the exhaustion and demoralization inherent in revising intimacy in a downward spiral as a disease progresses. Also, he or she may reach this "wall" sooner than other family members, who function at a greater distance. The well partner will need support for such a decision that addresses any feelings of blame, shame, and/or guilt.

Clinicians need to be aware that unlike in systemic illnesses, in many cognitive disabilities sexual desire remains completely intact. Unfortunately, a fundamental change in the capacity for intimacy may be so basic that the well partner permanently loses sexual interest in his or her mate. This is especially true when the man has the impairment, as women are less likely to separate sexuality from intimacy. Furthermore, a woman is more apt to assume a parental role with a disabled man than is the case when the situation is reversed. Having assumed a parentlike role, a woman is less likely to be sexually drawn to a partner who has become childlike. In contrast, the ill man may place great value on performing sexually as a way to bolster feelings of self-worth. Thus, the couple may become painfully out of sync in terms of their sexual relationship.

THE GENDER FACTOR

The gender of the ill partner and the caregiver is a critical dimension in understanding couples' dynamics with regard to chronic disorders. Research suggests that in traditional families, serious illness in the wife or mother presents the greatest overall risks to couples' and family functioning (Litman, 1974) because women generally serve so many of the practical and nurturant roles within families. Other research has found that husbands are more likely to hire a housekeeper to take over a disabled spouse's role, whereas wives tend to try to assume their husbands' roles despite the risks of overload (Zarit, Todd, & Zarit, 1986).

In the crisis phase it is useful to inquire whether either partner or the couple has preconceived ideas about who might become ill, dependent on the other, or die first, and how the other would survive. Often this is accompanied by fantasies about the kind of health problems a partner might develop, based on family-related illnesses, such as heart disease or cancer, or risky health habits, such as poor dietary patterns that may have been a source of conflict within a relationship. Typically, a couple's beliefs are gender related. Women are, on average, younger than their partners and have a greater life expectancy. For this reason women at midlife typically begin to rehearse the expectation that they may some day take care of or lose their partners (Neugarten, 1976). This gender-related difference in preparedness is reinforced by strong multigenerational patterns of caregiving by women. From this vantage point, men commonly have more difficulty adapting to a dependent partner, because illness or loss did not fit gendered social expectations. Men who are inexperienced as caregivers often are very anxious about taking care emotionally of themselves and their partner and children. This may be accompanied by feelings of anger on the part of the well partner for being put in an unanticipated position and by guilt on the part of the affected partner for failing to stay healthy and becoming a burden.

Men, socialized to be tough and invulnerable, often feel that being nurtured and dependent is acceptable, if at all, only when they are ill or injured. For many men their early memories of being nurtured are associated with mothering in periods of illness. The message from both parents and the larger culture was that they should be strong. Often illness and disability are experienced very ambivalently. On the one hand, powerful voices deride dependency and disability as evidence of infantilism and failure to fulfill the dominant male role of self-reliant provider for one's family. This is most difficult in conditions that are progressive and disabling, in which exerting control and remaining strong may have unavoidable limits. On the other hand, a chronic condition may provide many men with a sanctioned reason to be nurtured.

Because of gender socialization women and men often feel especially adept at different facets of coping. The psychosocial demands of a disorder can affect the experience of gender skew. For most men disorders that necessitate a high level of practical problem-solving, such as home-based kidney dialysis, are more in sync with their general sense of competence.

Men tend to tackle the practical or instrumental aspects of coping, avoiding the emotional side of their partner and themselves. Women are typically expected to tend to the emotional needs of their husbands, children, and others and to stifle their own needs. At the time of the initial illness crisis, couples tend to divide up coping tasks according to habitual patterns or stereotyped expectations. The risks are twofold. This division of psychosocial labor can become skewed and rigidified depending on who is the patient and who the caregiver and on role assignments according to gender. Clinicians can help couples distinguish patterns that served the initial crisis from those that are more adaptive over the long haul. In this sense, a chronic disorder gives couples an opportunity to reexamine habitual role constraints; this should be done with an understanding of the psychosocial demands of the disorder over time.

In one case, a woman had had cancer that was in remission for a number of years, during a period of rearing small children. Her husband was very supportive, but uncomfortable in handling sadness and the general emotional needs of the children. Throughout the illness, the wife had continued to monitor everyone's emotional needs while minimizing her own. As this woman's condition entered a terminal phase and she could no longer maintain her role as family nurturer, the husband felt ill prepared and overwhelmed by the emotional needs of his wife and children. An early intervention that would have helped this couple renegotiate their gender-defined roles in a more balanced way might have helped avert a double crisis in the final stages of the illness when they were facing impending loss and a need for role changes.

It is useful to ask couples how being male or female will determine how they will organize themselves with regard to an illness. Are there any roles they feel particularly suit them and others for which they feel unprepared? Inviting each to consider positive aspects of untried gender roles is beneficial. For men this may include allowing their softer side to emerge. For women, tackling the checkbook and insurance policies can enhance feelings of being able to manage finances. This type of questioning facilitates bringing thoughts and feelings about gender into couples' discussions about coping strategies. It especially can provide some sense of mastery and control to couples dealing with a physical condition about which they can do little or nothing to alter the medical course.

When couples present in a crisis later in an illness, often one partner actively needs to take over the other's role. For instance, in the above case, when the mother became terminally ill, the husband had to assume her nurturant parenting functions at a time when she was having to relinquish them permanently in the face of death. For the husband his fears of nurturing others was compounded by his sensitivity to his wife's acute suffering in watching her parenting roles being taken away forever. Early on, when illness is defined as an opportunity to rebalance roles regardless of the outcome, change is less crisis driven and tied to suffering and death.

In many instances a couple's crisis brought on by an illness or disability can lead to positive realignments that change basic beliefs guiding the relationship, as in the following case:

Sam and Alice presented for treatment eight months after Sam had suddenly developed a heart condition that left him disabled and unable to retain his job as a construction worker. Before this event, Alice had been at home full time, rearing their two small children, ages four and six. Although Sam could no longer work at his job, he was physically able to assume the role of house-husband. Initially, both Sam and Alice remained at home, his disability income enabling them to manage. When it became clear that Sam's disability was permanent, Alice expressed an interest in finding a job to relieve financial pressures. Sam resisted at first, feeling that child care and housework were appropriate only for a wife. He needed help rethinking his gendered, monolithic definition of family provider. With some encouragement, however, Sam agreed to try it. To his surprise, he enjoyed the time with his kids enormously, and the children loved it. Also, he became more fully aware of what he had missed with regard to his own father as he was growing up—a longing for closeness he had repressed since childhood. In spite of his disability, for the first time he felt a balance in his life he had never contemplated. "My job was important, but I'll only have one chance to spend time with my kids—while they are still young."

Here, a systemic intervention would also need to explore the wife's feelings of having to give up the satisfaction and bonds she had experienced in a primary parenting role. She is giving up the chance to spend time with her children while they are young and may not have a satisfying job situation to compensate for it.

Dramatic role shifts can also present problems for couples. In one situation, the husband, George, had sustained an injury that required a long period of rehabilitation at home before he could return to work. Until the injury, this couple had had clearly defined, traditional roles in which he supported the family financially and his wife reared the children. This arrangement had been satisfying for both. When George remained at home, he became involved with child care and parenting functions that had been the province of his wife, Janice. His style of parenting was more authoritarian than hers. Intense conflict and struggles over control and turf emerged as previous differences in parenting surfaced more forcefully. Both acknowledged that these differences were nothing new, but had been less consequential because roles were only minimally shared. This case highlights the need for couples to explore both the positive implications and potential conflicts in shifting roles assigned strictly by gender.

SEXUALITY

Chronic disorders can affect a couple's sexuality in a variety of ways (Kaplan, 1974; LoPiccolo & LoPiccolo, 1978; Schover & Jensen, 1988). Couples need clear information about how a particular disease or disability can be expected to affect sexuality physiologically. The fatigue caused by debilitating conditions or certain treatments, such as radiation and chemotherapy for cancer, are typically associated with diminished desire. Neurological complications from diseases such as diabetes, multiple sclerosis, or a spinal cord injury may interfere with erectile functioning. Antidepressants and medications for hypertension may compromise the ability to achieve orgasm.

Information about whether limitations will likely resolve or be permanent is useful. In situations that require caution for a period of time, such as after a life-threatening health crisis, couples function best when explicit guidelines are given concerning any necessary limits on sexual activity and how long they should adhere to them. Most couples are unaware of technological advances and clinical interventions available to ameliorate many physical causes of sexual dysfunction. One young married man with multiple sclerosis had lost his ability to maintain an erection five years earlier. At the time his neurologist said, "What can you expect? You've got multiple sclerosis." Living in a semirural area, the couple and doctor were unaware of new success with self-administered injections that could temporarily restore an erection for many afflicted patients. This case highlights the need for clinicians working with chronic disorders to keep up to date on technological advances related to sexual functioning. Learning how to give an injection is usually far less stressful than resignation to abstinence and a major long-term marital strain.

Almost any illness and disability can have secondary psychosocial effects on a couple's sexual life. Conditions with possible life-threatening recurrences can easily convert sexual exertion into a dangerous activity fraught with anxiety. Disfiguring conditions such as facial burns, strokes, or a mastectomy can arouse anxiety about attractiveness and/or diminish sexual feelings for both partners.

Breast and ovarian cancer are intimately associated with reproduction and cultural symbols of female sexuality. In Western culture women's breasts are emphasized as symbols of femininity and attractiveness, and loss or mutilation of a breast has significance for a woman's self-image and causes concern about loss of her desirability to her spouse. She may not want to be seen or touched and may not believe her husband's reassurances. Sensitive communication between partners about the meaning of the loss/change for each of them should be a priority of intervention. Losses caused by these conditions can shatter a woman's feelings of self-worth and make her feel unable to provide for her husband's needs for sex and offspring.

Breast and reproductive disorders confront some men with issues of their sense of entitlement to an intact woman who will bear their children and assure their immortality. Such feelings can be heightened by concerns of being judged failures by their male peers or fathers. One despondent young man whose wife's ovarian cancer and radiation treatment precluded having children stated, "I feel like I dropped the baton my father handed me."

Because illnesses easily disrupt a couple's sexual routines, those unaccustomed to communicating about their sexual life may need a crash course (Schover & Jensen, 1988). Couples may need help learning to communicate limitations, preferences, and emotions. A man suffering from chronic lung disease may find the customary missionary position too tiring; he needs to be able to communicate this to his partner. In addition, if his disability has necessitated his wife's becoming the primary wage-earner, he may associate her assuming a "superior" position during intercourse as symbolic of her new position in the relationship. This couple would need to discuss these issues to avert sexuality's becoming tainted by unacceptable role changes that challenge the foundation of his definition of masculinity.

For someone who expresses intimate feelings mostly through sexuality, a partner's illness can create a serious crisis; this is more common among men than women. In one case, after a woman's operation for a bleeding ulcer, the husband continued to demand sex as a way to maintain a sense of contact at a time of uncertainty. The wife, not wanting to hurt her husband's feelings, passively complied. Because of physical pain and unexpressed resentment at his insensitivity, she responded in a distant, unimpassioned manner. This increased his sense of desperation and redoubled his sexual demands, which only further angered his wife. In another situation, a wife felt in a double bind with her impotent husband: on the one hand, she thought that if she approached him in any way sexually, she would be labeled demanding, domineering, or castrating, and if she did not, she would be seen as cold, passive, maternal, or treating him like a child.

A man who suffers a life-threatening health crisis, such as a heart attack, that limits his sexual performance and who feels inadequate in other areas of intimacy, may respond in two extreme ways. He may totally withdraw into a depression or, against medical advice, attempt to reestablish his intactness and manhood by pressing for sex. A wife who wishes to protect her vulnerable partner may decline not out of a lack of interest, but out of fear of precipitating a fatal recurrence. This could be misread by the husband as confirmation of his inadequacy and cause him to angrily increase his efforts or engage in an extramarital affair or other destructive behaviors as a way to assert his intactness and express anger at his wife.

Sometimes sexual activity cannot be sustained physically or is beyond the psychological limits of a couple. Open discussion of this is often extremely difficult for couples. Well partners may find the realities of caregiving or visible impairment of their mate an impediment to sexuality. Often a well person's sexual withdrawal from a partner is fraught with feelings of shame and guilt, particularly if it is connected to underlying general feelings of ambivalence or to escape fantasies. Promoting open discussion can help avert the risk of general distancing from the relationship. Couples that can redefine intimacy and nurturance in terms broader than the purely sexual can successfully adapt to loss of the sexual component of their relationship.

Questions such as "If you were to view nonsexual nurturing as an acceptable compromise, how would that affect your feelings about the relationship?" can be used to explore possibilities. Clinicians can help promote a mutually caring, companionable relationship in other areas, with shared interests and pleasurable activities.

Extramarital relationships

How to deal with extramarital relationships in the context of chronic disorders is a particularly thorny question for clinicians. I subscribe to a nonjudgmental attitude, where the context of each situation requires careful consideration. Standards applied to physically healthy couples may not fit the excruciating long-term strains of couples facing illness and disability.

I have seen many instances in which an affair was destructive and hastened the end of a relationship. I have also seen a number of instances of protracted illness ordeals in which an affair allowed a well partner to sustain his or her commitment to caring for a spouse, particularly when a long-term disabling condition strikes early in the life cycle. One woman who took care of her severely disabled husband and reared three children over a 25-year period stated, "I loved him, and I was committed to the marriage, taking care of him and raising the kids. But his ability to reciprocate was limited, and sex was physically impossible. I was thirty years old when he was diagnosed. I had a lover for many years, but I never considered leaving my husband. He and the kids always came first." I would consider this woman's experience adaptive in light of the primacy of her commitment to her marriage and family. This does not mean that I advocate affairs. But in certain situations of serious illness, an extramarital relationship can be one option to sustain a commitment. This is most relevant when a couple's relationship has, of necessity, become exclusively one of patient and caregiver. Couples dealing with advanced dementias, brain injury, or terminal disease are examples.

Because a couple's relationship can become a constant reminder of illness and loss for both partners, an affair can express a need to escape the ordeal and find respite or be nurtured. A number of people have decribed how an extramarital relationship helped them reaffirm a feeling of being normal. Closeness with someone outside the ordeal was not tainted with all the issues of patient and caregiver. Sadly, often late in the chronic phase, couples have become so accustomed to these roles that they no longer find it possible to experience their relationship as separate from illness and adversity. For some, an affair may seem the only way to obtain a needed escape, to revitalize oneself and be nurtured by an intimate. If couples can develop early in a chronic condition ways to discuss needs for separateness and time that is not governed by patient and caregiver roles, these outcomes are less likely.

When a long-term severe disability precludes a sexual relationship between partners, occasionally couples openly negotiate an understanding that the well partner may meet sexual needs outside the relationship. This is an extremely delicate issue, one that requires a firm commitment to the primary relationship and sensitivity to discretion.

The advisability of disclosure of an extramarital relationship needs to be assessed within the context of the total clinical picture. When an affair is an expression of a dysfunctional relationship that contributes to further relationship deterioration, disclosure may be indicated, especially if the partner intends to continue it. On the other hand, disclosure of an affair may be counterproductive when it surfaces in situations such as severe cognitive disability or the final stages of an illness, during a time when the patient may already feel overwhelmed and the original partnership may no longer exist or be possible. When clinicians agree that a well partner has realistically assessed an illness situation, then the question of disclosure should be addressed in terms of "for what purpose." The need to confess to assuage guilt needs to be considered separately from disclosure as a way to restore or repair intimacy. In instances in which relationship possibilities may be limited, disclosure and the resulting pain may only heighten guilt for the caregiver.

Regardless of a decision about disclosure, a clinician can play a critical role in helping normalize an affair that has occurred under unusual and stressful circumstances. Such understanding from a professional can help alleviate the suffering of a well partner and counteract survivor guilt. In all such cases, clinicians really need to look at their own moralistic positions, which may not always be therapeutic.

BELIEF SYSTEM SKEW

As described in chapter 7, there is a range of fundamental beliefs that are significant when couples or families face illness and disability. In times of adversity, differences between partners can precipitate a relationship crisis. Particularly after an initial health crisis, couples have an opportunity to shift constraining beliefs in more healthful directions. Some couples choose to work on altering basic beliefs, as the following case illustrates.

Jack, age 33, and Katherine, a nurse, presented in a marital crisis with Jack very depressed and despondent that he had a disease he believed would control and drastically shorten his life. Diagnosed with a mild case of multiple sclerosis one year ago, he expected to be wheelchair-bound, demented, and seriously compromised in the fathering of his two small children. Katherine was intolerant of his attitude and thought he could lead a good life even with a chronic illness like MS, believing that "Disabilities become handicaps if you let them take over."

Jack's family background was significant in that, as he put it, "Everyone has a cross to bear, everything is a catastrophe, suffering brings status." When Jack was growing up, his father had a chronic anxiety disorder that had controlled the family. Since the diagnosis of MS, when Jack and Katherine visited Jack's family, his relatives granted his every wish: at the age of 33, he clearly had the biggest cross to bear.

Katherine's basic beliefs were, "When you get hurt, you get hugs and kisses, and then you get out there and fight, like my grandmother who escaped from the Nazis after being shot in the leg." Her parents had divorced when she was 10, and her mother had successfully obtained a job and reared the kids.

Their differences in fundamental beliefs about health issues and how to manage adversity were the focus of treatment. Each had very different legacies and scripts concerning control, the meaning of illness, and the rights and privileges of being sick that now came into full play during the crisis phase of an illness with an uncertain course. In Katherine, Jack could see values that would fit his script and others that would challenge him. Katherine, as a nurse, had a great capacity to give care, which his helpless side found attractive. In her belief in mastering adversity, Jack saw something foreign to his experience, but something he admired and wanted to learn. This difference, only an undercurrent before this health crisis, now expressed itself fully. Changing his values, which he did, meant relinquishing status with his family of origin and his desire for the kind of attention his father had received—but it also meant exchanging values that granted status at the price of shame for more empowering beliefs.

LIFE CYCLE SKEWS

Life cycle skews will be experienced most acutely at transition periods in their individual and couple life cycles, when normative developmental tasks of the next phase will have to be considered in the context of illness or disability. The disorder will, of necessity, need to be brought into bold relief at those times, often revealing stark differences in each partner's capacities to carry out life cycle goals. Manageable gaps can be experienced as unbridgeable chasms that threaten the core of the relationship. Open dialogue is especially critical at these times. Couples that master these challenges best are those with both the broadest and most flexible definitions of acceptable roles and those with alternative means of satisfying developmental needs.

Younger couples

Life cycle skews are most evident in couples at early stages of their development, when chronic disorders are most untimely. Most individual and collective dreams have yet to be lived out; the sense of loss and being robbed is more acute. Distinctions from age peers are often exquisitely apparent. Redefining personal and relationship goals in the context of limitations can strain both members. If disability or threatened loss is involved, the ill partner often becomes more aware of the pragmatic difficulty of achieving normative goals, such as beginning a family or pursuing career goals. He or she may not want to burden or disappoint the partner and therefore may minimize his or her actual limits. The well partner often realizes that the price of commitment to the relationship may mean forgoing key personal or relationship dreams, such as having children, or that achieving goals will require unusual persistence and possible hardship.

For a couple in which the wife had chronic pain from a severe accident, the decision to establish a family meant that each had to accept compromise. Because of his wife's disability, the husband needed to acknowledge that there would be an inherent skew regarding the practical tasks of parenting, so he would have to scale back his individual goals for career advancement. She needed to face her limits more directly, as she poignantly stated with regard to the first few months after their daughter was born, "Although I tried to prepare myself, it was a painful time for me. I had to accept my limitations in a way I never had to before."

Some couples may be unable or decide not to have children. Jim and Alice, in similar circumstances decided to forgo raising a family. As a result, Alice determined to expand her career aspirations. Although this was a healthy way for her to ensure that the relationship would not stifle all areas of her individual development, it heightened a sense of loss for her disabled husband, who now would not have children and who was unable to work at his occupation. Jim became very depressed. Alice assured Jim that even though he was disabled and could not work, her freedom to pursue some of her personal dreams strengthened her commitment to the relationship. Out of this process, Jim decided, for the first time, to become involved in community activities and volunteer work within his physical limits. Alice's plans had triggered a developmental crisis for him in which his individual life cycle choices between expansion of personal options or despondency were finally confronted. This couple's process was helped by the fact that the social stigma of remaining childless is lessening, and increasingly couples are expressing needs for generativity in other ways.

Clinicians can help couples anticipate life cycle nodal points at which issues of skew, autonomy, limits, and complexity will become heightened. Life cycle choices are key junctures at which couples can be helped to negotiate issues of separation and togetherness in a balanced and mutually respectful manner. As the last case suggests, it is often at these life cycle transitions that couples have an excellent opportunity for growth and redefining constraining aspects of a relationship.

In untimely conditions, couples have difficulty finding age peers with whom to share relationship concerns related to living with illness and disability at a particular life cycle stage. In this regard, younger couples tend to become more isolated. Generally, support groups are disease specific; less commonly, they are offered explicitly for couples; rarely are they organized according to stages of the life cycle. A cancer support group, although addressing many common concerns, may not meet the life cycle dilemmas of a younger couple. When feasible, clinicians can be extremely helpful by promoting networking among couples coping with chronic disorders at similar stages of development.

Just as healthy couples may avoid friends who are coping with serious illness, because of discomfort and fears of vulnerability, couples with a chronic disorder may also become avoidant and tentative, furthering their own isolation. They can become extremely self-conscious and insecure, and feel that their age peers cannot understand their situation. Often they are dealing with issues normal for later stages of the life cycle and experience being out of sync with peers. Sometimes initial tentativeness and fears by both well couples and those dealing with illness can become an escalating cycle of distancing that leads to breaks in relationships. Couples that can effectively circumscribe a condition without letting the disorder become their total identity can best counteract the tendency to isolate themselves. Just as both partners need to accept certain skews in their relationship as a necessary means of sustaining intimacy, couples dealing with untimely disorders may need to understand the differences between themselves and their peers to not escalate the social distancing process with friends. This allows them to stay engaged with friends and initiate communication about the impact of the disorder on important outside relationships.

Mid- and later-life couples

For couples in middle or later life, the transitions of launching children and retirement involve endings of major responsibilities that have occupied their lives for many years. The release from these commitments typically creates space for each partner to reevaluate his or her personal goals and their relationship as a couple. Fantasies and plans for the use of leisure time come to the fore, and compromises necessitated by a chronic condition may heighten feelings of being robbed. Plans, such as for travel, that needed to be deferred and have kept spirits up during arduous times now may need to be confronted as unrealistic. In our work-ethic–driven culture, all of us need to be reminded that life offers no guarantees, and that, when feasible, we need to build in pleasures, even small ones, at all phases of the life cycle.

Especially at midlife, leaving a relationship burdened by a long-standing illness may feel more possible, now that loyalties to parenting obligations no longer exist. In more serious and debilitating illnesses, long-unmet relationship needs interact powerfully with both keen awareness of one's mortality, that the hourglass is running out, and realization that there is still enough time to establish another life. As one woman put it, "I raised three kids by myself for the past twenty years while my husband was disabled; I want a chance to live while there is still time." This woman's feelings of anger and entitlement were counterbalanced by a sense of of guilt that she would be abandoning her helpless, disabled husband to life alone or in the care of her daughter, who would then unfairly inherit her burden.

Any decision to stay together or separate requires open discussion between both partners. Although anyone can experience these desires, men and women often see their options very differently. Men at midlife and retirement are more likely to leave or start an affair because of greater opportunities to find another partner. For both partners the risks of leaving, starting an affair, and depression are highest at these times.

To work effectively with such couples, clinicians need to be aware of biases that might align them with particular values or one partner concerning such issues as togetherness versus separateness. Also, clinicians should be mindful of any preconceived ideas they may harbor about older couples' being unchangeable or about illness as just a part of old age. Loss of a satisfying sexual relationship can be just as painful for older couples as for young ones. The realities of a couple entering late adulthood with years of stress and exhaustion from living with a chronic condition are very different from those of a healthy couple worrying about future infirmity. An older couple knowledgeable about life with chronic illness may be acutely aware of the reduced limits their relationship could withstand if the well partner were now to become ill or disabled. Such couples may need help addressing realistic fears about the need for a nursing home and being separated in the process. Fostering open patterns of communication and joint decisions about future eventualities is the best preparation for these critical life cycle junctures.

Gay and Lesbian Couples

Gay and lesbian couples facing chronic disorders must deal with issues related to social stigma in addition to all the same issues as heterosexual couples. A chronic or life-threatening illness, with its attendant need for health care, often forces a hidden or extremely private relationship to become public for the first time at a moment of great vulnerability. Experiencing cold or distant professional healers at a time of need can be a particularly poignant rejection. When gay couples face a highly stigmatized disorder such as AIDS, which society associates with a deviant life-style, the intensity of this experience is magnified tremendously. A gay couple being seen together in the hospital can represent for clinicians the first direct encounter with an intimacy so feared by many in society.

Health professionals may experience particular discomfort in dealing with the couple together. Homophobia and antipathy are more containable if the health professional can define a health problem as limited to a biological issue or a part of the body rather than the whole person and his or her intimate life. This kind of defense mechanism seriously compromises any therapeutic relationship. Clinicians, to be most helpful and "do no harm" to gay and lesbian couples, need to confront personal prejudice.

Couples may need help when a life-threatening health crisis brings their personal life and family of origin together for the first time. Sometimes a bitter family may try to wrest control of the situation and attempt to exclude the partner from caregiving or important rituals such as a memorial service. Since gay and lesbian couples' relationships are not legally recognized in most states, clinicians need to address issues related to disenfranchisement and exclusion from family leave policies and survivor benefits for the well partner and the lack of legal rights for visitation and sustained contact with the children of a partner who dies (Laird, 1993). In one case, the parents of a bisexual man who died from AIDS obtained a court injunction prohibiting further visits by his long-term male partner with their son's children from an earlier marriage.

Inclusion of Clinicians in the Couple's Relationship

For most couples the intimate fabric of their relationship is deeply private. Most partners have acknowledged and covert understandings about disclosure of their intimate life together. The ability to allow another person to see one's vulnerable side and frailties depends on a safe boundary that supports a primary relationship.

Chronic disorders often necessitate the intrusion of health professionals into the privacy of a couple's relationship. This is particularly true in cases of moderate or severe disability in which health care is delivered at home or when the ill member requires 24-hour care in a hospital or residential care facility. In essence, a second primary relationship can develop for the ill member with a health professional, for example, with a nurse who tends to his or her physical needs. This often occurs in a context of decreased physical contact with one's partner. A nurse's emotional comfort through nurturing physical contact with a disabled or debilitated person can contrast sharply with the emotional discomfort and distancing from physical contact that may have developed for a couple.

A professional assuming caregiving functions that have become burdensome or anxiety-ridden can help a couple's intimacy by removing certain tension-filled responsibilities from the well partner. For instance, for one man monitoring his wife's blood pressure following a stroke was a source of great anxiety. Although it was a simple procedure, he lived in fear that he would make a mistake and his wife would have a fatal recurrence. This led to hypervigilant monitoring of his wife that became a source of intense conflict and adversely affected their overall relationship. A regular visit by a nurse who assumed this responsibility solved the problem.

Although relief may be the predominant emotion for both partners in such a situation, divided emotions are not uncommon. Jealousy occurs frequently when intimate physical care (for instance, bathing, dressing) is provided by a professional who is the same sex as the well partner. Also, the patient may experience intense anger that the partner is no longer doing all the caregiving. This anger is connected to the inevitable separation process described earlier, a process that may be especially terrifying for the patient.

When physical caregiving is required, the implications for the couple's relationship of assumption of the relevant functions by the well partner or by a professional should be explored in advance. Particularly in conditions that can have life-threatening crises, the possible effects on the couple need to be discussed. In one instance, a husband who was a health professional agreed to monitor his wife at home for life-threatening infections during a high-risk period when her immune system was depleted after each high-dose chemotherapy treatment for cancer. In this situation a missed infection could be lethal in 24 hours. His wife wanted desperately to rest at home rather than wait out the recovery phase in the hospital. The health team responded to the patient's request to go home and encouraged the husband to agree to this cost-effective arrangement that this wife favored. The husband swallowed his fears rather than appear weak to his colleagues. Over time, the strain of this arrangement and the lack of open couple's discussion about the husband's fears increased his feelings of anger and of being controlled by the situation.

Conjoint and Individual Sessions

Intervention with couples coping with chronic disorders benefits from a flexible integration of individual and conjoint sessions. Because patterns of secrecy and mutual protection are so common, I routinely, as part of an initial assessment, meet with the couple together and separately. By doing this I can develop a better sense of the issues that can be openly shared and those that are closely guarded. Secret thoughts, feelings, and behaviors that are laden with shame, such as wishes to die, leave the relationship, or an ongoing clandestine affair often need to be shared privately with a neutral person before they can be discussed openly with a partner. This needs to be done within a systemic framework.

Individual sessions allow processing about which issues are best shared or kept private. A partner may feel guilty about a brief affair; yet it may be unnecessary, even cruel, to divulge this to the partner (Reibstein & Richards, 1993). And if sharing it is warranted, a private consultation can help a partner do it sensitively. For instance, in one case a brief affair occurred when a woman was feeling overwhelmed and unappreciated as a caregiver for her husband, who suffered from heart disease. Her anger about skewed nurturance was more significant than the affair. Several individual sessions helped reduce her guilt and her potential to be angry in a destructively reactive way with her self-absorbed husband. What was needed most was for her to express her needs and renegotiate the marital contract toward greater balance when conjoint sessions resumed.

In another situation, a woman experienced intense shame concerning her previously "perfect" husband's speech impediment that resulted from an accident. The husband's acceptance of his disability only heightened her sense of shame and blocked her from even mentioning her feelings, despite the fact that her ability to be close to her husband had been seriously affected. Individual sessions allowed her to express her feelings fully, be assured that they were normal, and then discuss them with her husband.

Couples dealing with chronic conditions often present individual issues that are more effectively handled separately. As mentioned earlier, couples have increased needs for separateness in the context of intimacy. This need may be isomorphically expressed in the relative usefulness of individual and conjoint sessions. For instance, one couple dealing with the husband's terminal cancer needed conjoint sessions to bring closure on relationship issues and plans for the funeral. At the same time, the husband required time alone to process personal feelings related to making peace with his own life, and his wife needed time to plan for a future without her husband. In terms of process, what was important for the couple was to be able to say to each other what they needed to discuss separately and why.

During medical crises or advanced stages of a progressive disease, each partner may need to operate in different worlds. This may impose severe limits on what a couple can realistically offer one another, particularly when the ill member is cognitively impaired or severely debilitated, for instance, following major surgery. A conjoint meeting may be helpful to acknowledge these limits. Nevertheless, each person may have separate and distinct issues that need prompt attention. Sometimes, during periods of hospitalization, the patient's needs may be met through an array of hospital staff, and the well partner may feel isolated and need additional support from the clinician. In these circumstances individual sessions can help balance an exclusive focus on the medically needy patient.

CHAPTER 11

Personal and Larger System Interface Issues for Clinicians

A MAJOR EMPHASIS of this book has been the quality of fit between different systems that interact with families facing illness and disability. This chapter will extend the Family Systems–Illness Model to examine clinical issues at the interface between the family, professionals, health-care contexts, and other societal institutions. I will discuss issues related to: (1) personal themes for clinicians working with illness, disability, and loss; (2) personal and professional boundaries with families; (3) the quality of fit between the family and provider system over the course of a disorder; and (4) some issues related to multiple and larger systems. I will emphasize issues for the clinician in this process.

Clinicians' Personal Themes

To understand our interface with families facing illness and disability, we need to address our own personal issues. In this regard it is crucial to take stock of our own belief systems and life cycle and multigenerational issues concerning illness and loss. This section will address dilemmas related to facing loss and personal limits in the context of work demands, while attempting to maintain a satisfying personal and family life.

HEALTH PROFESSIONALS' BELIEF SYSTEMS

To understand the fit between the family and health care professionals, clinicians and families need to be aware of the beliefs that guide professionals' attitudes and behavior. The same questions concerning beliefs asked of families are relevant to health-care professionals, including:

1. What is your attitude about your own and the family's ability to influence the course/outcome of the disorder?
2. How do you see the balance between your and the family's participation in the treatment process?
3. If there are basic differences in beliefs about issues such as control, how can these differences be reconciled?

Because of the tendency of most health facilities to disempower people and thus foster dependence, great sensitivity to family values is needed to create a therapeutic system. Many breakdowns in relationships between noncompliant or marginal patients and their care-providers can be traced to natural disagreements at this basic level that were not addressed.

Each clinician's health belief system represents a mixture of *personal, professional*, and *institutional beliefs*. Beliefs associated with the professional identities of physicians, nurses, psychologists, social workers, and family-systems-oriented consultants can vary considerably. For instance, psychiatrists' professional training is rooted in biomedicine, and the discipline has a strong interest in maintaining (or recapturing) its status as a *bona fide* medical subspecialty. This is in sharp contrast to the experience of most psychologists and social workers, whose basic training and professional identity are rooted more in the psychosocial. Similarly, the institutional beliefs guiding behavior in a hospital, public agency, or private office can be substantially different.

Professionals need to understand how they define their own competence or success. In the whole history of medicine and throughout medical training, the professional credo has been, and continues to be, overcoming disease and saving lives. When patients do not get better, we label them treatment failures and, as professionals, tell ourselves, "If we had been better clinicians, we would have saved the patient." As a result, we frequently label ourselves professional failures.

Only in recent years, with the advent of models for care of the chronically mentally and physically ill, have we begun to redefine our beliefs about successful outcomes. Hospice as a caregiving approach for the terminally ill and their families represents such a paradigm shift. As we professionals move away from equating chronicity and dying as failure, we facilitate family acceptance and mastery of those realities. For instance, to the extent that disorders such as schizophrenia are believed to be caused by pathological family transactions, it is likely that eventual chronicity will be defined as failure of both the family and clinicians. Recent psychoeducational models (Anderson et al., 1980, 1981, 1986; Falloon, Boyd, & McGill, 1984) are based on a belief that many chronic mental disorders are biologically based illnesses whose cure, at present, are beyond control of the family and the clinician. This helps free patient, family, and clinician from illness narratives that become increasingly marked by shame and failure.

Clinicians need to become aware of how their own family background affects their health beliefs and their interactions with families. It is useful for clinicians to take a personal inventory in terms of the types of beliefs described in chapter 7. Multigenerational beliefs and legacies about illness and loss are particularly important (see chapter 5). Areas of strength and vulnerability need to be identified, such as instances of overcoming adversity and unresolved loss issues.

One exercise I find useful to open exploration of personal beliefs is as follows:

1. Think about an important experience in your family with illness, adversity, or loss. Recall this experience and how it unfolded over time, and your personal involvement on a practical and emotional level.
2. What beliefs did you and your family use in that situation?
3. How did that experience affect your beliefs about such things as normality, mastery, control, optimism/fatalism, value of family efforts, etc.?
4. Did issues of blame, shame, or guilt surface in the family during this experience? I low were they handled? Were they resolved? What helped?
5. How does this experience affect your philosophy and work as a clinician?

FACING LOSS AND PERSONAL LIMITS

Working with illness and loss heightens awareness of our own mortality. A "we–they" attitude toward the families we encounter is impossible. We are helping families with issues that are inevitable in our own lives and families. For many mental health professionals, this is different from working with chronic mental disorders that we may have been spared in our own lives and families of origin; our own fears and vulnerabilities can be construed as more remote or unlikely and promote a "we–they" mindset.

Clinicians need to be cognizant of any issues related to loss that may complicate their clinical effectiveness. Obviously any personal situation of recent or threatened loss is likely to heighten feelings for a clinician working with similar circumstances. This is not inherently good or bad; rather, it requires an ability to be undefensively mindful of the impact of such situations. Clinicians commonly feel torn between their true feelings of overload and a professional belief in the need to remain objective and continue with any case no matter what the circumstances. To behave otherwise would be experienced as a shameful failure.

I am reminded of an experience during my training, when I was presenting a difficult case to a supervisor. I had recently made a home visit to a family in which the mother had recently been diagnosed with metastatic cancer. The supervisor broke in on my presentation of the case and said, "You're radiating ambivalence about this case all over the room. What is going on?" Only at that point did I tell her that my own mother had died four months earlier of a heart attack. In medical school I had been taught that you wall off personal experiences and just keep going. By attention to medical details one could more easily be distracted from personal emotional issues; here, where my explicit purpose was psychosocial, I could not defend myself the same way. The supervisor, who must have sensed my feelings of professional shame and personal sadness, told a story about when her own mother had died: she had felt unable to work effectively with certain cases and had transferred several of them to another clinician and declined others involving major loss for over a year. She did not tell me to transfer this case, but she was giving me permission to be human and acknowledge my limits.

This vignette suggests the importance of incorporating into training the need for self-understanding about illness and loss and acceptance of personal limits that are consistent with a positive professional self-image. When we do otherwise, we become isomorphic with family caregivers who have unrealistic self-expectations of competent caregiving and who see shared responsibility for caregiving or respite as shameful signs of weakness and failure. Our own inability to share our limits with each other can covertly communicate to families the same unwavering "tough-it-out" mentality. One of the most difficult tasks for well family members is to feel entitled to their own nurturance. Often the very thought generates intense shame because the caregiver burden is deemed a light one compared to a biological fight for survival. This view is a major contributor to well-person guilt and shame.

When we model the same behavior in our professional roles, we both generate feelings of shame related to our self-evaluation of our clinical performance and limit our clinical effectiveness. A major impediment to our sharing with each other our personal feelings about working with illness is the unacknowledged expectation that if we were to reveal our true feelings, we would be judged negatively by colleagues. Generally this fear represents a projection of our own shameful feelings about not living up to idealized and unachievable professional standards; it contributes to a hidden, shame-based, impaired professional self-concept in the context of working with emotionally demanding cases. In addition, if we are reticent about sharing these issues with family and friends, we can become truly isolated and alone with our suffering; and this can have far-reaching negative implications for long-term professional survival and general quality-of-life, which may be connected to the high rate of depression and suicide among physicians. Nevertheless, most health professional training promotes a stoic attitude, in which revealing feelings or vulnerabilities is discouraged.

In professional training, there is commonly a period of intense awareness of personal themes related to illness and loss. If they are not acknowledged and there is no opportunity to discuss them, these issues are, of necessity, repressed and go underground—otherwise it would be impossible to continue. This process of "psychic numbing" (Lifton, 1979) negatively affects our ability to remain sensitive and available to the emotional processes of families attempting to cope and adapt to serious illness, and is a major contributor to symptoms of burnout. Typically, clinicians who work with repeated loss, for example, in hospice or oncology units, encounter a psychological wall that represents a combination of immersion in death experiences of families, unsustainable personal standards of professional competence, and reawakening of personal themes related to loss. At this critical juncture, clinicians may either change jobs (usually with a sense of personal failure), develop a rigid, self-protective, hardened, clinical style, or actively reexamine basic issues related to life, death, and past losses.

In one hospice, the director of social services instituted a preventive group program for all new clinicians based on a developmental model of the typical psychosocial experience over the first year (P. Lynch, personal communication). In many respects the developmental tasks for the clinician mirrored those experienced by families in the crisis and chronic phases of adaptation to illness. On a cost-effectiveness basis, this program significantly reduced staff turnover and the use of sick and personal days and generally improved clinician morale and productivity.

It is extremely useful for clinicians who work with health problems to have an opportunity to discuss their belief system and how it influences their work with different patients or disorders. A conscious decision to incorporate this into case discussions or peer supervision groups has enormous payoffs. Difficulties with particular cases, overall job satisfaction, and issues of burnout can be intimately connected to underlying beliefs that are unexpressed. This is isomorphic with the kinds of complications that occur in families in which core beliefs have not been articulated among family members or with health providers.

It is most fruitful when relevant beliefs can be discussed within one's professional family (for example, in a clinic, unit, or department). However, institutional constraints can make this difficult unless a commitment is made to an ongoing process with ground rules that deal with concerns of vulnerability. Clinicians often feel uncomfortable about sharing personal feelings about loss with co-workers they will have to continue working with. Consciousness of hierarchy can inhibit airing vulnerabilities in front of a supervisor who is responsible for performance reviews of clinicians. Open discussion about such fears, perhaps with a consultant, can help a professional group decide the best approach. Sometimes, because of these institutional constraints, clinicians need to find alternatives, such as organizing a monthly peer group to talk about issues of common concern in working with illness and disability. In one city, oncology social workers formed such a group and hired a consultant, who met with them on a monthly basis.

In my experience, in teaching family therapy in medical schools and psychiatry departments, I have found that status and gender tend to block physicians from sharing their vulnerabilities with nonphysicians, such as nurses, psychologists, and social workers. The image of the male doctor as the technological expert in control further constrains self-disclosure by physicians. Even with the increase in women in medicine, many female physicians feel that to be accepted as equals in a traditionally male profession means being psychologically tough. More generally, issues of hierarchy and status severely restrict sharing among all disciplines (for instance, psychologists with social workers). Physicians usually do not want to let down their guard and potentially tarnish their professional image publicly with other professionals traditionally trained to look up to them; for instance, a nurse might question a doctor's objectivity or expertise with a case if she were aware of ambivalence stemming from a personal belief or experience. Unfortunately, most health-care systems minimize or disregard the need to invest time to address preventively personal concerns that emerge for clinicians at all levels and stages of health-care delivery.

Families often deny the need for respite or time to process emotional issues during early phases of an illness. A medical approach that is highly technologically focused promotes family beliefs that favor the practical side of coping. The need for respite and processing of feelings by all family members as an on-going developmental process over the entire course of an illness is frequently overlooked, becoming acknowledged only after signs of burnout or overload of unresolved feelings related to loss or threatened loss have become overt. And just as the ultimate cost to families is much higher when emotional issues are deferred, so such deferment is harmful to clinicians. Health and mental health professionals often adopt a "we haven't got time to talk about those issues" stance that parallels that of families.

Sadly, clinicians often know that they are heading for emotional burnout, but feel there is no space for attending to their emotional needs–and they are right. The combination of our cultural avoidance of issues related to loss and our current health-care system's profit orientation conspires to rigidify institutional structures that bypass the emotional needs of clinicians. Only when we more openly acknowledge that the stresses and strains on families coping with illness and disability apply also to clinicians involved in their care can we begin to implement a model of care that tends to the needs of clinicians.

The fact that most institutional philosophies and structures do not incorporate issues related to the psychosocial demands of disorders over time into the provider system is dysfunctional for families and clinicians alike. Families in a health crisis tend to shape their illness system in a manner modeled after that of the health-care team. As described in chapter 3, this becomes for families part of their initial crisis-phase "framing event." For example, when clinicians avoid or have no forum for discussing their own concerns related to living or working with threatened loss, then systems dynamics that inhibit such discussions will be overtly or covertly transmitted to families. Such dynamics will foster clinician interactions with patients and their families that are either distant or overinvolved. Distancing may occur because of a sense of danger in listening to family issues that are the same as those one is repressing or avoiding. This may take the form of avoidance of a particular patient, family, or painful topics. Overinvolvement or inappropriate personal sharing may occur with a family when there is no other outlet for burdensome feelings that would naturally arise in the process of working with chronic or life-threatening disorders.

Clinicians need to be particularly aware of situations in which their own fears about infirmity and loss collide with professional beliefs about competency, which can often lead to counterphobic behaviors. A clinician may express fears about loss of control triggered by a particular case by admonishing the patient or family that if they took more responsibility the patient would recover. Such a cavalier attitude in the face of an illness, such as Alzheimer's disease, that may have a relentless course conveys insensitivity in the face of an excruciating family ordeal. Vulnerable families are readily shamed by such behaviors, though they may reflect a clinician's own problem. They will be especially affected if such an attitude by a clinician dovetails with popular beliefs to which they have been exposed that promote taking responsibility for one's illness as a necessary step toward regaining health.

We need to be mindful of situations in which we become distant, overinvolved, or insensitive, and to make room in our professional belief system for these inevitable occurrences. Only then can we give ourselves permission to step back from a case to reflect and consult with colleagues. Otherwise, we replicate dysfunctional family dynamics, in which unacceptable feelings go underground and become expressed in personal physical or mental morbidity and destructive interpersonal behaviors.

The strain inherent in working with illness and disability often gets expressed dysfunctionally among colleagues. Commonly in high-stress work settings characterized by frequent loss, conflicts develop between clinicians, caused largely by feelings of being overwhelmed by the patients and families they are trying to help. Or, difficult patients and families are scapegoated. Both patterns resemble dynamics commonly seen in families coping with these problems over an extended period.

In one instance a hospice program hired a consultant because of intense staff infighting that had developed in recent months. A previous consultation had been unsuccessful because the consultant attempted to encourage expression of negative feelings among the staff, which only left the clinicians feeling more frustrated and helpless. The second consultant met first with the administrative and clinical directors. This discussion revealed that the program under new leadership had been enormously successful, but the increased service demands had overloaded the staff at the same time as many of the long-term personal issues described above were surfacing. The clinicians, having no vehicle for mutual support and reluctant to take their problems home, began to fight with each other. As with burdened families, affirmation and normalization by the consultant laid the foundation of a supportive environment for further discussion.

CLINICIANS' MULTIGENERATIONAL HISTORY

Using the Family Systems–Illness Model can help clarify situations in which clinicians may experience a particular sense of vulnerability with a family. Any multigenerational history of unresolved loss, inadequate coping, or issues related to blame, shame, or guilt can compromise clinical effectiveness. These feelings will be intensified if the case involves the same illness or a similar type of condition, in which some aspect of the experience elicits for the clinician something analogous to a sense of déjà vu or, if extremely painful, a post-traumatic stress reaction. For instance, witnessing a family struggle with a decision to institutionalize a patient with an advanced dementia can rekindle painful memories of the terminal illness of a beloved family member who needed nursing home placement. If this personal experience was tumultuous involving opposition by the patient and other family members and requiring the clinician to play a key role in this difficult decision (which is often the position of health and mental health professionals in their personal lives), the clinician may feel torn and off balance in his or her professional role in the current case. Just as family members' difficulties coping with a particular phase of an illness are often explained by a multigenerational history of a similar traumatic or unresolved circumstance, clinicians' sudden difficulty with a case may be related to surfacing of transgenerational experiences related to a particular phase of an illness.

I have been impressed that clinicians working with particular kinds of disorders or specialty services have a disproportionately frequent personal history of experience with that condition. When I consulted to the diabetes program at Yale New Haven Hospital, I was struck by the number of staff who had diabetes themselves or in their family history. This experience can be a source of great understanding and sensitivity. However, certain patients' dilemmas can trigger a resurfacing of issues and emotions related to the past or to current threatened loss. In these circumstances, we need to be cognizant of our own attempts to master the forces of uncertainty through our clinical practice.

Clinicians need to be aware of the roles they have played in their family of origin or nuclear family in situations of illness and adversity. Experiences as patient, caregiver, helpless bystander, or shielded child are examples of the kinds of roles that can fuel identifications with particular cases or family members. For instance, a clinician with a disabled spouse can show great empathy for the well spouse of a patient with a spinal cord injury; but he or she needs a thorough understanding of the strengths and vulnerabilities in his or her own illness system and marriage, disregard of which could lead to dysfunctional triangular inclusion and interactions with the patient and his or her spouse. For instance, if this clinician had ambivalent feelings and harbored unexpressed escape fantasies in his or her personal situation, he or she might unconsciously project such "unacceptable" feelings onto the well spouse of the patient. This identification and projection process could become linked dysfunctionally with the same ambivalent part of the well spouse and the need for respite or time away might become collusively encouraged in more dramatic ways that get acted out in an affair or premature separation by the well spouse.

A clinician who was in an overly responsible position in his or her family of origin, might gravitate toward assuming too much responsibility for patients' well-being or overlook the needs for respite of devoted caregivers. Similarly, a clinician who was in a rescuer position or felt helpless as a child to rescue a family member in a crisis could have difficulties, especially in illness situations, such as terminal cancer, that cannot be controlled. A clinician would be particularly vulnerable if he or she felt that he or she had failed as a rescuer (as with an alcoholic parent) and needed to make up for it now through his or her patients and their families. A clinician's difficulty in letting go because of such personal experiences could be misinterpreted by the patient's family as a need to persevere in the face of inevitable loss.

LIFE CYCLE TIMING

Clinicians are typically more affected by patients and families who are at the same stage of the individual and family life cycles as themselves. This is especially true for untimely conditions. A pediatric social worker who had worked closely with the oncology service noted increased difficulty with distancing from her clients after the birth of her first child. This kind of reaction is natural, but if denied, can seriously affect one's clinical performance.

Also, clinicians who had illnesses or were involved in a family illness at a particular phase of their own development may identify strongly with a family or a particular family member's situation that occurs at the same phase of the life cycle; or clinicians who had protracted illness in early adolescence that delayed personal autonomy from parents, might identify with teen-agers with disabling conditions. Such life cycle synchronicities can help explain extraordinary empathy as well as personal reactions of distancing or overinvolvement in a case.

ISSUES GENERATED IN THE CLINICIAN'S OWN FAMILY

A common dilemma for clinicians working with chronic disorders and loss involves maintaining a boundary between their professional life and their personal life and family. Clinicians often feel a skew developing between themselves and their family, particularly their partner or spouse. This is often heightened by other family members' not wanting to listen to the intimate experience of the clinician. Family members can feel imploded by reminders of disability, suffering, and loss that threaten well-sealed defenses of denial against existential fears of infirmity and death. Reactive distancing by a partner often occurs when a clinician has an intense need to share his or her experience and be nurtured; and, the clinician, in turn, can feel out of phase with everyone. He or she is attempting to cope psychologically with issues often reserved for later life, and may feel that no one can really understand what he or she is going through. This sense of aloneness and isolation can be terribly disheartening to professionals if they are not prepared for what is really a normal experience. Again, all these processes are isomorphic with those experienced by families coping with chronic conditions, which also feel isolated and out of phase with peers and close family members.

Another problem may arise when spouses or other family members feel that professionals give more time, attention, and nurturance to their patients than to their families. This is particularly common among, but by no means exclusive to, families of physicians. Often this pattern begins in training, with long hours at the hospital or being on call and the patient's needs always coming first. Family members can tolerate sacrificing their own needs for the sake of a relationship goal of successfully finishing professional training. Unfortunately, this skewed pattern often persists, fostering a long-term triangle involving a struggle among the professionals, their patients, and all other family priorities. Often families feel chronically neglected by comparison, and as a result, may resent listening to the personal concerns of professionals generated by their cases.

If an illness occurs in the clinician's family, powerful reactions such as jealousy may occur. In one situation, a terminally ill mother induced tremendous guilt in her daughter, a social worker, for giving more care and concern to her patients than to her own mother. The situation was further complicated by the uncertain course of the mother's illness and the geographic distance from her, which precluded regular visits, and knowing when to take an extended leave. The daughter's conflict was heightened by a professional ethos that involved colleagues' praising her for continuing on with all her clinical responsibilities ("not missing a beat") at a time of personal/family crisis. Systems need to provide support and time out for professionals to attend to caregiving needs in their own families. Professionals adopting this self-caring approach model for families the importance of reducing conflicting job demands to make space for quality time together as well as caregiving.

Clinicians and their family members benefit from open, frank discussion about expectations and limits of support. This is highly variable, depending on family communication styles. Each clinician needs to work out a level of sharing that fits his or her family relationships. Both expectations and reasonable limits of support often need to be established. For the families we treat, a chronic condition may represent the first time family members have had to discuss or negotiate limits and expectations of support. The same holds true for clinicians working with illness and disability. This is especially true for younger couples in which the subject of illness and loss may never have been broached.

Clinicians should anticipate that their experience working with illness may test previously understood boundaries in their personal relationships, particularly with a partner or spouse. Typically, such experience challenges the limits of a couple's conversational comfort zone. It is natural for the concerns confronting their patients to arouse anxieties about clinicians' own family life. Difficulties arise when a clinician's preoccupation with vulnerability, uncertainty, and/or loss in their own lives may be out of sync with their partner's current preoccupation. A young clinician dealing with a young terminally ill patient may become concerned about getting his or her own family affairs in order and drawing up a will–just in case. Raising this subject in one's own family can provide an opportunity for growth or precipitate intense conflict or a crisis.

Even for seasoned clinicians, exposure to a different type of disorder, for instance, one that is especially life-threatening or disfiguring, may evoke personal issues that have remained concealed when working with more benign conditions. A seasoned female clinician working for the first time with a patient who had just had a mastectomy found personal fears about vulnerability and rejection by her spouse surfacing powerfully. A male clinician with the same patient might worry about his spouse's vulnerability to breast cancer.

PSYCHOEDUCATION FOR CLINICIANS AND THEIR FAMILIES

Just as families need to be prepared for what they will need to face over the course of a condition, clinicians working with chronic illness and disability and their families need guidance concerning common issues that may surface in their personal life. From this vantage point, *any psychosocial orientation programs for clinicians would be improved by including their families.* From a systems perspective, this is analogous to the difference between interventions focused solely on the individual and those that include the larger system. A preventive systemic approach geared to the quality of life of the clinician and his or her family can help reduce clinician turnover and loss of work time and optimize professionals' family functioning.

Such a preventive psychoeducational orientation format for clinicians and their families can include the typical psychosocial demands of the kind of disorders a clinician will be working with. For example, Alzheimer's disease involves moderate or severe cognitive impairment, dependency, loss of control, and possible institutionalization. Clinicians involved in the care of patients with Alzheimer's disease and their families need information and support concerning such disorders, to which they are likely to become more sensitive in their own family life. In this regard, clinicians and their families need help in understanding how exposure to particular disorders can shape the kind of issues that become salient in their own lives. For a clinician and his or her spouse, learning about Alzheimer's disease provides an opportunity for discussion about what they might want done if ever one of them were in that position. Like families living with a disorder, clinicians exposed to serious illness have an opportunity for increased intimacy and greater appreciation of the present for themselves and their family. Also, normalizing the powerful influences that chronic disorders can have on all clinician's family members counteracts patterns of self-blame and unnecessary implications of clinician countertransference.

GENERAL GUIDELINES

The foregoing discussion suggests several guidelines for clinicians. Open communication about one's personal experience in working with chronic disorders is essential. There are a number of ways to accomplish this. Generally, clinicians will function best when support can be achieved in a balanced way from their professional and personal lives. In fact, accepting the fact that achieving total support in one area is unrealistic will help avert unavoidable disappointments.

For clinicians working in an institutional setting, building into the schedule an opportunity for processing personal experience is the best approach. Similar to the developmental needs of families, an initial orientation phase for new clinicians can serve as a base for involvement in ongoing group programs for long-term adaptation. As in any group process, disclosure of personal matters will need time to reach a comfortable level. However, the shared experience of common dilemmas of working with particular disorders or types of issues, such as loss, will facilitate this process. This is similar to a family support group in which dealing with a common disorder promotes disclosure. Also, clinicians usually entertain myths about what their colleagues would think about their struggles. As mentioned earlier, these beliefs typically represent projections onto co-workers of beliefs about unrealistic professional standards.

The Family Systems–Illness Model provides a framework for conceptualizing the needs of clinicians and a health-care team. First, clinicians will be more effective if they appreciate the culture and basic dynamics of the system they are working in. This includes patterns of communication about practical and emotional issues, problem solving, hierarchy and role differentiation, and so on. Second, they need a common understanding of the psychosocial demands over time of the different kinds of disorders they are treating. Third, they need to understand the belief systems, multigenerational patterns, and life cycle issues relevant to themselves and the program or institution in which they are working.

The effectiveness of psychoeducation or consultation to a program depends largely on understanding the evolution of developmental strains for each clinician, the health-care team, and any supporting institution. Use of this framework offers clinicians the same psychosocial map for their own experience that is provided for families. The model highlights common transitions and nodal points of strain at which cost-effective use of a consultant might be indicated.

CLINICIAN PSYCHOTHERAPY

Clinicians need to normalize the possibility that working with chronic disorders may stimulate the need for psychotherapy. Just as we strive to normalize such a need for average families coping with long-term conditions, we have to make room in our own experience for added support. Professional involvement with illness and loss is usually an added strain, particularly with certain patients or at different junctures of our own individual and family life cycles. Including psychotherapy as an acceptable option increases the range of choices for support and reduces anxieties about burdening family members or losing control in a professional situation. Self-exploration, in some form, of personal issues related to illness and loss should be included in one's training experience, regardless of discipline. Ultimately, one's comfort and effectiveness in working with families coping with illness and disability depends largely upon one's ability to accept one's own vulnerability and mortality and the inevitable loss of loved ones.

Boundary Issues

THE CLINICIAN'S PERSONAL BOUNDARIES WITH THE PATIENT'S FAMILY

Maintaining traditional patient–clinician boundaries is often more complex in chronic disorders. Traditional mental health guidelines are often more difficult to establish and maintain. There are several reasons for this. First, as discussed earlier, a "we–they" split between the clinician and the patient or family is illusory to the extent that we all have, or will inevitably have, to face illness, death, and loss. I think it is vital to distinguish a therapeutic humility based on common experience as humans from a professional boundary designed to preserve a therapeutic function. Most forms of family intervention are not based on fostering or preserving a transference relationship and therefore are less dependent upon strict rules about boundaries and self-disclosure. The Family Systems–Illness Model strongly advocates the use of normalization, which includes selective use of self-disclosure as an important therapeutic resource.

In New Haven, which is a small city, many families seeking my help knew that I had lost my first wife to cancer. Initially I was concerned that this would interfere with my helping families. As I examined my own feelings of vulnerability, I realized that my discomfort was connected to my professional training and beliefs that to maintain a therapeutic edge required keeping significant and not completely worked-through personal experiences outside the therapy relationship. Because I was anxious about how this knowledge might affect the therapeutic relationship, I would ask families directly about what it meant to them. I discovered that families valued the fact that I had "been there" and could probably empathize more directly with their situation. This was valuable in establishing rapport and making families feel comfortable. At the same time, I was aware that I maintained control over what I chose to disclose and that families were generally very respectful of personal boundaries.

The most significant aspect of self-disclosure has to do with awareness of for what purpose and for whose benefit the self-disclosure is intended. Generally, it is risky for clinicians to use self-disclosure as a vehicle for working through unresolved personal issues. This should be distinguished from the use of disclosure, when appropriate, of issues not completely worked through. One needs to be mindful when revealing personal information that one should think about the effect on all family members. Like the need for couples therapists to consider the impact of their own gender on both members of a couple, a therapist working with an illness situation needs to be mindful of the impact on a couple dealing with cancer of revealing that he or she either has a chronic illness or is or was a well spouse. In a high-conflict situation, a triangle can be fostered, in which the couple can perceive the clinician in alliance with the spouse with whom he or she shares a common history.

Second, work with families dealing with chronic conditions often requires clinicians to adapt to a number of settings, such as: office, hospital, intensive care unit, family home, extended-care facility, or hospice. Just as families learn to adapt their relationships to various unfamiliar settings, the clinician must do the same. Flexible expectations about boundaries and intrusions will facilitate clinician comfort. With conditions requiring frequent hospitalizations, such as kidney failure, the family needs to adapt to unavoidable transitions and intrusions. If we rigidly enforce a traditional boundary around the therapeutic process, we severely restrict our options to help families at critical junctures, where our rules become incompatible with external realities.

Families frequently invite clinicians to participate in important family rituals. At other times, clinicians may need to participate in rituals, such as a memorial service, for their own as well as the family's sense of closure. Families are very appreciative when clinicians who have been involved in a family member's care take the time to join the family in saying good-bye. Clinicians often avoid this kind of participation, because of fear they may possibly lose control and cry. This fear is usually not the family's concern. Rather, it often reflects a clinician's conflict with beliefs about professionalism that dictate a certain level of objectivity and personal composure. At the end of a protracted illness, family closure and healing are promoted by a transformation of the professional's role from a technological one connected with health-care settings to a more basic human one by joining the family at the graveside or in the family's home.

In one family, in which the mother died after a bone marrow transplant for leukemia, the husband invited me to listen to a piano recital given by his two young daughters in the home, with friends and extended family present. This event affirmed the life of their mother, who loved music. It also brought me into the family's expression of continuity and hope for the future, even in a time of great sadness. This poignant ritual facilitated their closure with me, and mine with them. It helped me see their belief in recovery, which would have been much more difficult if my final picture of them had been the scene of mother's death in the intensive care unit.

In general, differences in beliefs between professionals and a family should be acknowledged. Pseudomutuality with a family can be as harmful as complete disregard of their beliefs. Families often believe that mental health professionals are, by training, not supposed to reveal their honest feelings. Pretending to agree with them feeds family beliefs about disingenuous professionals. Also, clinicians need to be aware of a belief system alliance with a particular member of a family. This occurs normally, but if such an alliance is hidden or denied, especially to oneself, it can preclude any chance of therapeutic neutrality.

INCLUSION OF CLINICIANS AND HEALTH-CARE INSTITUTIONS IN THE PATIENT'S FAMILY LIFE

Information and community resources

Because community resources and services can be so valuable in family coping with chronic conditions, clinicians should understand how a family's health beliefs influence its willingness to include professionals in its system and the family's overall health behavior within a community (Mechanic, 1978). Families need health-care professionals to provide adequate information about potentially helpful outside resources and linkages.

Clinicians should become familiar with the availability of and access to community resources relevant to the management of long-term conditions. This includes a range of primary and tertiary medical, rehabilitation, respite, transportation, housing, institutional, and financial entitlement services. It also includes potential support from friends, neighbors, self-help groups, and religious, ethnic/cultural, or other community groups.

It is very useful to inquire whether a family's previous experience with such resources been affirming or alienating? Is the family adequately informed about potential outside sources of help? Ignorance may reflect family isolation from the community because of factors such as geographic distance, lack of education (for instance, literacy), language barrier, poverty, race, or ethnic/religious differences from the wider culture. A family's willingness to use outside resources may be limited or facilitated by cultural/ethnic values, family dynamics, and their belief systems.

For example, rigidly enmeshed families tend to view the world as dangerous and threatening to their fragile sense of autonomy. Personal autonomy is sacrificed to keep the family unit intact. Control issues concerning management of a chronic condition will need to be defined within a framework of family exclusiveness that minimizes the role of outsiders. A chronic disorder presents a powerful dilemma for these families. The condition may necessitate frequent excursions beyond the family borders or require the inclusion of professionals in disease management. Any hope of establishing a viable family–health-care team relationship depends on exquisite sensitivity to this interplay of dysfunctional family dynamics and its belief system. In situations that warrant ongoing professional involvement or sustained care, such families will need active assistance and links to potential supports, plus help in overcoming mistrust.

Mutual accommodation

As discussed in chapter 9, healthy family adaptation to illness and disability involves balanced inclusion of the condition in all family processes.

Adjustment to health-care institutions, professionals, and treatment procedures are crucial elements of the adaptational process. One aspect of this developmental task involves psychological acceptance of the disorder and its implications. This needs to be distinguished from the extent of day-to-day inclusion of procedures, professionals, or institutions, which can vary enormously depending on the practical demands of a particular disorder. It can be as limited as a momentary reminder to take medications with breakfast or as extensive as round-the-clock care in a nursing home. Conditions that are highly uncertain and life-threatening, such as a heart attack, tend to foster greater dependence on professionals as permanent, included members in the psychosocial life of a family, regardless of day-to-day medical needs. Because disorders differ tremendously in their inherent intrusion on families and families vary widely in their capacity for or comfort with these inclusion processes, clinicians need to consider carefully both sides of this equation.

The family FIRO model developed by William Doherty and Nicholas Colangelo (1984) and derived from Will Schutz's (1958) Fundamental Interpersonal Orientations model is useful in understanding struggles for control and conflicts developing between families and clinicians. The model describes three core dimensions—inclusion, control, and intimacy—that constitute a developmental sequence. If issues related to inclusion, concerning bonding, boundaries, and shared meaning are not adequately addressed first, then issues of control and power will be difficult to resolve.

With hospital admission, the patient and family must adapt to a time-limited shift based on foreign turf. Control issues often center on the degree to which the health-care setting allows or encourages families to maintain aspects of their identity. This means both the permissible options of the hospital or unit and patient assertiveness in personalizing the hospital room and the overall experience. The fit between family rituals, such as bedside vigils, and rules of the hospital system for patient and family behavior is one example. Conflicting norms that occur at key junctures in the illness life cycle are particularly significant. This frequently surfaces as an issue of control that can severely impair the mutual acceptance and inclusion process between the health-care and family systems, as the following case vignette illustrates.

A family and close friends had gathered at the hospital the day after the patient had been diagnosed with inoperable cancer. It was a very emotional time for all concerned. Late in the day, several family members and friends had to leave. In the hospital lobby, as the father and son were saying good-bye to a male friend, the emotions that had been contained erupted, and the three men began to cry and hug each other. Within moments, the lobby receptionist had a hospital security guard (both were men) tell these three grieving men that they would have to move on. They were hastily ushered into an examining room adjacent to the lobby.

For the family, this was an incident they never forgot, and for which they never forgave the hospital. The hospital was making a statement about acceptable behavior: crying was not permitted in major public areas of the hospital. And the fact that it involved three men was considered as particularly disruptive to the equanimity the hospital wished to project at its gates. The metamessage was that men should not display their feelings because that conveyed a lack of control and weakness that undermined the image of normality the hospital wished to convey. This experience was central to the framing event of this family, particularly in its interface with the health system and the initial inclusion process; and it impaired the joining process and later became expressed in heightened control issues about treatment decisions between the physician and the family.

Besides the need for mutual understanding and sensitivity, this case highlights how interface problems need to be considered in the context of the history of the interactions between the family and the professional caregiving system. In the same way that a family's multigenerational history of experiences with illness and loss is vital to an initial assessment (chapter 5), so is the history of a family's encounters with health and mental health systems and professionals. It is essential to understand experiences that were particularly affirming or traumatic. This is analogous to the need for couples forming a new relationship to understand their own and their partner's prior experiences with intimacy so that strengths are affirmed and areas of vulnerability are acknowledged, rather than enacted dysfunctionally.

The act of inquiry about earlier experiences with health/mental health professionals and institutions is itself a first step toward healing negative legacies. The clinician is acknowledging the importance of the family history of previous experience of and relationships with health-care providers. Sometimes it is useful for families to write to or recontact professionals with whom they have had either very good or particularly disappointing or traumatic encounters. Closure may be needed in either instance before a patient or family can trust or move on to a new relationship. The dynamics are similar to unresolved multigenerational issues in families.

Sometimes young adults who have had lifelong conditions have difficulty forming a new relationship with adult programs because closure with pediatric clinicians never occurred. The importance of separation and loss issues with regard to a patient's "second" family is underestimated. In serious life-threatening conditions, such as cystic fibrosis, in which reaching adulthood is considered a therapeutic success, clinicians celebrate the medical triumph and minimize the relationship losses between them and family members that are the by-product of medical success. The true significance of previous relationships with professionals and health-care systems can be appreciated only by tracking the family's narratives. Useful questions include: "What did you like best about your relationship with Dr. Jones, or about your past hospital experiences?" and "What would you have changed about it?"

Dilemmas of home-based care

Where extensive home care is involved, clinicians—particularly nurses—may need to be incorporated into daily family life in the family's own territory. Again, conflicts about control often reflect problems of basic inclusion that have not been addressed by the clinician or the family. This inclusion process is compounded by the level of importance of the clinician to basic survival of the ill member. Highly cohesive families and those with strong beliefs in personal control typically have the greatest difficulty in accepting home-based and protracted or permanent institutional care. Plans for such intensive care need to include discussion with the family about the meaning to them of incorporating a professional. For an elderly couple, a live-in nurse can simultaneously be a source of desperately needed respite and a first-time intrusion on the couple's privacy after fifty years.

Sometimes the arrival of a clinician can create a triangle in a dysfunctional relationship.

In one case, a nurse entered a home where an elderly terminally ill woman was being cared for by her daughter. Although the nurse was medically necessary, the daughter was extremely resentful of her attempts to exercise any control. She was clearly an unwelcome guest in the eyes of the daughter. The nurse became exasperated as the interactions between the two became increasingly contentious. As the clinician described the case, it became clear that this particular daughter had never felt affirmed by her critical mother, who, she thought, favored her two sisters.

As commonly happens in a situation with an aging parent, a sibling who has felt rejected and still seeks approval becomes a primary caregiver, envisioning the caregiving situation as a final attempt to get what he or she needs from the parent. Often this kind of situation does provide a real opportunity for reconciliation and relationship closure between family members. In this case the mother had not responded to her daughter's efforts. The arrival of the nurse, which the mother welcomed, for the daughter represented a re-creation of old triangular conflicts in which she had witnessed her siblings being favored and interference with her attempts to get close to her mother. And just as she had done repeatedly while growing up and as an adult, she fought with her perceived rivals (her sisters and now the nurse) rather than express her feelings of rejection directly to her mother.

In this case, the nurse had not connected how her arrival represented an interference with the daughter's single-minded mission to take care of her mother. Also, the nurse's arrival signaled that time was running out. As frequently happens, the daughter's despair about impending loss was displaced onto a clinician. Here, the physician was not available, so the clinician involved in the immediate care became the target of family rage about impending loss and the limits of control.

I suggested that the nurse begin by affirming how much the daughter had done and noting that sometimes it is hard not to be fully appreciated (a feeling with which a home health-care nurse can easily identify). This led to a shift and immediate softening on the daughter's part, who then confided to the nurse her relationship difficulties with her mother. After this joining of forces, the sharing of roles could be negotiated more smoothly. Also, the nurse was included in the system in a way that potentially enabled her to intervene with regard to the real issue, help the daughter accept the limits of her relationship with her mother, or include a family consultant.

This kind of long-term unresolved family dynamics needs to be distinguished from issues related to acceptance of transition to a new stage of a condition. Often the need for home-based or 24-hour care symbolizes the transition to a terminal phase. Family resistance to acceptance of this fact can easily be expressed toward a clinician as anger, distancing, or struggles for control. It is important to inquire whether the professionals' and family's understanding of the meaning of more extensive care is in sync. If the inclusion of professional caregivers represents a transition to a more terminal phase, helping families cope with that fact can aid in preventing conflict among family members and with clinicians.

Fit among Clinicians, Health-Care Systems, and Families

ILLNESS PHASE-RELATED ISSUES

Just as families can experience strain in accommodating to different settings, professional disciplines, and individual clinicians, there can be an ongoing change in fit between a clinician and a family in different contexts and at different phases of the illness. One should think about the fit of beliefs as an evolving phenomenon that changes over the course of a disorder, particularly in relation to the illness, individual, and family life cycles. Nodal points or transitions in these life cycles are key junctures at which a clash of beliefs may emerge or increase to dysfunctional proportions.

Since the typical goal of a medical workup during the *crisis phase* is a diagnosis, the meaning of symptoms are often objectified in a narrow biological way. In this context, family belief systems can become, for professionals, an extraneous distraction from the central medical task. Moreover, the failure of clinicians to acknowledge the patient's and family members' belief system or explanation of the illness can signal a disrespect for the patient and family, hubris in the face of alternative viewpoints, and failure of health-care providers to acknowledge the importance of the psychosocial in relation to the technological dimension. Unfortunately, a technological imperative has become a fundamental belief of professionals, for many disciplines even synonymous with professionalism.

During a *health crisis*, the patient may be admitted to the most technologically sophisticated part of a health system, such as the intensive care unit. For all concerned, there is a heightened focus on the competition between technology and disease. In this context, beliefs about success easily become technologically focused within a battlefield mentality. In such situations it requires the utmost skill for clinicians and families to remain sensitive to issues of quality of life, personal dignity, and compassionate care as core beliefs that need to be sustained throughout a chronic illness, not left at the doors to the intensive care unit. Typically, the patient's room is so full of high-tech equipment that there is no space to personalize. One hurried, normally sensitive physician exclaimed bluntly, "Get that picture (a family photo) out of the way so I can see the monitor." In this pressured instant, a monolithic professional belief about competency superseded all others at the expense of the well-being of the family and of the physician's relationship with its members.

Normative differences among family members or between family and professional or institutional health beliefs may become destructive conflicts during a health crisis, as in the following instance, in which I was called to consult on a case in an intensive care unit.

The head nurse for the ICU called for me to intervene with a patient and his mother who were disrupting the unit because the mother insisted on remaining at her son's bedside. The ICU's customary rules limited family visits to ten minutes. Also, the highly emotional arguing among the patient, his wife, and his mother about this issue was a further annoyance that was impossible to manage.

The patient, Stavros H., a successful professional in his early forties, had been admitted to the ICU with symptoms of intractable angina. Stavros, a first-generation Greek-American, had been married for twelve years to Dana, who was from a Scandinavian background. A long-standing smoldering triangular conflict had existed for the couple in terms of Stavros's divided loyalties between his strong relationship to his family of origin, particularly his mother, and his spouse. When Stavros was admitted to the hospital with heart disease, his mother began a 24-hour vigil by her son's hospital bed, so she could tend to him at any hour. Dana greatly resented her mother-in-law's seemingly intrusive behavior. Mrs. H. criticized what she perceived as Dana's emotional coldness and relative lack of concern. Stavros felt caught between his warring mother and wife and complained of increased symptoms.

Before beginning my consultation, I became acutely aware of the multiple layers of conflicting beliefs and positions, including my own, that were at issue in this situation. Because the request was made by the head nurse to me in my capacity as a consultation-liaison psychiatrist, a basic understanding was that I should fulfill my loyalty to the hospital. This meant restoring an optimal environment for the ICU to carry out its normal medical functions of caring for acutely ill patients in life-threatening situations. From the unit's perspective, the mother was interfering with the ICU's basic mission of providing state-of-the-art technological care. From this vantage point, the Greek mother's continuous presence and emotionality constituted the problem, whereas the "unemotional" wife who felt comfortable keeping her distance was seen as a healthy ally of the unit. Therefore, in the triangular conflict among the family members, the unit inadvertently had chosen sides. And, the covert assumption was that I should see and intervene in the situation accordingly—through the lens of the unit's primary purpose and the kinds of family beliefs and behaviors that would support that mission.

Both the family and the ICU expected me to determine who was normal and who was sick. For the family, which had lived with this smoldering triangular conflict for years, this crisis brought their problem to professional attention for the first time. The family saw me as a powerful tie-breaking vote that would resolve its long-standing feud. Both his mother and wife lobbied for my vote, while Stavros looked on in torn dismay.

In this case all concerned behaved according to their own cultural norms. In Greek culture, it is normal to maintain close ties to one's family of origin after marriage and expected that a mother would tend to her son in a health crisis. A son would be disloyal not to allow his mother that role. This sharply differed from the Scandinavian traditions of the wife. Each side considered the other pathological, creating a conflictual triangle with the patient caught in the middle.

In this situation it was vital first to affirm normative multicultural differences that had reached an emotional crescendo during a health crisis. Essentially, I announced there was no need for a vote since I saw everyone behaving normally. My position added new information that created an unexpected alternative belief that the family had never considered. This helped promote a transformation of process from blaming, and pathologizing to one of accommodating different, equally legitimate cultures. This intervention allowed the beliefs and values of all family members to be affirmed, which then facilitated a process of mutual acceptance.

The mother had accurately perceived the medical team's alliance with her daughter-in-law. This had only heightened her reactivity to the unit, which, in turn, increased the unit's reactive attempts to control her in a mutually escalating cycle. Further, she assumed that I would have undivided loyalty to the hospital and, therefore, would side with the unit and Dana. Removing the issue of identifying the locus of pathology allowed a team problem-solving approach. I was able to address Stavros and his mother in the following manner: "The unit and I really understand how important your being together at this time is for both of you. Do you think you could help the unit out by compromising a little so that it can give you the best medical care possible?"

My intervention in this case involved psychosocial shuttle diplomacy. Discussion with the ICU staff about my view of the family was coupled with requests for some flexibility on its part to the extent that the technological medical care could be delivered without significant compromise. I suggested that affirming the mother's values would enable her to work with the unit rather than in opposition to it. Interestingly, my position of neutrality and normalization opened discussion among unit staff about their own personal family values. Some unacknowledged cultural differences among the staff were openly communicated for the first time. This increased the cultural sensitivity and flexibility of the unit in subsequent cases.

In this case my own personal and professional belief system was an important consideration. My cultural background was more in sync with the Greek side of this family, in the sense that rituals such as bedside vigils are a common Jewish tradition. This could easily have interfered with my maintaining neutrality with the family, since loyalty as expressed through ritual was a central theme in this situation. Also, it could have created problems with my relationship to the ICU, since my tendency to ally with the mother and son about appropriate ritual would have been in opposition to the coalition between the ICU and Dana. In this way the conflict within the family could have been acted out isomorphically between the unit and me. My tendency to ally with the Greek side of the family could have been further intensified by prevailing professional beliefs about optimal mental health. Mental health professionals are generally taught to value open communication and full expression of feelings. Here, the mother–son relationship was more open and expressive than those involving Dana. Reinforcement of that value in this situation could have been easily interpreted as an alliance with the Greek side of the system.

Transition points

It is common for differences in beliefs or attitudes to erupt at major treatment or illness transition points. For instance, the murky boundary between the *chronic and terminal phase* highlights the potential for professionals beliefs to collide with the family's. The attitudes and behaviors of the health-care team can either facilitate or hinder this process for a family. A health-care team that continues heroic efforts to control the death of the patient can convey confusing messages. Families may not know how to interpret continued lifesaving efforts, assuming there is real hope when virtually none exists. Physicians can feel bound to a technological imperative that requires them to exhaust all possibilities at their disposal, regardless of the odds of success.

Often physicians feel committed to this course for ethical reasons, a "leave no stone unturned" philosophy, or because of concerns about legal liability. Is the medical team having its own difficulties letting go? Strong relationships with certain patients can be fueled by identifications with losses, often unresolved, in health professionals' own lives. Health-care professionals and institutions can collude in a pervasive societal wish to deny death as a natural process truly beyond technological control (Becker, 1973). Endless treatment can represent the medical team's inability to separate a general value placed on controlling diseases from its beliefs about participation (separate from cure) in a patient's total care.

Professionals need to examine closely their own motives for treatments geared toward cure rather than palliation, particularly when a patient may be entering a terminal phase. And professionals' self-examination needs to be done in concert with careful understanding of families' belief systems.

ETHICAL DILEMMAS

The convoluted web of ethical and legal dilemmas surrounding decisions about control over life and death is one of the most difficult areas for clinicians and families. Since 1991, the Patient Self-Determination Act dictates that all patients admitted to hospitals and nursing homes be given information concerning advance directives that cover such areas as any desired limits of treatment, including do-not-resuscitate orders; and who has the authority to make decisions for the patient in the case of severe incapacitation. It is essential that clinicians encourage open dialogue among family members and with involved clinicians. We need to be very mindful of our own personal and professional beliefs in these areas so that we do not impose our values on families. This is particularly significant when there is disagreement among family members and a clinician voicing an opinion prematurely or too forcefully may create an inadvertent coalition with one part of the family system or shut down a family process that needs to continue. I think it is very important and beneficial for clinicians to have some type of professional peer forum to discuss difficult cases and common ethical dilemmas.

Euthanasia

The issue of euthanasia is highly controversial. Whatever our personal feelings regarding this subject, we should remember that families in hopeless situations often discuss it and sometimes do take matters into their own hands.

In one case a man with a terminal form of cancer who was admitted for possible brain and bone metastases informed the consulting psychiatrist and the oncologist that if medical tests confirmed widespread disease, he was going to go home and commit suicide. He was not clinically depressed. Further, he said that he and his wife (they had no children) had discussed this fully and with other close friends and family. He had no psychiatric history and had led a satisfying personal and professional life. The clinicians felt torn. On one hand, they knew mental health law pertaining to suicidal patients. On the other, they both felt that patients with terminal illnesses involving great suffering should have control over how and when they chose to end their life. In this instance, the two physicians decided not to document the patient's comments, leaving him and his family with final control over the decision. Fortunately, this man's medical tests were normal.

In the Netherlands for the past twenty years, patients with terminal conditions, their families, and physicians can negotiate the terms for ending life. One man with terminal cancer articulated most poignantly the issue of personal rights to choose a peaceful end to unbearable suffering:

> I don't see the point of suffering for nothing. . . . Initially, the fear of death and the unknown sucked away so much of my energy. When I was assured that I was allowed to hold my life in my own hands until the last second, then this energy that I had used for this fear was set free to use for fighting the cancer. . . . My energy was set free by the real human attitude, not moralistic one, of my doctor. . . . I felt that I had always been responsible for myself and that the last part (of my life) should be included." (PBS, Frontline 1993)

Multiple and Larger Systems Interface Issues

Families coping with chronic disorders often need to deal with multiple treating systems and clinicians. Because these systems are often disengaged from one another and conflictual in their purposes and interactions, a family's need for cohesion in the face of adversity conflicts with these larger system dynamics. For example, the financial goals of insurance companies or managed care systems can be fundamentally at odds with a physician's goal of quality care. Unfortunately, the family pays the financial and the psychosocial price. A family systems consultant can help reduce the disengagement process by providing the psychosocial equivalent of the family physician as a medical case coordinator when a number of specialists are involved in continuing care.

An initial family consultation should include an assessment of the various interlocking layers of clinicians and systems that are currently involved and outlining the anticipated course of the condition and what other systems will become part of the process. A systems consultant, functioning as a bridge between the health-care system and the family, may have the best perspective on and opportunity to understand the implications of this complex interface for a family. In this role, the clinician needs to function flexibly as psychosocial interpreter, shuttle diplomat, mediator, and advocate.

In situations of ambivalence or differences over important decisions, isomorphic replications easily occur among interfacing systems. When dysfunctional unresolved conflicts exist within the family, different clinicians or systems can become isomorphically aligned with these warring parts of the family. If a family is divided about the need for nursing home placement of a deteriorating aging parent, clinicians or services may argue by proxy about the same issue. Similarly, a family given inconsistent advice about the need for a placement may develop a family debate that mirrors unresolved issues emanating from professionals. An effective systems intervention will require understanding these kinds of dynamics when family and provider systems interact.

Sometimes a systems intervention may involve a meeting of family and professionals together with the family systems consultant. This is easiest to suggest if the initial framing event about the consultant's role has been defined as collaborative. This can be accomplished in the referral process, when the consultant and primary medical provider meet together briefly with the family as a way to introduce the former's involvement within a team model. When this is not convenient, the same groundwork can be established by the family systems consultant's having early contact with the health-care team. This process, which communicates a functional flexible boundary among professionals, needs to be sensitively balanced with family needs for confidentiality regarding personal issues.

Often health professionals think that mental health professionals are unapproachable. In situations of chronic disorders, ongoing, multiple system involvement that includes other professionals is inevitable. Because of this fact, strict traditional rules about communication among a therapist, other professionals, and family members can become dysfunctional and heighten tendencies toward disengagement. For instance, when family members disagree about the possibility of loss, helping them establish family priorities that are uninformed by medical advice might be destructive and irresponsible. When working with chronic disorders, mental health clinicians need to examine how their rules for therapy may need to be adapted to meet ongoing interface issues.

Conclusion: Principles for Family-Oriented Programs and Policies

Living well with the stresses and uncertainties of illness and disability can be a monumental challenge. The model I have described offers a way to meet this challenge and make the inevitable strains more manageable. In our postmodern era we are encouraged to think contextually and respect multiple realities and perspectives. In this sense, each family's experience with illness and disability is unique and cannot be reduced to a clinical formula. Yet, there are predictable issues that can help us guide a family's quest for meaning and mastery of the challenges, and promote both the professionals' and family's needs for empowering and for functional narratives about the illness experience.

Any family that has lived with illness and disability understands at some basic level that clinical care and effective coping and adaptation can best occur within a healing environment that is family-centered, contextual, and, above all, collaborative. When we ask ourselves or our loved ones what we would want in a personal health crisis, there is a great deal of consensus within our diversity. Attending to the longitudinal psychosocial pattern of a condition within a multigenerational, life cycle, and belief system context can provide the kind of structure—a common language that facilitates collaborative, creative problem solving and quality of life for families facing serious health problems.

To this end, we need family-centered health policies and programmatic initiatives (Elliott, 1993). The following principles are imperative to support families coping with illness and disability (Rolland, 1993b):

- Policies should address the immediate and long-term needs of families and their members facing a health crisis and its sequelae.
- The definition of family should be broad enough to encompass the diversity of family forms in contemporary society.
- Families facing chronic conditions need health-care reforms that reimburse preventively oriented family and relational-centered mental health

services. Access to psychosocial care should be guaranteed and reimbursed on the same basis as physical health care.

- More resources must be directed toward the prevention of the psychosocial problems associated with chronic disorders. The efficacy of routinely offering a family psychosocial consultation at the time of diagnosis or early in the crisis phase of a serious health problem should be documented by research.
- Policies that advocate comprehensive home and community-based care should become part of the system, thereby reducing institution-based care. These include expanded provisions for rehabilitation and long-term care supporting the caregiving roles provided by families while protecting their job and economic security.
- Policies concerning continuing life-support and euthanasia need to be advanced. The realities of these complex decisions need to be addressed, not just from technological and ethical perspectives, but also in terms of the profound impact on family well-being and resources.
- Efficient collaborative family-centered models that include health-care institutions, providers, the workplace, and patients and their families need to be implemented as a way to significantly improve the quality of care, reduce direct and indirect costs, improve productivity, and enhance family well-being (Bloch, 1993).
- Basic knowledge about family dynamics and the developmental demands of various health problems over the life course of an illness or disability should be included in the education of all health and mental health professionals.
- Innovative programs should be implemented to address workplace and family caregiving needs. These should include flexible work arrangements that accommodate the immediate and long-term demands of illness and disability while maintaining the continuity of home and work life equitably for both men and women.
- Programs should be sensitive and flexible to accommodate the different cultures of families and meet the needs of families at various life cycle stages.

Above all, we must advocate for a humane, responsive system of health care that provides this vision of care not as a privilege but a basic right for all patients and their families.

References

Abramson, L., Garber, G., & Seligman, M. E. P. (1980). Learned helplessness in humans: An attributional analysis. In J. Garber & M. E. P. Seligman (eds.), *Human helplessness: Theory and applications*. New York: Academic Press.

Adams, J. E., & Lindemann, E. (1974). Coping with longterm disability. In G. V. Coelho, D. A. Hamburg, & J. E. Adams (eds.), *Coping and adaptation*. New York: Basic Books.

Ader, R. (ed.) (1981). *Psychoneuroimmunology*. New York: Academic Press.

Akamatsu, J., Stephens, M. A., Hobfoll, S., & Crowther, J. (eds.) (1992). *Family health psychology*. Washington, DC: Hemisphere Publishing.

Anderson, C. M. (1982). The community connection: The impact of social networks on family and individual functioning. In F. Walsh (ed.), *Normal family processes* (1st ed.). New York: Guilford Press.

Anderson, C. M., Hogarty, G. E., & Reiss, D. J. (1980). Family treatment of adult schizophrenic patients: A psychoeducational approach. *Schizophrenia Bulletin*, 6, 490–505.

Anderson, C. M., Hogarty, G., & Reiss, D. (1981). The psychoeducational family treatment of schizophrenia. In M. Goldstein (ed.), *Interventions with families of schizophrenics*. San Francisco: Jossey-Bass.

Anderson, C. M., Reiss, D., & Hogarty, G. (1986). *Schizophrenia and the family*. New York: Guilford Press.

Anderson, H., & Goolishian, H. A. (1988). Human systems as linguistic systems: Preliminary and evolving ideas about the implications for clinical theory. *Family Process*, 27, 371–93.

Antonovsky, A. (1979). *Health, stress, and coping*. San Francisco: Jossey-Bass.

Antonovsky, A., & Sourani, T. (1988). Family sense of coherence and family adaptation. *Journal of Marriage and the Family*, 50, 79–92.

Baker, L., Minuchin, S., Milman, L., et al. (1975). Psychosomatic aspects of juvenile diabetes melitus: A progress report. In *Modern problems in pediatrics*. White Plains, NY: S. Karger.

Bateson, G. (1972). *Steps to an ecology of mind*. New York: Ballantine.

Bateson, G. (1979) *Mind and nature: A necessary unity.* New York: Dutton.

Beavers, J., Hampson, R., Hulgus, Y., & Beavers, W. R. (1986). Coping in families with a retarded child. *Family Process, 25,* 365–78.

Beavers, W. R., & Hampson, R. B. (1990). *Successful families: Assessment and intervention.* New York: Norton.

Beavers, W. R., & Voeller, M. N. (1983). Family models: Comparing and contrasting the Olson circumplex model with the Beavers systems model. *Family Process, 22,* 85–99.

Beavers, W. R., & Hampson, R. B. (1993). Measuring family competence: The Beavers systems model. In F. Walsh (ed.), *Normal family processes* (2nd ed.). New York: Norton.

Becker, E. (1973). *The denial of death.* New York: Free Press.

Benson, H. (1979). *The mind/body effect.* New York: Simon & Schuster.

Berger, P., & Luckmann, T. (1966). *The social construction of reality.* Garden City, NY: Doubleday.

Bishop, D. S., & Epstein, N. B. (1980). Family problems and disability. In D. S. Bishop (ed.), *Behavior problems and the disabled: Assesssment and management.* Baltimore, MD: Williams and Wilkins.

Bloch, D. A. (1993). The "full-service" model: An immodest proposal. *Family Systems Medicine, 11,* 1–9.

Borden, W. (1991). Stress, coping, and adaptation in spouses of older adults with chronic dementia. *Social Work Research and Abstracts, 27,* 14–22.

Borysenko, J. (1987). *Minding the body, mending the mind.* New York: Bantam Books.

Boss, P., Caron, W., Horbal, J., & Mortimer, J. (1990). Predictors of depression in caregivers of dementia patients: Boundary ambiguity and mastery. *Family Process, 29,* 245–54.

Boss, P., Caron, W., & Horbal, J. (1988). Alzheimer's disease and ambiguous loss. In C. Chilman, E. Nunnally, & F. Cox (eds.), *Chronic illness and disability: Families in trouble series,* Vol. 2. Beverly Hills, CA: Sage Publications.

Boss, P., & Greenberg, J. (1984). Family boundary ambiguity: A new variable in family stress theory. *Family Process, 23,* 535–46.

Boszormenyi-Nagy, I. (1987). *Foundations of contextual family therapy.* New York: Brunner/Mazel.

Boszormenyi-Nagy, I., & Spark, G. (1973). *Invisible loyalties: Reciprocity in intergenerational family therapy.* New York: Harper & Row.

Bowen, M. (1976). Theory in the practice of psychotherapy. In P. J. Guerin (ed.), *Family therapy: Theory and practice.* New York: Gardner Press.

Bowen, M. (1978a). Family reaction to death. In M. Bowen, *Family therapy in clinical practice.* New York: Jason Aronson.

Bowen, M. (1978b). *Family therapy in clinical practice.* New York: Jason Aronson.

Bradley, C. (1979). Life events and the control of diabetes mellitus. *Journal of Psychosomatic Research, 23,* 159–62.

Breslau, N. (1983). The psychological study of chronically ill and disabled children: Are healthy siblings appropriate controls? *Journal of Abnormal Child Psychology, 11,* 379–91.

Brody, E. M. (1974). Aging and family personality: A developmental view. *Family Process, 13,* 23–37.

Broyard, A. (1992). *Intoxicated by my illness.* New York: Fawcett Columbine.

Byng-Hall, J. (1988). Scripts and legends in families and family therapy. *Family Process, 27,* 167–81.

Cadman, D., Boyle, M., & Offord, D. (1988). The Ontario Child Health Study: Social adjustment and mental health of siblings of children with chronic health problems. *Developmental and Behavioral Pediatrics, 9*(3). 117–21.

Campbell, T. L. (1986). *Family's impact on health: A critical review and annotated bibliography.* National Institute of Mental Health Series DN No. 6, DHHS Pub. No. (ADM) 86-1461. Washington, DC: U. S. Government Printing Office. (Also available in *Family Systems Medicine,* 4[2][3], 135–328.)

Cantor, M. (1983). Strain among caregivers: A study of experience in the United States. *The Gerontologist, 23,* 597–604.

Carter, E. A., & McGoldrick, M. (eds.) (1989). *The changing family life cycle: A framework for family therapy* (2nd ed.). New York: Allyn & Bacon.

Chesler, M., & Barbarin, O. (1987). *Childhood cancer and the family.* New York: Brunner/Mazel.

Chilman, C. S., Nunnally, E. W., & Cox, F. M. (eds.) (1988). *Chronic illness and disability: Families in trouble series.* Beverly Hills: Sage Publications.

Chodoff, P., Friedman, S. B., & Hamburg, D. A. (1964). Stress, defenses and coping behavior: Observations in parents of children with malignant disease. *American Journal of Psychiatry, 120,* 743–49.

Christie-Seely, J. (ed.) (1984). *Working with the family in primary care.* New York: Praeger.

Clayton, P. J., Halikas, J. K., Maurice, W. L., & Robins, E. (1973). Anticipatory grief and widowhood. *British Journal of Psychiatry, 122,* 47–51.

Cleveland, M. (1980). Family adaptation to traumatic spinal cord injury, response to crisis. *Family Relations, 29,* 558–65.

Cole, R. E., & Reiss, D. (1993). *How do families cope with chronic illness?* Hillsdale, NJ: Lawrence Erlbaum Associates.

Coleman, S. B., & Stanton, M. D. (1978). The role of death in the addict family. *Journal of Marriage and Family Counseling, 4*(1), 79–91.

Combrinck-Graham, L. (1985). A developmental model for family systems. *Family Process, 24,* 139–50.

Combs, G., & Freedman, J. (1990). *Symbol, story and ceremony: Using metaphor in individual and family therapy.* New York: Norton.

Cousins, N. (1979). *Anatomy of an illness.* New York: Norton.

Cousins, N. (1989). *Head first: The biology of hope.* New York: Dutton.

Coyne, J., & Fiske, V. (1992). Couples coping with chronic and catastrophic illness. In J. Akamatsu et al. (eds.), *Family health psychology.* Washington, DC: Hemisphere Publishing.

Croog, S. H., Shapiro, D. S., & Levine, S. (1971). Denial among male heart patients: An empirical study. *Psychosomatic Medicine, 33,*385–97.

Crouch, M. A., & Roberts, L. (eds). (1987). *The family in medical practice: A family systems primer.* New York: Springer-Verlag.

Daniels, D., Miller, J. J., Billings, A. G., & Moos, R. H. (1986). Psychosocial functioning of siblings of children with rheumatic disease. *Journal of Pediatrics, 109,* 279–383.

Davies, R. K., Quinlan, D. M., McKegney, P., & Kimball, C. P. (1973). Organic factors and psychological adjustment in advanced cancer patients. *Psychosomatic Medicine, 35,* 464–71.

Dell, P. F. (1985). Understanding Bateson and Maturana: Toward a biological foundation for the social sciences. *Journal of Marital and Family Therapy, 11,*1–20.

Derogatis, L. R., Abeloff, M. D., & Melisartos, N. (1979). Psychological coping mechanisms and survival time in metastatic breast cancer. *Journal of the American Medical Association, 242,* 1504–08.

Doherty, W. J., & Baird, M. P. (1983). *Family therapy and family medicine: Towards the primary care of families.* New York: Guilford.

Doherty, W. J., & Baird, M. A. (1986). Developmental levels of physician involvement with families. *Family Medicine, 18,* 153–56.

Doherty, W. J., & Baird, M. A. (eds). (1987). *Family-centered medical care: A clinical casebook.* New York: Guilford.

Doherty, W. J., & Colangelo, N. (1984). The Family FIRO model: A modest proposal for organizing family treatment. *Journal of Marital and Family Therapy, 10,* 19–29.

Dohrenwend, B. S., & Dohrenwend, B. P. (eds.) (1981). *Stressful life events and their contexts.* New York: Prodist.

Duvall, E. (1977). *Marriage and family development* (5th ed.). Philadelphia: Lippincott.

Eisenberg, M. G., Sutkin, L. C., & Jansen, M. A. (eds.) (1984). *Chronic illness and disability through the life span: Effects on self and family.* New York: Springer.

Elliott, B. (ed.) (1993). *Vision 2010: Families and healthcare.* Minneapolis: National Council on Family Relations.

Elliott, G. R., & Eisdorfer, C. (1982). *Stress and human health: Analysis and implications of research.* New York: Springer.

Engel, G. L. (1977). The need for a new medical model: A challenge for biomedicine. *Science, 196,*129–36.

Engel, G. L. (1980). The clinical application of the biopsychosocial model. *American Journal of Psychiatry, 137,* 535–44.

Epstein, N. B., Bishop, D. S., & Levin, S. (1978). The McMaster model of family functioning. *Journal of Marriage and Family Counseling, 4,* 19–31.

Epstein, N., Bishop, D. Ryan, C., Miller, I., & Keitner, G. (1993). The McMaster model: View of healthy family functioning. In F. Walsh (ed.), *Normal family processes* (2nd ed.). New York: Norton.

Erikson, E. H. (1950). *Childhood and society.* New York: Norton.

Erikson, E. H. (1959). Identity and the life cycle. *Psychological Issues, 1,* 1–171.

Falloon, I. R. H., Boyd, J. L., & McGill, C. W. (1984). *Family care of schizophrenia: A problem-solving approach to the treatment of mental illness.* New York: Guilford.

Fiske, V., Coyne, J. C., & Smith, D. A. (1992). Couples coping with myocardial infarction: An empirical recommendation of the role of overprotectiveness. *Journal of Family Psychology, 5,* 4–20.

Foerster, H. von (1981). *Observing systems.* Seaside, CA: Intersystems Publications.

Framo, J. L. (1976). Family of origin as therapeutic resource for adults in marital and family therapy: You can and should go home again. *Family Process, 15,* 193–210.

Framo, J. L. (1992). *Family-of-origin therapy: An intergenerational approach.* New York: Brunner-Mazel.

Friedman, S. B., Chodoff, P., Mason, J. W., & Hamburg, D. B. (1963). Behavioral observations on parents anticipating the death of a child. *Pediatrics, 32,* 610–22.

Fulton, R., & Gottesman, D. J. (1980). Anticipatory grief: A psychosocial concept reconsidered. *British Journal of Psychiatry, 137,* 45–54.

Futterman, E. H., Hoffman, I., & Sabshin, M. (1972). Parental anticipatory mourning. In B. Schoenberg, A. Carr, A. Kutscher, D. Peretz, & I. Goldberg (eds.), *Psychosocial aspects of terminal care.* New York: Columbia University Press.

Gerber, I., Rusalem, R., Hannon, N., Battin, D., & Arkin, A. (1975). Anticipatory grief and aged widows and widowers. *Journal of Gerontology, 30,* 225–29.

Gergen, K. (1985). The social constructionist movement in modern psychology. *American Psychologist, 40,* 266–75.

Glasersfeld, E. von (1987). *The construction of knowledge.* Salinas, CA: Intersystems Publications.

Glenn, M. (1987). *Collaborative health care: A family-oriented model.* New York: Praeger.

Glick, I. O., Weiss, R. S., & Parkes, C. M. (1974). *The first year of bereavement.* New York: John Wiley & Sons.

Goffman, E. (1986). *Stigma: Notes on the management of spoiled identity.* New York: Simon & Schuster.

Goldner, V. (1988). Gender and generation: Normative and covert hierarchies. *Family Process, 27,* 17–33.

Gonzalez, S., Steinglass, P., & Reiss, D. (1989). Putting the illness in its place: Discussion groups for families with chronic medical illnesses. *Family Process, 28,* 69–87.

Gottman, J. M., & Katz, L. F. (1989). Effects of marital discord on young children's peer interaction and health. *Developmental Psychology, 25,* 373–81.

Gottman, J. M., & Levenson, R. (1992). Marital processes predictive of later dissolution: Behavior physiology and health. *Journal of Personality and Social Psychology, 63,* 221–33.

Gould, R. L. (1972). The phases of adult life: A study in developmental psychology. *American Journal of Psychiatry, 129:* 521–31.

Griffith, J., & Griffith, M. (1994). *The body speaks.* New York: Basic Books.

Griffith, J., Griffith, M., & Slovik, L. (1990). Mind-body problems in family therapy: Contrasting first- and second-order cybernetics approaches. *Family Process, 29,* 13–29.

Grolnick, L. (1972). A family perspective of psychosomatic factors in illness: A review of the literature. *Family Process, 11,* 457–86.

Haley, J. (1976). *Problem-solving therapy.* San Francisco: Jossey-Bass.

Hamburg, B. A., Lipsett, L. F., Inoff, G. E., & Drash, A. L. (eds.) (1980). *Behavioral and psychological issues in diabetes* (NIH Publication No. 80-1993). Washington, DC: U.S. Government Printing Office.

Harder, L., & Bowditch, B. (1982). Siblings of children with cystic fibrosis: Perceptions of the impact of the disease. *Children's Health Care, 10*, 116–20.

Henao, S., & Grose, N. (eds.) (1985). *Principles of family systems in family medicine.* New York: Brunner/Mazel.

Herz, F. (1989). The impact of death and serious illness on the family life cycle. In E. A. Carter & M. McGoldrick (eds.), *The family life cycle: A framework for family therapy* (2nd ed.). Boston: Allyn and Bacon.

Hoffman, L. (1989). The family life cycle and discontinuous change. In E. A. Carter & M. McGoldrick (eds.), *The changing family life cycle: A framework for family therapy* (2nd ed.). Boston: Allyn and Bacon.

Hoffman, L. (1990). Constructing realities: An art of lenses. *Family Process, 29*, 1–13.

Holmes, T. H., & Rahe, R. H. (1967). The social readjustment scale. *Journal of Psychosomatic Research, 39*, 413–31.

Hsia, Y. E., Hirschorn, K., Silverberg, R., & Godmilow, L. (eds.) (1979). *Counseling in genetics.* New York: Alan R. Liss.

Huygen, F. J. A. (1982). *Family medicine: The medical life history of families.* New York: Brunner/Mazel.

Hyman, M. (1975). Social and psychological factors affecting disability among ambulatory patients. *Journal of Chronic Diseases, 28*, 99–216.

Imber-Black, E. (1991). Rituals and the healing process. In F. Walsh & M. McGoldrick (eds.), *Living beyond loss. Death in the family.* New York: Norton.

Imber-Black, E., & Roberts J. (1992). *Rituals for our times.* New York: HarperCollins.

Imber-Black, E., Roberts, J., & Whiting, R. (eds.) (1988). *Rituals in families and family therapy.* New York: Norton.

Ireys, H. T., & Burr, C. K. (1984). Apart and a part: Family issues for young adults with chronic illness and disability. In M. G. Eisenberg, L. C. Sutkin, & M. A. Jansen (eds.), *Chronic illness and disability through the life span: Effects on self and family.* New York: Springer.

Jackson, D. D. (1965). The study of the family. *Family Process, 4*, 1–20.

Jung, C. (1964). *Man and his symbols.* New York: Doubleday.

Kaplan, D. M. (1968). Observations on crisis theory and practice. *Social Casework, 49*, 151–55.

Kaplan, H. S. (1974). *The New Sex Therapy.* New York: Brunner/Mazel.

Kasl, S. V. (1982). Social and psychological factors affecting the course of disease: An epidemiological perspective. In D. Mechanic (ed.), *Handbook of health, health care and the health profession.* New York: Free Press.

Kazak, A. (1989). Families of chronically ill children: A systems and social ecological model of adaptation and challenge. *Journal of Consulting and Clinical Psychology, 57*, 25–30.

Keeney, B. P. (1983). *Aesthetics of change.* New York: Guilford.

Kellerman, J., Rigler, D., & Siegal, S. E. (1977). Psychological effects of isolation in protected environments. *American Journal of Psychiatry, 134,* 563–67.

Kleinman, A. M. (1988). *The illness narratives: Suffering, healing, and the human condition.* New York: Basic Books.

Kluckhohn, F. R. (1960). Variations in the basic values of family systems. In N. W. Bell & E. F. Vogel (eds.) *A modern introduction to the family.* Glencoe, IL: The Free Press.

Kobasa, S. C. (1979). Stressful life events and health: An inquiry into hardiness. *Journal of Personality and Social Psychology, 37,* 1–11.

Koocher, G., & McDonald, B. (1992). Preventive intervention and family coping with a child's life-threatening or terminal illness. In J. Akamatsu, M. A. Stephens, S. Hobfoll, & J. Crowther (eds.), *Family health psychology.* Washington, DC: Hemisphere Publishing.

Kubler-Ross, E. (1969). *On death and dying.* New York: Macmillan.

Kubler-Ross, E. (ed.) (1975). *Death: The final stage of growth.* Englewood Cliffs, NJ: Prentice-Hall.

Laird, J. (1993). Lesbian and gay families. In F. Walsh (ed.) *Normal family processes* (2nd ed.). New York: Norton.

Landau-Stanton, J. (1993). *AIDS, health and mental health: A primary sourcebook.* New York: Brunner/Mazel.

Laqueur, H. P. (1980). The theory and practice of multiple family therapy. In L. Wolberg & M. Aronson (eds.), *Group and family therapy.* New York: Brunner/Mazel.

LaShan, L. (1977). *You can fight for your life: Emotional factors in the causation of cancer.* New York: Evans.

Lazarus, R. S. (1991). *Emotion and adaptation.* New York: Oxford University Press.

Lazarus, R. S., & Folkman, S. (1984). *Stress, appraisal and coping.* New York: Springer.

Lefcourt, H. M. (1982). *Locus of control* (2nd ed.). Hillsdale, NJ: Lawrence Erlbaum Associates.

Lerner, H. G. (1989). *The dance of intimacy: A woman's guide to courageous acts of change in key relationships.* New York: Harper & Row.

Levenson, H. (1973). Multidimensional locus of control in psychiatric patients. *Journal of Consulting and Clinical Psychology, 41,* 397–404.

Levenson, H. (1974). Activism and powerful others: Distinctions within the concept of internal-external control. *Journal of Personality Assessment, 38,* 377–83.

Levenson, H. (1975). Multidimensional locus of control in prison inmates. *Journal of Applied Social Psychology, 5,* 342–47.

Levine, S. (1987). *Healing into life and death.* New York: Doubleday.

Levinson, D. J. (1978). *The seasons of a man's life.* New York: Knopf.

Levinson, D. J. (1986). A conception of adult development. *American Psychologist, 41,* 3–13.

Lifton, R. J. (1975). Preface. In A. Mitscherlich & M. Mitscherlich (eds.). *The Inability to mourn.* New York: Grove.

Lifton, R. J. (1979). *The broken connection.* New York: Simon & Schuster.

Lindemann, E. (1944). Symptomatology and management of acute grief. *American Journal of Psychiatry, 101*, 141–48.

Litman, T. J. (1974). The family as a basic unit in health and medical care: A sociobehavioral overview. *Social Science and Medicine, 8*, 495–519.

Locke, S. E., & Gorman, J. R. (1989). Behavior and immunity. In H. I. Kaplan & B. J. Sadock (eds.), *Comprehensive textbook of psychiatry/II*. Baltimore, MD: Williams and Wilkins.

LoPiccolo, J., & LoPiccolo, L. (1978). *Handbook of sex therapy*. New York: Plenum.

Macklin, E. (ed.) (1989). *AIDS and families*. New York: Haworth.

Madsen, W. (1992). Problematic treatment: Interaction of patient, spouse and physician beliefs in medical noncompliance. *Family Systems Medicine, 10*, 365–85.

Matthews-Simonton, S., Simonton, C. O., & Creighton, J. L. (1978). *Getting well again*. New York: Bantam Books.

Maturana, H. R., & Varela, F. J. (1987). *The tree of knowledge: The biological roots of human understanding*. Boston: Shambhala.

Matus, I., & Bush, D. (1979). Asthma attack frequency in a pediatric population. *Psychosomatic Medicine, 41*, 629–36.

McCubbin, H. I., & Patterson, J. M. (1982). Family adaptation to crises. In H. I. McCubbin, A. Cauble, & J. Patterson (eds.), *Family stress, coping and social support*. Springfield, IL: Thomas.

McDaniel, S., Campbell, T., & Seaburn, D. (1990). *Family-oriented primary care: A manual for medical providers*. New York: Springer.

McDaniel, S., Hepworth, J., & Doherty, W. (eds.) (1992). *Medical family therapy: A biopsychosocial approach to families with health problems*. New York: Basic Books.

McGoldrick, M., & Gerson, R. (1985). *Genograms in family assessment*. New York: Norton.

McGoldrick, M., Pearce, J. K., & Giordano, J. (1982). *Ethnicity and family therapy*. New York: Guilford.

McGoldrick, M., & Walsh, F. (1983). A systemic view of family history and loss. In M. Aronson & L. Wolberg (eds.), *Group and family therapy 1983*. New York: Brunner/Mazel.

McGoldrick, M., Anderson, C. M., & Walsh, F. (eds.) (1989). *Women in families: A framework for family therapy*. New York: Norton.

McKeever, P. (1983). Siblings of chronically ill children: A literature review with implications for research and practice. *American Journal of Orthopsychiatry, 53*, 209–218.

Mechanic, D. (1978). *Medical sociology* (2nd ed). New York: Free Press.

Meyer, R. J., & Haggerty, R. J. (1962). Streptococcal infections in families: Factors altering individual susceptibility. *Pediatrics, 29*, 539–49.

Minuchin, S. (1974). *Families and family therapy*. Cambridge, MA: Harvard University Press.

Minuchin, S., Baker, L., Rosman, B. L., Liebman, R., Milman, L., & Todd, T. (1975). A conceptual model of psychosomatic illness in children: Family organization and family therapy. *Archives of General Psychiatry, 32*, 1031–38.

Minuchin, S., Rosman, B. L., & Baker, L. (1978). *Psychosomatic families: Anorexia nervosa in context*. Cambridge, MA: Harvard University Press.

Mishel, M. (1988). Uncertainty in illness. *Image, 20*(4), 225–32.

Moldofsky, H., & Chester, W. J. (1970). Pain and mood patterns in patients with rheumatoid arthritis: A prospective study. *Psychosomatic Medicine, 32,* 309–18.

Moos, R. M. (1977). *Coping with physical illness*. New York: Plenum.

Moos, R. M. (ed.) (1984). *Coping with physical illness. 2: New perspectives*. New York: Plenum.

Natterson, J. M., & Knudson, A. G., Jr. (1960). Observations concerning fear of death in fatally ill children and their mothers. *Psychosomatic Medicine, 22,* 465.

Neugarten, B. (1976). Adaptation and the life cycle. *The Counselling Psychologist, 6,* 16–20.

Oliveri, M. E., & Reiss, D. (1982). Families' schemata of social relationships. *Family Process, 21,* 295–311.

Olson, D. H. (1993). Circumplex model of marital and family systems: Assessing family functioning. In F. Walsh (ed.), *Normal family processes* (2nd ed.). New York: Norton.

Olson, D. H., Russell, C. S., & Sprenkle, D. M. (eds.) (1989). *Circumplex model: Systemic assessment and treatment of families*. New York: Haworth.

Parkes, C. M. (1976). Determinants of outcome following bereavement. *Omega, 6,* 303–23.

Parkes, C. M., & Weiss, R. S. (1983). *Recovery from bereavement*. New York: Basic Books.

Parsons, T., & Fox, R. C. (1952). Illness, therapy and the modern American family. *Journal of Social Issues, 13,* 51–4.

Patterson, J. M. (1988). Chronic illness in children and the impact on families. In C. S. Chilman, E. W. Nunnally, & F. M. Cox (eds.), *Chronic illness and disability. Families in trouble series,* Vol. 2. Newbury Park, CA: Sage Publications.

Patterson, J. M. (1989a). Illness beliefs as a factor in patient-spouse adaptation to treatment for coronary artery disease. *Family Systems Medicine, 7,* 428–42.

Patterson, J. M. (1989b). A family stress model: The family adjustment and adaptation response. In C. N. Ramsey (ed.), *Family systems in medicine*. New York: Guilford.

Paul, N. L., & Grosser, G. (1965). Operational mourning and its role in conjoint family therapy. *Community Mental Health Journal, 1,* 339–45.

PBS (1993). *Choosing death: A health quarterly Frontline special*. Aired March 23. Chicago: WTTW-TV.

Pelletier, J. (1977). *Mind as healer, mind as slayer*. New York: Dell Books.

Penn, P. (1983). Coalitions and binding interactions in families with chronic illness. *Family Systems Medicine, 1* (2), 16–25.

Piaget, J. (1952). *The origins of intelligence in children* (translated by M. Cook). New York: International Universities Press.

Pinkston, E., & Linsk, N. (1984). *Care of the elderly: A family approach*. New York: Pergamon Press.

Pless, I. B., & Perrin, J. M. (1985). Issues common to a variety of illnesses. In N. Hobbes & J. M. Perrin (eds.) *Issues in the care of children with chronic illness.* San Francisco: Jossey-Bass.

Ramsey, C. N., Jr. (ed.) (1989). *Family systems in medicine.* New York: Guilford.

Rando, T. (1983). An investigation of grief and adaptation in parents whose children have died from cancer. *Journal of Pediatric Psychology, 8,* 3–20.

Rando, T. A. (1984). *Grief, dying and death.* Champaign, IL: Research Press.

Ransom, D. C. (1983a). On why it is useful to say that "The family is a unit of care" in family medicine. *Family Systems Medicine, 1*(1), 17–22.

Ransom, D. (1983b). Random notes: The legacy of the Peckham experiments. *Family Systems Medicine, 1,* no. 4, 104–8.

Ransom, D., Fisher, L., & Terry, H. (1992). The California family health project: II. Family world view and adult health. *Family Process, 31,* 251–69.

Register, C. (1987). *Living with chronic illness: Days of patience and passion.* New York: Free Press.

Reibstein, J., & Richards, M. (1993). *Sexual arrangements: Marriage and the temptation of infidelity.* New York: Charles Scribner's Sons.

Reiss, D. (1981). *The family's construction of reality.* Cambridge, MA: Harvard University Press.

Reiss, D. (1983). Sensory experience and family process: Perceptual styles tend to run in but not necessarily run families. *Family Process, 22,* 289–308.

Reiss, D., Gonzalez, S., & Kramer, J. (1986). Family process, chronic illness, and death: On the weakness of strong bonds. *Archives of General Psychiatry, 43,* 795–804.

Reiss, D., & Kaplan De-Nour, A. (1989). The family and medical team in chronic illness: A transactional and developmental perspective. In C. Ramsey, Jr. (ed.), *Family systems in medicine.* New York: Guilford.

Resnick, M. (1984). The social construction of disability and handicap in America. In R. Blum (ed.), *Chronic illness and disabilities in childhood and adolescence.* Orlando, FL: Grune and Stratton.

Richardson, H. B. (1945). *Patients have families.* New York: Commonwealth Fund.

Roberts, M. C., & Wallander, J. L. (1992). Family issues in pediatric psychology: An overview. In M. C. Roberts & J. L. Wallander (eds.), *Family issues in pediatric psychology.* New York: Earlbaum.

Rolland, J. S. (1984). Toward a psychosocial typology of chronic and life-threatening illness. *Family Systems Medicine, 2,* 245–63.

Rolland, J. S. (1987a). Chronic illness and the life cycle: A conceptual framework. *Family Process, 26,*203–21.

Rolland, J. S. (1987b). Family illness paradigms: Evolution and significance. *Family Systems Medicine, 5,* 467–86.

Rolland, J. S. (1988a). Family systems and chronic illness: A typological model. In F. Walsh & C. Anderson (eds.), *Chronic disorders and the family.* New York: Haworth Press. (Also available in *Journal of Psychotherapy and the Family, 3,* 1987, 143–68.)

Rolland, J. S. (1988b). A conceptual model of chronic and life-threatening illness and its impact on the family. In C. Chilman, E. Nunnally, & F. Cox (eds.),

Chronic illness and disability: Families in trouble. Beverly Hills: Sage Publications.

Rolland, J. S. (1990a). Anticipatory loss: A family systems developmental framework. *Family Process, 29,* 229–44.

Rolland, J. S. (1990b). The impact of illness on families. In R. E. Rakel (ed.) *Textbook of family practice.* (4th ed.). Philadelphia: W. B. Saunders.

Rolland, J. S. (1993a). Mastering family challenges in serious illness and disability. In F. Walsh (ed.), *Normal family processes* (2nd ed.). New York: Guilford.

Rolland, J. S. (1993b). Families and health crises. In B. Elliott (ed.), *Vision 2010: Families and health care.* Minneapolis: National Council on Family Relations.

Rolland, J. S., & Walsh, F. (1988). Blame, shame and guilt: Family belief systems in chronic and life-threatening disorders. Paper presented at 46th Annual Conference, American Association for Marriage and Family Therapy.

Rolland, J. S., & Walsh F. (1994). Family therapy: Systems approaches to assessment and treatment. In R. E. Hales, S. Yudofsky, & J. Talbott (eds.), *American psychiatric press textbook of psychiatry* (2nd ed.). Washington, DC: American Psychiatric Press.

Rosen, E. (1990). Families facing death: Family dynamics in terminal illness. Lexington, MA: Lexington Books.

Ruesch, J., & Bateson, G. (1951). *Communication: The social matrix of psychiatry.* New York: Norton.

Sargent, J. (1985). Physician-family therapist collaboration: Children with medical problems. *Family Systems Medicine, 3,* 454–66.

Satir, V. (1964). *Conjoint family therapy.* Palo Alto, CA: Science & Behavior Books.

Sawa, R. (1985). *Family dynamics for physicians: Guidelines to assessment and treatment.* New York: Mellen.

Scheinkman, M. (1988). Graduate student marriages: An organizational/interactional view. *Family Process, 27,* no. 3, 351–68.

Schmale, A. H., & Iker, H. (1971). Hopelessness as a predictor of cervical cancer. *Social Science and Medicine, 5,* 95–100.

Schoenberg, B., Carr, A., Kutscher, A., Peretz, D., & Goldberg, I. (eds.) (1974). *Anticipatory grief.* New York: Columbia University.

Schover, L. R., & Jensen, S. B. (1988). *Sexuality and chronic illness.* New York: Guilford.

Schutz, W. C. (1958). *FIRO: A three-dimensional theory of interpersonal behavior.* New York: Holt, Rinehart & Winston.

Seaburn, D., Lorenz, A., & Kaplan, D. (1992). The transgenerational development of chronic illness meanings. *Family Systems Medicine, 10,* 385–95.

Seligman, M., & Darling, R. (1989). *Ordinary families, special children: A systems approach to childhood disability.* New York: Guilford.

Selye, H. (1956). *The stress of life.* New York: McGraw-Hill.

Sheehy, G. (1976). *Passages: Predictable crises of adult life.* New York: Dutton.

Siegel, B. S. (1986). *Love, medicine and miracles.* New York: Harper & Row.

Simon, R. (1988). Chronic illness as a therapeutic metaphor. *Family Systems Medicine, 6,* no. 3, 262–76.

Simonton, C. O., Matthews-Simonton, S., & Creighton, J. (1978). *Getting well again.* Los Angeles: J. P. Tarcher.

Simonton, C. O., Matthews-Simonton, S., & Sparks, T. F. (1980). Psychological intervention in the treatment of cancer. *Psychosomatics, 21,* 226–33.

Slater, S. B., Sussman, M. B., & Stroud, M. W. (1970). Participation in household activities as a prognostic factor for rehabilitation. *Archives of Physical Medicine and Rehabilitation, 51,* 605–11.

Sluzki, C. (1992). Transformations: A blueprint for narrative changes in therapy. *Family Process, 31,* 217–31.

Sontag, S. (1978). *Illness as metaphor.* New York: McGraw-Hill.

Sontag, S. (1988). *AIDS and its metaphors.* New York: Farrar, Straus & Giroux.

Sourkes, B. M. (1982). *The deepening shade: Psychological aspects of long-term illness.* Pittsburgh: University of Pittsburgh Press.

Stein, R., & Jessop, D. (1982). A noncategorical approach to childhood chronic illness. *Public Health Reports, 97,* 354–62.

Steinglass, P., Bennett, L. A., Wolin, S. J., & Reiss, D. (1987). *The alcoholic family.* New York: Basic Books.

Steinglass, P., & Horan, M. (1988). Families and chronic medical illness. In F. Walsh & C. Anderson (eds.), *Chronic disorders and the family.* New York: Haworth.

Stoneman, Z., & Berman, P. W. (1993). *The effects of mental retardation, disability and illness on sibling relationships.* Baltimore: Paul H. Brookes Publishing.

Strauss, A. L. (1975). *Chronic illness and the quality of life.* St. Louis: Mosby.

Strong, M. (1988). *Mainstay: For the well spouse of the chronically ill.* Boston: Little, Brown.

Sussman, M. B., & Slater, S. B. (1971). Reappraisal of urban kin networks: Empirical evidence. *The Annals, 396,* 40.

Swanson, D. W., & Maruta, J. (1980). The family's viewpoint of chronic pain. *Pain, 8,*163–66.

Taylor, S. (1989). *Positive illusions: Creative self-deception and the healthy mind.* New York: Basic Books.

Thomas, E. J. (1970). Problems of disability from the perspective of role theory. In P. Glasser & L. Glasser (eds.) *Families in crisis.* New York: Harper & Row.

Tritt, S. G., & Esses, L. M. (1988). Psychosocial adaptation of siblings of children with chronic medical illnesses. *American Journal of Orthopsychiatry, 58,* 211–19.

Turk, D., & Kerns, R. (eds.) (1985). *Health, illness and families: A life span perspective.* New York: Wiley.

Turnbull, A., Patterson, J., Behr, S., Murphy, D., Marquis, J., & Blue-Banning M., (eds.) (1993). *Cognitive coping, families and disability.* Baltimore: Paul H. Brookes Publishing Company.

Vernick, J., & Karon, M. (1965). Who's afraid of death on a leukemia ward. *American Journal of Diseases of Children, 109,* 393–7.

Viney, L. L., & Westbrook, M. T. (1981). Psychosocial reactions to chronic illness related disability as a function of its severity and type. *Journal of Psychosomatic Research, 25,* 513–23.

Walker, G. (1983). The pact: The caretaker-parent/ill-child coalition in families with chronic illness. *Family Systems Medicine, 1*(4), 6–29.

Walker, G. (1991). *In the midst of winter: Systemic therapy with families, couples and individuals with AIDS infection.* New York: Norton.

Wallston, B. S., Wallston, K. A., Kaplan, G. D., & Maides, S. A. (1976). Development and validation of the health locus of control (HLC) scale. *Journal of Consulting and Clinical Psychology, 44,* 580–85.

Wallston, K. A., & Wallston, B. S. (1978). Development of the multidimensional health locus of control (MHLC) scales. *Health Education Monographs, 6*(2), 160–70.

Walsh, F. (1989a). The family in later life. In B. Carter & M. McGoldrick (eds.), *The changing family life cycle: A framework for family therapy* (2nd ed.). Boston: Allyn & Bacon.

Walsh, F. (1989b). Reconsidering gender in the marital "quid pro quo. " In M. McGoldrick, C. Anderson, & F. Walsh (eds.), *Women in families.* New York: Norton.

Walsh, F. (1993a). Conceptualization of normal family processes. In F. Walsh (ed.), *Normal family processes* (2nd ed.). New York: Guilford.

Walsh, F. (ed.) (1993b). *Normal family processes* (2nd ed.). New York: Guilford.

Walsh, F. (in press). *Promoting healthy family functioning.* New York: Guilford.

Walsh, F., & Anderson, C. M. (1988). Chronic disorders and families: An overview. In F. Walsh & C. Anderson (eds.), *Chronic disorders and the family.* New York: Haworth.

Walsh, F., & McGoldrick, M. (1988). Loss and the family life cycle. In C. J. Falivoc (ed.), *Family transitions: Continuity and change.* New York: Guilford.

Walsh, F., & McGoldrick, M. (eds.) (1991a). *Living beyond loss: Death in the family.* New York: Norton.

Walsh, F., & McGoldrick, M. (1991b). Loss and the family: A systemic perspective. In F. Walsh and M. McGoldrick (eds.), *Living beyond loss: Death in the family.* New York: Norton.

Watzlawick, P. (ed.) (1984). *The invented reality.* New York: Norton.

Weakland, J. (1977). "Family somatics": A neglected edge. *Family Process, 16,*263–72.

Weil, A. (1983). *Health and healing: Understanding conventional and alternative medicine.* Boston: Houghton Mifflin.

Weingarten, K. (1991). The discoveries of intimacy: Adding a social constructionist and feminist view. *Family Process, 30,* 285–305.

Weisman, A. (1984). *The coping capacity: On the nature of being mortal.* New York: Human Sciences Press.

Weiss, S. M., Herd, J. A., & Fox, B. H. (eds.) (1981). *Perspectives on behavioral medicine.* New York: Academic Press.

White, M., & Epston, D. (1990). *Narrative means to therapeutic ends.* New York: Norton.

Wiggins, S., Whyte, P., Huggins, M., Shelin, A., Theilmann, J., Bloch, H., Sheps, S., Schechter, M., & Hayden, M. (1992). The psychosocial consequences of predictive testing for Huntington's disease. *New England Journal of Medicine, 327* (20), 1401-5.

Wolff, C. T., Friedman, S. B., Hofer, M. A., & Mason, J. W. (1964). Relationship between psychological defenses and mean urinary 17-hydroxy corticosteroid excretion rate. I. A predictive study of parents of fatally ill children. *Psychosomatic Medicine, 26,* 576–91.

Wolin, S., Bennett, L. Noonan, D., & Teitelbaum, M. (1980). Disrupted family rituals: A factor in the intergenerational transmission of alcoholism. *Journal of Studies of Alcoholism, 41,* 199–214.

Wolin, S. J., & Bennett, L. A. (1984). Family rituals. *Family Process, 23,* 401–20.

Wood, B. (1993). Beyond the "psychomatic family": A biobehavioral family model of pediatric illness. *Family Process, 32,* 261–78.

Wood, B., Boyle, J. T., Watkins, J. B., Nogueira, J., Zimand, E., & Carroll, L. (1988). Sibling psychological status and style as related to the disease of their chronically ill brothers and sisters: Implications for models of biopsychosocial interaction. *Developmental and Behavioral Pediatrics, 9* (2), 66–72.

Wortman, C., & Silver, R. (1989). The myths of coping with loss. *Journal of Consulting and Clinical Psychology, 57,* 349–57.

Wright, L. M., & Leahey, M. (1987). *Families and chronic illness.* Springhouse, PA: Springhouse Corporation.

Wright, L. M., & Nagy, J. (1993). Death: The most troublesome secret of all. In E. Imber-Black (ed.), *Secrets in family and family therapy.* New York: Norton.

Wright, L. M., Watson, W. L., & Bell, J. M. (in press). *Families, beliefs, and health problems.* New York: Basic Books.

Wynne, L. C., Shields, C. G., & Sirkin, M. (1992). Illness, family theory, and family therapy: I. Conceptual issues. *Family Process, 31,* 3-18.

Wynne, L. C., & Wynne, A. R. (1986). The quest for intimacy. *Journal of Marital and Family Therapy, 12,* 383–94.

Wynne, L., McDaniel, S., and Weber, T. (1986). *Systems consultation: A new perspective for family therapy.* New York: Guilford.

Zarit, S. M., Todd, P. A., & Zarit, J. M. (1986). Subjective burden of husbands and wives as caregivers: A longitudinal study. *The Gerontologist, 26,* 260–66.

Zborowski, M. (1969). *People in pain.* San Francisco: Jossey-Bass.

Index

Abeloff, M. D., 29
Abramson, L., 8
Acute-onset diseases, 2, 22–23
Adaptability. *See* Family adaptability
Ader, R., 3
Adolescence: autonomy in, 111–12, 213,
  215–16; chronic disorder in, 213, 215–16,
  219
Adult-onset disorders, 190
Adversity, history of coping with, 83
Affective issues, management of, 87
Age at onset, significance of, 41
Aging parents, caring for, 226–34; enmesh-
  ment and, 231–33; ethnic traditions of,
  228; by families with small children,
  229–30; gender and, 228, 229; home-
  based care and, 286–87; institutionalization of, 234, 275, 293; last parent, 233–34;
  multigenerational patterns of, 97–98,
  227–28; open discussion of, 227–28, 234;
  resented parent and, 231; by single-parent family, 230–31
AIDS, 5, 10, 25, 28, 31, 65–66, 70–71, 102,
  129, 148–50, 152–53, 155–56, 193–94, 205,
  244, 264–65
Akamatsu, J., 5
Alcoholism, 5, 153, 160
Alzheimer's disease, 5, 24, 25, 31, 35, 67, 84,
  152, 170, 174, 183, 229–30, 242, 245, 274,
  279
Amputation, 26
Amyotrophic Lateral Sclerosis, 52–53
Anderson, C. M., 5, 8, 69, 205, 269
Anderson, H., 9, 128
Anger: couples with chronic disorder in
  partner feeling, 239–40; of siblings,
  218–20; in terminal phase, 181–82
Angina, 172
Anorexia nervosa, 10
Anticipatory grief, anticipatory loss versus,
  165, 166

Anticipatory loss, 165–95, 208; anticipatory
  grief versus, 165, 166; belief systems
  and, 167, 191–94; chronic disorder in
  child and, 212; chronic disorder in early
  adulthood and, 216; in chronic phase,
  175–77; clinician and, 195; cognitive loss
  and, 173–74; in crisis phase, 174–75;
  families with chronic disorders and, 125;
  "if" and "when" of death and, 171–72;
  information on nature of disorder from
  physician and, 168–70; mastery over,
  194; outcome and, 28–29; overemphasis
  on, 194–95; progressive diseases and,
  170–72; quality of life and, 194–95; relapsing illnesses and, 172–73; societal
  stigma and, 193–94; systems-oriented
  model viewing, 166; terminal phase and,
  177–84, *see also* Hospice; time line and,
  168–74; time phase of illness and, 167;
  varying salience of, 166. *See also* Anticipatory loss, family life cycle approach to
Anticipatory loss, family life cycle approach to, 184–91, 194; adult-onset disorders and, 190; childhood-onset disorders and, 188–89; multigenerational
  issues and, 184–86, 189; nodal points of
  for couple, 190–91; out-of-phase illness
  and, 186; present and future timing with
  life cycle and, 186–88; transitions and,
  187–88, 194
Antonovsky, A., 3, 138
Anxiety, in terminal phase, 181–82
Arrival phase, hospice and, 179–82
Arthritis, 24, 28, 50–51, 245
Assessment: normative perspective on,
  63–64; time phases schema and, 54–55;
  uses of family ritual in, 159. *See also*
  Family functioning
Asthma, 10, 21, 27, 29, 38, 41–42, 66, 88–89,
  99, 111, 129, 136, 172, 214, 215
Attention, siblings' need for, 220–21